DANCING WITH GODDESSES

DANCING

WITH

GODDESSES

ARCHETYPES,

POETRY,

AND

EMPOWERMENT

ANNIS PRATT

INDIANA UNIVERSITY PRESS
BLOOMINGTON AND INDIANAPOLIS

The paper used in this publication meets the minimum requirements of American National Standard for Information Sciences—Permanence of Paper for Printed Library Materials, ANSI Z39.48-1984.

Manufactured in the United States of America

Library of Congress Cataloging-in-Publication Data

Pratt, Annis, date

Dancing with goddesses : Archetypes, poetry, and empowerment / Annis Pratt.

p. cm.

Includes bibliographical references (p.) and index.

ISBN 0-253-34586-3 (alk. paper).—ISBN 0-253-20865-3 (pbk. : alk. paper)

1. English poetry—History and criticism. 2. Archetype (Psychology) in literature. 3. American poetry—History and criticism. 4. Medusa (Greek mythology) in literature. 5. Aphrodite (Greek deity) in literature. 6. Artemis (Greek deity) in literature. 7. Authorship—Sex differences. 8. Goddesses in literature. 9. Women in literature. 10. Bears in literature.

I. Title.

PR508.A66P73   1994

821.009'353—dc20   93-28442

1 2 3 4 5 99 98 97 96 95 94

and this one is for
Henry
my companion on our great adventure
into the darkest forests

CONTENTS

Contents

PART THREE

WHERE THE WILD THINGS ARE

Preface: Blackbirds in a Pie

On a dark November night in 1985 I was teaching a series of poems about Medusa to my undergraduate students at the University of Wisconsin. I had them discussing the poems in their groups of ten or so, as I usually do; but that evening while they were in the small groups, I went out into the hall and put on a big cardboard mask of Medusa, complete with tusks, brightly colored snakes for hair, and glaring, fearsome eyes. I then leapt back into the classroom, my arms extended wide in a threatening gesture. One student began to vomit, several others moaned and put their heads in their laps, and another rushed to the window as if to jump out. Later that term one student sent me a wild and violent poem in which she identified me with Medusa and called me a "fat red umbilical cord." I had neglected to take the enormously powerful psychic force of archetypes into account in my classroom simulation of Medusa: my students, most of whom were women in their twenties, needed only my Medusa mask and my threatening gesture to transfer their feelings about the frightening power of their own mothers onto me, a forty-eight-year-old woman wielding professorial control over them. Their age is one at which one of the primary psychological issues is differentiation from the mother, accomplished by scorn and rebellion or by sheer physical distancing; the time to face up to and absorb her power comes later in their lives, after they have established their identity with the help of women role models whom they can dissociate from maternal images. In conflating my professorial affect with the fearsome Medusa, I had impersonated an archetype too overwhelming for them to cope with at their stage of psychological development. That dark November evening was a stunning reminder that archetypes are not mere literary tropes but powerful catalysts which can spark explosive responses in the psyche.

It is astonishing how easily twentieth-century undergraduates respond to goddesses who belong to a mythological system far removed from their religious or secular experience. In my next pedagogical experiment I desisted from goddess impersonation, asking instead that the students complete the statement "I saw Aphrodite on State Street last Saturday night, and she . . ." I had given them some introductory background about Aphrodite's self-determined sexuality, with its suggestion that we women can say yes or no to sexual invitations according to our own desires—self-permission which, oddly enough, undergraduates in the late 1980s often greeted as astonishing news. The short essays were rather sad. One student wrote admiringly about a freewheeling Aphrodite dressed in black velvet wielding sexual power from her bar stool but made it clear that this was an archetype alien to her own experience because she would not feel safe in copying it in our town. An undergraduate responding to the same exercise in Oshkosh, Wisconsin, wrote that

> I saw Aphrodite last Saturday and she was doing two things, one overtly and one covertly. On the conscious level, she was laughing loudly, drinking, coming onto men, and all in all appearing to be a "cool," with it young woman. On the other level, however, the one inside, she was filled with doubt and misgivings, insecure about her worth, especially her body, and trying desperately to please.

The note of wistfulness is striking, as if Aphrodite were something lost and perhaps irretrievable. Even after only the briefest of introductions, nonetheless, the Aphrodite archetype could stir up feelings about their sexuality which these women had not quite faced before.

When a suburban Detroit high school which had asked me to introduce students to archetypes let me know that my Aphrodite exercise would be inappropriate, I tried Artemis out on the class. These students had been given only the standard description of Artemis as a virgin huntress, stressing her "chastity," and I told them little more than that she was a goddess of women who love nature. Their short notes on "When I go to (a favorite place in nature) I feel . . .," which were written on the spot, revealed the way these highly pressured teen-aged women sought solace in and accorded reverence to the green world. Most striking was one rebellious soul who announced that "When I cruise Woodward (a local commercial boulevard) in my Thunderbird I feel powerful and have fun looking for guys in the other cars," reflecting the sexual prowess of the Artemis archetype, which often appears in medieval literature as a hunter and seducer of men, a characteristic which has not been featured in the introductory material used in the high school.

Although my focus in this book will be on how literary archetypes recur in poetry, my classroom experiences suggest that archetypes are psychological rather than aesthetic in origin, stimulating personal responses in the individual who encounters them. Even though the classical archetypes of Medusa, Aphrodite, and Artemis belong to a Greek and Roman mythology remote from our everyday modern experience, they clearly embody suggestions about feminine power to which, as we shall see, both men and women respond at a profound psychological level. The bear archetype, which will be my fourth example in this book, derives from much more immediate sources than classical mythology—from European folklore and fairy tale as well as contemporary popular culture and, in the case of a good many North Americans, from direct experience. In all four cases, these archetypes can call up features not necessarily associated with their appearances in the historical period within which the poet is writing, suggesting that they are not entirely determined by European mindsets but embody qualities which earlier cultures accorded them. In each section of this book I will outline the earlier appearances of these qualities, which I have termed the deep background of each archetype.

In my career as an archetypalist (which began with a study of Dylan Thomas published in 1970) I have become increasingly doubtful that archetypes can be understood as mere facets of an overwhelmingly powerful masculine ideology determined by Judeo-Christian and classical paradigms. Dylan Thomas's works gave me my first hint that there are other mythic systems than these feeding into modern literature: I found that I could elucidate his recondite symbology in the context of pre-Christian Welsh concepts about nature, humans, life and death, and language which differed from standard European paradigms. It became clear that in addition to the historically modern signature and the personal or individual signature shaping Thomas's archetypes, I should consider their deeper background in the myths and religions of pre-Christian Wales.

During the period that I was writing about Dylan Thomas I became active in the feminist movement in Georgia, and went to teach at Spelman College, a part of Atlanta University, where exciting rediscovery and accumulation of bibliographies about "forgotten"

African American as well as women writers was flourishing. As I began to read widely among these writers (few of whom had ever been assigned in my undergraduate years at Smith College and none of whom I was assigned in any of my Columbia University graduate courses) I realized that trying to explain women's use of archetypes in terms of standard (masculine) myth criticism was like trying to fit square critical pegs into literary holes of another shape altogether. In my reading of 328 women's novels which constituted my data for *Archetypal Patterns in Women's Fiction* (1981) I applied many elements of C. G. Jung's, Northrop Frye's, and Joseph Campbell's descriptions of myth patterns to women's texts, but I learned to discard those elements which separated and objectified women and "the feminine" and which did not serve to illuminate the novels, and to substitute new hypotheses arising out of the material. Because masculine myth paradigms did not precisely fit literature by women, I found it useful to let women's fiction suggest its own archetypal patterns, and it was in this way that I discovered the value of an inductive method in feminist criticism. Since we women dream dreams and create imaginary universes of our own, I never felt that Jung, Frye, or Campbell should be the only one to describe the patterns which dreams and imaginary universes take. Nor was I worried that doctrinaire Jungianism would force me to compromise my feminist intentions; rather, I learned to use previous archetypal theories as hypotheses which I modified when women's novels suggested deviations from them. Since the most frequent deviations had to do with the feminine authorship and content of women's texts, I hypothesized that women's fiction differed significantly from men's, a luxurious presumption in that I did not systematically compare and contrast fiction by gender during my blissfully gynocentric vacation from masculine literature, a hiatus I intend to remedy in the present volume. Poetry is a much more primitive form than prose, deriving from the preliterate stage of both species and individual development; since it also accords archetypes a more central, structural role than does fiction, I realized that poetry should provide my next field of research. This time, however, I would compare texts by men and women in order to delineate the gender differences which, I hypothesized, would take the form of contrasting approaches and attitudes to a limited set of four archetypes.

During my study of women's fiction it had become clear that even the most conservative women writers wove into their texts strands of a fully human possibility contradicting the gender norms they overtly accepted, and that even the most feminist women authors were burdened by patriarchal prescriptions for women's behavior, especially women's sexuality. These conflicting tendencies produced an ambivalence of tone, irony in characterization, and disjunction in plotting in women's novels between 1700 and 1978 which mirrored women's dialectical experience in patriarchy. This experience, however, did not always get stuck in an eternally dualized conflict: often a new synthesis, in which women absorbed and transcended gender dualities and approached a complex, holistic selfhood, was either described or implied.

I thus found that women's novels could be elucidated better if I assumed that the archetypes they encoded in their texts embodied apatriarchal psychological possibilities than if I read them merely as reactions to a culturally determinist status quo. Some kind of forgotten code or buried script seemed to underlie the normative plots which women authors internalize from a "culture" whose hegemony seems a lot less absolute than we have suspected. During this period we were busy setting up our women's studies program in Wisconsin and establishing feminist criticism in our literature departments, out of a desire to make feminist scholarship a viable academic field and to integrate women's literature and feminist criticism into our departmental curricula. Since women's literature manifested a heavy patriarchal content, we spent much of our literary study in critical consciousness raising, delineating the sticky web of patriarchal constraints pervading texts; meanwhile, in women's studies, we devoted much of our energy to analyzing our oppression.

This consciousness raising, with its revelation of the complex and multiple restraints patriarchy imposes upon the development of selfhood in women, took place during the rise of critical schools which posited cultural determinism, with the result that we often felt overwhelmed by a dominant masculine culture which we might critique but which we took as the only context in which we ever had lived or breathed; sometimes we accorded such power to patriarchy that we even described our women's speech as silence and our presence as absence. We became more and more like the blackbirds baked in the pie and set before the king, convinced that the crowded, hot, sticky patriarchal crust was our whole world—past, and present, and to come—and that we had lived forever in an engulfing masculine pie under the threat of being eaten alive by the king and his men. My analysis of archetypal patterns in women's literature, however, suggested to me that our literature is not entirely determined by patriarchy but is structured from a tension between our cultural and our authentic selves, and that our authentic voices are not merely reactive but are endowed with qualities independent of patriarchal prescriptions about selfhood. We had been taught that women's literature was marginal and that even the idea "woman" was a masculine invention; but as we read more and more of our writing it seemed that these margins imploded into centers radiating the feminist values of control of our own sexuality, intellectual inventiveness, love of community, and a marvelously creative but practical competence. As I discovered this subversive imagery of a totality of self as an apatriarchal countertext in women's writing, I developed the hypothesis that our drive toward the fullest possible realization of our emotional, rational, creative, sexual, and political capacities is sufficiently powerful to undermine the gender norms of patriarchy. Like Emily Dickinson, I began to feel that being nobody in culture had its advantages, our implosive marginality more and more exhilarating and our nowheres eccentric only to the dreary patriarchal frogs chorusing away in bogs which seemed ever less appealing.

I have never denied that our blackbird songs (and those were British and melodic, not American and squawking blackbirds) were affected by the hot oven, claustrophobic enclosures, and terrifying masculine threat in patriarchy. These factors have an effect upon our performance, to be sure, disrupting our harmony and making it difficult for us to sing and not gasp our last, but we have not always been cooked inside a patriarchal pie: how and what we sing is as dependent upon the lives we might normally live in the wild as upon the artificial confines of our captivity. Ultimately, authentic blackbird modulation derives from the natural environment organic to the well-being of blackbirds. Just as a discerning ornithologist would want to study that natural environment, so we as women's studies scholars and feminist critics need to entertain the hypothesis that women's ungratified desires may spring from a drive for totality of self that is not only psychologically healthy but which has been accorded greater value in earlier periods than in the culture we presently inhabit.

As I found myself shifting from consciousness raising about our oppression to the unconsciousness raising which constitutes archetypal analysis, I discovered feminist alternatives latent in our literary texts which seemed to represent values recovered from a wide variety of apatriarchal religious and mythological systems. Although I had once found the idea of a pre-Judeo-Christian "Mother Goddess" religion posited by turn-of-the-century myth scholars appealing, during the period that I was writing this book, feminist theologians made it clear that such a construction is a fancifully monotheistic conflation of much more diverse and polytheistic myths and belief systems. There was no denying, however, that elements of these systems had somehow found their way into poets' responses to archetypes from the medieval through to the contemporary period. To avoid spending the rest of my life writing a key to all poetic mythologies, I have limited my sample almost entirely to poetry written in English; however, if my categories fit, I hope that scholars will want to test them out on poetry in other European and world literatures.

In this study I will use poems by men and women to illustrate that elements of preclassical and non-European myth systems can shape and structure poetry in English. Although I will speculate occasionally about the psychological basis for archetypal responses, I will not focus on how archetypal symbols are passed on from age to age or between culture and culture, a matter best left to students of instinct and cognition or of iconographic transmission.

Not all of the most feminist (which I define as woman-valuing) responses are to be found in the remote past. For just one example, I will explain in part two how Aphrodite's aura of independent feminine sexuality remained constant in Aphrodite and Venus archetypes until about 1700, before which women were considered as sensual as men (only with less control over our sexuality) and after which, for economic reasons, our sensuality was denounced as unfeminine. Nor are the blackbirds here in the crust with us all female. Women are not the only people to long for a world more psychologically healthy than patriarchy: the archetypal experience of an authentic and holistic selfhood for women, interwoven in a dialectical fashion with overlayers of gender prescriptions, shapes many poems by men as well as by women. As I read further in men's poetry, I realized that gender norms inhibit the psychological growth of men, too, and that poems by men contain protests against restrictive concepts of what is "masculine" and what is "feminine" as well as visions of a better way of living.

Thus my hypothesis that the differences I had postulated in my study of women's fiction would hold true when I compared poetry by women and men began to crumble, a process which accelerated when I added Canadian poetry to my sample. In the fall of 1981 I was invited to a Dialogue of Feminist Critics held at York University in Toronto to present a paper on "Affairs with Bears/Amours avec des ours," which represented my initial exploration of an archetype recurrent in Canadian literature and in the folklore of Canadian Native Peoples, the story of a woman who makes love to a bear. After my presentation a conservatively dressed middle-aged woman rose from the audience to query politely how I could talk about making love to that bear? In reply I went back over my entire archetypal hypothesis with many learned flourishes, but she raised her hand again and said she didn't mean how could a woman make love to a bear but how could Marian Engel's heroine make love to that particular bear? Some other bear, apparently, would have been an acceptable partner for this activity, but that one, she reminded me emphatically, had the mange. Thus in the very first year of my work on the present volume I realized that the Canadian archetypal consciousness was going to be a wild card in my pack.

The Canadian government likes to encourage professors from the United States to study Canadian culture and to include it in their course curricula and research. I had already completed the first two chapters of part one, covering British and U.S. poets' approaches to Medusa, when I received a grant from the Canadian Embassy to add a new set of texts to my mix. I found that male and female poets in Canada approach the Medusa archetype with less gender polarization than do their British and U.S. counterparts. I also discovered that the Canadian critic Northrop Frye significantly altered the quest patterns and archetypal narratives he had described as applicable to non-Canadian literature when he dealt with Canadian materials; so not only did the Canadian joker in the pack disrupt my hypothesis about gender differences, but I also had to rethink the impact of a specific natural landscape upon responses to my four archetypes. Since I discovered that Canadian differences depend to an important degree upon an internalization of attitudes toward nature shared by Canadian Native Peoples, I decided to explore the poetry of these Native Peoples and to include works by Native American poets as well in my field of research. Out of this project came my chapters "Medusa in Canada," "Romancing the Stone," "Archetypal Patterns and Native American Poetry," and "Bear," my comparison/contrast of the bear archetype in British, U.S., Native American, Anglo-Canadian, and Canadian Native Peoples' poetry with which I conclude this book, as well as a whole new definition of the archetypal process as an interaction among humans, animals, and nature.

Up to this point I had been defining archetypes as complex variables which recur in a wide variety of religious, artistic, and literary structures, with the variations in a given poem determined by the archetype's deep background interacting with both the historical or cultural context and the poet's individual signature, which I defined as the impact of his or her personal psychology and gender. I was assuming, however, that these variable symbols and narrative patterns were entirely human inventions, originating somewhere in our minds among the neocortical, limbic, and instinctual functions. As one might suspect, my experience of a Canadian and native American poetry in which bears talk to humans and humans talk to bears raised some interesting questions about the anthropomorphic derivation of archetypes, challenging my presumption that symbols and archetypes have a single point of origin, in the human mind. One might argue, of course, that these poems, in which nature and animals dialogue with people, are human inventions; however, many of the poets were writing as if this was not the case, as if they were not just speaking for themselves or the human race but functioning as skilled communicators with a nature they perceived as an active, autonomous respondent. I thus found myself entertaining the hypothesis that such poems can tell us as much about how the earth relates to us as about how we relate to the earth.

Although I have never been much taken with Jung's quasi-religious location of archetypes in a kind of Platonically transcendent collective unconscious, I am just as uncomfortable with theories that accord absolute superiority and primacy to human cognition by insisting that nothing on Earth, not even the earth itself, comes into existence until human beings find words for it. Between 1980 and the present, feminist theologians as well as myth scholars and environmentalists were also questioning traditional European assumptions that mind should dominate matter, spirit be valued over body, and human beings have primacy over a planet we did not think into existence, while creation theologians and ecologists (including both men and women) were positing hypotheses about the relationship between human beings and nature which I found applicable to many of the poems I was examining.

I will introduce the hypotheses of archetypalists such as Jung, Erich Neumann, and James Hillman, of myth critics such as Frye, and of mythologists such as Campbell, as well as the concepts of feminist theologians such as Carol Christ and Judith Ochshorn, feminist neo-Jungians such as Jean Shinoda Bolen and Christine Downing, and feminist archaeologists such as Marija Gimbutas, where they seem to fit the poetry I am analyzing. It seems appropriate to my inductive method to examine such hypotheses where they illuminate my data rather than to summarize my deviations and derivations from them in a theoretical introduction.

Finally, I should explain how I selected the sample texts which provide the data for my archetypal hypotheses. Have I not, one might query, selected just those poems which serve my eco-feminist belief system, and aren't I thus, as subjectively as any deductive theorist, working from my personal presumptions about the right relationship between men and women, human beings and nature? I hope that in this prefatory narration about how I came to vary my initial hypotheses about gender difference and how my whole archetypal apple-cart was upset by Canadian animism I will have indicated my open-mindedness, but only my reader's attentive companionship as we read poems about Medusa, Aphrodite, Artemis, and bears can provide the proof of the pudding, which, as in any inductive endeavor, must be in the eating.

In choosing my sample of more than four hundred poems, I would like to have read every poem about these four archetypes in English before arriving at my archetypal hypotheses. But I feel that the sample of poems listed under each archetype in the *Chicorel Index to Poetry in Anthologies and Collections* and *Granger's Index to Poetry*, the standard reference sources, hardly brought me anywhere near such a goal, since many poems by women, African Americans, and Native Americans are not included in the anthologies upon which *Chicorel* is based and *Granger's Index* is structured on a similarly limited set of sources. Most useful in finding poems about the three goddesses was Helen H. Law's *Bibliography of Green Myth in English Poetry*, the most recent edition of which ends in the 1950s. It was thus necessary to let my colleagues far and wide know that I was searching for poems about my four archetypes, and to turn my intrepid student runners and research assistants loose in the library stacks to conduct a page-by-page search through anthologies and collections by individual authors. Meanwhile my undergraduate students delved into poems about the goddesses, examined the impact of the archetypes on their own experience, and helped me to collect instances of the bear archetype in poetry, folklore, and popular culture.

The result is a sample of texts which certainly does not exhaust the entire field of poems about these archetypes; what I hope is that my readers, as they did with *Archetypal Patterns in Women's Fiction,* will apply my hypotheses to texts that they uncover in their own research. There is interesting work to be done on many more archetypes in poetry (such as mermaids, geese, turtles, unicorns, and toads), the pursuit of which (should the planet survive) ought to keep us all as happy as queens and kings for many years to come.

Acknowledgments

Since the scholarly life of an archetypalist can be a rather solitary one, I am enormously grateful to friends who have supported my work on this volume during the past ten years, especially to Estella Lauter of the University of Wisconsin–Green Bay, who not only provided moral support but also, together with Carol Rupprecht, edited and published in their pioneering anthology, *Feminist Archetypal Theory*, my essay on the differences between feminist archetypal theory and the theories and methods of Jung, Frye, and Lévi-Strauss. Other friends whose faithfulness kept me going include Cathy Davidson, Linda Wagner, Bob Adolph, Martin Bickman, Jeffrey Steele, Claudia Card, Nancy Vedder-Shults, Sunshine Jones, and Sister Ann Wittman.

Linda and Cathy urged me to extend my field of study to Canadian literature, while Bob Adolph provided reading lists of Canadian authors and saw to it that I was invited to York University to present my findings on affairs with bears. Barbara Godard of York University encouraged my efforts by publishing my bear article in her anthology *Gynocritics/La Gynocritique* and inviting me to return to Toronto to share my research results with her students. Joan Coldwell of McMaster University in Hamilton, Ontario, inspired my impulse to study Medusa as a maternal archetype in twentieth-century poetry and provided useful lists of poems about Medusa; while Maïr Verthuy of Concordia University in Montreal helped me to obtain Canadian fellowship support. I am grateful to Dr. Norman T. London, Academic Relations Officer of the Canadian Embassy in Washington, and to the Government of Canada for the Faculty and Institutional Research Program's grant to conduct my research on archetypes in Canadian poetry.

I found it very helpful to be able to travel to other universities to give lectures about my archetypal methods and findings and to engage in discussion about them: I want to thank Barbara Hill Rigney of Ohio State University, Columbus; Robert Daniel of Kenyon College; Maryanne Ward, Judith Elkin, and Donn Neal of the Great Lakes

Colleges Association, who invited me to be keynote speaker at their conference at Wooster College; Mary Robinson of the University of Illinois at Urbana; Susan Crowl of Ohio University in Athens; Doug Thorpe of St. Mary's College in South Bend, Indiana; and Dennis Compton of the Murphy Center for Languages and Literature at Hendrix College in Arkansas for inviting me to speak on their campuses.

My student library assistants David Mosely and Jennifer Steinberg gathered examples of poems about the three goddesses, while Susan McMorris, a graduate student in Classics, developed an outline of Aphrodite in Greek and Roman mythology which proved invaluable to my understanding of the archetype. My graduate assistants Kristen Laine and Wendy Osterweil were ingenious in finding poems about Artemis and bears: when we realized we needed to conduct page-by-page searches for poems not specifically on the archetypes, Kristen and Wendy developed skills in recognizing cognate poems in which the archetypes did not appear by name.

It will be clear from my preface that teaching archetypes to undergraduates can be an intense project, and I am not only profoundly grateful to my students who suffered and grew in the process but also owe deep thanks to Jean Saul Rannells, who as a graduate student in Continuing and Vocational Education at the University of Wisconsin developed a method of coding the impact of archetypes on the process of individuation in undergraduate students, a project which became her dissertation, "The Individuation of Women through Study of Deity Images: Learning from a Jungian Perspective" (1986). Jean did not merely take notes; during our Medusa crisis she developed exercises and workshops to enable students to deal with such powerful psychological figures, while reassuring me that I was not driving the students mad but helping them with "soul-making."

Eleanor Amico, while a graduate student in Religious Studies at the University of Wisconsin writing her dissertation, "The Status of Women at Ugarit" (1984), provided me with useful materials on Tiamet, Ishtar, and snakes for the deep background of the Medusa archetype. I am also grateful to Lise Papetti for her work on masques, E. Jan Jacobs for her contributions on crones and witches, Pat O'Hara for material on the Rossettis, Mary Ann Ross for her help with classical sources, and Sherry Reames, who chased down a medieval hymn. Finally, Adena Bargad's research on feminist student develop-

Acknowledgments

ment not only provided me with fresh ideas for teaching but also nudged me toward the topic for my next book, which will be on transformational pedagogy.

Nancy Pilzner-Dougherty photocopied and sent me articles on developments in feminist and neo-Jungian psychology during the entire period of composition, which was enormously helpful in keeping me current with recent changes in Jungian theory and clinical practice.

My undergraduate students were especially intrepid in their hunt for bear archetypes, and I received valuable material for my last chapter from work done in class by Marla Schneiderman, Helen Klebesadel, Anne M. Campbell, Gretchen Oppriecht, Terri Matzke, Sara Knutson, Susan M. Rees, and Diane Friberg.

Ten years is really a very short time to complete a key to all mythologies; the speed with which I was able to write the final drafts of this book, as well as the amelioration of my dyslexic tendencies and total disappearance of my writing block, is due to my daughter Lorien's urging me to learn word processing and to her installation of my computer and thoughtful tutelage in its use. My daughter Faith's humor and insight sustained me mightily during this period, and my thirty-four-year relationship with Henry Pratt, to whom I dedicate this book, not only survived but flourished, even during one potentially explosive period when each of us was writing a book simultaneously on the same computer.

Acknowledgments

Excerpts from "Medusa" from *The Blue Estuaries* by Louise Bogan. Copyright © 1968 by Louise Bogan. Reprinted by permission of Farrar, Straus, & Giroux, Inc.

"Desert Elm," from *The Catch* by George Bowering, McClelland and Stewart, 1976. Reprinted by permission of the author.

"Attis: Or, Something Missing," from *Collected Poems* by Basil Bunting, Oxford University Press, 1978. Reprinted by permission of the publisher.

"To Judith Asleep" by John Ciardi. Reprinted by permission of Myra Ciardi for the Ciardi family estate.

"Medusa" by Rachel Blau DuPlessis, copyright © 1980 by Rachel Blau DuPlessis. With the permission of the author. Originally published in *Wells* (New York: The Montemora Foundations, 1980).

"The Death Grapple," "The Black Goddess" and "The White Goddess," from *New Collected Poems* by Robert Graves, Oxford University Press, 1975. Reprinted by permission of Oxford University Press and A. P. Watt, Ltd. on behalf of the Trustees of the Robert Graves Copyright Trust.

"Medusa, Smiling," from *On Women Artists: Poems 1975–1980* by Alexandra Grilikhes, Cleis Press, 1981. Reprinted by permission of the publisher.

"The White Witch," from *Saint Peter Relates an Incident* by James Weldon Johnson, copyright © 1917, 1921, 1935 by James Weldon Johnson, copyright renewed © 1963 by Grace Nail Johnson. Used by permission of Viking Penguin, a division of Penguin Books USA, Inc.

"Canoe Trip" and "A Country without a Mythology," from *The Wounded Prince and Other Poems* by Douglas LePan. Used by permission of the Canadian Publishers, McClelland and Stewart, Toronto.

Excerpts from *Chosen Poems*, by Audre Lorde, used by permission of W. W. Norton and Co.

Excerpt from "Witch Woman" by Amy Lowell, in *The Complete Poetical Works of Amy Lowell*. Copyright © 1955 by Houghton Mifflin Co., © renewed 1983 by Houghton Mifflin Co., Brinton P. Roberts, and G. D'Andelot Belin, Esq. Reprinted by permission of Houghton Mifflin Co. All rights reserved.

Excerpts from "Near the Ocean" from *Near the Ocean* by Robert Lowell. Copyright © 1967 by Robert Lowell. Reprinted by permission of Farrar, Straus, & Giroux, Inc.

"Notes from Furry Creek," "Coast Range," and "A Stone Diary," from *A Stone Diary* by Pat Lowther, copyright © Oxford University Press Canada 1977. Reprinted by permission of the publisher.

"Love Songs to Joannes," from *The Last Lunar Baedecker* by Mina Loy. Reprinted by permission of Roger L. Conover, literary executor to the estate of Mina Loy and editor, *The Last Lunar Baedecker*.

Acknowledgments

"The Man," from *Against Nature: Wilderness Poems* by Judith McCombs. Reprinted by permission of the author.

"And When My Love Calls" and "A Navy Blue Afro," from *Music from Home: Selected Poems* by Colleen McElroy (Carbondale: Southern Illinois University Press, 1976), reprinted by permission of the author; and *Queen of the Ebony Isles*, pages 67–68, copyright © 1984 by Colleen J. McElroy, reprinted by permission of Wesleyan University Press and University Press of New England.

"The Pride" by John Newlove, from *The New Oxford Book of Canadian Verse*, Oxford University Press, 1982. Reprinted by permission of the author.

Dream Work by Mary Oliver, copyright © 1986 by Mary Oliver. Used here with permission of the Atlantic Monthly Press.

Lines from "Moving Out" are reprinted with permission of Macmillan Publishing Company from *The Woman Poems* by Joel Oppenheimer, copyright © 1975 by Joel Oppenheimer.

The Moon Is Always Female by Marge Piercy, copyright © 1980 by Marge Piercy. Reprinted by permission of Alfred A. Knopf, Inc.

"Medusa," from *Ariel* by Sylvia Plath, © 1966 by Harper and Row. Reprinted by permission of HarperCollins Publishers and Faber and Faber Ltd.

"The Muse as Medusa," from *Collected Poems (1930–1973)* by May Sarton. Reprinted by permission of W. W. Norton and Company.

"Considerations on Indo-European Culture," from *Dowry* by Janet Beeler Shaw. Reprinted by permission of the author.

"The Dreamers" and "The Children Asked Me to Kill You," from *Wilderness Images* by St. John Simmons. Reprinted by permission of Fiddlehead Books.

Excerpts from *Poems of Dylan Thomas* copyright © 1939 by New Directions Pub. Corp., 1945 by the Trustees for the Copyrights of Dylan Thomas. "A Winter's Tale" was first published in *Poetry* and is reprinted by permission of New Directions.

"The Girls" copyright © 1986 by Diane Wakoski. Reprinted from *The Rings of Saturn* with the permission of Black Sparrow Press. Excerpt from "No More Soft Talk," from *The Motorcycle Betrayal Poems* by Diane Wakoski, Simon and Schuster 1971. Reprinted by permission of the author.

Excerpts from "Hartico" by Anna Walters copyright © 1975 by Kenneth Rosen. Reprinted from *Voices of the Rainbow*, edited by Kenneth Rosen, published by Seaver Books, New York, NY.

Excerpts from *Inanna*, Harper and Row 1983, reprinted by permission of Diane Wolkstein.

PART ONE

MEDUSA

The Muse and Her Artist, *Helen Klebesadel, 1989. Watercolor, 30" x 11". Reproduced with permission.*

1.

The Other Side of a Mirror:
The Deep Background of
the Medusa Archetype

*I*t wouldn't be so bad if, like blackbirds in the pie, we only sang our own blues about our own lives, but our personal songs are always being thrown off tune by the discords of our mothers' experiences. For students, for poets, and for archetypal critics as well, the Medusa archetype is difficult to confront psychologically. The problem is that the wildly raging female with reptilian hairdo and terrifying eye is no mere cartoon stereotype constructed as a patriarchal slur upon powerful women: when we look at the Medusa we see in her eye our mother's rage, a rage often visited upon us as daughters. My mother, for example, had a birth name which she renounced when she suffered a trauma (I have never known what) at five years old, when she took to her bed, announcing she would never eat or breathe again until everyone called her a new name, after her father. So the unhappy, angry, but very real child remained undeveloped at the core of an ultra-"feminine" personality which she cultivated as an especially compliant daughter, perhaps in an attempt to substitute herself for a little brother who had died before she was born. Underneath this beautiful but dependent woman, beloved by many friends, there lurked the child she had repressed, for whom she named me. When I was a child she would sometimes fly into rages against me completely out of the blue, and then, looking into her eyes, I would see a glaze come over them, and in that brown reflecting pool a child would appear whom I did not know, but who I now realize was her own self she had abandoned. Medusa, the archetype I will be concerned with in this section of my book, focuses the emotions we felt about our mothers as powerful, often angry, wounded figures and elicits attitudes toward them which spring from a prelinguistic era in our lives when we were entirely dependent upon them.

The continuity of Medusa evident in her perennial appearances in fantasy movies, comic books, science fiction, and video games derives from the way that the archetype engenders our powerful emotional responses. In the summer of 1988, I found a Medusa head carved in stone guarding a Roman well deep in the forest near Cologne, signaling with her snaky hair, threatening eye, and decapitation that harm should keep away from the place she is guarding. She is also used as a negative icon, repulsing evil spirits, by Greek bakers, who to this day like to have glaring Medusa heads forged onto their oven doors to avert spirits that will make the bread fall.

One's recognition that the power and danger of angry women radiates from the Medusa head does not depend upon knowledge of classical mythology. Emily Erwin Culpepper has noticed how "a popular feminist button reproduces a Gorgon face [which] contains no words, for it needs no explanation of what it is. This face is self-explanatory. The father of an acquaintance saw this button on the book bag I carry. He had never heard of Gorgons nor seen a picture of one and asked me what it meant. I asked him to tell me first what he thought it meant. Immediately he replied, 'It means: Keep Out!' " (22–23).

Women are not always repelled by Medusa but sometimes empower ourselves by identifying with her. Culpepper goes on to demonstrate that the Medusa archetype is no mere decorative feminist icon in telling how she repelled a male intruder, who pushed into her apartment and began to attack her, by calling up her own "Gorgon spirit." Realizing that she should not have opened the door, she found herself shouting "GET OUT! GET OUT!" and felt that "I am staring him out, pushing with my eyes too. My face is bursting, contorting with terrible teeth, flaming breath, erupting into ridges and contours of rage, hair hissing. It is over in a flash." When she looked in a mirror a few minutes later, "What I saw in the mirror is a Gorgon, a Medusa, if ever there was one" (24). Culpepper has empowered herself by identification with the archetype, calling upon her internal Medusa to help her fight off a rapist. Whether she functions as an image of aversion or of empowerment, Medusa clearly evokes powerful emotional responses.

My intention in this first part of the book is to look closely at a few nineteenth-century poems which are structured upon this most "negative" feminine archetype in order to raise some initial questions about gender differences in archetypal response. I want to consider whether there is any feminist archetypal baby in all that patriarchal bathwater at all; that is, if women's poems provide any examples of feminist reenvisionings of Medusa, do these arise from a subversive reworking of myths which were originally patriarchal and created only to express masculine responses to powerful women? Does the archetype contain or provoke a response which empowers us because it reminds us of the feminine power we would like to have, or does it somehow evoke traces of apatriarchal feminine power which human beings might have once experienced?

I would define such archetypes as galvanizing psychological complexes which, far from being rigid either in content or effect, vary according to individual experience and cultural context. Although I am certainly out of sympathy with C. G. Jung and his disciple Erich Neumann's masculine perspectives upon Medusa as a typical "Terrible Mother" in a "Terrible/Great Mother" polarity, we need to assess their explanations of her threat before undertaking a feminist archetypal reading of poems about her.

Jung valued the unconscious as a locus of potentially empowering archetypes not only in individuals but also in artistic, religious, and literary systems, and he posited the healthy self as integrating conscious and unconscious facets of the personality. He valued "femininity," which he associated with the unconscious, urging his male patients to get in touch with their "animas," or more emotional sides, in order to repair the psychological damage of excessive masculine rationalism. Jung was the product of a gender-polarized Victorian Switzerland and, even more important, of the kind of European education which insisted upon categorizing all phenomena into pairs of opposites. Thus, no matter how much he valued the unconscious and the instinctual, emotive side of the personality, he tended to place them on the downside of a seesaw, with consciousness, rationality, and masculinity on the up end: "Although man and woman unite," he insisted, "they nevertheless represent irreconcilable opposites which, when activated, degenerate into deadly hostility. This primordial pair of opposites symbolizes every conceivable pair of opposites that may occur: hot and cold, light and dark, north and south, dry and damp, good and bad, conscious and unconscious" (*Psychological Reflections* 94). Jung and Neumann perceive consciousness itself as masculine, so that, as Neumann puts it, "the masculine has identified itself with consciousness and its growth wherever a patriarchal world has developed. . . . But in general consciousness sees the unconscious symbolized as feminine and itself as masculine." Thus, Neumann reasoned, both men and women who "participate in this development of consciousness" and therefore possess "a symbolically male consciousness" experience the maternal feminine at the core of our infantile memories and of the collective unconscious as the "Terrible Mother" (148). We shall see as this study progresses that both Jung and Neumann tried to get their patients to balance out this perception of the feminine as "terrible" by coming to terms with their unconscious lives; but their masculinist warp and their tendency to dualize prevents them from achieving a truly integrative psychology.

While Jung readily admitted that he and his colleagues suffered from their masculine bias, recognizing that "the elementary fact that a man always presupposes another's psychology as being identical with his own aggravates the difficulty and hinders the correct understanding of the feminine psyche" (*Psychological Reflections* 97), and although he encouraged his female colleagues to conduct research from their own perspective, his descriptions of the most important archetypes remained distorted by masculine bias.

We can see such a distortion in the archetypal narrative of the rebirth quest or journey which Jung set forth in *Symbols of Transformation* as the basis for psychological health at the midlife crisis. As I explained in the article "Archetypal Approaches to the New Feminist Criticism," in this journey Jung's male hero crosses the threshold from the conscious to the unconscious world in an attempt to come to terms with his internal nature, understood not only as his personal psychology but also as the collective unconscious whose patterns correspond to such cultural paradigms as the resurrection of Jesus and the rebirth of the sun from the sea. The male hero journeys from the day-to-day world first into the realm of his "shadow," a collection of personal antisocial tendencies, his opposite or wicked self. These invert his good-citizen persona, but as he moves more deeply into the unconscious the shadow changes sex, merging with his buried feminine tendencies, or anima, to form a powerful "autonomous complex," which Jung terms the "dual mother" or "terrible mother." The hero's problem is to struggle with this powerful feminine component in his self, to absorb her import, master her autonomous control over his impulses, and then return, regenerated or transformed, to everyday life.

The "mother" in the male quester is "terrible" only in the sense that he fears and resists her; in battling with her and overcoming her, in Jung's process, he is able to absorb her feminine power as an element in his reborn, androgynous self. There is nonetheless a lot of intergender conflict as well as usurpation of "femininity" infecting this rebirth process, and the archetype derives a conflictual tone from Jung's definition of male and female as eternally battling contraries.

But what happens when the woman hero quests into her unconscious? To start with, the "shadow" realm for women is infected with self-repudiation and self-loathing for any manifestation of feminine sexuality—a social inheritance, as we shall see, from very recent nineteenth-century gender norms. Some women poets describe encounters with an apatriarchal "green world lover" who represents a healthy heterosexual Eros, an archetypal figure who combines antisocial shadow with the "animus" (internal "masculine" element) and who sometimes takes the form of Pan, Dionysus, or the horned god of the Celts. This positive male figure is far less common than a much more patriarchally infected male lover or husband whose gynophobia destroys his victim's psyche before she can win through to the deeper layers of her unconscious. Anima, or internal femininity reinforced by maternal memory, plays a similarly central role in women's as in men's psychological quests; should the woman hero prevail she must come to terms with a powerful feminine element resident at the core of her psyche. Although, like male questers, women often fight this terrifyingly powerful female archetype, the encounter is different from men's in its meeting of same with same, of daughter with mother, resulting in a woman/woman destruction or empowerment.

I do not believe that all myths merely reflect a masculine cultural ideology to which women have never contributed. My hypothesis is that given the thousands of years human beings have existed, the patriarchal pie is only a recent context for the formulation of responses to archetypes, and these recent responses constitute only a thin over-layer hiding much more feminist attitudes. Poetry, I believe, is our primal literary genre, popular long before the invention of reading and writing and long antedating prose as a means for religious celebration. If we consider that we are living in the same kinds of bodies and with brains identical to those of our ancestors at least thirty thousand years ago, it is possible to suggest that recurrent symbols call up responses whose characteristics may derive as much from our remoter past as from more recent culture. In this chapter I will set a few exploratory examples of poems about Medusalike figures against Medusa's deeper archetypal background in order to suggest how we can read women poets as responding both to her particular historical signature and to their own unrequited desires about feminine power.

"The Other Side of a Mirror"

Although it will not be my practice to an-alyze an entire poem, I want to start with one complete poetic text in order to demonstrate the kinds of readings I base my hypotheses upon. Mary Elizabeth Coleridge was twenty-one years old when she sat down to write "The Other Side of a Mirror" in 1882, right in the middle of one of the most difficult periods for women in our entire history.

I sat before my glass one day,
    And conjured up a vision bare,
Unlike the aspects glad and gay,
    That erst were found reflected there—
The vision of a woman, wild
    With more than womanly despair.

Her hair stood back on either side
    A face bereft of loveliness.
It had no envy now to hide
    What once to man on earth could guess.
It formed the thorny aureole
    Of hard unsanctified distress.

Her lips were open—not a sound
    Came through the parted lines of red.
Whate'er it was, the hideous wound
    In silence and in secret bled.
No sigh relieved her speechless woe,
    She had no voice to speak her dread.

And in her lurid eyes there shone
    The dying flame of life's desire,
Made mad because its hope was gone,
    And kindled at the leaping fire
Of jealousy, and fierce revenge,
    And strength that could not change nor tire.

Shade of a shadow in the glass,
    O set the crystal surface free!
Pass—as the fairer visions pass—
    Nor ever more return, to be
The ghost of a distracted hour,
    That heard me whisper, "I am she!" (137)

The first thing to notice about this striking poem, written by a young woman trying to find a way to be a poet and an intellectual within the rigid gender prohibitions of Victorian England, is that it is not explicitly about Medusa. It contains sufficiently Medusean features, however—the hair on end, the grimacing masklike face, and especially the "lurid" eyes—to suggest that the woman behind the mirror is a close relative of the Gorgon. As first-person narrator, Coleridge enframes her poem in two ritual assertions, her invocation in the first stanza of a spirit from behind the mirror and, in the final stanza, a "rite of riddance" begging the figure to depart. In that she is acting as a "conjurer," one who has the power and the skill to bring a figure up out of a dark reflecting recess in an act of scrying, Coleridge establishes herself as active and powerful rather than passive and victimized; at the end of the poem she also presumes a magician's power of bidding a hostile spirit to leave her alone. She makes it clear that the ordinary light-hearted "aspects glad and gay" a young woman might be expected to cast upon her mirror have no power to entrance her when below these lurk someone far more interesting, a "wild woman" she is unafraid to face. As we shall see toward the end of this book, when Coleridge had arranged her poetic and intellectual life in the manner she wanted, she expressed her entrancement with wild women even less ambiguously. At this stage in her life it is important to note the courage with which, as a young woman, she faces what is lurking behind the normatively sweet and feminine reflections of her mirror.

She describes the archetype she has conjured up in three central stanzas, one about hair, one about lips and mouth, and one about eyes, approaching these features in a tone that blends fear with a sense of awe at the power of the woman within. Although the qualities and characteristics set forth in these central stanzas are mainly negative— "face bereft of loveliness," "the hideous wound," "her lurid eyes"— each negative quality encases a positive value that empowers Coleridge as much as it repels her: "What once no man on earth could guess" (a well-kept women's secret), "in silence and in secret bled" (again, a concealed wound stoically endured), "the dying flame of life's desire" (at least the desire burned brightly enough to empower her). This encapsulation of a powerful quality within a negative construct is particularly evident in the first and last enframing stanzas: "The vision of a woman, wild / With more than womanly despair" expressing an unwomanly quality Coleridge does not reject; and "The Ghost of a distracted hour, / That heard me whisper, 'I am she!' " couching her strongest assertion in a direct and simple statement encoded within a welter of negative constructions.

Far from ambivalent about the wounded, despairing woman on the other side of her mirror, Coleridge identifies with her, only lightly concealing the emphatic self-definition of her last stanza beneath the expressions of fear and terror that go before. This viewpoint is especially interesting in a young woman whom Edith Sichel described as nice to a fault, who "would write in odd corners, in odd postures, at odd moments, so as to escape detection" and who "would allow anyone to interrupt her. Any bore in human form who made a claim upon her seemed more important than what she was about" (21). It is also notable that Coleridge managed to avoid women's ordinary fate of marriage and childbirth and spent her life in pursuit of intellectual and poetic companionship; she was much admired by Robert Bridges, and by no means a recluse.

Coleridge gets quite happily carried away by the antisocial content of her vision, not only empathizing with her wild woman's wounds and despair but identifying with her power. As Sandra M. Gilbert and Susan Gubar note in using this poem as one of the touchstones for their analysis of nineteenth-century women writers, Coleridge's identification with the woman behind her mirror attests to "an invincible sense of her own autonomy, her own interiority" (16). Gilbert and Gubar, however, read the poem quite differently than I do: while I see Coleridge perceiving only "glad and gay" normative images of womanhood on the mirror's surface and rejecting them to affirm the wild woman behind it, they read both the angelic good girl and the demonic " 'monster' . . . whose Medusa-face also kills feminine creativity" as patriarchal in origin. The Medusa archetype has certainly accreted many layers of gynophobic response since its adoption by the Greeks; I will argue, however, that women poets empowered themselves from signals embedded in the archetype long before the Victorian age.

Although there is no implicit maternal content in Coleridge's Medusalike archetype, at this phase in her life she is clearly weighing the kinds of feminine choices modeled for her, perhaps by her mother as well as by other women of her acquaintance. Earlier in the century, Elizabeth Barrett Browning, in her 1856 poem about the growing up of a woman poet, has Aurora Leigh ascribe specifically Medusan qualities to a painting of her dead mother. The portrait on which the young Aurora meditates throughout her childhood was done after her mother's death by an artist who refused to paint the pale English shroud and substituted, instead, a bright red brocade blouse, so that, as Aurora puts it,

> Therefore very strange
> The effect was. I, a little child, would crouch
> For hours upon the floor with knees drawn up,
> And gaze across them, half in terror, half
> In adoration, at the picture there,—
> That swan-like supernatural white life
> Just sailing upward from the red stiff silk
> Which seemed to have no part in it nor power
> To keep it from quite breaking out of bounds.

Again, the woman poet's horror is overweighed by fascination, not just a child's natural ghoulishness but an attraction to the power in the color red in contrast to the deathly and pure whiteness. Just as the wounded mouth seems menstrual in "The Other Side of a Mirror," the color red in Browning suggests as an emblem both of feminine bodily power and feminine reproductive suffering. Aurora's perception of her mother is highly dualized, the "supernatural white life" of the neck intended to suggest the divine as opposed to the earthly red garment; and Browning consistently polarizes both the symbol and Aurora's response to it:

> And as I grew
> In years, I mixed, confused, unconsciously,
> Whatever I last read or heard or dreamed,
> Abhorrent, admirable, beautiful,
> Pathetical, or ghastly, or grotesque,
> With that still face . . . which did not therefore change,
> But kept the mystic level of all forms,
> Hates, fears, and admirations, was by turns
> Ghost, fiend, and angel, fairy, witch, and sprite,
> A dauntless Muse who eyes a dreadful Fate,
> A loving Psyche who loses sight of Love,
> A still Medusa with mild milky brows
> All curdled and all clothed upon with snakes
> Whose slime falls fast as sweat will; or anon
> Our Lady of the Passion, stabbed with swords
> Where the Babe sucked; or Lamia in her first
> Moonlighted pallor, ere she shrunk and blinked
> And shuddering wriggled down to the unclean;
> Or my own mother, leaving her last smile
> In her last kiss upon the baby-mouth
> My father pushed down on the bed for that,—
> Or my dead mother, without smile or kiss,
> Buried at Florence. (256–57)

However exaggerated this romantic necrophilia may seem, the paradoxical responses are typical of a child's ambivalence toward the overpowering figure of her mother. The strikingly sensual attributes which Aurora reads into the painting have the tactile concreteness of childhood perception, in that she is equally fascinated by the milk conflated with reptilian slime and her mother's hair "clothed upon" with snakes, a paradoxical yoking of qualities we would ordinarily consider opposites. Her response to snake slime and curdled milk is not repulsion: Aurora is attracted to and fond of all of the associations with her mother's portrait. Like Mary Elizabeth Coleridge, Browning acknowledges women's identification with a Medusa archetype which ought to repel any right-thinking nineteenth-century man or woman. Neither Coleridge's nor Aurora's affections cling to merely the "glad and gay" aspects of their vision; quite the contrary, the wild, wounded, reptilian aspects of the feminine seem to be equally fascinating.

Coleridge's and Browning's attraction to a feminine archetype who seems to be both fiend and angel bears the signature of the nineteenth century's propensity for binary feminine archetypes, like the angel/demon dyad that Nina Auerbach has recognized as a popular Victorian symbol which appeals to women as both a nightmare and an "avenue of power": one of the most powerful creations of the Victorian cultural imagination, she writes, "is an explosively mobile, magic woman, who breaks the boundaries of family within which her society restricts her. The triumph of this overweening creature is a celebration of the corporate imagination that believed in her" (1–2). By identifying Medusa and other such monstrous images as vehicles of power for Victorian women, Auerbach acknowledges the archetype as a source of feminist strength; I would like to explore the possibility that this source is not only the rebellion that would result from any woman's natural desire to subvert Victorian gender constraints but also constitutes a recognition of the code of feminine empowerment which the archetype carries into the nineteenth century from its earlier history.

Although Browning and Coleridge are making use of a polarized feminine symbol popular in the nineteenth-century imagination, their responses deviate from the sense of "otherness" which nineteenth-century male poets accord to the archetype. My suspicion is that the women poets' polarized Medusas are not so much a corroboration of the Jungian model as a parallel case arising out of the nineteenth century's proclivity for dualizing women. The women poets' attitudes to Medusa's dualities are quite different both from Jung's and from the attitudes of male poets, however; when we turn to Shelley and Keats, we find them taking an entirely different tone toward the archetype than do Coleridge and Browning.

Where Coleridge looked at her wild woman in a mirror, Shelley, in "On the Medusa of Leonardo Da Vinci in the Florentine Gallery"

(1819), is taking the same stance as Browning, describing a painting. Although his Medusa is female, he describes her as "it" through most of his poem, which he structures upon binary images of beauty and ugliness ("Its horror and its beauty are divine," for example, and " 'Tis the tempestuous loveliness of terror") until the penultimate line, where he identifies "it" with "A woman's countenance, with serpent-locks, / Gazing on death in heaven from those wet rocks." Speaking in the distanced third person of "the gazer" (upon the painting), Shelley identifies the Medusa's beauty rather than her ugly snaky hair as her most frightening aspect: "Yet it is less the horror than the grace / Which turns the gazer's spirit into stone," rather than her

> Hairs which are vipers, and they curl and flow
>   And their long tangles in each other lock,
> And with unending involutions shew
>   Their mail'ed radiance, as it were to mock
> The torture and the death within, and saw
>   The solid air with many a ragged jaw. (IV: 23)

Like Coleridge, Shelley recognizes and even to a certain degree empathizes with Medusa's suffering; however, his stance remains that of a horrified observer.

Shelley thrills to the conflation of death and serpent life and to the mixture of feminine beauty with danger, but however attracted he may be, he maintains the stance of the aesthetic observer. We find the same poetic stance taken toward paintings of Medusa in less famous poets of the nineteenth century such as Edgar S. Fawcett, who wrote a similarly dualized sonnet about her in 1878, yoking lovely "lips that a god were worthy alone to woo; / Round chin, and nostrils curved in the old Greek wise" with ideally "warm soft gold" hair out of which "Coils of lean horror peer with many a fold, / With sharp tongues flickering in flat clammy heads!" (181). Her appealing beauty is the primary attractant of this kind of Medusa, covering something ugly, reptilian, and frightening. I will argue in chapter 5 that this splitting up of feminine beauty from feminine sensuality is a unique and recent psychological trend in European sexual history, arising from the necessity for wives to be absolutely chaste or sexless in the capitalized marriage market, a trend so disruptive of natural human instincts that the nineteenth-century poets expressed it in terms of the enraged and dangerous Medusa buried under the mien of any lovely woman you might meet. In this context it is not surprising to find male poets engaged in a kind of horrified attraction/repulsion while women poets cannot help but identify with the feminine plight the archetype encodes.

John Keats's *Lamia,* a narrative poem written in the same year—1819—as Shelley's poem about da Vinci's Medusa, provides a more extended, detailed example of the romanticized snake goddess. In this case the figure is that of a Lamia, who in some accounts started out as a beautiful queen in Libya but who had a relationship with Zeus which led to Hera's jealous slaying of her children. She is reputed to have taken up kidnapping children after this punishment, an activity which links her to Lilith, a goddess who in Hebrew legend steals away other people's children. In Keats's poem Hermes changes the snake Lamia into a beautiful girl as a reward for helping him pursue a nymph he loves. The Lamia is in love with Lycius, who is enchanted by her mortal beauty and makes love to her, hidden away from society. In a gender reversal of the Psyche-Eros plot, Lycius, like Psyche, wants more than sexual intercourse with his lover; he wants to marry her so as to boast of his conquest before his friends and enemies. Meanwhile his tutor Apollonius, who represents the quality of rationality opposed to sensual entrapment, recognizes Lamia's reptilian underside and tries to save Lycius by forcing him to see it. He succeeds, and the poem reaches its tragic end as Lycius dies of the shock. The paradox of reptilian horror lurking beneath feminine beauty structures *Lamia* as it does the other nineteenth-century lyrics by male poets, but in adapting the Lamia legend Keats brings into focus a less rigidly dualized, earlier archetypal narrative which accounts for her being a snake in the first place in terms of victimization by Zeus and Hera.

Like the Lamia, Medusa, in some archetypal narratives, had not always been a Gorgon but had been turned into that horrific creature through the jealousy of an Olympian goddess. In these myths Medusa was an especially beautiful priestess in the temple of Athena, until she made love to or (in some accounts) was raped by the sea god Poseidon. Then Athena, in her fury or jealousy, turned her into an ugly Gorgon who could never attract the god again. This is the version underlying L. Morris's *Epic of Hades* (1879), in which the sympathetic poet recounts Medusa's first-person story of her predicament: "I was a priestess once," she tells him, singing "my cold pure hymns" to the "virgin ear" of the goddess Athena, though longing for the happier dances and songs of "the neighboring shrine / Of Aphrodite." Into her dissatisfactions Poseidon comes "Like a god," and "How should a virgin know / deceit, who never at the joyous shrine / of Cypris [Aphrodite] knelt"? "For innocence / The gods keep all their terrors," she admits: her sexual naiveté has led to her victimization and to Athena's punishment. Morris's conclusion, spoken by Medusa, has to do with his century's unhealthy refusal to acknowledge the sensuality of ordinary women:

> We are made to love—
> We women, and the injury which turns
> The honey of our lives to gall, transforms
> The angel to the fiend. For it is sweet
> To know the dreadful sense of strength, and smite
> And leave the tyrant dead with a glance; ay! sweet,
> In that fierce lust of power, to slay the life
> Which harmed not . . . (156–57)

Now resident in hell, Medusa's only redeeming memory is of Perseus using her severed head as a "shield / Of chastity" to destroy the monster who held Andromeda captive. Medusa ends her monologue advising tender young women who have been raped and left in "despair / And shame and all abhorrence, while he goes / His way unpunished" to help other victims. Interestingly, Morris's final association is between Medusa and the Magdalen, fallen (sexually victimized) women whom he urges to redeem themselves by their empathy for others in their same sexual plight.

Whereas Morris accepts the idea that a young woman may be "fallen" but still be worth helping, many Victorians considered amarital sexuality unforgivable in a woman. We find this psychologically destructive assumption underlying the works of Christina and Dante Gabriel Rossetti, sister and brother poets who acted out in their lives the era's divergent attitudes toward male and female sexuality. In his "Aspecta Medusa" (1865 or 1867), Dante Rossetti describes Andromeda, "by Perseus saved and wed," obsessed with the desire to "see the Gorgon's head,"

Till o'er a fount he held it, bade her lean,
And mirrored in the wave was safely seen
   That death she lived by.
Let not thine eyes know
Any forbidden thing itself, although
It one should save as well as kill: but be
Its shadow upon life enough for thee. (123)

Dante Rossetti does not explain why Andromeda should want to see Medusa's head in the first place, though within the context of poems like Mary Elizabeth Coleridge's, as well as in his definition of Medusa's head as a "shadow upon life," it is clear that Andromeda is curious about her own sexuality, which Victorian norms for women had relegated to her "shadow" or unconscious. For Christina Rossetti, who tried to live a naturally sensual life in a family which considered sensuality and goodness anomalous when combined in an unmarried woman, the split is personally destructive. "The World" (1854) is split into irreconcilable day and night spheres, personified as a "soft, exceedingly fair" goddess who woos the poet "by day" but who becomes "Loathsome and foul with hideous leprosy, / And subtle serpents gliding in her hair" at night. Christina Rossetti cannot accept her brother's advice to Andromeda to look only at the shadow of the nocturnal Medusa because she knows that the reality Medusa embodies is more central to her life than the "glad and gay" normative surfaces, which, like Mary Elizabeth Coleridge, she rejects as less vital than the Medusa under the mirror: "By day she stands a lie," asserts Rossetti, "by night she stands / In all the naked horror of the truth" (Bernikow 126). It is not Medusa herself who is horrible; the horror results from Rossetti's introjection of Victorian distaste for a natural feminine sensuality which characterizes her daytime goddess, whom she associates with "Ripe fruits, sweet flowers, and full satiety." Where nobody would consider her brother unmanly for carrying out his sensual desires, his sister's desires make her unwomanly, a cultural repudiation which makes her split her entire "World" into tormenting opposites.

The Victorian insistence that innocence and sensuality were opposite qualities and that no one who enjoyed sensuality could be considered pure in heart underlies the pathetically dualized archetype of child/horrible female in Thomas Gordon Hake's "Infant Medusa" (1894). Speaking, oddly enough, in the voice of Poseidon, Hake has him announce that

> I loved Medusa when she was a child,
> Her rich brown tresses heaped in crispy curl
> Where now those locks with reptile passion whirl,
> By hate into dishevelled serpents coiled.
> I loved Medusa when her eyes were mild,
> Whose glances, narrowed now, perdition hurl,
> As her self-tangled hairs their mass unfurl,
> Bristling the way she turns with hissings wild. (28)

Poseidon is, after all, the one who kissed the innocent mouth which "curved with amorous spell," and thus (according to the Athena/ revenge version of the legend) brought about her punishment. Hake's sonnet, nonetheless, remains objective, structured upon Medusa's transformation from lovely child to Gorgon, with his expressions of horror rather blandly issuing from the lips of her lover-rapist Poseidon. In this strange paradox resides the stance of the male poet toward the Medusa element in Victorian sexuality, insisting that the only quality conventionally appropriate for brides was sexless innocence, to the extent that even within marriage a wife's unfolding sensuality would be considered (even by the husband who stirred her up) impure, an unwomanly loss of innocence. I will go more deeply into this question of unhealthy sexual prohibitions in my chapters on Aphrodite; with regard to male and female poets' approaches to Medusa, it is important to note that in the nineteenth century both genders seem to be infected by a dichotomous archetypal signature which arises from a rupture of normal sensuality.

At this initial stage in my gender comparison it is clear that the women's attitudes are colored by a kind of maternal bonding, an attraction to Medusa's sameness, while the men stand at more of a distance, horrified at the possibility of being tempted by Medusa's feminine allure. Keats and Morris, nonetheless, are quite sympathetic to Lamia and to Medusa, whom they perceive as victims of wrongful responses to feminine sensuality. Although all eight of these nineteenth-century Medusa poets stand back to observe and describe the archetype without suggesting exactly what should be done about her, they recognize that Medusa is a wounded feminine archetype and that her wound is inflicted by a split between her bodily integrity and nineteenth-century ideas about feminine sexuality. It is easy for the twentieth-century literary critic to blame the Victorian sexual mores for Medusa's wounds and to overlook the way that nineteenth-century poets adapt elements of the classical Medusa's plight to convey their pity, and sometimes even their outrage, at her fate.

The Beautiful Medusa

Many classical legends suggest that Medusa was beautiful before she was ugly, that she was a priestess before she was a Gorgon, and that her integrity had been ruptured by the Olympian divinities Athena and Poseidon. My thesis is that these explanatory narratives suggest an underlayer of earlier valuation of Medusa beneath the gynophobic, Persean perspective. This valuation is evident in the qualities that Perseus steals from Medusa. He takes away her head, whose reptilian blood turns out to be magically healing, and out of her severed neck arises Pegasus, whom Perseus also steals in a usurpation of her poetic powers; in a number of versions he presents her severed head as an ornament for Athena's shield. In the stories which tell of Medusa's beauty before Athena punished her, we also can detect earlier versions at odds with Perseus's perspective.

Some traces of these are sufficiently persistent in the Medusa archetype to find their way into early modern Europe. In a fifteenth-century tapestry Perseus is depicted riding away on Pegasus and bearing a shield with Medusa's head on it while Medusa, a lovely, naked maiden with two beautiful young sisters, stands pierced by an arrow with her blood dripping down into the river. The arrow has been shot by cupid from the back of Pegasus while her two lovely sisters look on, one riding a swan and the other a dolphin. Christine de Pisan, in her *Book of the City of Ladies* (1405), wrote that

> Medusa (or Gorgon) was celebrated for her outstanding beauty. She was the daughter of the very wealthy king Phorcys whose large kingdom was surrounded by the sea. This Medusa, according to the ancient stories, was of such striking beauty that not only did she surpass all other women—which was an amazing and supernatural thing—but she also attracted to herself, because of her pleasing

appearance—her long and curly blond hair spun like gold, along with her beautiful face and body—every mortal creature upon whom she looked, so that she seemed to make people immovable. For this reason the fable claimed that they had turned to stone. (203–204)

The legends of Medusa's original beauty, which began with the classical versions and lasted into the Renaissance, survive in modern popular culture, as evidenced in a Betty Crocker Home Library volume, *The Pleasures of Crewel*, published in 1972, which suggests how women can, using "bronze crewel wool for the head, face and hair," embroider a "modern version of the mythical Medusa Head [which] uses flowers, a bird and a butterfly in place of the traditional snakes. An improvement, don't you agree?"

It was while doing the research for "Aunt Jennifer's Tigers: Notes towards a Preliterary History of Women's Archetypes," in which I looked at the history of women's needlework, that these recent recognitions of Medusa's beauty suggested to me that the archetype has undergone a process of degradation, a superimposition of gynophobic perspectives over attitudes which persist in valuing women. The question which the embroidery evidence raised was whether the beautiful Medusa degraded by Athena and beheaded by Perseus carries historical traces from earlier mythologies which give greater value than the Greeks and other Europeans did to a threatening one-eyed female associated with snakes.

When nineteenth-century and early-twentieth-century archaeologists began discovering artifacts which suggested the worship of goddesses on a worldwide scale, many myth scholars began to dream of a kind of golden world of feminine hegemony before a patriarchal fall. In the perspective of the classical scholar Jane Ellen Harrison, for example, the Perseus-Medusa interaction could be read as evidence of the tension between images representative of Greek and antecedent cultures in which goddesses and snakes were more highly valued. Studying Greek literature and religious practice in a volume called *Mythology*, Harrison posited two interacting layers, which she described as "southern," of Anatolian and Cretan derivation, in which a "dominant Mother-God" was worshipped, and a "northern stratum which is Indo-European" and has the "Father-God," in a "patrilinear" system (62). Using Harrison's data, Joseph Campbell postulates in *Occidental Mythology* a process by which the northern stratum, characterized by a militant, father-God-oriented and patriarchal dualism, ravished the "essentially organic, vegetal, non-heroic view of nature" characterizing the "older mother myths" (21). Both Harrison and Campbell assume a monolithic, dominant "matriarchy" antedating patriarchy, with the system of "Mother Right" in control, just as the myth scholar J. J. Bachofen had postulated earlier. In recent years this concept, that a matriarchal "Mother God" as dominant as the patriarchal "Father God" existed as a mirror image of masculine monotheism, has been superseded by data illustrating the polytheistic religious systems prevalent from prehistoric to classical times, which are characterized by a more equal distribution of power between genders. Judith Ochshorn, for example, contrasts the polytheistic religions of the Middle East to monotheistic Judaism and Christianity, and suggests that far more positive attitudes toward femininity characterize polytheistic than monotheistic religions (73–75). Similarly postulating gender equity for polytheistic religions practiced in the prehistoric cultures antedating the Greeks, archaeologist Marija Gimbutas ascribes gender equity to "Old Europe" of 6500–3500 B.C.E.:

> In Old Europe the world of myth was not polarized into male and female as it was among the Indo-Europeans and many other nomadic and pastoral peoples of the steppes. Both principles were manifest side by side. The male divinity in the shape of a young man or a male animal appears to affirm and strengthen the forces of the creative and active female. Neither is subordinate to the other; by complementing one another, their power is doubled. (237)

We should note that the religion of such Indo-European groups as the Greeks and the Celts was polytheistic, like that of the Old European cultures they replaced. Any student of Greek or Celtic mythology can discern the contrast to Judaic and Christian monotheism in their many goddesses, queens, and even female military heroes, like the Celtic woman warriors who were said to fill their hair with lime to make it stand on end so that they could terrify their enemies, or the women warriors who, Tacitus suggests, were typical of the lack of gender distinction in the British military system. In Greek mythology, however, the power of women is often perceived as unpleasant (Hera's divisive jealousy, for example) or inimical to good (male) values, the categorical classical mind finding anomalies like the sphinx, hydra, and Medusa especially unwholesome mixtures of the chthonic or earthy with the human. Goddesses are revered in Greek myth not as symbols of women's holistic powers but as a split-off feminine function: Aphrodite standing for Eros, for example, while Athena is "chaste" but wise, Artemis wild but "chaste," etc. The perpetual gender conflict among Greek gods and heroes and Greek goddesses and mortal women, which often takes the form of narratives about stealing women's powers, establishes a tension between the sexes which characterizes Greek polytheism and differentiates it from the equally polytheistic mythologies of the ancient Middle East (Amico 545).

Gimbutas recognizes that it was of primary interest to the Greeks and other Indo-European invaders to assert their more male-dominant, masculine religious system over the local gods and goddesses representing, in her interpretation of archaeological findings, more gender-equal mythologies. Although her analysis is a bit monolithic, she provides an interesting hypothesis for analyzing poetic texts in which patriarchal strata are underlain by feminist perspectives. She thus describes the invading Achaean Greeks as promulgating a "masculine world view" which is

> that of the Indo-Europeans, which did not develop in Old Europe but was superimposed upon it. Two entirely different sets of mythical images met. Symbols of the masculine group replaced the images of Old Europe. Some of the old elements were fused together as a subsidiary of the new symbolic imagery, thus losing their original meaning. Some images persisted side by side, creating chaos in the former harmony. Through losses and additions new complexes of symbols developed which are best reflected in Greek mythology. . . . The study of mythic images provides one of the best proofs that the Old European world was not the proto-Indo-European world and that there was no direct and unobstructed line of development to the modern Europeans. The earliest European civilization was savagely destroyed by the patriarchal element and never recovered, but its legacy lingered in the substratum which nourished further European cultural developments. The old European creations were not lost; transformed, they enormously enriched the European psyche. (237–38)

Although there is still no historical proof of exactly what happened in human history to enable patriarchal cultures devoted to hierarchical dominance to undercut more gender equal and peaceable human societies, there is general agreement that cultures which are nomadic or threatened by scarcity tend to be less egalitarian than village cultures which have long been settled in the cultivation of their gardens (Sanday 171–211). Whatever the cause of the rise of patriarchy, however, archaeologists, classical scholars, and historians, as well as anthropologists comparing European to alternative cultures, have suggested that patriarchy is neither inevitable nor entirely successful in imposing its values on the cultures, classes, and genders it attempts to subjugate; the crust of the pie is much less thick than we blackbirds had realized. Thus Gimbutas's concept of interacting layers of images provides an interesting model for a literary analysis of the dialectical interaction of patriarchal with feminist imagery in poems about goddess archetypes.

Whereas Harrison and Gimbutas suggest two strata interacting in Greek mythology, anthropologist-linguist Paul Friedrich posits multiple lines of imagery interbraided in Greek gods and goddesses, with strands from "oriental" (Middle Eastern) and Mycenaean and Minoan religions woven into the "Proto-European culture of Southern Russia and the Danubian plain that has been reconstructed for about the close of the fourth millennium" (52). When a literary critic studies one goddess archetype, she needs to be aware of this complex superimposition of one set of images upon another, in order to determine whatever preclassical attitudes the archetype contains in interaction with its more classical contents. Analyzing the deep background of the Medusa archetype provides a *reculant pour mieux sorter*, a stepping back in order to leap forward into a clearer understanding of how the classical perspective continues to be undermined, both by its preclassical content and by the desires it elicits during later periods of literary adaptation.

The key to the deep background underlying the classical Medusa lies in the motifs which always accompany her. Most important are her snakes, but the staring eye and the severed head also occur both in the interbraided Middle Eastern archetypes and in Celtic mythology. Finally, her association with stone, which I will consider only in passing here, becomes especially important in chapter 3, where I examine Medusa in Canada.

<table>
<tr><td>Symphonies of
Snakes</td></tr>
</table>

The accompanying chart demonstrates the far more feminist perspective taken toward women associated with snakes in both Middle Eastern and Old European mythological systems than in later periods.[1] By "more feminist" I mean attitudes more accepting than ours of a combination of power and prowess in a woman's body and of her alliance with a deeply revered animal appreciated for its association with wisdom and generativity. In the pre-Biblical Middle East the snake, as Joseph Campbell remarks in *The Power of Myth,* was "the symbol of life throwing off the past and continuing to live" and of "immortal energy and consciousness engaged in the field of time, constantly throwing off death and being born again." The snake was a sacred animal in Eastern and Native American religions (45–47). It has, in contrast, been considered disgusting and dangerous rather than wise and generative in most European mythologies since classical times, the object of terror and horror, as we noted in nineteenth-century poems about Medusa.

Greek horror of Medusa derives as much from distaste for anomaly as disgust for snakes, the Greeks feeling a profound aversion to anything combining two opposites in one being, especially if those opposites are from the supposedly distinct categories of the human and the nonhuman. Such an anomalous conflation in the body of a woman—women being considered threatening to human development and prone to allegiance with the chthonic or primal, earthy realm—was especially threatening. Thus for the Greeks the snake's Middle Eastern association with intellect falls away entirely, so that the archetype is considered distastefully nonrational. In the Old Testament, as Campbell reminds us,

> our story of the Fall in the Garden sees nature as corrupt; and that myth corrupts the whole world for us. Because nature is thought of as corrupt, every spontaneous act is sinful and must not be yielded to. You get a totally different civilization and a totally different way of living according to whether your myth presents nature as fallen or whether nature is in itself a manifestation of divinity . . . (99)

Hellenized Christian theology inherited the Greek distaste for snakes as nonrational and for women with snakes in their hair as disgusting anomalies, an attitude which it conflated with the Augustinian insistence that nature and the human body are ontological enemies of the soul.

CENTURIES OF SNAKES

OLD EUROPE

MIDDLE EAST

10,000 B.C.E.

Upper Paleolithic Snake and bird goddess in Magdalenian and Upper Paleolithic sites (Gimbutas 144).

Neolithic and Chalcolithic (Copper Age) "The snake and its abstracted derivative, the spiral, are the dominant motifs of the art of Old Europe" (Gimbutas 93).

1

5000 B.C.E.

Snake goddess decorated "with stripes or snake spirals, while her arms and legs are portrayed as snakes or she is entwined by one or more snakes" (Gimbutas 101).

"The snake characteristics were emphasized by parallel or zigzag lines,

9000–7000 B.C.E.

Sites at Hacilar, Musa Dag, Jericho reveal widespread worship of female divinities (Mellaart in M. Stone 15). "Art makes its appearance in the form of animal carvings and statuettes of . . . the Mother Goddess."

4000 B.C.E.

Sumeria "The Goddess Nidaba, the scribe of the Sumerian heaven, the Learned One of the Holy Chambers, who was worshipped as the first patron deity of writing, was at times depicted as a serpent" (M. Stone 199).

Inanna also connected to serpent worship (Langdon in M. Stone 199).

1. Classical Cucuteni bird, or snake goddess. Cucuteni A period of northern Moldavia, circa the end of the fifth millenium B.C. NAM Bucharest inv. no. 5730. Pub. V. Dumistrescu, "La Civilisation du Cucuteni," *Berichten van de Rijkdienst voor het audheidkundig Godemonderzoek* 9 (1959); fig. 10, 2. Author's line drawing from photo in Marija Gimbutas, *The Goddesses and Gods of Old Europe,* 141.

dotted bands, and most frequently, by snakes spiralling over the body and by a 'snake-spiral' coiffure" (Gimbutas 145).

1600 B.C.E.

Minoan and Mycenaean Domestic snake cult widespread in houses at Knossos; associated with birds, no sacrifice associated with snake goddess. "Lady of the Dead" and "Goddess of Fertility" primitive fusion of chthonic underground with area from which plants grow up.

2

610 B.C.E.

Ancient Greek Pythia at Delphi, sits on tripod stool coiled about by Python, which is female in early accounts. Apollo murders Python and takes over shrine with male priests (M. Stone 203).

Classical Mythology Athena (pre-Greek name) intimate with snakes (Harrison in Gimbutas 148). De-

Before 3100 B.C.E.

Predynastic Egypt Cobra goddess Ua Zit, known to Greeks as Buto. Patron deity of all lower Egypt. Hieroglyphic sign for goddess is a cobra (M. Stone 201).

3

2800 B.C.E.

On Byblos, a Canaanite site where goddess and her cobra were worshipped, "one headband, adorned with the rising cobra, was constructed so that the snake would emerge from the forehead of the person who wore it, as the Eye of Wisdom" (M. Stone 208).

2000 B.C.E.

Revival of Sumeria Ningishzida now male serpent god (Campbell 283).

1830–540 B.C.E.

Babylonia Tiamet, a dragon or serpent goddess, is the first divine

---

2. The serpent goddess. Typical statuette from Knossos in Crete, circa 1700–1500 B.C.E. Author's line drawing.
3. Cobra goddess Ua Zit (named Buto by the Greeks), seventh century B.C.E. Statue from Dessuk, Egypt. Courtesy of the University Museum of the University of Pennsylvania. Author's line drawing after photo in Merlin Stone, *When God Was a Woman*, fig. 10.

scendant of Minoan snake goddess. Hera, a double of Athena, originally dominates Zeus: "Her hair curls like snakes in many of her portrayals, and a snake winds or zigzags vertically in the middle of her skirt" (Gimbutas 150). "Both, Hera and Athena, are true heiresses of the Old European Pantheon."

being, possessing the Tablets of Destiny, which Marduk claims after murdering her (M. Stone 200).

Biblical Mythology Job 26:13 and Psalm 104 give accounts of Yahweh doing battle with serpent Leviathan. "The biblical description of Yahweh's conquest of the primeval serpent may well have been simply another version of the by now familiar tale of the Indo-European male deity defeating the serpent of darkness, the Goddess" (M. Stone 109).

Which brings us to Eve's conversation with the Snake of Wisdom and Knowledge in the Garden of Eden.

4

In his therapeutic practice Jung attempted to heal this rupture between the mind and instinct, body and soul, which had become especially psychologically destructive during the Victorian period. He attributes this pathology not to such archetypes as the snake (which he understands both as the unconscious manifestations of insanity and as "normal types of fantasy") but to the inability to integrate one's consciousness with one's unconscious:

> The pathological element does not lie in the existence of these ideas, but in the dissociation of consciousness that can no longer control the unconscious. In all cases of dissociation it is therefore necessary to integrate the unconscious into consciousness. This is a synthetic process which I have termed the "individuation process," . . . Accordingly, the therapeutic method of complex psychology consists on the

4. A typical caduceus used as a medical symbol: mating snakes around a winged staff. Author's line drawing.

> one hand in making as fully conscious as possible the constellated
> unconscious contents, and on the other hand in synthetizing [sic]
> them with consciousness through the act of recognition. (*Archetypes
> and the Collective Unconscious* 40)

Thus when Jung goes on to write about "dragons and serpents" as
deriving from "the threat to one's inmost self," he locates the threat in
"the danger of the newly acquired consciousness being swallowed up
again by the instinctive psyche, the unconscious" (166). Although he
retains some of the traditional classical and Christian attitudes to
snakes, Jung nonetheless understands snake archetypes as potentially
healthy if they can be integrated by the conscious self.

In examining the layered imageries found in classical archetypes it
is helpful to consider Paul Friedrich's dating system, which he uses to
trace Aphrodite images from Old Europe (7000–3500 B.C.) through
Proto-European (5000–3000 B.C.) and pre-Greek (2000 B.C.) strata to
the Minoan civilizations, which directly affected both pre-Olympian
and Olympian (classical) mythologies. Friedrich argues that close
contact between Crete, a direct heir of Old European (non-Indo-
European) mythology, and the Greek-speaking Myceneans or
Achaeans created a synthesis of "Late Helladic" mythologies, which in
turn passed into the Homeric synthesis of classical mythology (23–
28).

Nearly all accounts identify Medusa as one of three Gorgon sisters,
all daughters of Ceto and Phorcys, who also parented a serpent who
guards the golden apples of the Hesperides (sacred to Hera in her
pre-Olympian form) and will preside over the end of the world (see
Campbell, *Occidental Mythology* 153). They are Titan in descent,
grandchildren of Gaea, who was one of the four pre-Olympian gods
who represented the earth, the heavens, the hills, and the seas
(Campbell, *Primitive Mythology* 102). Gorgons are described as not
only having serpents for hair but, in some accounts, also wearing
serpents at their girdles whose heads stick forward from the goddesses'
waists with their tongues flickering. These suggest an association
between Gorgons and the snake goddesses of Cretan palaces
documented by Sir Arthur Evans and other scholars of Cretan and
Mycenean religious practices.[2] Describing the kind of snake imagery
typical of Minoan Crete, for example, H. E. L. Mellersh notes that

"although there is obvious poetry in these snakes, there is no suggestion of an evil or frightening potency, as there is in the Greek Medusa head with writhing snakes for hair." Mellersh goes on to note that in Minoan Crete, snakes were symbols of protection, "becoming a useful scavenger and pet on a par with the farm yard cat" (95). As a Gorgon, Medusa is thus part of a triple goddess clearly related to the snake goddesses of Crete and to earlier archetypes valuing snakes as powerful animal familiars.

I have mentioned Hera's pre-Olympian origins, and one account of her rebellion against her patriarchal husband, Zeus, relates to her snake-Gorgon connection. Angry when Zeus gave birth to Athena through his forehead, Hera took revenge by bearing a "monstrous child" named Typhaon, whose nurse was the "female serpent" or dragonness called Delphyce, who presided over a sacred spring at Delphi. That the queen of the gods should express her rebellion against the male god's usurpation of reproductive powers by bearing a dragon-serpent child may have to do with the superimposition of snake-loathing Achaean over earlier snake-revering attitudes. The dragonness at Delphi, moreover, provides an interesting analogy to the Gorgon Medusa, in that she is a powerful feminine archetype associated with snakes whose powers are usurped, like Medusa's, by a male (in her case, Apollo).

Merlin Stone suggests that Mycenaean artifacts underlying the classical temple at Delphi reveal worship practices similar to those surrounding the snake goddess of Crete. At Delphi a goddess imparted her oracles to a priestess called Pythia, who sat upon a tripod (birthing) stool around which coiled a snake called Python. "Though in later Greek writings Python was male," Stone asserts, "in the earliest accounts Python was described as female" (203). Joseph Fontenrose, in *Python: A Study of the Delphic Myth and Its Origins*, mentions versions of the Apollo/Python myth in which Apollo fought a "she dragon" at Delphi, as well as variations in which "a dragon named Python, who guarded the shrine for the goddess, opposed Apollo on his arrival" (15). Fontenrose also associates the Amazon tribes with snakes and snake worship, identifies Lamia as a beautiful African queen turned into a monster by Hera, and lists many analogies between the legends of the Lamia and Medusa, noting that "both were queens in Libya. Medusa's very name means queen" (285). Diodorus

Siculus, writing in about 60 B.C.E., identifies Medusa as queen of a tribe of Amazons called Gorgons:

> But the Gorgons, grown strong again in later days, were subdued a second time by Perseus, the son of Zeus, when Medusa was queen over them; and in the end both they and the race of the Amazons were entirely destroyed by Heracles, when he visited the regions to the west and set up his pillars in Libya, since he felt that it would ill accord with his resolve to be the benefactor of the whole race of mankind if he should suffer any nations to be under the rule of women. (II: 257)

Since Libya, in North Africa, is one of the reputed sites of Amazon kingdoms and some accounts identify Gorgons with Amazon queens, several interesting links between snake goddesses, Gorgons, Amazons, and the classical Medusa seem evident. We shall see later in this book how African goddesses serve as "dark mother" archetypes to empower African American poets and how the terrifying maternal element of the goddess plays a key role in the quest of both men and women poets for psychic health.

These legends, which constitute the deep background of the Medusa archetype, talk of a before and after, a time when she was a powerful queen before she was attacked by Greek gods and heroes. Her original power is suggested in the fact that in all of these accounts Medusa is frightening to males precisely because she is a source of capabilities they want to usurp. Thus Apollo seizes the strategic political oracles at Delphi when he gives the ancient temple of the snake god or goddess over to his priests, and thus Perseus garners a rich medley of poetic and healing powers when he decapitates Medusa. The archetypal narratives surrounding the Perseus-Medusa conflict make it clear, moreover, that even in classical myth she did not start out as a Gorgon or snake monster but as a mortal woman punished, like Lamia, for making love to/being raped by a god. Although in some accounts Athena turns Medusa's hair into snakes out of jealousy that Medusa's hair is so beautiful, in others Athena punishes Medusa after discovering her *in flagrante delicto* with her own lover, Poseidon. Since there are stories of a rivalry between Poseidon and Athena over who will be the deity of Athens, Athena's concern with Poseidon's love life is political as well as erotic.

An even more interesting dimension suggests itself if we remember that Gorgons are often associated with the sea and that Poseidon is a sea god worshipped as the consort of one of the snake goddesses in the temples of Crete. Vincent Scully has pointed out that Potnia, a goddess prominent in Crete, was hailed at Pylos as "Divine Mother" and that "most of the surviving dedications of offerings are to her and Poseidon, apparently her consort and possibly identified with the living king himself" (41). This suggests an analogy between Medusa and the Mother Goddess of the Minoans; analogies between Gorgons, Medusa, and the Cretan snake goddess seem to enrich the deep background of the Medusa archetype. Finally, Medusa's alliance with Poseidon suggests one final aspect of the Cretan snake goddesses: their association with water and water gods, analogous to the snake and bird goddesses whom Marija Gimbutas describes as having special importance during the Old European historical period when the area suffered from an arid climate.

We can thus discern a cluster of archetypal motifs involving Medusa, snakes, gorgons, snake goddesses, oracular Pythons, and Poseidon as god of the sea, which occur in Greek myth in gender conflict with a contrasting set of motifs involving Athena or Perseus or Apollo as the Olympian antagonist interested in curtailing/usurping these powers. In the manner suggested by Harrison, Campbell, and Gimbutas, classical Medusa myths, whether they involve Athena's punishment or Perseus's murderous quest, are based on the conflict between these two sets of mythic images. When with the aid of archaeological scholarship and the researches of prehistorians we look into the deep reaches of history behind the mirror, we can discern radically different perspectives on Medusa than those proffered by classical mythologies concerned with justifying the overthrow of everything she represents.

To summarize the kinds of materials outlined in the chart, goddesses in the form of snakes or closely associated with snakes have been revered since the Paleolithic era as deities of wisdom and sagacity in combination with earthly power and regeneration. Neolithic Linear Pottery decoration, according to Gimbutas, was covered with "symphonies of snakes" revered for their "mysterious dynamism," "extraordinary vitality and periodic rejuvenation," and perennially associated with women: "Some vases flaunt a gigantic snake winding or

A Neolithic snake goddess. Dimini period at Sesklo near Volos, Thessaly. Excavated and published by Tsountas, 1908. Courtesy of the Ministry of Culture of the Hellenic Republic. Athens National Museum: 36, inv. no. 5937. From Marija Gimbutas, Goddesses and Gods of Old Europe.

stretching over 'the whole universe,' " writes Gimbutas, "over the sun or moon, stars and rain torrents; elsewhere the snake winds above or below a growing plant or coils above the pregnant mother's belly" (95). Nidibaba of Sumeria, patron divinity of writing, was worshipped as a snake, as was the cobra Goddess Ua Zit in the predynastic period of Egypt. These figures, associating snakes with power, wisdom, sexuality, and rebirth, have a lot to do with what happened in the Garden of Eden. Finally, the presence of snakes at so many oracular shrines may derive from the quality of snake venom as a stimulator of the hallucinatory visions considered crucial to prophecy; once a priestess has systematically immunized herself to its more deadly effects this venom induces a trance from within which makes oracular pronouncements. The practice of snake handling among both African American and white Christians in the American South, in religious ceremonies accompanied by falling into a trancelike state, may be a folk variation on this ancient practice.

It is possible to read Athena's role in Medusa's downfall in two entirely different ways. One feminist reading of Athena's betrayal of her priestess understands Athena as the masculine-identified woman, the queen bee we know from office politics, who makes herself into an honorary male not only through her intelligence and skill and deft mimicry of fashionable masculine jargon and behavior but also by cutting down other women. In this reading Athena, a local divinity antedating the Olympian mythological system, is replaced under the invading masculine culture by a kind of Stepford wife look-alike, who has been reborn through the head of Zeus and who devotes herself to patriarchal purposes, providing heroes like Perseus the equipment they need to destroy more chthonic goddesses like Medusa.

The argument for a pre-Olympian Athena is well founded. According to Gimbutas, both Athena and Hera were originally Old European Snake goddesses; in Bronze Age shrines, for example, Gimbutas describes Hera with her hair curled like snakes and a snake zigzagging vertically in the middle of her skirt in the sign associated with thunder, storms, and water, while Karen Elias-Button, in "Athene and Medusa: A Woman's Myth," documents Athena's association with the Libyan goddess Neith, a cognate of the African Lamia, and suggests that Athena/Medusa was one goddess: "Not only was Athena addressed as *Pallas Athene Parthenos Gorgo Epekoos* (Pallas Athene, Virgin, Gorgon-like, Listening-to-prayer), she was also called, by Sophocles, *gorgopis* or 'gorgon-eyed' and, in Elis, 'she who petrifies.' She was also referred to in Greek drama as *medousa*, meaning 'ruleress' or 'queen' " (120). Instead of stressing the enmity between the patriarchalized Athena and the prepatriarchal Medusa, Elias-Button provides an alternative feminist reading in which she describes the "Athene/Medusa constellation" as a single, powerful archetype which classical mythmakers did not succeed in dividing and conquering. "If Perseus is seen as merely a kind of 'hit-man' for Athena," Elias-Button argues, "then it becomes obvious that it is the Athena/Medusa constellation that lies at the center of this myth. The two female figures represent two aspects of a single self, and Perseus acts only a minor, auxiliary role" (120).

Tobin Siebers, in *The Mirror of Medusa*, agrees with Elias-Button about this unified Medusa/Athena archetype, suggesting that "Medusa and Athena merge, combining impiety and piety, savageness and civilization, monstrosity and divinity," and concludes that "the evolution of the Gorgoneion suggests that the seemingly antithetical figures of Medusa and Athena are only two different expressions made by the same face" (15, 24). Although the Perseus story certainly attempts to sunder these two aspects of a unitary mother-goddess, Elias-Button insists that it does not teach the lesson that

> the Mother must be irrevocably destroyed. Instead, just as the story of Demeter and Persephone can be seen as one of ongoing separation and reunion, so in the myth of Athene and Medusa the two aspects of the single self are constantly involved in a process of renewal, resulting here, not in a primitive reunification with the all-embracing maternal, but in an active, creative transformation of powerful, unconscious energies; carried out by a self-contained and magnificent feminine consciousness. (123)

Elias-Button describes the relationship between Athena and Medusa as one of quest, a journey in which we try to learn how to transform our unconscious energies into intellect without letting either one overwhelm or destroy the other. Her reading, like mine, is based on an understanding that classical goddesses are subjected to a process of splitting and degradation that does not wholly succeed, first, because of their deeper background in preclassical myth systems which gave greater value to wide-ranging feminine powers, and second, because the psychological elements they represent cannot be sundered in a healthy human life.

This interpretation of snake and snake goddess archetypes as having to do with psychological integrity makes it necessary to question Freud's attitude toward Medusa and snakes. I would not deny that snakes have phallically suggestive shapes: Gimbutas, for example, notes that snake ornamentation of Old European artifacts frequently exploits an analogy between snakes and phalluses. We have to remember, however, that in Old European polytheism masculinity and femininity are understood as complementary rather than conflictual or hierarchical elements of the personality; hence the snakes coiling around the breasts and buttocks of female statuettes can be seen as expressing masculine in balance with feminine sensuality. Sandor Ferenczi, following Freud's interpretations of genitalic imagery in Medusa, is influenced more by European gynophobia than by ancient Middle Eastern attitudes when he identifies the Gorgon head as "the terrible symbol of the female genital region, the details of which are displaced 'from below upwards'. The many serpents which surround the head ought—in representation by the opposite—to signify the absence of a penis, and the phantom itself is the frightful impression made on the child by the penis-less (castrated) genital. The fearful and alarming staring eyes of the Medusa have also the secondary meaning of erection" (360). Leaving aside the fact (which I will elaborate on later) that Medusa's eye is traditionally associated with wisdom and magical force, several questions arise concerning Ferenc-zi's perspective. Principally, one needs to ask to whom the female genitals look so fearful; why they are considered to be without sexual attributes (penis-less); and why the association of snakes with the penis should make us view Medusa as an object either of phallic worship or dread of castration.

It has never been entirely clear to me why a snake should be more like a penis than an intestine or, for that matter, the vagina. Phillip Slater, for example, takes issue with Ferenczi's idea that snakes are substitute penises. "Despite Freud's ingenuity in dealing with the problem," he argues, "it seems more likely that the snakes of the Medusa head are not compensatory phallic, but are a source of fear, and represent an aspect of the vagina itself." Slater also mentions a custom among Australian Aboriginal women of making a long string from their pubic hair, anointing it with vaginal blood, and thus transforming it into a snake which they send to destroy their victims (20 n. 5). One can argue that early worshippers of snakes and snake goddesses were not anthropomorphic but animistic, appreciating the snake for its fascinating manner of copulating with its own kind in huge groups (an activity represented in much-diminished form in the symbol of the caduceus with two snakes copulating around a pole). People have always felt that the snake had some kind of rebirth power because of the way it sheds its skin and emerges regenerated from it. If the snake is associated with wisdom through the hallucinogenic properties of its venom, and with sexuality and regeneration through these images of copulation and rebirth, the Freudian interpretation seems too narrowly masculine to account for the combination of feminine sexual prowess and sage womanly prophecy it brings to the Medusa archetype. Such a conflation of sexuality, wisdom, political acumen and generativity in women and goddesses would profoundly threaten patriarchal cultures, which would then feel the need to split these qualities up into separate goddesses or heap disgust upon goddesses who combine them anomalously. We shall see in the next chapter how Siebers's and Elias-Button's emphasis upon the unity of consciousness and primordial power in Medusa suggests a feminist archetypal reading of twentieth-century poems about her which is much more apt than the conflictual relationship between feminine power and murderous heroics in the Perseus and Athena versus Medusa narratives.

The Eye of Wisdom

According to Jane Ellen Harrison the daughters of Phorcys were called "the Grey Ones or Old Ones, Graiae" who were "fair of face though two-thirds blind and one-toothed; but the emphasis on the one tooth and the one eye shows that in tooth and eye resided their potency, and that in this they were sisters to the Gorgons" (*Prolegomena* 193–94). I associate the image of the "one eye" shared by the three beautiful Old Ones with the "eye of wisdom" mentioned in the chart (Middle East, 2800 B.C.E.) as represented by a cobra emerging from the forehead of a Canaanite goddess. Traditionally located in the middle of the forehead, this "third eye" (which Hindu and gypsy women still use) is wiser and sees more deeply than the traditional two eyes most mortals are endowed with. Buffie Johnson has described such an eye as the central feature of Inanna-Ishtar, who has her own Eye Temple at Tell Brak in eastern Syria. It dates from 3000 B.C.E. and

> is crowded with countless figures of the Eye Goddess. High on the walls of the dramatic interior, great eye-faces alternate with symbols of the gate guarded by Inanna's reed bundles. Her special role was evidently to stare back an attacker at the gate. Punctuating the design are rosettes, vorticles of petals that look like eyes with lashes (the vagina surrounded with hair). The design, which displays three symbols with similar meaning, is repeated around all the walls. The shrine overflows with hundreds of variations of the eye figure, each apparently a votive presentation. Alone on an altar is an enormous pair of hypnotically staring eyes that resembles nothing so much as a pair of opera glasses. (70–71)

A similarly powerful eye goddess presided over courts and over justice as Maat, the "All-Seeing Eye of ancient Egypt," whose attribute of the powerful eye was, according to Barbara Walker, eventually transferred to a male god as the "Eye of Horus." Walker suggests that although an eye goddess was worshipped as Mari throughout neolithic Syria and Mesopotamia, she was also degraded by Christian and Jewish masculine monotheism into "the evil eye," although this remained associated with women. Both Muslims and Christians, in Walker's explanation, "diabolized the female spirit of the All-Seeing Eye. Old women were credited with the ancient Goddess power to 'overlook'—to curse someone with a glance. Witches had to enter courts backward, to deprive them of the advantage of a first glance," while "in the most patriarchal societies it is customary to insist that 'proper' women keep their eyelids lowered in the presence of men. In 19th century Islamic Iran, it was believed that every woman above the age of menopause carried the evil eye. Old women were not permitted in public appearances of the Shah" (*Woman's Encyclopedia* 294–95).

As in the case of Medusa's reptilian hair, we can see two perspectives in operation here: on the one hand, a hatred and terror of the eye as a source of "evil," a patriarchal perspective undoubtedly shared by many women; and, on the other hand, a reverential attitude toward the qualities of wisdom and justice which the eye symbolizes. Both perspectives come together in the custom of wearing little jewels representing "the evil eye" which paradoxically ward off evil or bad luck. As in the case of Emily Culpepper's Gorgon emblem, the eye of wisdom has survived in folk and popular culture as endowed with the power to avert trespass and misfortune.

The folklore of the eye of wisdom also persists in European literature. Hazel E. Barnes notes that Virgil and Dante, in Dante's *Inferno*, perceive Medusa as characterized by an "Eye of Judgment," radiating a "divine judgment which fixes the sinner for eternity, with no further possibility of redemption, in the place which his life has prepared for him." Goethe's *Faust*, similarly, "underscores the idea that Medusa's head represents the Eye which appraises my conduct and condemns it." Such fear of Medusa's judgment certainly is like the feelings we experienced as children when coming up for punishment before a powerful parent or teacher, feelings similar to those which an Egyptian suspect might feel when coming before an "all-seeing" judge.

Conversely (though in a way consonant with the substitution of reverence for fear in responses to Medusa) Barnes goes on to argue that artists have often considered the "Gorgon's look the apotheosis of artistic achievement," by which "the transformation of flesh into stone might be viewed, not as a passage from life to death but as the imposition of beauty and form upon the chaotic flux of experience" (32–34). The power of the eye, especially the female one, to "kill with a glance" or to radiate an arresting fascination that stops you in your tracks, is a later courtly development on this feminine power to transfix. The maternal power over both life and death, our mothers' ability when we are infants and young children to determine whether we survive or perish, merges here with magical power attributed to the eye of a goddess who can kill or bless or, literally, petrify you with her glance. Poets, like children, are in special awe of this maternally Medusean glance; as Barnes notes, Medusa's ability to transform chaos into permanent aesthetic structures probably accounts for her association with poetry through being the mother of Pegasus. A powerfully wise and creative woman poet conflates our feelings about our mothers and our teachers and about magically incanting enchanters like witches and nuns in a way that echoes Medusa's power. As we shall see, twentieth-century poets such as Louise Bogan and May Sarton concentrate more on this petrifying artistic power in the Medusa archetype than on her snakes, admiring and yet fearing her ability to transmute that which lives and moves into immortal stone.

The Mask of Medusa

Jane Ellen Harrison explains Medusa's face as merely a "prophylactic mask" concealing a beautiful and powerful goddess, probably used to frighten off those who were not ready to be initiated into her mysteries. Harrison felt that, to the Greeks, Medusa represented "the Ugly bogey-Erinys-side of the Great Mother," her Gorgon face masking an earlier "potent goddess, not as in later days a monster to be slain by heroes . . ." (*Prolegomena* 193–94). Tobin Siebers notes that

> although Medusa petrifies her beholder, the mask of Medusa has been widely associated with the neutralization of fascination. As the most efficacious amulet against the evil eye, the Gorgoneion accompanied the Greeks and Romans in every walk of life. They placed it on their clothing, jewelry, tools, money, and buildings. Aristophanes men-

tions that it was found near the heart of most Athenian households. Along with great owls and ugly comic men, the mask of Medusa was also placed on ovens used to bake pottery. (8)

The Romans took Medusa medallions and ornaments to Britain with them; there the archetype underwent underwent a syncretistic conflation with a "cult of the head" popular among the Celts. Ann Ross points out that "the theme of the head . . . goes right through Celtic religious tradition and is found, not only as a separate cult, but bound up with all other cults" to the extent that, "because of its link with all other cults, its symbolic use over the entire Celtic area, insular and continental, and the longevity with which it was imbued with significance, the human head is given first place as being the most typical Celtic religious symbol" (61). Nor is this a merely generalized severed head that is so recurrent a Celtic archetype; in Roman Britain an Indo-European solar divinity "became crystallized" because of the classical influence

into a staring, serpent-wreathed symbol of evil-averting power. Placed on temple porticos, eaves of buildings, and shields, in the same contexts as those in which the Celtic 'tête coupée' was exhibited, the symbol of the Gorgon head shared with the Celtic heads in apotropaic powers, but had lost the divine association of the Celtic heads. Celtic heads, frequently horned, were often associated with thermal waters and with the sacred serpent. The Medusa heads likewise tended to be linked with healing springs, while their serpent associations are constant. In this respect, the assimilation of classical to native imagery is a simple matter. The native could clearly make concessions to the classical Gorgon-type, while retaining the symbolism and significance of the divine head, making the symbol acceptable to Roman and native alike. Deeply indigenous native cults could thus be comfortably masked under the image of Medusa, only the individuality of expression, the vigour of execution and the male sex of the heads betraying their nonclassical origin. (90)

I have quoted Ross at length because it is crucial to understand how the Medusa archetype accreted Celtic attributes in Roman Britain, creating a continuity between classical and Europagan mythological systems. Many Medusa heads are found in places where there are special fountains—as at Bath, with its warm springs—suggesting an even deeper archetypal background in the pre-Indo-European cultures which also held these sites sacred. Thus the Renaissance was not the first culture in Britain to syncretize classical archetypes but offered to the more recently arrived Anglo-Saxon and Norman peoples a continuation of a much longer archetypal tradition with which the Celts still inhabiting the British Isles were already familiar.

The supposedly forbidding Medusa head became increasingly beautiful in European iconography, as exemplified in the tapestry Medusa whose "head" Perseus is carrying away on Pegasus, leaving the three lovely sisters behind. This does not mean that by the fifteenth century women were considered less of a threat than in the classical period: in both eras when women were feared for their beauty as well as for anomalous alliances with animals. Feminine beauty frightened Greek as well as Renaissance men every bit as much as Gorgon ugliness, since it tempted them to succumb to the potent sexuality which was considered an important feminine feature until much later in history. Hazel Barnes notes that although a "monstrous ugliness" characterized early Gorgons, by the Hellenistic era Medusa had become "a truly deadly beauty . . . a face which it is death to look upon but which lures it to us, a representation of *fascination* with the ambivalent meaning which the English word holds for us today" (36). Christine de Pisan could remind her readers of Medusa's surpassing loveliness in 1405 because feminine sensuality came to be considered anomalous, a monstrous crime against womanhood, only just prior to the nineteenth century. To put it another way, the "aspects glad and gay" which Mary Elizabeth Coleridge allows her despairing, wounded Medusa to subvert might not have seemed so unthreateningly innocent in earlier periods before feminine beauty came to be associated with sexual purity. Although the enormous power which Coleridge, Browning, Keats, and Shelley discern in the wounded Medusa would have been recognized in all periods as representing the possibility of maternal anger and the threat of feminine revenge, only in the eighteenth and nineteenth centuries does this rage become directed against norms denying sensuality as a natural attribute of women.

For poets, Medusa is an important archetype of feminine creativity, especially when this creativity is thwarted. In "The Muse as Medusa" Karen Elias-Button attributes Medusa's appeal both to her preclassical powers and to our feelings about our mothers. Referring to Medusa as "the Terrible Mother" (in Neumann's fashion), she notices that many women poets choose Medusa as a "goddess considered responsible during the Neolithic age for the underside of creative renewal, to represent the potential sources of female transformation," so that Medusa comes for many twentieth-century poets to serve as "a metaphor for powers previously hidden and denigrated, collective powers we are finally beginning to reaffirm and claim for ourselves. Medusa becomes for us, in a process that involves more than a simple inspiration, a muse" (193–94). Since most women poets have experienced their mothers in moods when they were furious at patriarchy, their coming to terms with maternal victimization and maternal anger, both of which are suggested in the Medusa archetype, also involves facing up to their own feelings about culture, a probing of their own acultural feminine depths without which they cannot write. We shall see in the following chapter that, for men as well as for women, the key to psychological survival as well as to poetic maturity is a face-to-face encounter with Medusa's personal and archetypal meaning. Each poet must complete a painful quest to understand and to forgive Medusa; only by looking into her eyes and understanding what lies beneath them can we enter the healing seas of the unconscious from which rebirth is possible.

2.

Medusa in Twentieth-Century British and U.S. Poetry

My brief comparison/contrast of nineteenth-century poems about Medusa by men and women raises the question of the relationship between a poet's personal signature, his or her contemporary historical context, and the deep background of the archetype. If women were wholly determined by a monolithic patriarchy, one would expect their nineteenth-century poems about Medusa to manifest disgust at the powerful and angry Gorgon rather than a recognition of her as muse, "an image of the poet," as Cheryl Walker puts it, who "represents that violated wild self whose power is felt as the spirit of poetry" (42). Writing within a culture whose distaste for natural feminine sensuality was intense, these poets nonetheless felt empowered by perceiving themselves and even their mothers as Medusa, whom they approached as a "violated wild self" lurking beneath day-to-day existence in patriarchy. Following Paul Friedrich's demonstration in the case of Aphrodite, I suggest that the content of a classical archetype consists of many strands in which earlier responses toward the archetype are interbraided with its historical and personal signatures, so that it is possible to posit a seditiously feminist subtext as an active element affecting poetic composition.

This does not mean that I believe in a fixed, ahistorical meaning for archetypes in the manner that Jung has so often been accused of.

Medusa in Twentieth-Century British and U.S. Poetry

Although I agree with Jung that similar responses to archetypes recur over a wide range of human history and cultures, I find that his analysis of such recurrent responses is often limited to masculine feelings, without sufficient analysis either of what Medusa might have been feeling or of women's attitudes to her. If women poets were determined by Perseus's heroic posture of fear transcended by attack and triumphant usurpation, we would either perceive Medusa as horrible and take on Perseus's attitude, or identify with her helplessness, anger, and victimization. If we were entirely determined by the patriarchal pie we could only masculinize ourselves, on the one hand, or, on the other, sing Medusa blues about our anger and victimization. In this chapter I will assess the degree to which masculine feelings characterize twentieth-century women's poems about Medusa, within the context of a comparison/contrast between poems by men and women along a scale of attitudes from loathing to reverence and awe.

The hypothesis that archetypes are entirely patriarchal in content would suggest that male poets must approach Medusa with Perseus's perspective. Jung's and Neumann's definition of the hero's interaction with the "Terrible Mother" seems constructed upon this attitude; although they define (male) psychological health as transcending terror of the more frightening aspects of femininity in order to get in touch with "the feminine" within the male psyche, there is something Persean both in their perception of "feminine" powers as profoundly alien and in their plans to psychoanalytically usurp these powers. We shall see that twentieth-century male poets who are well read in myth adapt Jung's and Neumann's intention of usurping Medusa's powers but get transfixed by the "Terrible" side of the "Terrible/Good Mother" when they are unable to transcend their presumption that "the feminine" and women are ontologically "other."

There is much more of a carry-over into the twentieth century of Victorian repulsion against feminine power, especially feminine reproductivity and sexuality, than popular assumptions about "modern" sexual liberation might suggest, carry-overs which probably account both for the applicability of Jung's prescriptions to twentieth-century men's psychological problems and to contemporary male poets' inability to deconstruct the Victorian content of Jungian theory. For example, in 1973 Robert Bly outlined a fourfold "Great Mother" based on two poles of feminine energy: the "Good Mother" versus the "Death Mother" and the "Ecstatic Mother" versus the "Tooth Mother." Following Neumann, Bly describes the male poet's task as seeking out the "Ecstatic Mother" as a muse who contains the feminine energy necessary for poetic composition: "All of my poems come from the Ecstatic Mother; everyone's poems do. Men in patriarchies try to deny the truth that all creativity lies in feminine consciousness; it is part of the fight with the Mother. But if the Mothers are immense force fields, then men are receiving magnets, who fly about in inner space. The masculine soul in a woman is pulled in a similar way" (*Sleepers Joining Hands* 40). Bly is suggesting a simple inversion of the poet/mother relationship for the woman poet, with her goal (implicitly) the "ecstatic father" and her danger, correspondingly, some kind of killing phallus. Bly's image of men as magnets flying about within the inner space of an enormous and threatening mother suggests an infantile rather than an adult consciousness, so that his goal of a mature relationship to "the feminine" is undercut by his feeling that she is not only much more powerful than he is but an antagonistic "other." At this stage of his thinking, Bly's descriptions of being petrified or, even more frighteningly, being cut apart by the teeth within the "tooth mother's" vagina, suggest a stance of alienation from "the feminine," a stance common to many male poets of the time. It is important to note that in his work on the "Iron John" archetype in the 1980s Bly posited a same-sex archetype as the key to the empowerment of both men and women.

The horrific nature of the Medusa archetypes we will encounter in the category of "fear and loathing" should not blind us to the fact that they represent only one extreme, gynopobic end of a continuum that includes much more positive attitudes. Not only will we find that women as well as men write poems consumed by loathing of Medusa, we will also find men as well as women revering her feminine power as a source of healing. Although the Medusa is most often negative for male poets, it will become clear in my discussion of Aphrodite, Artemis, and bears that being frightened by goddess archetypes is a necessary phase which one must pass through and which represents a failed stage in one's quest for personal transformation. It will also become clear that the negative perceptions of Medusa I treat in this chapter comprise, as Jane Ellen Harrison put it, erroneous terrors of a mere prophylactic mask to frighten off those not ready for initiation.

For an example of the extreme, negative end
of the continuum of poetic attitudes about
Medusa let us consider Joel Oppenheimer's
Woman Poems, which is based on the Neumann-
Bly precepts. In "Moving Out," Oppenheimer expresses his terror of a
woman from whom he averts his gaze but who nonetheless turns him
to stone. His attitude at the outset seems respectful enough: he prays
to "holy mothers" to "save me from your sister" who "sits always in the
corners of my eyes." Although he is frightened of the "sister," she is
part of his psyche as of one of his own internal attributes. In a manner
appropriate to Bly's prescriptions, Oppenheimer tries to stand firm in
her presence, courageously determining not to flinch, not to hide his
eyes or turn away, though he anticipates that this confrontation will
lead to a horrific denouement:

> if she turns me
> to stone i will stand
> not moving, but i will not
> turn myself to stone.
> if she strips me bare i
> will be naked, but i will
> survive. if she
> strips the flesh from
> my bones with her teeth
> my bones will stand as
> monument to her and to my
> stand. if she bites me
> in pieces, i will be in a heap
> at her feet, at the center
> of the cave. (7–8)

He intends to "enter that cave" to address the "holy mother / of life,
holy mother / of death" so that he can join in the dancing, though he
anticipates that he "may slip / into the teeth" in the "center of the
cave." In precisely the fashion outlined by Bly and Neumann, Op-
penheimer declares his intention to transcend the fact that "i am
afraid of the mother who bites" and "move toward / the mother who

dances, / or stand suspended / between them," understanding himself as "the hanged man / who was the fool," but whose "foolish" stepping beyond the bounds of masculinity into the cave of the mother will initiate him as "magician."

Despite the sincerity of Oppenheimer's prayers to the "holy mothers" for protection, in subsequent poems he displays profound discomfort with "the feminine." In "Screaming Poem," for example, he identifies "the woman inside me" who, by no means beneficent or psychologically healing, "claws at / my innards." It becomes clear in a group of poems about childhood and breasts that Oppenheimer's relationship to his internal anima or "feminine" muse is that of the Wolf who ate Red Riding Hood's grandmother: the consumer of an indigestible supper. In "Child Poem," "Meat Poem," and "Breast Poem" he perceives the muse/Medusa/mother as a food item, "meat of the beloved / beside us in the night," or "i hold / my wife's flesh, her / meat, I cry aloud, mother do not forsake me." Oppenheimer has conflated the maternal with the sexual, so that he mixes his infantile experience of his mother's breast with adult heterosexuality, then projects this confusion between nursing and intercourse onto an image of the mother as someone who, consumed by a ravening appetite, threatens to bite and tear and swallow him up. So intense is Oppenheimer's conflation of his own hunger and feminine sexuality that he projects his own desire to devour onto women, to the extent that he describes disembodied breasts chasing him through his campus.

Although Medusa imagery is implicit in these "terrible" and "devouring" archetypes, Medusa emerges explicitly in "Mirror Poem," personified in all the "women i love" who wear mirrors attached to their clothing in a fashion of the 1970s. Oppenheimer no longer approaches these women as the Persean poet-hero in quest of magical power from the dancing/toothed mother and muse; now he accuses them of deflecting his attention by use of the mirrors: "women i love and / watch these days" use "bits of / glass in their / sleeves" "to keep / my eye glancing / off." Whereas in his previous poems he has been in control of his gaze, of his power to image the women who threaten to devour him, in "Mirror Poem" he realizes that women have taken back his weapon and will use it to "blind me, stop me, cold as stone." I would suggest that when Oppenheimer confronts real women rather than projections of his own attitudes, his profound disgust with a Medusean totality of feminine selfhood that includes maternal and sexual power keeps him paralyzed and distanced from women. Unable to bring his own gynophobia to consciousness, he translates his hostility toward women to women's antagonism toward him, with the result that his ability to assimilate the archetype as muse is undermined.

I have begun my analysis of male Medusa texts with Oppenheimer's poems because of his detailing of an extreme attitude found in less explicit form in other poems of masculine fear and loathing. It is also significant that it was written in the 1970s, which deters us from assuming that attitudes toward women improved much as the twentieth century went along. Oppenheimer's approach to Medusa is not very different, for example, from Basil Bunting's in his 1931 poem "Attis: Or, Something Missing." In his approach to the goddess Cybele (who castrated her son Attis so that no one else could love him) Bunting, like Oppenheimer, mixes loathing and reverence:

> Praise the green earth. Chance has appointed her
>   home, workshop, larder, middenpit.
>   Her lousy skin scabbed here and there by
>   cities provides us with name and nation.
> From her brooks sweat. Hers corn and fruit.
>   Earthquakes are hers too. Ravenous animals
>   are sent by her. Praise her and call her
>   Mother and Mother of Gods and Eunuchs. (8)

In a second section of the poem which he calls "Variations on a theme by Milton," Bunting conflates the castrating Cybele with his wife and with Gorgon Medusa, all three out for revenge against the male. Bunting identifies himself with Attis as victim of castration, "grieving for his testicles!" cut off by the overpowering mother.

In his association of Cybele/Medusa with an unpredictable natural world, Bunting allies himself with a number of poets who write about nature as terrifying enclosure. Thus Joseph Auslander, also in the 1930s, wrote two poems on this figure. In one ("Medusa Twice"), he declares that he has come back "from gazing / On love that gasps for breath," a "love" which he identifies with Medusa: "I watched the eyeballs glazing / With the Medusa Death" (51). In the other ("Strange Mother"), he starts off with a dispassionate description of a "Nature [which] bears no grievance" and cherishes "No grudge." Auslander has been filled with "a sulky anger at birth" and bitterness at

Medusa's hegemony, understanding himself as "her fretful man-child" who will fall asleep in a death which is but an element in her uncaring natural scheme.

Identifying with Perseus in his quest to kill Medusa, Howard Nemerov, in a poem called "Hero with Girl and Gorgon" from the 1970s, perceives himself as "child" hero who must outwit both "the three grey hags" and Medusa. Nemerov is so horrified by his victim that he "cut[s] backward in aversion from the cold / Brow's beauty and the wide unpitying gaze." Again we have a sense of the male poet deploring Medusa's inattention to his needs, a maternal indifference to the child's heroics which we also see in Auslander and Oppenheimer. Nemerov perceives Medusa's power to punish him even after he has murdered her: his hero is "paralyzed to silence in the stone," destroyed by the "great head swung by the serpents" he triumphantly holds.

Since Medusa is immortal, killing her is no final triumph for Nemerov's Perseus, any more than an attack on nature itself would benefit Auslander or their disgust for her would aid Oppenheimer or Bunting on their quests. The Persean desire to destroy Medusa structures these poems upon a deadlocked antagonism. James Merrill's 1940s "Medusa," similarly, starts off describing the Medusa head as mere marble statue, "blind in its own right" but nonetheless presiding over the summer. Merrill's marble Medusa has somehow fallen from grace; now, however, he and his companions are blinded and petrified. The occupants of the garden have been paired off for love but now are in a depleted state that he blames on the Medusa while calling for her murder. Like Bunting and Oppenheimer, Merrill associates Medusa with a heterosexual relationship gone sour, his murderous intent arising from a bad experience of nature and sexuality.

The pathology implicit in these approaches derives from the male poet's disassociation of himself from his own natural sensuality and his blaming this upon either a maternal figure or a woman lover, or both fearsomely conflated, whom he then sets out to excoriate or kill. The alienation of the spirit from the body and human beings from our own natural sensuality is rooted deeply within European culture, derived, as Joseph Campbell has suggested, from "the biblical condemnation which [Americans] inherited from their own religion and brought with them, mainly from England. God is separate from nature, and nature is condemned by God." Campbell finds this attitude mistaken. We ought rather to "think of ourselves as coming out of the earth, rather than having been thrown in here from somewhere else," he reminds us; "you see that we are the earth, we are the consciousness of the earth" (*The Power of Myth* 32). In my hypothesis, male poets stuck in murderous antagonism against women and nature or deadlocked in a fatal complicity with them are experiencing a profound dysfunction of their natural drive toward more healthy relationships to their own mothers, to nature, and to women. Thus in "Fragments of Perseus," Michael McClure identifies Medusa not as something to be blamed on women but as "the horror of my mind / BLOWN UP / within / my body and MADE / INTO FLESH!" (17). I read such poems not merely as misogynistically stereotyped but also as examples of healthy human relationships gone awry. I would argue that the very intensity of the male poets' discomfort springs from their unrealized but powerful need to find better ways to be with women than those fostered in a patriarchy whose norms are psychologically destructive to men as well as to women.

One murderous poem about Medusa presents an interesting question about the impact of race on one's perception of archetypes. My reading of "Perseus" by the African American poet Robert Hayden, in which he perceives Medusa's "sleeping head with its great gelid mass / of serpents torpidly astir" as a "hated truth the mind accepts at last," is that he has conflated onto the Medusa figure all that blacks most fear in whites and in the punishments whites mete out upon black men for approaching white women and that he wishes to destroy this figure (58). In Countee Cullen's "Médusa," similarly, the Gorgon's threat is not her ugliness but her dangerously seductive beauty. "I know it was a lovely face I braved," Cullen insists at the end of a poem in which a reference to "abuse / Heaped on a tree of all its foliage thinned" implies a lynching. In a sonnet from the same collection he associates his Persean stance with the African American poet's heroic attempt to fight a white culture that would destroy him: "Thinking himself a Perseus, and fit to brook / Her columned throat and every blandishment" (153). As in the case of Christian hymns used to encode black rebellion, Hayden and Cullen seem to be recasting the classical legends whites value in disguised subversions of white culture. Directing their hatred at a remote classical archetype may be evidence of their distaste for femininity, but it may also be a way of encoding their distrust for white women, who could seduce them into castration and lynching.

These poems by African Americans do not mention Medusa's maternal element; nor do they identify the archetype with specific wives or lovers. In Robert Lowell's "Near the Ocean," dedicated to his wife, Elizabeth Hardwick, the conflation of the maternal and the sexual once again dominates the Medusa imagery. Lowell identifies with "the hero" Perseus, standing "stunned by the applauding hands" and lifting "her head to please the mob," but this image is quickly replaced by that of a brother and sister who "wait before their mother," whom the brother calls "old iron-bruises" and wishes to kill, though he knows that if he does the deed

> his treadmill heart will never rest—
> his wet mouth pressed to some slack breast,
> or shifting over on his back . . .
> The severed radiance filters back,
> athirst for night-life—gorgon head,
> fished up from the Aegean dead,
> with all its stranded snakes uncoiled,
> here beheaded and despoiled. (42)

Lowell recognizes that murdering his mother will not cure him of projecting her attributes onto his lovers, and the rest of the poem describes his relationship to his wife as one of hopeless complicity with feminine qualities which disgust him—"menstrual blood / caking the covers / when they woke," to cite but one example. Locked forever in an uncomfortable and uncomforting embrace near an Atlantic Ocean afloat with condoms, Lowell can only hope for sleep or for the childlike holding of his wife's hand:

> A hand, your hand then! I'm afraid
> To touch the crisp hair on your head—
> Monster loved for what you are,
> till time, that buries us, lay bare. (48)

Lowell's complicity with a Medusa wife he simultaneously loves and finds monstrous might seem, at first blush, simply a misogynism; male poets, however, are not alone in their fear and loathing of Medusa.

Mythologist Kathleen Raine, for example, often takes a misogynist perspective, applying male distrust of goddesses to herself. Although she recognizes their power, she often conceives of feminine archetypes in negative terms: Kore locked forever in a Hades of nothingness, Eurydice perceived only as Orpheus's shadow, and goddesses with whom she identifies herself described as loathsome. Thus in "The Pythoness," about the figure who in some legends was a priestess empowered by snakes, Raine describes herself as "that serpent-haunted cave / Whose navel breeds the fates of men." Far from celebrating feminine generativity, she deplores women's powers over birth and death, calling herself a "feared and longed-for burning place" in a "low polluted bed." Although it might be possible to read this as a bold declaration of outrageousness in the manner that, as we shall see, African American women poets identify with African goddesses, in the context of Raine's tendency to identify with the negative side of dualized feminine archetypes I would read this as self-degradation, redeemed only by the fact that sons are born out of her female squalor. We shall see in the chapters on Aphrodite that Raine perceives herself as men describe her; believing in her "glad and gay" beauty's intrinsic evil and disregarding the deeper contents of her mirror, she consistently punishes herself for men's stereotypical projections. We shall also see that she shares a symptom with many women poets who have not been able to assimilate the maternal archetype: a deadlocked, cyclical posture of self-blame and defeat.

Nor is Raine alone among women poets who perceive Medusa through gynophobic lenses. Marya Zaturenska's "Head of Medusa" depicts Perseus's murder of Medusa as a good thing, both for her victims and herself, since it prevents her from turning men and other living things into stone. Zaturenska depicts Medusa as worn out with the loneliness of "knowing that all who look on her will die," calling herself "this loathesome thing no men desire" (33). Even when naming Medusa's ugliness, women poets tend to remain in some way identified with her. The pain of Raine's self-loathing, for example, is palpable, and Karen Lindsey writes about a Medusa she accepts as a terrifying female who affirms the empowerment that comes from absorbing her import. Thus at the end of her "Medusa" she asserts that "the legends are wrong. / it is those who do not look / who turn to stone." In this interesting twist to a poem which initially seems to degrade Medusa, Lindsey affirms the importance of facing up to an archetype she has been distancing herself from.

Women poets such as Raine who seem to sympathize with Medusa's male victims, as well as those like Zaturenska and Lindsey who try to distance themselves from her, try to superimpose the masculine signature of the archetype, men's perspectives upon Medusa, onto quite different feminine responses, so that there is a contradiction between their loathing for Medusa and their tendency to identify with her. A different kind of loathing characterizes women's poems which focus on Medusa's maternal element, in which the poet endows Medusa with feelings about maternity and, specifically, about her own mother. Even though these poems express fear of Medusa, there is a crucial gender difference between a woman consumed by loathing for the Medusa archetype and a man's hatred for it, based upon men's sense that Medusa is "other" in contrast to women's identification with her. Thus Lowell's approach toward his mother/wife differs from Sylvia Plath's to her mother along gender lines, Plath fearing fusion and Lowell disgusted by complicity with something alien or monstrous.

Like her fellow New England poet Robert Lowell, Sylvia Plath associates Medusa with the ocean. In Plath's case, as both Joan Coldwell and Sister Bernetta Quinn have cogently argued, the association is with the Medusa jellyfish, whose Latin name, Aurelia, is the same as her mother's, and with the ocean's salty, amniotic chemistry. Plath's "Medusa" was written in October 1962, at a time when, as Quinn reminds us, Plath was frantically trying to disassociate herself from her mother, who had been trying to reach friends by cable and telephone to check up on her daughter in London. Quinn suggests that Plath encoded her mother as Medusa/jellyfish to disguise her rage against her; the relationship between them had entered a dysfunctional state in mother-daughter psychology, that of fusion.

The issue of disassociating oneself from one's mother in a specifically physical and sexual way, crucial in a woman's young adulthood, is prevented if the mother intrudes upon her daughter's adult sexuality. "The mother as Gorgon," writes Coldwell, "is something different from the potential castrator of her sons that [Margaret] Laurence's Stacey feared in herself: here it is that more familiar projection of the mother, however loved, who seems, through her expectations and concern, to stand in the way of her daughter's full self-realization.

Plath's poem attempts an exorcism of that figure in order for her true self to be born" (430). It is the threat of interference in her marriage as well as of her mother's attempts to live through her achievements that makes Plath identify her mother with a dangerous Gorgon. The summer before she wrote "Medusa," her mother had witnessed her fights with her husband, and Plath felt it crucial that her mother stay away while she tried to sort out her life. Thus in "Medusa" she fears her as "unnerving head" and "lens of mercies" (the eye of judgment), threatening to engulf her back into her "old barnacled umbilicus" and "placenta / Paralyzing the kicking lovers." The poem represents Plath's desperate resistance to the threat of fusion, of having her sexual maturity overwhelmed by her mother:

> I am sick to death of hot salt.
> Green as eunuchs, your wishes
> Hiss at my sins.
> Off, off, eely tentacle!
>
> There is nothing between us. (*Ariel* 40)

Although I tend to read this last line as Plath's successful distancing from her mother, my students, coming from an earlier developmental stage still threatened by maternal fusion, read it as a statement of hopeless fusion. A third reading, which could be woven into this multiple ambivalence, would be the kind of "I am she!" recognition we noted in Coleridge's declaration of identity with Medusa. Whereas Coleridge was empowered by an image of apatriarchal selfhood behind her normatively feminine mirror, however, Plath does not feel the permission to make it on her own that Coleridge did; moreover she is too weak psychologically to identify with Medusa, who threatens a destructive engulfment.

Coldwell agrees with Quinn that Plath had made earlier poetic attempts to take Medusa's power to herself through poems she wrote at college envisioning the Gorgon as muse. Coldwell cites Plath's "Perseus, the Triumph of Wit over Suffering" (about a painting by Paul Klee) as "one of a group of poems [Plath] described as 'breaking open my real experience of life in the last five years.' The poem is, as its title suggests, an allegory, in which Medusa stands for all of human suffering," a self, Coldwell argues, "that is weighed down by the sufferings of life [and which] must be killed for the positive self to be released. . . .

Her comic picture of the decapitated Medusa in this poem amounts to a self-portrait, very similar in its disgust, particularly over the pouting, disconsolate mouth, to the comments Plath made about a photograph of herself, 'an ugly dead mask,' she pasted into her diary" (430). At this stage in Coldwell's analysis, we could understand Plath's earlier self-portraits as companion pieces to the later portrait of her mother as Gorgon, representing self-hate for the Medusean qualities she would later attribute to her mother. There is a further dimension Coldwell notices in Plath's college poem and diary, however. In the earlier Perseus poem, Medusa as intense mental suffering is said to " 'stiffen all creation,' ambiguous terms, where creation means both the world and the power to create, and stiffen suggests both petrifaction and bracing. Such ambiguity is at the heart of Plath's aesthetic creed." Coldwell notices that although such a paralysis can be read as "writer's block," "the same term, and the process of petrifaction, take on positive connotations in the creation of art. . . . It is looking straight at the tragic Medusa, accepting Medusa as muse, that allows the petrifaction in art to occur, with the bracing of the will to overcome the suffering" (431). Paradoxical as it may seem, it is precisely this kind of frozen, stunned state of life fixed in stone that many poets associate with Medusa's creative inspiration as muse.

| *The Petrifying Medusa* | Hazel Barnes has analyzed Medusa's capacity to turn everything living to stone in terms of Sartre's existential theory about a "universal de- |

sire . . . to fix the self into a hard steadfast entity—like a stone—so that one might be what one is, forever, instead of having continuously to pursue the self as a freely-existing self-making creature must." Art, after all, triumphs over life by impos-ing form "upon the flux of experience," and fulfills a human desire "to fix once and for all the essence of the ever-changing existent." Such an attitude, Barnes asserts, is also informed by a neurotic "desire to identify one's being with a petrified Self beyond the reach of the 'Other' " (40). Barnes interprets Medusa's petrifying gaze as a two-way force, empowering the gazer to create art while being a petrified victim of her gaze. Aesthetically, the poem or artifact becomes a way of simultaneously giving in to, assimilating, and "petrifying" or transfix-ing the threatening Medusa in the form of art. A poet like Plath, thus,

fixes the Medusa as a way of transcending a sense of personal engulf-
ment by the mother.

Psychologically, Barnes adapts R. D. Laing's understanding of
"the Medusa complex" to further explain the poet's posture before the
Gorgon: "As with the Oedipus complex of Freud, the Medusa com-
plex, for Laing, represents a cluster of emotions and experiences
which form part of the life of even the healthy and 'normal' person. If
mismanaged it may become the foundation of the schizophrenic per-
sonality and psychosis." For Laing, a person suffering from "ontologi-
cal insecurity" has trouble identifying as a separate existence, fearing
" 'engulfment,' in which he is lost in others; implosion, whereby his
empty self might be crushed by the impingement of reality; and
petrifaction. It is the third of these, of course, which Laing develops in
terms of the Medusa complex" (27–28).

A sense of petrifaction, or being blocked and unable to function,
also typifies the traumatic state of the victim of rape, who is suffering
from a total intrusion analogous to engulfment in the maternal. A
number of women poets who express disgust with Medusa's character-
istics while identifying with her victimization focus on her rape experi-
ence. Among their poems is Ann Stanford's "Medusa," in which the
poet identifies with the Gorgon as rape victim but perceives her fury as
revenge upon her tormentors by petrifaction. Medusa's Gorgon char-
acteristics of snaky hair and frightening stare spring from her anger at
being raped; thus the speaker's horror of Medusa's attributes derives
from sympathy with her victimization by "the stinking breath, the
sweaty weight, the pain, / the quickening thrust" of rape. We sense
here a blockage and paralysis similar to Plath's college work; in my
reading, Stanford's Medusa undergoes a rape-trauma paralysis which is
reinforced by the further degradation of being pregnant, having con-
ceived during the rape a "monster seed growing beneath my heart."
Although the poem ends with despair, Stanford breaks free from her
loathing of Medusa by identifying with her anger at being victimized,
the tension between what a woman would normally desire and what
has been done to her engendering both protest and the poet's act of
embedding Medusa in poetry.

It is Medusa's rage that empowers Stanford's rendition of the
archetype, a righteous anger we might associate with Medusa's tradi-
tional power as all-judging eye of wisdom to turn the living into stone.
We can find this same blend of aesthetic petrifaction and revenge in a

statue of Perseus by the French sculptor Camille Claudel, who had been Rodin's lover and collaborator until he married someone else and withdrew his patronage of her work. Without financial support, Claudel became angry at the world and eventually was committed to a mental institution for paranoid symptoms. Louise Witherell has described Claudel's statue of Perseus (sculpted in 1898 when she was trying to disassociate herself from Rodin) as a self-portrait, with the handsome naked hero triumphantly holding up "her own puffy, middle-aged head as the head of Medusa, complete with an expression of profound horror" (6). It is this Medusa as victim, her Gorgon characteristics a response to rape or betrayal, that characterizes Stanford's "Medusa."

There is, moreover, a level in Medusa's deeper archetypal background that sets a precedent for aesthetic revenge by sculpture. Sculpturing or carving in stone, after all, has been a central activity of religious systems during most of the history of the human race, and even when human beings have not carved or painted their beliefs on stone they have selected special stones as sacred objects. Barbara Walker suggests in *The Crone* that the stone of Scone, the sacred Black Stone of Mecca, and other "Crone Stones" are examples of human beings' tendency to locate the sacred in rocks and stones, a tendency which explains Medusa's "petrifying look [which] may have symbolized the 'turning to stone' of the dead, in the form of a grave pillar, or funerary portrait statue" (57). Walker associates the traditional head of Medusa with "female wisdom," her ability to turn living beings to stone with her power to endow immortality, a capacity related to the wise old woman's transformative power at birth and death.

A poem in which the poet is arrested in horror at a Medusa image, such as Shelley's poem about Leonardo's painting, is in and of itself a kind of Keatsian "thing of beauty" or enduring aesthetic object, eternally arresting what had been fluid and changing. This understanding of Medusa informs Willoughby Weaving's "Medusa Awake," in which the reader is warned to "beware" of a Gorgon with

> Elf-locks? Serpents! writhing hair,
> Features lovely—fell and cold
> From the black pool's mirror shine
> Beauty—horror—both divine! (53)

Weaving's 1916 poem is similar in attitude and content, if not in style, not only to the poems of Keats and Shelley but also to William Merwin's "Ode: The Medusa Face" written in the 1950s, suggesting a lack of evolution in male attitudes toward Medusa over the nineteenth and twentieth centuries. Merwin takes the persona of Perseus, who boasts about having "deprived / Three hags of their one eye," only to wonder forever whether "stone is upon me / Healing me, clotting time until I stand / Dead" (46). The heroic Perseus is unsure whether it is Medusa's "lithe hair" which has stiffened or himself "Amazed" into petrifaction. These poems convey the male poet's sudden arrest before the Medusa archetype, a gaze into the eye of wisdom which transfixes both poet and Gorgon.

The twentieth-century poem that most clearly embodies the power of the Medusa archetype to paralyze the poet while endowing the moment of his or her gaze with immortality is perhaps Louise Bogan's 1923 "Medusa," in which, as Deborah Pope was the first to notice, the immobilized landscape is an image of Bogan's feeling about her own natural body (17). Informed by an early childhood experience when she was momentarily blinded by the shock of discovering her mother with a lover, Bogan approaches a "house, in a cave of trees" where "everything moved," while in the natural world "sun and reflection wheeled by." Bogan images the traumatizing realization of maternal sexuality as

> the bare eyes were before me
> And the hissing hair,
> Held up at a window, seen through a door.
> The stiff bald eyes, the serpents on the forehead
> Formed in the air.

As a result of this perception of her mother, nature itself is transfixed for Bogan, so that "This is a dead scene forever now" where "Nothing will ever stir." However, as my students have often noted, the result is not entirely negative, since at the denouement of the poem nature is arrested in an immortal state.

> The water will always fall, and will not fall,
> And the tipped bell make no sound.
> The grass will always be growing for hay
> Deep in the ground.

> And I shall stand here like a shadow
> Under the great balanced day,
> My eyes on the yellow dust, that was lifting in the
> wind
> and does not drift away. (*The Blue Estuaries* 4)

What has been seen is fixed forever, and although the maternal Medusa in her terrifying sexuality has proved too much for the gazer, that which she gazes upon has become immortalized through her experience. Bogan's difficulties arise from her inability to assimilate the totality of feminine selfhood—the feminine power and sexuality as well as feminine victimization—inherent in the maternal Medusa. As I shall suggest in the chapters on Aphrodite, this divorce of the maternal from the sexual is a recent phenomenon in sexual history, one that causes extreme psychological difficulties for those trying to come to terms with a holistic feminine personality.

Robert Graves, like Robert Lowell and Louise Bogan, finds the conflation of the maternal and the sensual problematic. Male poets often fail to separate their early ideas about maternal sexuality from their heterosexual experiences; like the "White Goddess" he places at the center of his myth theory, Graves's Medusa mixes maternal and sexual elements in a manner which makes his relationships to real women conflictual. In "The Death Grapple," for example, he equates lovemaking with fighting a snake and confronting a hungry female lion:

> Lying between your sheets, I challenge
> A watersnake in a swoln cataract
> Or a starved lioness among drifts of snow.
> Yet dare it out, for after each death grapple,
> Each gorgon stare borrowed from very hate,
> A childish innocent smile touches your lips,
> Your eyelids droop, fearless and careless
> And sleep remolds the lineaments of love.
> (*New Collected Poems* 268)

Stuck in the Victorian ascription of either childlike innocence or whorish concupiscence to women and the corollary presumption that a woman one makes love to must belong to the latter category, Graves experiences sexuality as inexorably antagonistic. His Medusa is simultaneously childlike and wicked, her eyes exhibiting both the powerful Gorgon stare and "drooping," infantile features. Graves may be projecting onto his lover the childlike state in which he first perceived maternity while attributing to her the frightening power a boy perceives in his mother. There is, moreover, a Persean trait to his "challenge" of the Gorgon, which he conceives of as an adventure in the poetic quest to win inspiration from his muse. Karen Elias-Button reminds us of Graves's claim in *The White Goddess* "that Perseus undertakes the slaying of the Gorgon to steal from her the power to understand the sacred alphabet" ("Athene and Medusa" 120). It is hardly surprising that Laura Riding, a woman poet who was one of Graves's lovers, wrote of men from whom "we must steal death and its wan splendors / From the women of their sighs we were," recognizing the destructive status for a woman poet of being "forgeries of ourselves" in men's reconstructions of our reality (77).

Graves agrees with Harrison's definition of the frightening Gorgon face as merely a mask covering a face which true initiates are unafraid to approach. And, as we shall see, Graves's antagonism to Medusa does not characterize his poems about other goddesses in which he is able to recognize that his distaste for the darker side of femininity is something he needs to work through. For Graves, as for most British and American male poets, the Medusa archetype is dominated by her negative content, distancing them from any blessings that might lurk behind her mask.

Women poets who have internalized patriarchal values also perceive Medusa in a negative light. In a 1971 collection Diane Wakoski associates both snakes and Medusa with patriarchal ideas about feminine beauty, norms which prevent her from celebrating her own femininity. In "No More Soft Talk," a revenge poem against a lover she finds in her bed with somebody else, her description is similar to Bogan's traumatic vision of her mother and her mother's lover. In Wakoski's poem fluid snakes rather than a frozen landscape embody her feelings:

> Yes, yes,
> a bed full of snakes all bearing new young,
> a bed full of slashed wrists,

a bed of carbines and rifles with no ammunition,
a bed of my teeth in another woman's fingers.
(*The Motorcycle Betrayal Poems* 66)

The snakes represent a sexuality which infuriates the poet and drives her toward revenge; they do not represent her sexuality, notably, but the danger to her well-being of somebody else's.

Earlier in the poem Wakoski had wondered "how a woman / can be a rock, / when all she wants is to be soft, / to melt to the lines / her man draws for her"; in spite of this desire to conform to masculine demands, and although she cannot identify with the Medusean snakes, she reappropriates Medusa's stony power to rebel against her lover. In her anger Wakoski metamorphoses from soft to exploding rock, "a volcanic mountain," sufficiently self-determined to declare that when her anger/lava cools she will become a hard rock that he can love "if you can / I will not make it easy for you / any more" (68).

Although she appropriates the Medusean rock imagery in order to empower herself, Wakoski associates snakes with something threatening and external to her own selfhood. They are not alien to a femininity she admires in her friends, however. In "The Girls" she associates a love of snakes with slim, beautiful women and her own distaste for snakes with her perception of herself as "ugly duckling." Although her "slender and chic" women friends love to handle snakes, Wakoski would be terrified even of finding "a harmless little black / fellow / curled in the grass." She conflates her feeling that "I have never been / one of the girls" and her fear of snakes with her sense that men don't accept her either:

> Men see me as the Medusa,
> with vipers hissing around my hair.
> How ironic
> I have always been so afraid
> of snakes . . . (*The Rings of Saturn* 23)

The irony of this text does not derive so much from Wakoski's quite natural fear of snakes (which is shared by many men and women) as from her simultaneous internalization of what men say about her and her inability to feel sisterly with women. By accepting men's ideas about beauty she shares in their alienation from the blessings of

Medusa. By asserting a volcanic anger, Wakoski, like Riding, begins to reclaim Medusa's power, a process she carries much further in her 1991 collection, *Medea, the Sorceress,* in which she identifies with both Medea and Medusa. In this collection she transcends her fear of snakes to characterize herself as someone who sits at a blackjack table in Las Vegas with a "snake coiling around my neck," and signs her letter to a friend in the name of "Yr lady of the coiling light." We shall see in later chapters how she tries to turn the corner from patriarchal determination to self-definition by coming to terms with her feelings about her mother.

Whereas Raine, Riding, and Wakoski seem overwhelmed by what men think about women, Rachel Blau DuPlessis tries in her "Medusa" to work through a devastating maternal victimization. The process involves reenacting the trauma while inventing a new language to embody Medusa's pain and power. DuPlessis describes Medusa with images of ugliness similar to Plath's: "flat-faced," "splay eye," "crosst tongue," "cavern slug," "hair-face" (42). Here, however, these rough images do not express disgust but the poet's willing immersion in feminine/maternal corporeality, as part of a quest both for personal transformation and for poetic inspiration in a mother tongue. DuPlessis begins her poem by recounting Medusa's victimization in Persean third-person terms ("She is the thing he / flickers with his light," 42), then switches to Medusa's/her mother's point of view to reenact Perseus's attack ("Everywhere / I see / inside me / Man / poised," 44), in empathy with the terrible experience of maternal rape:

> A cave of pain   a howling mouth
> it is
>   dark
>   the emptied self
> Striking my head on the rock my mother. (46)

At the same time she places the blame squarely where it belongs:

> Stole
> they
> eye of my mother
> stole they teeth
> mother.

> Broke the moon box
> where she keep
> the deep socket
> of the child set solid. (47)

Using nonsense and infantile syllables, DuPlessis as daughter undertakes the quest for the raped and robbed mother in the deepest places of nature and of her unconscious:

> What is this thing
> this ancient middenstead?
> All stark.
> It is a stone.
> Its lips are stone.
> Its eyes are mica mirrors. (48)

Having named and resisted men's attempts to dominate Medusa's sexuality and generativity, DuPlessis undertakes the final stage of the Demeter/Kore quest, which for a daughter is to transcend her mother's experience in patriarchy by assimilating her authentic feminine powers.

The Empowering Medusa

Jane Ellen Harrison notes that the Demeter/Kore celebration, an annual Greek religious ritual at the end of September, was "almost uncontaminated by Olympian usage," deriving from pre-Hellenic practices in Thrace and Crete (*Prolegomena* 120). Jung concurs that

> the Demeter-Kore myth is far too feminine to have been merely the result of an anima-projection. . . . Demeter-Kore exists on the plane of the mother-daughter experience, which is alien to man and shuts him out. In fact, the psychology of the Demeter cult bears all the features of a matriarchal order of society, where the man is an indispensable but on the whole disturbing factor.

In fact, Jung argues, "in the formation of the Demeter-Kore myth the feminine influence so far outweighed the masculine that the latter had practically no significance. The man's role in the Demeter myth is really only that of seducer or conqueror" (*Archetypes and the Collective Unconscious* 203, 184).

Although the classical Demeter/Kore archetypal narrative, and the Eleusinian rituals derived from it, had to do with the mother's rescue and bringing back to life of her raped daughter, the mother/ daughter quest can work either way, from mother to daughter or daughter to mother. Jung identifies this woman/woman quest, in which mothers and daughters mutually empower each other, as the core of women's psychological maturation:

> We could therefore say that every mother contains her daughter in herself and every daughter her mother, and that every woman extends backwards into her mother and forwards into her daughter. . . . An experience of this kind gives the individual a place and a meaning in the life of the generations, so that all unnecessary obstacles are cleared out of the way of the life-stream that is to flow through her. At the same time the individual is rescued from her isolation and restored to wholeness. All ritual preoccupation with archetypes ultimately has this aim and this result. (*Archetypes and the Collective Unconscious* 188)

We have seen that in "The Muse as Medusa," Karen Elias-Button recognizes that twentieth-century women poets tend to seek out powers hidden in "denigrated" archetypes, and she goes on to insist that the exploration of archetypes like Medusa can lead behind patriarchy to deeper levels of feminine psychology. Well aware of the scorn cultural determinists visit upon those who value the deeper background of images which they consider stereotypically sexist, Elias-Button denies that our research is "a relinquishment of ego development in the name of cyclicity and romantic unconsciousness," defining feminist archetypalism as an engagement in "a reaching-back to the myths of the mother, to find there the source of our own, specifically female, creative powers" ("The Muse as Medusa" 193). It is Hecate (who, as we shall see in the chapter on Artemis, is often a Medusa cognate), wandering through the dark underworld with her torch, who witnesses Pluto dragging Persephone down to hell and tells Demeter how to find her daughter. Demeter, Hecate, Persephone, and Medusa can all be defined in psychological terms as integral elements in a quest for wholeness that each mother and each daughter must undertake.

When we juxtapose the preclassical background of the Medusa myth to the way women poets claim Medusa as mother, we can begin to understand how the archetype enables women to cast aside what men think about us in order to celebrate our mothers and ourselves. This cannot be done, however, without an acceptance of one's mother's corporeality and an overcoming of our repulsion about their bodily lives as well as our terror at their victimization. Women poets who loathe Medusa tend to be father-identified: valuing our mothers' experiences as women is a very difficult task in patriarchy, where it is much more logical to denounce them and identify with our fathers and their culture.

I suggested in the first chapter that one compromise is to affirm Medusa's victimization and power simultaneously, as in the vivid case of Mary Elizabeth Coleridge. In the late 1940s Edith Sitwell published a series of poems in this tradition, in which powerful feminine archetypes like the Bee Priestess, Medusa, and Venus help her to transcend what men have said about goddesses and to achieve personal transformation. Her "Hymn to Venus" will form an important part of my discussion of Aphrodite in a later chapter; it is crucial to recognize here that in her "Medusa's Love Song," which comes immediately before "Hymn to Venus" in *The Canticle of the Rose,* she understands Medusa and Venus as aspects of one other. In her title she affirms Medusa's erotic identity, recognizing her original status as priestess of Athena, companioned in her salad days with other "amaryllideous girls of burning."

Medusa is asked by a personification of "Day" to change it into stone, so that the grief and suffering of the war can be soothed by petrifaction. Day begs that those "who hourly die" and the "children fleshless as Adam" of the war-torn streets be turned to stone through Medusa's pity for them. Medusa refuses to do this because she remembers her own youthful springtime; she has not forever been rigid but has experienced the fire and fluidity of life. Medusa's gift is not to turn day and its fluidity to night and stone but to keep the day alive with "the blood that is fire and is Fate, the blind impulse," so that it can avert her fate of being unable any longer to feel "the warm heart of Aprils and apricots." These vital, earthy joys are no longer hers, but she will not petrify the war-torn "Day" because she values the sun and fire and regeneration that it will continue to experience. As we shall see in my analysis of "A Hymn to Venus," Sitwell describes the love goddess there as "Beyond the seeds of petrifaction, Gorgon of itself," thus positing Medusa and Venus as complementary aspects of a single archetype. A sense of enormous vitality underlies Medusa's rigidity in Sitwell's "Medusa's Love Song," as well as memory of her previctimization sensual joy, so that the poem hovers between the aesthetic stasis of Bogan's and the empowerment which DuPlessis achieves by transcending Medusa's victimization to claim her as both mother and muse. The uniqueness of Sitwell's vocabulary, which is her "eccentric" stylistic signature, obscures from all but very careful readers the element of self-empowerment in her Medusa/Venus archetype.

Whereas one feels a suffering and victimization in Bogan's celebration of a landscape petrified by Medusa's gaze and Sitwell's celebration of Medusa empowerment is obscured by her style, other women poets more openly claim Medusa as muse. In an exchange of letters and poems between 1964 and 1980, for example, Alexandra Grilikhes and May Sarton shared their recognition that Medusa is not the negative creature men deplore but a source of poetic inspiration. In one letter Grilikhes noted that "particularly for the woman artist, the Muse is nothing but Medusa turned backwards. You face the implacable force in yourself with which you must find how to live, Medusa, the terrible unknown that one mines and one mines, and of whom the end never comes. You use it rather than let it turn you to stone. Medusa, for you if you choose; she isn't outside you" (73). Sarton's "The Muse as Medusa" seems to be an answer to and expression of Grilikhes's insight. Sarton declares that she has looked Medusa "straight in the cold eye" but has not been "punished, was not turned to stone," and that she thus questions "the legends I am told," namely patriarchal distrust of Medusa. Like Robert Lowell and Sylvia Plath, Sarton is a New England poet who associates Medusa with the jellyfish that stings her prey into paralysis before eating it, but when "I came as naked as any little fish, / Prepared to be hooked, gutted, caught," Sarton declares, she was not killed but allowed to "swim my way / through the great deep, and on the rising tide," even "though you had power marshalled on your side." Sarton distances herself from Medusa's rigidity, however. "You chose / to abdicate by total lack of motion," she accuses. "But did it work, for nothing really froze?" Although, like Sitwell, she perceives fluidity beneath Medusa's mask, she does not identify with the archetype as Sitwell does but establishes her distance and perhaps enmity as a freely swimming "little fish." In the final verse, which seems similar to Coleridge's final stanza, Sarton has not assimilated the power of a "face" she confronts:

> I turn your face around! It is my face.
> That frozen rage is what I must explore—
> Oh secret, self-enclosed, and ravaged place!
> This is the gift I thank Medusa for.
> (*Collected Poems* 332)

In her disassociation of Medusa's "frozen rage" from the healing oceanic fluidity she escapes to, Sarton seems unresolved, or just setting out, on her quest for self-understanding, moving toward assimilating Medusa as her muse but, like Bogan, remaining on the threshold of the "ravaged place" the archetype inhabits. In an interview between Jenny and Mrs. Stevens in her pivotal novel *Mrs. Stevens Hears the Mermaids Singing*, Sarton paraphrases Grilikhes again in her identification of Medusa's face with her own, but she goes on to project both Medusa and rage upon her friend Dorothea, a woman whose mind Stevens associates with "masculinity." Here we find a clue, I believe, to Sarton's deadlock over Medusa: in defining not only intellect but also creativity as "masculine" (Mrs. Stevens thinks you can't have children and be a poet and that there could never have been a female Dylan Thomas) Sarton internalizes patriarchal dualism to remain identified with the father culture. I think that her poem about Medusa ends without assimilation of Medusa's feminine empowerment because Sarton persists in associating creativity, art, and intellect with a "masculinity" that can only be achieved by renouncing one's womanhood.

Within the context of our understanding of the maternal content of the Medusa archetype and of women poets' need to come to terms with their mothers' experiences in patriarchy, I read Sarton's indeterminate ending as having to do with both father-identification and an uncompleted rebirth journey to assimilate the maternal elixir. In "Medusa, Smiling," which Grilikhes wrote subsequent to her correspondence with Sarton, we find a contrasting recognition that the quest for Medusa must include these maternal issues. The poem is a formal, reverential prayer to Medusa as "great lady" whom she recognizes as

Fond
mother, stone
mother, with me now
in weariness, in
dark
water I see you now Medusa
see your face at last
with my face
in your eyes, gleaming (73)

an outcome which suggests Grilikhes's quest for healing successfully reconciles mother with self in the Medusa archetype. Whether they feel blocked by a negative Medusa, like Plath, Wakoski, and to a lesser extent Sarton, or conceive of her as empowering, like DuPlessis, Sitwell, and Grilikhes, there is a sense of enormous effort in the poetic quest for a maternal blessing. Not only "the legends we are told" about Gorgon Medusa but even more our difficulties in developing a self-hood from the ruins of our mothers' lives in patriarchy make our attempts to approach Medusa complex and painful.

The Black Medusa

The sense of deadlock that white women poets experience when trying to assimilate Medusa contrasts to the way African American women poets affirm Medusalike goddesses derived from African mythology. I will discuss the relationship between African American women poets' use of African goddess archetypes and their sexuality in a later chapter; here we need to consider the Medusan qualities which help African American women poets distance themselves from white culture, reconcile themselves with their mothers, and empower themselves archetypally.

There is a scene at the end of Toni Morrison's novel *Beloved* in which Beloved (the murdered daughter who has returned to live with the mother who killed her) comes out on the porch to confront a crowd which has gathered to exorcise her. They see her as tall, very black, fully pregnant, and coiffed in a beautiful Afro, which looks like thick, coiled vines. Morrison seems to associate Beloved's curls with Medusa's snakes in a manner consonant with Libyan prototypes of

Medusa (see chapter 1). In the late 1960s, when students at a black women's college where I was teaching began to renounce straightening their hair in conformity with white standards of beauty and to cultivate the "natural," or Afro, the responses of shock in both white and African American middle-class communities included revulsion against what is primal and "uncivilized," especially when associated with women. The students, however, found in their "naturals" an affirmation of African feminine power and beauty, a quality which recent African American writers such as Doris Davenport have described as "Afracentric . . . the state of being comfortably, wholly female and Black at once . . . a word which encompasses spiritual and material, political and social realities, with Black wimmin's perspectives and visions as a norm" (13). In "A Navy Blue Afro," Colleen McElroy recognizes the Medusan element in the Afro style as a quality of this Afrocentric feminism which fashionable women have tried to repress:

> you have seen them
> all those fake Furies
>   coiffured
>   powdered
>   and costumed
>   their Medusa hair tamed
>   and dressed in new money
> they are so rich
> they piss in droplets (*Music From Home* 76)

McElroy contrasts these women and their bad faith attempts to assimilate to white norms of beauty to "the girl with the navy blue hair" whose "blackness sings to me" with authenticity and power.

African American women poets have developed outrageously powerful women heroes analogous to the snaky-haired goddess archetype. Colleen McElroy, in her series of "Dragon Lady" poems, subverts a comic book stereotype proffered by white patriarchy, replacing it with powerful feminine archetypes. In *Queen of the Ebony Isles* she describes an "old woman" who "follows me from room to room / screams like my mother angers like my child," who "has seen too many comic strips / believes she's as deadly lovely / as Dragon Lady and Leopard Girl." The old woman demands that she make love and dance and participate in both creation and destruction:

> on midnight-blue nights she screams
> into the eyes of the moon twirling her war machine
> like some Kamikaze pilot

She insists that the poet "play the game" of life. At this phase McElroy
still resists the nonconforming old woman who is trying to serve as her
guide into personal transformation:

> when she looks into the mirror from my eyes
> I want to float away unscathed
> drift like patches of early morning fog
> she thinks I stay because I love her
> one day soon I'll move while she's sleeping (68)

But in subsequent poems she empowers herself by identifying with the
Dragon Lady. The key to McElroy's success consists in conflating the
Dragon Lady with her own mother. The poet cannot be inspired to
speak in her own authentic voice until she comes to terms with her
mother as muse and completes a quest into her maternal memories
buried in the deeper reaches of her psyche. Although there are no
specific Medusa images in McElroy's successful daughter/mother quest,
she is reconciled to those very maternal rages which Plath and Sarton
cannot handle.

The link between the archetypal Medusa, African goddesses, and
assimilating maternal power is even more explicit in Audre Lorde's
poetry. The key to Lorde's quest for poetic and sexual inspiration
consists (as she puts it in "Black Mother Woman") in being able to
peel "away your anger / down to its core of love." I will return to this
poem when I discuss the black Aphrodite; it is important to note here
that Lorde's assimilation of her mother's anger and thwarted power is
closely related to several Medusalike figures she celebrates in her
poetry. As Estella Lauter has reminded us, for Lorde the "Black
mother" represents "the source not only of poetry but of all creativity.
Affirming that it is a resource available to men and to whites, she
associates it again with chaos, saying that if we (humankind) do not
learn its lessons, we run the risk of committing the same cultural
mistakes all over again" ("Eros and Creativity" 5). Lauter quotes *Sister
Outsider*: "we must never close our eyes to the terror, to the chaos
which is Black which is creative which is female which is dark which

is rejected which is messy which is. . . . Sinister, smelly, erotic, confused, upsetting . . ." (101). Lorde entirely subverts the negative "Terrible Mother" white psychoanalysts find so troubling, affirming and assimilating a terror which consists in her natural, feminine power and a destructiveness which manifests a world-creating chaos.

In "Oya," written in the name of a Yoruba goddess of "the river Niger, tornadoes, strong winds generally, fire, lightning, and buffalo" (Gleason 1), Lorde conflates her own "mother asleep on her thunders" with Oya. In this poem from the 1970s, Lorde recognizes with considerable trepidation that she can conquer only if she accepts and loves the destructive maternal aspects; her attitude remains awed and respectful to the black mother figure as she develops her selfhood so that by 1986, in "Call," she is writing much more familiarly and with far less fear about such an African archetype as "Aido Hwedo," the rainbow serpent. She reenvisions the kind of multifaceted snake goddess (like Ua Zit in Nidaba and the Old European snake goddess who antedated Athena and Hera) which constitutes the deep background of the Medusa archetype. As a rainbow serpent Aido Hwedo combines all colors in its power, constituting an archetype which Lorde identifies as "a representation of all ancient divinities who must be worshipped but whose names and faces have been lost in time." In extending this archetype's empowerment to white men and women as well as to her African American brothers and sisters, Lorde creates a black mother goddess out of African and personal materials and approaches her in a manner at the most positive end of our scale of attitudes toward Medusa. Most striking is her subversion of the stereotypical, racist association of blackness with evil and darkness with destruction to offer the black goddess as a healing archetype available to us all.

| Gender Differences |

But what about African American male poets who write about Medusa? As we have seen in the cases of Robert Hayden and Countee Cullen, these poets tend to associate the classical Medusa with the threat of being lynched/castrated through seduction by white women. We shall see in assessing these poets' approach to the Aphrodite archetype that James Weldon Johnson similarly warns African American men to beware "the white witch," and

Cullen introduces an evil white woman interloper who disrupts the idyllic marriage in "Ballad of the Brown Girl." Like most white male poets, African American male poets reflect patriarchal definitions of Medusa, focusing on her negative qualities. When these poets bring their African roots into a poem, however—as in Cullen's "Ballad of the Brown Girl," where the brown bride's "wild blood sings" as she asserts her "dark wrath," or "A Song of Praise," in which his lover is empowered by her "soul of Africa" into a "barbaric dance" and a mood of "arrogance"—they celebrate empowering feminine archetypes. We shall see in a later chapter how Cullen, Jean Toomer, Langston Hughes, and Don Lee use African archetypes to transcend "Terrible Mother" attributes derived from white culture; only when an African American male poet is infected by an overdose of European thought, as in the case of Imamu Amiri Baraka's existential paradigms about women and the body, do we find the misogyny more characteristic of white male poets.

The black archetypes I have described in this chapter as Medusa cognates enable African American poets to get much closer to a holistic goddess figure than can white men and women poets, who tend to perceive Medusa much more negatively. I would suggest that the level of distrust in approaching Medusa has to do with the degree to which a poet perceives himself or herself as engulfed in the patriarchal pie. Marginalized African American poets seek African archetypes which are more empowering to them than those available to whites through a traditionally classical mythology. The African goddesses these poets draw upon, for example, are less dualized than the classical Medusa, conflating thunderstorms, generativity, political prowess, and sexuality into a powerfully feminine archetype analogous to ancient snake divinities and to goddesses such as the Sumerian Inanna. To put it another way, for white poets the deeper Medusa archetypes are buried under many more layers of patriarchy than is the case for African American poets, who have never been fully assimilated during the few centuries they have been reluctantly enclosed within white culture.

It seems evident that the further poets think they live from the center of patriarchal culture, the more intensely they are empowered by apatriarchal feminine archetypes. This hypothesis may, at first blush, seem naively romantic or even degradingly sentimental about the "noble savage" stereotype. I have found, nonetheless, that it not only holds true in the case of African American poets' recourse to African archetypes but, as I will illustrate in the next chapter, also accounts for significant differences in the way Anglo-Canadian poets approach Medusa. Since I will postulate that these Canadian differences are influenced by the theology of Canadian Native Peoples, the question of the "noble savage" fallacy, along with Native American accusations of "white shamanism" against non-native poets' usurpation of Native American theological materials, will remain a prominent concern of this volume.

Women poets divide into two groups in this chapter: those who loathe the image (which they share of themselves with men) in their mirrors, and those who look beneath the image to discern someone more psychologically healthy than the female monster Perseus saw. French theorist Hélène Cixous would account for women's ability to see behind the patriarchal surfaces to our position outside of culture:

> Now women return from afar, from always: from "without," from the heath where witches are kept alive; from below, from beyond "culture"; . . . The little girls and their "ill-mannered" bodies immured, well-preserved, intact unto themselves, in the mirror. Frigidified. But are they ever seething underneath! . . . Here they are, returning, arriving over and again, because the unconscious is impregnable. They have wandered around in circles, confined to the narrow room in which they've been given a deadly brainwashing. You can incarcerate them, slow them down, get away with the old Apartheid routine, but for a time only. As soon as they begin to speak, at the same time as they're taught their name, they can be taught that their territory is black: because you are Africa, you are black. Your continent is dark. (247)

Here again we have what looks like a stereotypical association of Africa with psychological darkness and danger, a description of the unconscious in terms of blackness that seems insulting to African Americans. However, in the context of Audre Lorde's definition of the "dark mother" as characteristic of a powerful black womanhood accessible to nonblacks, we can read Cixous's declaration that "the Dark Continent is neither dark nor inexplorable" and her insistence that "it is still unexplored only because we've been made to believe that it was too dark to be explorable" as affirmations of empowering marginality. The world of the unconscious, the background deeper than patriarchy, is symbolized for Cixous in Medusa herself: "You only have to look at the Medusa straight on to see her. And she's not deadly. She's beautiful and she's laughing." We have seen that a woman poet's ability to break through to Medusa has to do with facing her mother "straight on" in order to negotiate a passage toward psychological maturity.

Cixous's interpretation of the archetype as potentially empowering for women is markedly different from the existential assumption that Medusa, like women and nature, is ontologically "other," a view characterized, for example, by Kimon Friar, whom Barnes describes as convinced that Medusa is at one and the same time "pure form" and "art for art's sake" and, paradoxically, "that portion of Evil before which every artist must shudder in temptation. He stares not into the moral or the immoral eyes of humanity, but into the blank and amoral gaze of nature" (38). For someone with Friar's attitude, normal psychological maturation as well as a healthy relationship to one's own body and to nature will inevitably be blocked.

It is clear that there are significant gender differences between white American and British men and women poets in their approaches to Medusa, causing them to structure poems based upon the archetype in significantly variant ways. These differences cannot be simplistically described as a masculine loathing versus a feminine reverence for Medusa; as we have seen, both men and women can be awed or horrified by her. Their attitudes deviate, nonetheless, according to gender, with the men drawn into a fatal complicity with the "other," her femininity understood as dangerously different, while women poets, even if equally horrified by her, are drawn toward a fusion based upon identity. These differences seem determined by the simple psychological variants of a girl's and a boy's feelings about the mother, with the boy's experience of establishing himself over and against the mother as different and the girl's of trying to identify as a self in spite of sameness. Thus, to review but one example, Oppenheimer and Plath both fail in their quests for Medusa because they remain too childlike. But there is a crucial difference between Oppenheimer's infantile hunger for the breast and body of his lovers and Plath's inability to transcend the threat of maternal engulfment. Although neither of them is able to assimilate maternal sexuality, their quests fail in different ways, in that her danger is sameness and his otherness, paralleling deviations between a girl's and a boy's developmental psychology (Chodorow 92–110).

Since both men and women poets find the Medusa/mother at the heart of their psychological journeys, both seek her as muse. Although we rarely find poems in which a male poet seeks a male muse, women, like men, seek empowerment and inspiration in Medusa. From the British and American white sample alone we might establish significant gender differences in relationship to the Medusa archetype; the African American poets, however, throw a spanner into this simplistic hypothesis, which, as I will demonstrate in the next chapter, is also challenged by Canadian archetypal attitudes.

3.

Medusa in Canada

I showed in the preceding chapter how British and U.S. poets respond to the Medusa archetype on a scale from horrified antagonism to identification. Male poets are more likely to perceive her as "other," an entirely alien being, with whom they may nonetheless feel a disquieting complicity, but their attitudes vary from horror to sympathy. Although women poets share the male fear of Medusa inherent in her classical archetype, they often identify with her outrageous power as well as with her victimization. So many poems are structured upon Medusa as to suggest that the archetype links a mythical to a personal content, that of childhood experience of the mother. British and U.S. poems show clear variations along gender lines, undoubtedly determined by the different personal impacts of the mother-son and mother-daughter bond.

I have suggested that Jung's and Neumann's theories about the good/bad mother archetype (with its implication that women and the unconscious are facets of masculine consciousness) derive from a traditional hierarchical dualism. Since traditional European attitudes about nature tend to be conflated with feelings about women, nature shares with women the down side of this polarity, dominated by mind and masculinity. These attitudes lead to the theory that neither women nor nature have any real existence without reference to men and to culture, which in literary theory leads to a corollary assumption that not only women and natural objects but even the idea of a human self are linguistic inventions.

Canadian poets adopt strikingly different stances to the natural world than do British and U.S. poets. The differences derive from the unique Canadian attitude toward the natural world. The principle difference in Canadian poetry is its resistance to anthropomorphic subordination. Although Canadian poets associate a terrifying female-ness with their landscapes, their conviction that nature is nonhuman and insubordinate modifies their approach to feminine archetypes. One would expect that a nature so much stronger than human beings would evoke a kind of Sartrean alienation, a sense of being a tiny consciousness lost in vast and mindless extension. Many Canadian critics posit initial hypotheses about poet and landscape in Canada which suggest this kind of existential stance, but as they explore their material these same critics induce hypotheses more appropriate to a non-European attitude toward the environment.

W. H. New notes these critics' frequent suggestions that "the land becomes a stronger presence than the human figures in Canadian fiction, a character in its own right, an actor as well as an activating power in the psychological and metaphysical dramas being unveiled." Poets must abandon traditional subjective biases in dealing with such a nature, taking on an "empirical realism" which subverts normal "modes of structuring points of view" (xii, xxi). Warren Tallman, similarly, describes Canadian writers leaving European mythologies behind to reinvest "Old Mother North America" with her indigenous divinities (253).

In the introduction to *Marked by the Wild: An Anthology of Literature Shaped by the Canadian Wilderness*, Bruce Littlejohn and Jon Pearce cite a number of Canadian critics on the importance of nature to Canadian literature, asserting that "if there is one distinguishing element that sets Canadian literature apart from most other national literatures, it is the influence of the wild" (11). A national literature in which nature rather than culture takes the foreground is likely to contain archetypes quite different from traditional ones.

Northrop Frye provides the most important example of a critic whose hypotheses vary when he deals with Canadian literature and when he deals with the classics and the traditional European canon. He urges critics concerned with Canadian poetry to find new hypotheses for it: "Certain critical principles are essential for dealing with Canadian poetry which in the study of English literature as such are seldom raised. Unless the critic is aware of the importance of these

principles, he may, in turning to Canadian poets, find himself un-
expectedly incompetent, like a giraffe trying to eat off the ground"
(*The Bush Garden* 163). According to Frye, Canadian poetry is not
determined as much by other poetry as by the obdurate Canadian
landscape: "it is not a nation," he insists, "but an environment that
makes an impact on poets, and poetry can deal only with the imagina-
tive aspect of that environment." Whereas in "older countries" human
beings and nature have adjusted to "some kind of imaginative har-
mony," for Canadians "the land of the Rockies and the Precambrian
Shield" creates a "profoundly unhumanized isolation" (*The Bush Gar-
den* 164).

In his writings about classical and European literatures Frye
assumes that culture is both different from and dominant over nature,
but in his analyses of Canadian literature he describes nature as the
determinant of culture. This is not a chronological evolution in Frye's
thinking; rather, he seems to have been so faithful to a genuinely
inductive method that he shifts his hypotheses when dealing, even
simultaneously, with different literatures. Like a number of Canadian
critics, Frye describes the nineteenth-century Canadian writer's atti-
tude toward nature as one of terror before an absolutely alien otherness
and describes recent Canadian poetry as similarly dominated by
"themes of desolation and loneliness, and more particularly of the
indifference of nature to human values, which I should say was the
central Canadian tragic theme" (*The Bush Garden* 171).

Although in his criticism of European and classical literatures Frye
works from the presumption that literature is primarily derived from
other literature, he notices the disjunction of Canadian poetry from its
literary antecedents: "The imaginative content of Canadian poetry,
which is often primitive, frequently makes extraordinary demands on
forms derived from romantic or later traditions" (*The Bush Garden*
173–74). It is important to note that he is saying this in 1956, only a
year before the publication of his *Anatomy of Criticism*; thus he is
postulating entirely different paradigms simultaneously.

In the conclusion to *Literary History of Canada* (1976), Frye
distinguishes between the relationship between literature's "detached
and autonomous mythology" and society's "corresponding mythology"
in Canadian as opposed to American and European literature. Where-
as the "sentimental or nostalgic pastoral myth" characterizing non-
Canadian literature "increases the feeling of separation between sub-

ject and object by withdrawing the subject into a fantasy world,"
Canadian literary myth "starts with the identifying of subject and
object," or human beings with nature in a manner distinct from the
traditional European separation (354). "Everything that is central to
Canadian writing," Frye asserts, "seems to be marked by the im-
manence of the natural world" (357–58). In an essay from the previ-
ous year, Frye deplores the Christian conviction that "the gods that
had been discovered in nature were all devils," from which "it fol-
lowed that a natural religion like that of the Indians simply had to be
extirpated if the Indians were to realize their human potential," and
tells an anecdote about a doctor and an Eskimo lost in the Arctic
tundra. "What with the cold, the storm, and the loneliness, the
doctor panicked and began shouting 'We are lost.' The Eskimo looked
at him thoughtfully and said 'We are not lost. We are here.' A vast
gulf," Frye concludes, "between an indigenous and an immigrant
mentality opened at that point: the possibility of eventually closing
that gulf is the main theme of what follows" ("Haunted" 26–27).

As a result, the rebirth pattern Frye had postulated as typical of
the "total verbal order" which had informed his *Anatomy of Criticism*
in 1957 as well as his *Secular Scripture* of 1976—written simultaneously
with the Canadian essays—varies for his Canadian sample. In the
traditional rebirth quest the hero starts out in a culturally determined
"green world," which is a pastoral or an Edenic setting, and moves
through adventures of combat with natural and (often) female mon-
sters toward a denouement in which society reaffirms its norms.
Although Frye notes a tension between the hero's rebellious desire for
freedom and society's concerns, the outcome is his accommodation to
culture. The hero's excursion is understood, moreover, as an inward
one, the monsters and nature emanating from his unconscious, with
his quest conforming to such traditional religious paradigms as rituals
and sacraments.

Nature, in this archetype of rebirth, is subordinate to and a
vehicle of spirit, as well as a dispensable realm to be overcome or
transcended in the soul's quest for salvation. When Frye describes the
Canadian rebirth journey, nature and culture remain separate but
nature is no longer a building brick of culture. Rather it has become a
primary force in its own right to which the hero must accommodate.
"A poetic consciousness formed within the leviathan of Canadian
nature," Frye writes, "feeling that it belongs there and can no longer

think of itself as a swallowed outsider, would naturally be preoccupied with two themes in particular: the theme of descent into the self [earlier Frye] and the theme of forming, within that self, an imaginative counterpart of what is outside it" ("Haunted" 41). Frye contrasts the Jonah-punished-by-being-swallowed-by-the-whale trope, in which Leviathan embodies all that Hebrews most feared in nature, to the Canadian vision of a hero who succeeds in his quest journey only insofar as he is willing to come to terms with the whaleness of the whale, the essence of the natural world.

In the quest archetype Frye describes in *Anatomy*, an (implicitly male) hero wrestles with an alien realm where nature, the unconscious, and the feminine are aspects of himself. The outcome is both internal and cultural, an apotheosis of the hero won by his overcoming and, sometimes, absorbing the contrary forces of his own personality which represent the separation of subject from object Frye had noted as typical of the traditional European pastoral myth. In the Canadian rebirth journey the hero, who is as often female as male, approaches nature, seeking a harmonious balance between the human and the natural universe. In his analysis of James Reaney's "The Heart and the Sun," Frye describes this process as an encounter with "something casual and expected in nature [which] goes through a vortex or gyre into the mind, and creates there a riddle of experience which cannot be assimilated to any set of human or social values. Like the gods of polytheism, it is neither good nor evil, but may be either or both" ("National Consciousness" 53). "Good and evil" belong to traditional attitudes about the enmity between spirit and matter, the rejection of the human and the world's body by the Christian attempt to free the soul from their toils. Frye would agree with Joseph Campbell's statement discussed earlier, that alienation from nature is an unhealthy result of the mind-body and spirit-matter splits of Christianity.

I have adopted Frye's inductive method, his willingness to discard unsuitable hypotheses when new material varies, as a central element of my critical method. If a given body of poetry—whether by women, Canadians, or Native Peoples—does not fit the literary theories or descriptions of literary conventions which I thought would apply, I attempt to describe it in its own terms. Attention to Canadian literature's variations from traditional paradigms liberates us from intimidation by the idea that European patriarchal concepts are givens.

Canadian nature's resistance to anthropomorphism can be exemplified by contrasting the use of landscape in several New England Medusa poems already discussed with that in the Canadian poems which form the sample for this chapter. In Robert Lowell, May Sarton, and Sylvia Plath the specifically named Medusa figure embodies poets' powerful emotions—horrified complicity (Lowell), rage (Sarton), and terror of being fused with one's mother (Plath). The seascape, correspondingly (along with other traditional Medusan motifs, such as snakes, oceanic rocks, and fatally seductive eyes), provides extended metaphors and metaphysical symbols expressing these psychological themes. In Canadian poetry an unnamed Medusa is more likely to be merged into the landscape, background becoming foreground as primary attractant, a kind of mesmerizing but not necessarily human outcrop. Whereas in a British or American poem about Medusa rocks might be vehicles for the theme, in Canadian poetry they are more apt to be the primary focus. Thus D. G. Jones begins "For Eve" with what looks like background—the music waves make, "Washing, washing in on the stones," but in the second stanza he focuses on "the one stone, emerging / Wet in the sunlight." Nature leaping into the foreground as actor can also be seen in Earle Birney's "November Walk near False Creek Mouth," in which the dialogue of rock and sea is dominant over human voices, the "sculptor sea," which "repeats what it said / to the first unthinking frogs / and the green wounds of the granite stones," relegating mere human contributions to the background (20, 22). Only in Canada, it seems to me, does a poet like Jones compliment his love by likening her to rocks: ". . . your beauty like a generous stone" (20–21). I shall demonstrate in this chapter, as well as in chapter 8, the unique way rocks work their way into Canadian love poetry.

Although E. J. Pratt's presentation in *Towards the Last Spike* of the Precambrian Shield as a kind of petrified Grendel's dam is most often proposed as a prototype of Canadian attitudes to nature (with Margaret Atwood, for example, describing this creature as a " 'thing' not exactly human but at least a female, a sort of reptile made of rock" [*Survival* 200]), it seems to me that Pratt's archetype, like that of the New England poets, is more anthropomorphic than many rock/female symbols in Canadian literature. More typically, the rockbound Canadian Medusa is far less humanized, less likely to contain the projected fears of human beings than to represent a strictly impersonal power, in contrast to American and British poetry in which the landscape around Medusa expresses her power, the details of setting her effects. Canadian poems do not all differ from British and American ones to the same degree. As in my earlier sample, poets approach rocks or stone/women (or even stone/men) with attitudes varying on a scale from hostility through complicity to attempts at identification, from hatred to awe and respect. Some poets adopt more European and Jungian approaches than others, personifying the Medusa and projecting emotions upon her; at the other end of the scale, a significant number of poets approach the rocky archetype in a manner similar to Native Peoples'. Since the Canadian landscape dwarfs both male and female poets with its nonhuman power, one would expect them to respond in a more comparable manner than British and American ones, necessitating careful attention to the relative roles of culture and gender in comparing poems by Canadian men and women.

It is among Canadian male poets that we find the closest analogues to the reviled Medusa of classical mythology. In St. John Simmons's "Dreamers," for example, the poet, like Perseus, murders a Medusalike woman in order to usurp her powers. The speaker appropriates the generative powers of the woman he hates: he bleeds, endures contractions, and gives birth, associating placenta and umbilicus ("a blue snake / tangled in the trees, wrapped around rock") with himself, and rock and stone with the woman:

> My woman
> with eyes of black stone
> throwing back at me
> the dulled vision of meadows.

Here, as in many British and American poems by men, the landscape absorbs Medusa's effect, while the poet assimilates her vitality by killing her and appropriating her attributes to himself:

> I would like to carve
> the darkness from her eyes,
> spread the mica soul
> into a malleable sheet
> and polish it
> with my fur. (51)

Like Medusa's head, the woman's powers are trophies empowering her murderer.

In another poem, "The Children Asked Me to Kill You," Simmons approaches a hated wife and mother to transform her (after submitting her to a slow and painful death by exposure) into an aesthetically pleasing object:

> And I will take some few bones back,
> bones so white and smooth
> they will seem grotesque pebbles from the stream,
> and I will hang them in the yard
> where the children, happy in their stoic innocence,
> may ring them like Buddhist chimes. (53)

Although Simmons's attitude to the "Terrible Mother" depends upon traditional attitudes to the Medusa archetype described by Jung and Neumann, making Simmons closer to a U.S. poet like Joel Oppenheimer than to many of his Canadian counterparts, something about his use of stone imagery renders his Medusa more than merely projective. Her "eyes of black stone" and "mica soul," her bones "like grotesque pebbles," conform to a peculiarly Canadian use of rock imagery. Perseus, it will be recalled, earned not only Medusa's head as his reward for her murder; he was also given the horse Pegasus, born out of her severed neck, which gave him the power of poetic composition. Thus in "The Invention of Mythical Beasts," Simmons's rewards for killing a woman are animals "clear and cold as quartz" and elements which are a "sea of obsidian eyes" enabling the poet to repeat their import "in stone."

Other male poets whose attitude is less hostile than Simmons's make the same association of Medusa's allure with her ability to endure as an object of petrifaction, frozen into stone in a kind of Keatsian immortality. Thus in one of the very few Canadian poems which I have found constructed specifically upon the classical Medusa myth, Daryl Hine's "Tableau Vivant," the poet is sympathetic to Medusa's entrapment in her own effect, having always to dream "of petrified forests, / . . . / Or of the mate that she will never meet / Who will look into her eyes and live" (65). Like a number of British and U.S. male poets, Hine is compassionate about the loneliness of turning everyone you look at into stone. The way that the rock imagery embodies a power which is simultaneously female and nonhuman strikes me, however, as specifically Canadian, the focus on her "agate gaze" suggesting as much fascination with the agate as with the gaze. I do not mean to imply that there are no traces of the usual attitudes toward the classical Medusa in this or in other Canadian poems. The nineteenth-century poet Charles Heavysege, in "Sonnet Sequence from Jephthah's Daughter," alludes to fate as "Gorgon-visaged, dire necessity" (6), and Richard Outram assumes Medusa's persona in "Tattooed Lady," where, after the manner of the terrible/beautiful woman archetype, she lures a lover to a "stone-blind" intercourse in the classical manner (194). Far more typical of twentieth-century Canadian poetry is A. J. M. Smith's "Narrow Squeak," in which the sorry plight of Keats's hero of "La Belle Dame Sans Merci" becomes transformational because the speaker is turned to stone: "stone my heart, it stopped my breath / I dropped like stone, I dropped down dead." The victim, unlike Keats's wan and deathly knight, revives in a much improved condition, no longer fading under the aegis of the "bloodshot moon" of the first stanza, but reborn through petrifaction (48).

Barbara Godard has noticed that "in A. J. M. Smith's poetry, stones are frequent images. 'The Lonely Land' and all his other northern poems are stone poems; his other poetry is filled with images of jewelry. They are directly related to the creation of beautiful artifacts, by implication the poem" (letter to the author, 1985). Since many of the stones which appear in the imagery of Canadian poetry are jewels—as in the case of agate and obsidian—poets quest not only for Medusa-turned-to-stone but also for Medusa-as-jewel or artifact. I will argue, however, that the petrifying Medusa is a less anthropomorphic archetype in Canadian than in British and U.S. poetry, the aesthetic stasis which Hazel Barnes accords to her less of a factor than intrinsic natural qualities.

George Bowering's elegy for his father, "Desert Elm," provides an interesting variation on the woman poet's association of her mother with Medusa. Although Medusa is not named, stone moves into the foreground so that Bowering endows his father with the qualities of stone more than the stone with the qualities of the father. At his father's death the poet "thought of a rock, not quite round . . . be / ginning to crack," and considers "The earth he made me on," "all rocks & all round rocks, all stones / rolled together," an earth which

"is not brown but grey, grey of / stones, the flat stones round to the eye
/ looking straight down." Whereas in classical Medusa poems the poet
must avoid looking into Medusa's eyes lest he be turned into stone,
Bowering absorbs the power of his father's land by "Staring straight
into his eyes." Thus in the last stanza the dead father, the father's
eyes, the poet's daughter's eyes, and Canadian stones are all associated
together as the forces which survive death:

> In the ocean light of the ward window his
> eyes are barely blue & deep in his head
> like my daughter's. He woke again to see
> me smiling at him, his head straight in
> the pillow, a rock nearly round. In the
> desert the rocks simply lie upon each other
> on the ground, a tree is overturned out
> of the ground, its shallow widespread roots
> coiled around small rocks. By these fruits
> we measure our weight & days. (379–84)

The stones are not merely symbols of the father's eyes or the family's
land but represent being in their own right, their natural experience
approximating but not subordinate to the human experience, rock and
dying father given equal gravity in the poet's imagination. Even when
Canadian male poets begin with apparently traditional Medusa
archetypes, something in their situation is likely to bring the rocks
into the foreground as a transformational power which poets disassoci-
ate from human qualities. This does not necessarily lead to the ex-
istential alienation of human consciousness from a vast uncaring
nature. As I shall suggest later in this chapter, poets are more likely to
perceive nature as amenable to the needs of human beings if
approached in its own terms.

If Canadian attitudes toward nature differ in the ways I have
suggested, will Canadian poetry display less difference along gender
lines than British and U.S. poetry does? There are, for example, a
good number of poems by Canadian women which reverse the "stone
woman" archetype of the male poets along gender lines, the woman
poet approaching a stone (or ice or snow) man who guards a desired
treasure. Thus in "Summer Landscape: Jasper" Dorothy Livesay de-
scribes mountains as "cold husbands" whose impotence renders them

"remote as brotherhoods / bereft of women" (25); and Margaret Atwood, in "River," approaches an "Ice / Man" the way Perseus approaches Medusa, to go "rigid in your sad / mirror while I look" (*The Animals* 25). P. K. Page, in "Mineral," describes a woman's loss of her lover in terms of his petrification: "Now he is mineral to her . . . Mineral his going and his having gone," so that at the end, "Nothing's real but mineral: cold touch, sharp taste of it / lodged foreover in her routed house" (193). Women do not perceive these inversions of the Pygmalion/Galatea legend negatively. Thus we have Miriam Waddington's enjoyment, in "Love Poem," of her lover's trans-formation into "a marbled palace / of many rooms" which results from their passion, her "kissing your body / making it white as stone" (150), representing a not infrequent outcome of Canadian intercourse.

Waddington's petrification of her lover parallels Simmons's lapi-dary activities. Making the lover into a stone object suggests a pattern of sexual exploitation which also characterizes Michael Ondaatje's "Women Like You," where "stone mermaids" with "stone hearts" once carved by men are approached by the frustrated male poet, who resents their preference for rock lovers. "They answer to no one / take the hard rock / as lover" (284–85). As I shall illustrate in chapter 8, what is remarkable in this activity is not so much the similarity between poets of different genders as their common assumption that lovemaking results in petrifaction and that petrified lovers (or even just plain rocks) are sometimes preferable to lovers in the flesh.

Women poets also like to escape from lovers to nature. Susan Musgrave avoids a human lover in "Songs of the Sea-Witch" by wrapping herself in the snake skin of a masculine Lamia or snake god, retreating "cold in the slime of the / snake-seraph with his head dress / and fangs" (*Songs* 35–36). Although Musgrave's reptile might seem analogous to Pratt's female monster, gender creates an important difference in that Musgrave retreats *from* a human lover *to* the snake, having already identified herself with the "Sea-Witch," a female nature power. To Pratt, in contrast, the stone female remains intrac-tably other, feared by the men who drive spikes into her flesh in order to probe for minerals.

Women poets sometimes approach stone females as "terrible" or "good" mothers after the manner described by Jung and Neumann. Thus Musgrave uses "Terrible Mother" imagery in "One-Sided

Woman" while recognizing the frightening female as her mother: "the person inside her / is beating the walls— / knocking on stone" (*Grave Dirt* 17–21). Like Medusa, the "one-sided woman" is fatal to men. For women, however, the petrified woman is a vehicle for rebirth. Musgrave's conflation of womb and stone enclosure is a typical Canadian coupled image, similes between flesh and rock being so common that poets seem to assume the readers' unsurprised acceptance of them. Thus Atwood expects that the reader will not find the linkage of stones and flesh unbelievable when, in "Black Stone Mother God," she approaches a rock/mother archetype as something "you like, want / to be like" (*Two-Headed Poems* 90). Similarly, when Gwladys Downes, in "The Return," makes a "bargain with the goddess" to "drink stone / eat silence . . . and she / would give me air" (97), she takes it for granted that imbibing stone is desirable.

Female poets seem at ease with the idea that wombs have stone walls and that stone is an empowering elixir, but both genders put as much emphasis on relating to rocks as on relating to the opposite sex. Even in apparently traditional classical allusions such as those of Daryl Hine and A. J. M. Smith, the fascination of stone occupies male poets. Thus in "Identification Question" we find Robert Kroetsch likening a woman's "face when she came" to "the Medusa in her snaky hair, stone writhing" (166), because for him, as for so many other Canadian writers, Medusa is made of stone as well as being capable of turning others to stone, and, however terrifying, her petrifaction is perceived as a part of sex.

Stones play a similarly unique role in poems about lovemaking and about the quest for inspiration, with stone imagery often used to describe a paradoxically petrified and potent intercourse or as a linguistically inspiring elixir. It seems that poets' peculiar relationship to the Canadian landscape leads them to write poems in which stone women and stone men make weirdly satisfying love as a matter of course and in which poetic inspiration consists of speaking in a fresh, pebbly idiom. I am not acquainted with any other national literature in which one is unsurprised to find a woman poet saying, as Pat Lowther does in *A Stone Diary:*

> By the turn of the week
> I was madly in love
> with stone. Do you know

how beautiful it is
to embrace stone
to curve all your body
against its surfaces (9)

The idea of stones having intercourse with each other is not entirely
unique to Canadian literature; Isak Dinesen recounts, for example, a
Danish story about "big stones at the bottom of the sea which came on
land upon full-moon nights, shining wet, hung with sea-thong and
mussels; they ran a race, and copulated, on the shore" (241). What is
striking about stone imagery in Canadian love poetry is the assump-
tion that being like or turning into stone is a happy by-product of
intercourse.

We have seen how, in "Women Like You," Ondaatje resents
women's affinity to rock, and how many women poets flee from male
to stone lovers or just to stones. Susan Musgrave's "Sea-Witch" fol-
lows a progression from humanized to nonhuman nature, as her affair
moves from dreaming about stone, to both lovers becoming stone, to
the poet transcending the relationship with her own stoniness intact.
Although in "One-Sided Woman" Musgrave remains ambivalent
about feminine promiscuity, fearing a terrifying woman with "eyes like
stones / that water / could not reach" (21), she aspires nonetheless to
the solid, stonelike quality of the archetypal figure. Like Musgrave,
Phyllis Webb both dreads and admires the Keatsian stasis of rock. In
her "Tall Tale" a "seagirl" and a whale make eternally arrested love in
an underwater cave. Two hundred years of intercourse have meta-
morphosed them into "brutal artifacts of stone," but the lovers,
through a combination of sexual longevity and petrifaction, have
achieved apotheosis as "stone gods," illustrating the "moral" that
although "loving flesh will quickly demise" it can "secrete a skillful
shell and stone and perfect be" (155–56).

Whereas in the traditional Medusa myth the hero avoids being
turned to stone and in British and U.S. poems about Medusa the poets
fear that she will turn them to stone, in these Canadian poems being
turned to stone is an intrinsic quality of Medusa herself, an elixir for
successfully approaching her, and is to be expected in lovemaking. I
do not mean to suggest that any of these stone/flesh images should be
taken with entire seriousness, but their ubiquity in Canadian litera-
ture, even as flights of metaphysical wit, suggests an interesting

application of Frye's theory about the impact of the environment upon the Canadian imagination.

Dorothy Livesay's "On Looking into Henry Moore" is less of a tourist piece than a poem, like "A Tall Tale," about petrifaction. Looking "into" the holes of the Moore sculpture, the poet prays that the sun "Turn me to stone," desiring the statue's "Passivity in fire / and fire in stone." Her transformation requires an androgynous, Jungian balance between "Female and male" so that she can "rise alone" as a reborn personality. The diction, however, is Canadian stone in the metaphorical mode (517–18). In "Fortunes" Miriam Waddington chooses stone as a means of transcending a confusion of ethnic identities by going out "to cry my anger to the stone-blind fields," which tell her who she is. Through immersion in the Canadian landscape, Waddington is changed from lost exile into indigenous Canadian: "no longer a bewildered princess, / but a wonderful living statue of marble stone" (120–21). Waddington accepts herself as a Galatea, but her Pygmalion is no human sculptor; rather, she achieves rebirth under the aegis of the rocky Canadian landscape.

Poets' association of stone with sexuality and rebirth seems related to the idea that by assimilating stone a poet can be linguistically inspired. Undoubtedly because of Atwood's concern in her critical writings with attitudes toward the Canadian landscape, her poetry provides interesting examples of both metaphoric and metamorphic use of stone imagery. In two poems about pioneering Atwood contrasts early settlers' feelings of alienation from the land, taking a male persona in one and a female point of view in the other. In "Progressive insanities of a pioneer" Atwood's male character goes mad resisting the landscape: "disgusted / with the swamp's clamourings and the outbursts / of rocks," he is unable to hear the language of his new environment. Canadian nature turns his assumptions topsy-turvy: "his foot sink[s] / down through stone," rupturing his preconception that "The land is solid." Most important, nature is doing the talking, its "clamours" and "outbursts" having nothing to do with human language; "Things / refused to name themselves, refused / to let him name them" (The Animals 39). Atwood is probably satirizing what Frye terms the "Cartesian ego, the sense of man as a perceiving subject totally different from everything else in nature, by virtue of his consciousness," which leads to the assumption that human ideas have more reality than nature and that nature only comes into existence when named by humans ("National Consciousness" 69).

In a sequence of poems based on Susanna Moodie's *Roughing It in the Bush,* Atwood depicts a woman settler in the Upper Canada of the 1830s who gradually abandons European preconceptions to adjust to Canadian nature on its own terms. In "Resurrection" Susanna recognizes that the

> dormant stones lie folding
> their holy fire around me
> (but the land shifts with frost
> and those who have become the stone
> voices of the land
> shift also and say
> god is not
> the voice in the whirlwind
> god is the whirlwind
> at the last
> judgement we will all be trees.
> (*The Journals of Susanna Moodie* 58–59)

Susanna realizes that divinity does not use matter as a vehicle for expressing transcendence over it; rather, divinity is immanent within matter, god being, as for the Yoruba, a whirlwind, and people must be metamorphosed into rocks and trees in order to be in harmony with it.

Vehicle and tenor, image and import, exchange places in Atwood's poetry, with rocks sometimes standing for human experiences and human experiences as often representing rocky qualities. Although Atwood sometimes uses stones as metaphysical conceits (as, for example, in "After the Flood, we," where pebbles seem to be metaphors for sperm [*The Circle Game* 12]), they are just as likely to speak for themselves. In her sequence "Some Objects of Wood and Stone," words are similes for stones: the characters gather pebbles "in shapes / as random and necessary as the shapes of words." Although at first glance the stones seem containers of human sentiments, it becomes clear that the rocks are speaking their own language, which resembles the shapes of human words. Atwood's use of metamorphosis differs from the frozen-into-immortality petrifaction described by Louise Bogan and William Merwin, whose Medusas were much more anthropomorphic than Atwood's metamorphosed divinities. Atwood's poets are not inspired by Medusa as muse but by rocks themselves; by holding pebbles in their hands the human speakers acquire a fresh, polished diction, a poetical dialectic of equal interchange between human and stone being, the synthesis being a "flight of words" as much in the language of rocks as of humans, analogous to the interchange lovers achieve by turning each other into stone during intercourse. Or, as F. R. Scott puts it, Canadian poets desire "only a moving / with no note / granite lips / a stone throat" (483).

Like so many other Canadian poets, Atwood shifts within a single poem or sequence from a vision of nature as empty of meaning to an affirmation of the intrinsic being of matter. Thus in "Totems," the first poem in "Some Objects of Wood and Stone," she perceives native symbols as masks empty of import; but in "Carved Animals," the final poem in the sequence, the text is structured upon totemistic concepts, the exchange of human and stone being which takes place when natives carve animals. Both native stonecarvers and Canadian poets seek inspiration in a dialogue with stones. This activity represents animistic religious assumptions that are markedly different from the Judeo-Christian attitudes toward nature. Atwood's approximation of native religious attitudes is typical of many Canadian poets who (as Frye, Tallman, and other Canadian critics have noted) develop a non-Western approach to nature through assimilating indigenous belief systems. Although the whole question of nonnative Canadian poets' use of native metaphysics is so vast as to require a later chapter, the way poets approach stones, as well as their quests for stone/women and their modification of the classical Medusa archetype, can be clarified by reference to indigenous theologies.

Prehistoric peoples used rock to create petroforms in Manitoba, for example; while more recently, many tribes carved sacred objects out of stone. Stone heads not unlike the Roman and Celtic sun gods and Medusas also characterize the culture of ancient peoples in the great Plains region. There are Iroquois legends about stone giants who could turn you into stone by looking at you; and the Iroquois also tell of Ia Do Da Ho, a wicked chief, enemy of the Iroquois confederacy, who is usually shown with snakes in his hair and has survived as a popular figure in contemporary Iroquois stonecarving.

Canadian poems about "special" stones are common to both native and nonnative literature. Robert Kroetsch's "Stone Hammer Poem," Susan Musgrave's "Dream Song," and Victor Coleman's "Fish: Stone: Song" provide examples of the latter. The particular kinds of animation accorded to stones in the sample I have surveyed in this chapter—the quality of femininity or motherhood, for example, and of poetic inspiration—can also be found in native attitudes toward rock. There are, of course, as many ways of approaching rock as there are indigenous theologies. Anne Cameron suggests a link between the prehistoric petroforms and native theologies in a chapter called "Stones" in *Daughters of Copper Women*, when she goes in detail into the way certain tribes of coastal British Columbia used special marking stones to measure solar and astronomical phenomena and returned to specially constructed stone circles to get in touch with the powers from which they felt themselves to have originally derived (99–106). I will return in chapter 10 to the fraught question of white shamanism, Native Americans' accusation that whites are trying to usurp their religious symbols.

Pat Lowther's "Stone Diary," which provides perhaps the most detailed description of a Canadian woman poet empowering herself through rocks, ceases to seem like a freak approach to nature when considered in the context not only of rock imagery in Euro-Canadian poems but also of indigenous animism. Like Atwood, Lowther describes a progression from the European view of nature as alien to an assimilation of nature's attributes for a transformation. After a week spent "madly in love / with stone," Lowther begins to experience metamorphosis:

> Today for the first time
> I noticed how coarse
> My skin had grown
> But the stones shine
> With their own light,
> They grow smoother
> And smoother

Although in "Notes From Furry Creek" she acknowledges the distinction between human flesh and the essence of stone, she transforms herself by identification:

> reaching the centre
> you become
> stone, the perpetual
> laved god. (367)

Lowther engages with an (implicitly male) stone god, undergoing the same kind of androgynous and alchemical transformation as Livesay in "On Looking into Henry Moore" and Waddington in "Fortunes." Her quest is to abandon human personality and plunge into total identification with rock, enduring a breakdown in order to break through to rebirth:

> The mountains reject nothing
> But can crack
> Open your mind
> Just by being intractably there. ("Coast Range" 367)

Lowther is not talking about the kind of cracking up that frantic settlers experience when "bushed" or driven mad by the alien Canadian landscape; she enters, rather, into the empowering petrifaction that is Canadian nature to its poets. This merging with stones is neither exploitative nor anthropomorphic: rocks remain rocks and women women, the interchange dependent, after the animistic manner, upon each approaching the other from distinct realms of being.

Few recent Canadian poets project psychic attributes onto the environment in the manner of Jung and Neumann; rather, they abandon the anthropomorphic along with the pastoral, romantic, and existential approaches to nature. Canadian poetry embodies a transition from regret for the European culture left behind to affirmation of the Canadian landscape, along with a shift from European smugness about the superiority of mind over matter toward a more cautious appreciation of nature's intrinsic essence. The difference between the many Canadian poems in which both men and women are empowered by achieving a harmonious relationship with stone and British and U.S. poems about Medusa is easier to understand in the context of Canadian attitudes to nature. The very fact that Medusa goes so often unnamed in Canadian poetry, with rock emerging as more important than her classical attributes, conforms to Frye's descriptions of rebirth quest patterns in Canadian literature.

The difference between the classical Medusa and the Canadian stone/woman archetype may also derive from the quite different attitude toward heroism in Canada which Frye and a number of other critics describe. In the classical archetype, Perseus set forth to destroy Medusa and assimilate her powers as part of a series of adventures by which he proves himself worthy. One's sympathy is supposed to be with Perseus in this narrative, although, as I have documented, both women and men are very likely to sympathize with Medusa. The hero, or Perseus, fades into the background in Canadian poems about stones and stone/women, the subjective poetic persona replacing him as quester. Only in very few instances in Canadian poetry have I found his traditional inimical gynophobia intact as a poetic attitude, a shift in perspective which may be explained, at least in part, by Canadian attitudes toward hunter and victim.

Whether because of a sense of inferiority in the face of exile from European culture or because of the colonial and thus necessarily subordinate posture toward England or the obdurate quality of the Canadian landscape, the traditional paradigm of hero-hunted-victor dominating an enemy-prey-victim shifts to identification with the victim. Thus Frye notes a "theme of metamorphosis, where the victorious human actually becomes the defeated animal" ("National Consciousness" 53), and Margaret Atwood develops this shift in attitude into a scale of victim identifications. Having noted, like Frye, that in Canadian literature "the proper response" to the environment is "double-natured . . . not simple escape but further exploration resulting in an increased self-knowledge" ("Canadian Monsters" 103), in a chapter of *Survival* entitled "Nature the Monster" Atwood constructs a series of phases in Canadian victor-victim relationships, each of which correlates to a phase of "victimization" discussed in a previous chapter. In position one (correlating to denying being a victim) she postulates an attitude of looking to nature as a Divine Mother while simultaneously being eaten alive by mosquitoes. Position two (correlating to admitting you are a victim) involves accepting that Canadian nature is neither divine nor maternal. Position three, which relates to this acceptance of victimhood as a given, can lead to the decision to attack nature before she/it attacks you but can be transcended in position four, resolving to be a creative nonvictim by taking a stance toward nature quite similar to the one Frye describes. "What does nature look like from Position Four?" asks Atwood. "Well, it isn't the Divine Mother . . . and it isn't Nature the evil monster. It exists as itself, I suspect, but not as a collection of separate but inert objects; rather it exists as a living process which includes opposites: life and death, 'gentleness' and 'hostility' " (63).

The important thing about position four as a context for the nature imagery I have studied in this chapter is that it expresses an attitude which is simultaneously very old in human consciousness and yet being rediscovered in recent decades. Taking nature for itself, a common assumption both in preclassical times and among native peoples, has not been a favorite Judeo-Christian posture in recent centuries. Correspondingly, taking one's body on its own terms, understanding oneself as needing to be in harmony with nature, was valued in prehistoric times but has only recently regained favor in Europe and America. From Atwood's position four, as she notes, "man himself is seen as part of the process; he does not define himself as 'good' or 'weak' as against a hostile nature, or as 'bad' or 'aggressive' as against a passive, powerless Nature. He can accept his own body, including its sexuality, as part of this process. . . . Since he does not see life as something that can only be maintained inside a fortress and at the expense of shutting out Nature and sex, he is free to move *within* space rather than in a self-created tank *against* it" (63).

I am not suggesting that it is only in Canada that we find poets suddenly transcending Judeo-Christian dualism through naturistic synthesis of good and evil, life and death. As I have shown in previous chapters, there is a good deal of this approach on the scale of attitudes toward Medusa in other literatures as well. What is striking about Canadian poetry is that it provides so many examples of poets uncomfortable with the traditional categories who recognize this indwellingness of being. "From the deer and fish in Isabella Crawford's 'The canoe,' " writes Frye, "to the frogs and toads in Layton, from the white narcissus of Knister to the night-blooming cereus of Reaney, everything that is central in Canadian writing seems to be marked by the imminence of the natural world" (Conclusion 358).

A further factor which may contribute to this attitude is that the English were not the only settlers in the new land but were accompanied and often preceded by French pioneers. Although it is unfortunately beyond the scope of this study to develop a comparison of French and English Canadian poems about various archetypes, such an inquiry would be interesting in light of the different approach to nature taken by French Canadians. In *Exiles and Pioneers* T. E. Farley suggests a crucial difference between the way a French pioneer is "rooted in Canadian soil," which was perceived as "sacred and alive with indigenous ghosts" (22), and the sense of exile experienced by the English. Loyal to a culture disdainful of the "primitive" and politically estranged from the United States, where "manifest destiny" gave permission for wholesale genocide, the English could not be unaware of the greater ease with which the French, long encouraged by their church to intermarry with the Native Peoples, not only adapted themselves to the environment but adopted native attitudes toward it.

Thus when Canadian poetry in English produces a Medusalike stone divinity who has shed her classical identity and attributes to take on those of the Canadian landscape, one can suspect a French as well as a native influence on the archetype. This divinity is a powerful, prelapsarian force embodying generative vitality, immortality, and creativity. As I shall demonstrate in the following chapters, these qualities characterize the Middle Eastern, Old European, and preclassical versions of Aphrodite and Artemis, whose "paganism" consists in a synthesis of the divine and the material. In the Canadian poems which I have studied here, the poets sometimes project human qualities onto this stone being, as in the case of male poets endowing it with femininity and of women poets writing about male stone lovers. As many poets, however, are entirely nonprojective, approaching rock as rock, assuming that its powerful qualities will flow back into human lives without becoming human in themselves. This peculiar metamorphic approach, in which the poet recognizes the power of rocks to affect human lives in entirely nonhuman terms, characterizes nearly all of the poems which I have surveyed. Even when Simmons and E. J. Pratt and (in two instances) Livesay and Atwood remain at a distance from the stones onto which they have projected qualities of the opposite sex, they are nonetheless comfortable with the idea that humans have stone qualities. Most striking of all, I find no significant differences in point of view and attitude along gender lines: there are as many projective female poets as nonprojective, and the male poets seem as comfortable empathizing with and even turning into stones as the women do.

What seems to be happening in Canadian literature is a breakdown of the European paradigm which locates men and mind on one side of a dualism and women and nature on the other. Nature is so much a force in its own right in Canada and so powerful over human lives that men and women poets have more in common in their responses than they do in England and the United States. To put it another way, the Canadian cultural signature undermines the European dualism of certain archetypes, giving Canadian poets a less encoded access to their deeper backgrounds in non-European cultures. I shall demonstrate in the third part of this book on Artemis, moreover, that there are interesting analogies between Canadian attitudes to the wild and the wild attributes underlying archetypes which have endured in European literatures to the present day.

PART TWO
APHRODITE

Women's Mysteries—The Crane Dance, *Monica Sjöö, 1976. Oil on hardboard, 4' x 8'. Reproduced by permission. The artist states:*
"*I wove together motives from ancient Goddess cultures: in the centre is 'sleeping priestess' of the Hypogeum in Malta (sub-terranean tomb/womb/ temple where priestesses commune with the spirits of the ancestors in incubating dreams) and she sleeps on Maltese double spiral altar found in the Tarxien temple nearby. Women initiated the movements of the cranes in dances and here are two present-day young African women still dancing the crane dance sacred to the Goddess. Cranes fly across the body of primordial Egyptian Goddess with upraised arms and finally I've portrayed owl goddess Lilith who is a winged air spirit. The breasts moulded on a menstrual blood red background are from murals in Çatal Hüyük in Anatolia (ancient Turkey) c. 7000 B.C.*"

4.

The Deep Background of the
Aphrodite Archetype

The three chapters on Medusa should have laid to rest the idea that archetypes are ontological absolutes. We have seen that Medusa is so ruptured by the Canadian natural environment that she can hardly be defined as eternally recurrent in the same form. Our childhood experiences seem to establish attitudes toward frightening and powerful female figures which color our poetic representations of the Medusa archetype. Women's recognition and admiration of feminine power, in spite of our culture's profound distaste for it, seems to make our responses significantly different from men's. My introduction of Canadian poetry, however, disrupts the hypothesis that approaches to the archetype are always differentiated by gender, since the impact of an overpowering natural environment makes the responses of male and female poets far less distinct.

Although it could be argued that Canadian attitudes toward nature are themselves cultural constructs, the poems suggest a nature that is not controllable by human beings and thus not mediated by culture. If in my British and American sample of poems about Medusa women poets disrupt the received Greek archetype because of their admiration for female power, both sexes in Canada stand in such awe of nature that they disrupt traditional European paradigms about its subordination to culture. To return to my blackbirds-in-the-pie analogy, women poets in England and America and poets of both sexes in

Canada realize that the pie crust is sufficiently penetrable to enable them to perceive, sing about, and perhaps even fly away to the world outside the window.

This flexibility in the Medusa archetype, its variation under gender and national pressures, raises the question of whether it is less archetypal than thematic. Is there sufficient sameness and recurrence left for Medusa to be universal? In terms of Marie Louise von Franz's definition of archetype as a skeletal or basic structure retained over a long historical period, the perennial fascination of Medusa may consist in the psychological responses of both poet and audience to female power, responses which retain their force throughout Middle Eastern and European religious history from elements with prehistoric characteristics as well. The many instances in recent literature in which Medusa occupies the core of a poem as the unifying subtext make her archetypal in the literary sense of a recurrent symbol shaping a wide variety of literary structures. She is empowering because she reminds us that women are powerful: "The discovery of a mythical pattern that in some way one feels is connected to one's own life," suggests Christine Downing, "deepens one's self-understanding. At the same time, the discovery of the personal significance of a mythic pattern enhances our understanding of the myth and its variations" (26). Recognition of the power in one's own feared and admired mother, especially within the context of a culture that has done much to degrade her/our bodily sensations, is both a disturbing and, hopefully, a healing experience.

Von Franz notes what she calls "fantastic theories of survival and migration" of goddess imageries from ancient to modern times but does not think that we need to rely on these theories to explain archetypes, which she considers perennially welling up in the human psyche, symbols which we are constantly "recreating from the unconscious" (9). Whether responses to goddess archetypes derive from the universal experience of the powerful mother or carry within them a stimulus to the remembrance of some maternal divinity, they endure as archetypes through their ability to galvanize a response in both poet and audience.

If this is true of Medusa, who was taken as a destructive figure by the Greeks and other Europeans, how much more true of Aphrodite. If Medusa constellates responses to the problem of separation and differentiation from one's mother, Aphrodite is about the experience of feminine sexuality. For heterosexual men, this means coming to terms with the impact of a lover upon the personality, and for women it entails coming to terms with one's own sensual nature. Poems about Aphrodite are structured upon a tension between the archetype's joyous sensual connotation, the contemporary attitude toward feminine sexuality, and the individual sexual experiences of the poet.

When I send my students to the library to decide what is most typical about Aphrodite according to standard myth reference sources, they list "trickery," "seductiveness," and "power over men" and conclude that "she was a real floozy." The degradation of Aphrodite from a golden divinity celebrating feminine sexuality to a threatening (and silly) seductress has been internalized from the intellectual history of Europe into the heads of contributors to the standard myth reference sources. It is because we are likely to lose sight of the qualities Aphrodite once represented that I will devote this chapter to a study of elements in the classical archetype that come from preclassical sources.

To determine whether there are significant textual differences between male poets, who approach the archetype as an embodiment of feminine attractants, and women poets, who must deal with contradictions in the archetype between their natural sensuality and European culture's gradual repression of feminine sexuality, I will focus my second chapter on Aphrodite (chapter 5) on a comparison/ contrast of poems about the archetype by men and women writers from the Middle Ages to 1900. That chapter is followed by a chapter each on male and female poets in the twentieth century and a chapter on love poetry in Canada.

| *The Aphrodite Archetype* | One of the most important goddesses interbraided into the classical Aphrodite is Inanna. The cycle of Inanna is a group of narrative |

poems, hymns, and prayers which establish her as an important goddess in a pantheon worshipped in the city-state cultures of Sumer and Akkad during the third millenium B.C.E. A love song sung by Inanna to her lover Dumuzi during their courtship expresses a joyous and powerful feminine sensuality:

> What I tell you
> Let the singer weave into song.
> What I tell you,
> Let it flow from ear to mouth,
> Let it pass from old to young:
> My vulva, the horn,
> The Boat of Heaven,
> Is full of eagerness like the young moon.
> My untilled land lies fallow.
>
> As for me, Inanna,
> Who will plow my vulva?
> Who will plow my high field?
> Who will plow my wet ground?

When Dumuzi replies that "Great Lady, I, Dumuzi the King, will plow your vulva," she joyfully responds, "Then plow my vulva, man of my heart! / Plow my vulva!" (Wolkstein and Kramer 36–37).

Inanna's love song is part of her courtship of Dumuzi. As a girl, Inanna leans against an apple tree to admire her body:

> She leaned back against the apple tree.
> When she leaned against the apple tree,
>   her vulva was wondrous to behold.
> Rejoicing at her wondrous vulva
>   the young woman Inanna applauded herself. (12)

In another story in this cycle, she usurps the Me, which are fundamental principles of order, from her father, Enki, after she drinks him under the table. These principles include the "throne of kingship," "the art of lovemaking," "the holy shrine," "the art of the hero," and "the art of power," as well as "the plundering of cities," "deceit," "kindling of strife," "counselling," "the giving of judgments," and "procreation" (16–18). She takes these in her boats to her own court at Uruk. In another courtship lyric, she is preparing herself for a marriage that is both an establishment of her reign in political terms and an expression of achieving full adult sexuality. Her unabashed delight in proffering her "horn," or vulva, to be "plowed" attests to her culture's acceptance of feminine sexuality, of women's enjoyment of our own bodies.

The Deep Background of the Aphrodite Archetype

Not all feminist scholars are pleased by Inanna's love song. Elizabeth Fisher finds her request to be plowed "not a happy thought, certainly, in contemporary terms," although she notes that "it must be remembered that the English language has a built-in prejudice which tends to make male sex active and female passive" (287). Caught in this contemporary bias she herself recognizes, Fisher assumes that Inanna's acceptance of her "body as land to be cultivated" entails submission, that her love song to Dumuzi thus is an "exhortation to male potency," a declaration of "the birth of phallocracy" with its "image of utilitarian sex and women's passive role" (288).

That a modern woman writer should read a poem in which a powerful woman celebrates her genitalia and calls out for sexual intercourse as a declaration of submission tells us more about "modern" attitudes toward feminine sexuality than about the way people in Sumeria five thousand years ago might have felt about lovemaking. Reviewing Wolkstein and Kramer's *Inanna, Queen of Heaven and Earth*, which I have been quoting, Tikva Frymer-Kensky objects that they have interpreted Inanna too humanly, more as a personalized goddess than as a symbol. Following Thorkild Jacobsen, Frymer-Kensky prefers to read Dumuzi as the "spark of Life" and Inanna as "the power of the storehouse," participating in a ritual marriage which achieves "the coming together of the fertile spark of nature with human husbandry." She also objects to the conflation of a diversity of goddess types into a single "moon goddess" and reads the Sumerian Inanna as basically a "male image (an image probably shared by women) of an eternally young, eternally sexually available female" (64), sharing Fisher's presumption that celebrations of feminine sexuality originate in the male mind.

As Eleanor Amico has pointed out in her study of women in the northern Canaanite city-state Ugarit, "When people tell a story, they share their ideals, if not the reality of their lives. . . . From myths we might not get actual present-day social customs, but we do find out what is conceivable in a culture" (58–59). Elaborating on this statement in a letter to the author, Amico comments that "sexuality in the time these poems were composed was obviously not imbued with dominance/submission as today. For instance, in no way can Inanna be construed as 'giving herself' to Dumuzi. Instead, because he meets her sexual need she confers her power upon him. . . . This is not, however, female dominance over male, but that of a deity over a mortal, I would say." While it would be deviant in European poetry to depict it as natural and delightful that a young girl setting forth in life should applaud her vulva, it was clearly conceivable to the Sumerians that a girl should celebrate the dawn of her sexuality. Within the context of the Inanna story, which is about a forceful, self-reliant, politically powerful goddess so courageous and daring that she decides to descend on her own into the land of the dead, it seems to me that her love song can be read as an expression of Sumerian admiration of all women's sensual powers and not merely as a seductive trap to ensnare women for men's purposes. When Dumuzi betrays Inanna, first by seizing her throne when she is on a quest into the underworld and then by refusing to mourn her death, she returns to punish him, ordering him to the underworld in her place but mourning him bitterly nonetheless. Inanna's lament for the husband whom she has consigned to the underworld, prototypical of many laments for "dying gods" and later of Venus for Adonis, is thus more complex than one might expect. I would read it as not only her lament at the death of her lover but also as her grief that his seizure of her political prerogatives compels her to condemn him; Inanna's grief seems to blend sincere passion for the lost lover, unhappiness with his having betrayed her, and the complex decision of having to order his death herself.

Inanna's attitude toward sex can be further understood within the context of a rite of sacred intercourse characteristic of a number of Mesopotamian religions. This rite, although it had to do, as Frymer-Kensky suggests, with agricultural regeneration, identifies feminine as well as masculine Eros as the source of that outcome. The underlying idea of this rite is that intercourse is a powerful expression of immanence, a theological approach to spirituality or divinity resident within the human body and within the earth. Fisher notes that reverence for nature antedates archetypes of "a queen or a king of heaven," going back to a time when "the universe was viewed as a pantheistic collection of forces inherent in nature, forces that were female and male, animal and human, and combinations of both" (282). In such systems, as in the metaphysics of Native American and Canadian Native Peoples I mentioned in the previous chapter, nature or matter contains divinity. In Fisher's words, "The Mesopotamian pantheon of the fourth millenium showed the gods as immanent in nature, not rulers but expressions" (282); polytheistic religions celebrated the spirituality in dwelling within nature. According to E. O. James, Inanna's courtship of Dumuzi or Ishtar's of Tammuz is the prelude to a celebration of intercourse between a priestess representing the goddess and the king, who joins with her to endow the land with generation through this ritual lovemaking. In this rite of marriage, Inanna archetypally incarnates "the fertility of nature," while Dumuzi is "the embodiment of the creative powers of spring." James sees the sacred marriage as a ritual representing the transition from a cult of the "Great Mother," primarily associated with birth, to a cult of an "Earth-goddess" whose powers of generativity control agricultural cycles. She is thus "the source of generative power in nature as a whole and so became responsible for the periodic renewal of life in the spring after the blight of winter or summer drought. Consequently, she was a many-sided goddess, as in the case of Inanna-Ishtar, both mother and bride" (114–16). Describing a "Hymn to Ishtar as the planet Venus" which was "written for the cult of the deified king of Isin-Dagan" (c. 2258–37 B.C.E.), James notes that "throughout the Goddess is represented as taking the initiative. It was to her 'far-famed temple' that the king went, bringing to her cakes 'to set the table for the feast', and it was she who embraced her beloved husband. . . . Again, it was the Goddess who actually vouches the prosperity for the new year and the bounty which the ritual marriage secured" (116–17).

Is this "sacred marriage" in which priestess and king "identify with their divine archetypes" Mesopotamian culture's way of keeping woman in her place? In *The Sacred Marriage Rite* and an essay in *The Legacy of Sumer*, Samuel Noah Kramer argues that earliest Sumer was egalitarian and only later imposed subordination of women, as reflected in a much more patriarchal treatment of goddesses. Given the confusion of temple priestesses with "temple prostitutes," is this a ritual of sexual enslavement? One of the Me which Inanna joyfully celebrates usurping from her father is "the art of prostitution" and the attendance of "the cult prostitute" (Wolkstein and Kramer, *Inanna* 17). Should these be understood in the modern sense of a woman sexually enslaved for profit? Or are Mesopotamian "temple prostitutes" the kinds of priestesses who stood in for the goddess Inanna in the ritual marriages, and whose intercourse took place outside the boundaries of marriage and within the realm of a religion in which women celebrated their sexuality? E. O. James certainly suggests an insubordinate role for Inanna when he declares that "in Mesopotamia the kingship was vitally connected with a nuptial relationship between the local human ruler and the Goddess in which she was the dominant partner" (*The Sacred Marriage Rite* 117), but is this just an ancient way of putting the feminine on a pedestal while keeping real women down? Judith Ochshorn suggests that the power of the goddess reflected the real power of women in Mesopotamian culture. Concurring with James that the salient feature of the story is structured upon the "dominance of the goddess" who chooses the king and initiates the intercourse, she notes that

> still another feature common to all the Sacred Marriage rites was that the active sexuality of the goddess was portrayed only as good, and it was seen as a precursor to the blessing of the whole community. At least in the divine sphere, as expressed in this rite, female sexuality had no connotations of evil or danger for men. And the goddesses' sexuality was displayed as totally extra familial, i.e., it was nowhere linked to their own reproductive abilities nor was there any implication of monogamy on her part. The heart of the Sacred Marriage rite was Inanna/Ishtar's great power over life, fertility, and destiny, the energizing character of her sexuality in her aspect as the goddess of love and fertility, and her role in actively seeking out and sexually enjoying the king. (124)

Historian Gerda Lerner answers these questions, in "The Origin of Prostitution in Ancient Mesopotamia," by making a distinction between "cultic sexual service," which would involve ritual intercourse, and "prostitution," the commercialization of sexual favors (238). Both "sacred prostitution" and "commercial prostitution" took place near the temple. The first involved reverence for a goddess and her feminine sexuality, the second exploitation of women as sexual slaves. Commercial prostitution, according to Lerner, arose during the first millenium B.C.E. when slaveowners profited from renting out their female slaves as prostitutes and farmers, pauperized by centralization of agriculture, were forced to sell their female family members (247). Lerner also points out a development which has parallels in the eighteen and nineteenth centuries in Europe: that when "the virginity of respectable daughters became a financial asset for the family" the commercialization, or institutionalization of prostitution became a social necessity for men" (247).

In spite of this considerable scholarship on rites of sacred intercourse, there is evidence that scholars may have been relying on Herodotus's exaggerations. "There is a lot of criticism of Herodotus' account as inaccurate and from the point of view and preconceptions of a 'tourist' outsider trying to show how barbaric other cultures were," Eleanor Amico writes in a letter to the author. Nevertheless, perhaps the reason that modern readers of the Inanna poems have so much trouble grasping the nature of her sexuality is that we are looking at her through the lens of five thousand years during which every effort has been made to declare such a potent and authentic feminine sensuality suspect.

Elizabeth Fisher has outlined the sad history of the diminishment of the Inanna/Ishtar archetype from about 4000 B.C.E., when it still contained generative and sexual powers, to 3000 B.C.E., when the male role in procreation began to be stressed, to 2000 B.C.E., when the archetype became merely the seducer who arouses the male after which he, rather than she, brings plenty to the land. In this decline, Fisher argues, "phallocracy" is born, expressed in the image of the goddess as a ploughable field with all of her fecundity derived from the male seed (283–94).

Within the history of Indo-European myth, as in that of the Near East, we find rituals in which a powerful and immortal woman empowers a mortal man through intercourse. Wendy O'Flaherty traces the narrative pattern of an immortal male forcing intercourse (rape) upon a mortal woman back to its inverse archetype in Indo-European mythology, a ritual in which a mare goddess "invigorates the aging King by her annual ritual copulation with him." This horse goddess is "an awesome and dangerous creature," a "source of power" who is "whole, integrated: the proto-Indo-European goddess of dawn is also simultaneously maternal, sororal, and erotic," and parallels Inanna and Ishtar, "both of whom were said to copulate with horses." In Greece she survives in Leda, "herself a bird goddess as well as the victim of a bird god. . . . Aphrodite, too, is associated with the goose or swan or winged horse and is both a danger and a benefactress to her mortal lover" (212).

In a process similar to Fisher's description of the gradual decline of Inanna and Ishtar until they are objects of subordination within a male religious metaphysics, O'Flaherty outlines the gradual degradation of this immortal horse/bird goddess to a victim of rape:

Under the influence of a steadily increasing Indo-European androcentrism (or, to put it more bluntly, male chauvinism) the mare goddess was split into two parts, the good mother and the evil mother. At this time, also, the image of the mare was another already available Indo-European image of the goddess who mates with a mortal—the swan maiden. Finally, as the model of mortal woman and mortal man, the goddess was demoted to ignominious mortality and passivity. Now the helpless female was left hoping against hope that the great horse/swan god would deign to visit her (riding on his white horse). Now Leda awaits Zeus, awaits the moment when she may, in William Butler Yeats' words, "put on his knowledge with his power / Before the indifferent beak would let her drop." (212–13)

O'Flaherty identifies the splitting up of a holistic goddess into a polarized image of good and evil as an androcentric process inherent in later Indo-European consciousness, which suggests that when Neumann insists upon this two-featured female divinity he is reflecting not merely his cultural attitude toward women but also a mindset centuries in the making, by which archetypes like the mare goddess, which were originally associated with multifaceted political and spiritual feminine power, split into the white mare/nightmare duality, which men in patriarchy fear.

In O'Flaherty's Indo-European example, as in the case of Inanna in the Mesopotamian region, holistic goddesses are first celebrated and later diminished so that males can take credit for sexuality and generativity. The original idea that such qualities as sexual prowess could be integrated with political, economic, and theological power in the person of female goddesses undergoes transformation so that they become prizes for males or male gods who trick and conquer mortal and immortal women.

Looking back through the lens of centuries in which female sensuality has been usurped and put under male control (with political attempts to return reproductive rights to culture being only the most recent example), it is hard for us to understand the attitude either of the King singing hymns to Inanna so that he can enjoy stewardship of lands comprehended as her body or of the woman worshipper hoping to acquire Inanna's sensuality and generativity in order to enhance her own powers, whether as priestess or as wife. We will find, nonetheless, certain structures in later poems to Venus and Aphrodite which carry over from these original approaches to the goddess, in that poets take the point of view of a worshipper desiring empowerment from her, a heightening of being only possible through her grant. Classical hymns to Venus and Aphrodite often retain this mood of respect and propitiation. Women's celebration of self-initiated sexuality, similarly, underlies the classical assumptions about Aphrodite's "golden" enjoyment of sex, and survives in a muted way in the courts of love of medieval and Renaissance poetic traditions, as well as in Dante's, Chaucer's, and Boethius's praise for her as the central force holding the universe together.

The classical Aphrodite derives her sexual and generative powers from a source more directly accessible to the Greeks than Indo-European or Middle Eastern materials. As we have seen, archaeologist Marija Gimbutas has provided ample documentation of a culture in what she describes as "Old Europe," an area which includes Greece, that dates between 6500 and 3500 B.C.E. The powers which Gimbutas attributes to a bird and snake goddess who plays a key role in this culture may contribute to the subversive continuity of the Aphrodite archetype in European literature. It is interesting that this bird goddess, whom Gimbutas finds in so many digs, is frequently also a snake goddess, suggesting a preclassical conflation of the Medusa and Aphrodite archetypes. "The Snake Goddess and the Bird Goddess appear as separate figures and as a single divinity," Gimbutas writes. "Their functions are so intimately related that their separate treatment is impossible. She is one and she is two, sometimes snake, sometimes bird" (112). Although the snake is associated with water and the bird with air, they represent one nurturing, maternal archetype. "In contrast to the Indo-Europeans," Gimbutas continues, "to whom earth was the Great Mother, the Old Europeans created maternal images out of water and air divinities, the Snake and Bird Goddess. A divinity who nurtures the world with moisture, giving rain, the divine food which metaphorically was also understood as mother's milk, naturally became a nurse or mother" (142). The divinity, figured as a bird or snake in Old European statuary, was often incised with patterns representing thunder, rain, and meandering rivers, to represent the moisture which this region of Europe, very arid at the time, took as the force most necessary to life.

The Old European bird and snake goddess, like the snake goddesses antedating the classical Medusa in the Middle East and Crete,

Aphrodite riding a goose. Rhodes,
470-460 B.C.E. Photograph by Laurie
Platt Winfrey. Reproduced by courtesy
of the Trustees of the British
Museum.

were simultaneously sexual and generative, erotic and maternal. Gim-
butas suggests a direct link between these figures of birds with women's
breasts and women with bird's heads and the classical "Aphrodite
Urania," who, "born from the sea, was portrayed as flying through the
air standing or sitting on a goose or being accompanied by three
Geese" (149). O'Flaherty associates the classical Leda with the bird
goddess, considering her "a bird goddess as well as the victim of a bird
god. . . . Aphrodite, too, is associated with the goose or swan and is
both a danger and a benediction to her mortal lovers" (212). Using
Gimbutas's researches, Paul Friedrich develops a similar link between
the Old European waterbird goddesses and classical Aphrodite: "Many
archaic Greek representations of Aphrodite have birdlike heads or
eyes. Aphrodite herself can be seen as a humanized and rationalized
descendent from the Old European Water Bird—the queen of water
birds . . . [a] female goddess [which] incarnated the creative principle"
(11).

The Deep Background of the Aphrodite Archetype

For my purposes, the importance of Aphrodite's association with swans, geese, cranes, and ducks is their connotation of female sensuality, love, and lustfulness, which is also found in Hindu and Celtic variations of the archetype. Thus in Hindu legend both Krishna and the "milkmaids" who make love to him in a cosmic dance sometimes appear as swans, and in the swan cult of the Urnfield and Halstatt sites Celtic artifacts depict both male and female heroes turning into swans for amatory purposes. In "The Dream of Angus," for example, Angus seeks out Aillil in order to participate in her "Great Magic" of being a bird one year and a human the next. Described as a "powerful, many-shaped girl," Aillil is typical of many women in Celtic myths who undergo metamorphosis into swans (Ross 237). These Celtic swan goddesses share powers over sexuality and war with the multifaceted Inanna and Ishtar. They fly over battlefields, directing the energies of their favorites, and help these humans to achieve successful erotic exploits. Both male and female divinities occur as "bird lovers" of humans. "In the Irish tradition," Ross writes, "the role is not confined to men, both men and women appearing in the role of bird-lovers. Furthermore, the bird or bird-flock may bring about the desired situation without the lover himself (or herself) adopting bird form. There would seem to be a close link between birds and the sexual act in the case of divine or semi-divine beings . . ." (262).

One might speculate that the frequent appearance of swans, geese, and other birds in European love poetry has something to do with this ancient association of birds with sexuality. As in the case of Inanna in the Middle East and the mare goddess of the Indo-Europeans, however, patrilinear culture gradually diminishes the power of the bird goddess, whose sexuality is first bestowed upon, then shared with, and finally usurped by male divinities and heroes. In Arthurian legend, for example, swans are captured and brought to court to be used in chastity tests against adulterous wives, from whom they refuse to accept food (Ross 241). Since Celtic women originally practiced extramarital sex with impunity (Markale 77, 164), it seems clear that the patrilinear culture underlying later redactions, insisting upon wifely fidelity as an absolute value in a male inheritance system, seeks to undermine earlier practices by turning the swan, the avatar of amarital feminine sensuality, against women who enjoy sex outside of marriage. In Greek mythology, similarly, Aphrodite's swan gradually comes to be associated with Apollo, and the story of Zeus taking on the swan form to rape Leda (who was, according to O'Flaherty, a bird goddess in her own right), provides but one example of the degradation of earlier myths in which swans and swanwomen were archetypes for a feminine sexual power uncontrollable by men.

Both the sexual, martial, and politically powerful Inanna and the life-renewing, generative Old European bird goddess resemble the omnipotent Aphrodite of Homer's Hymns, Hesiod's descriptions, and the first book of Lucretius's *De Rerum Natura.* These classical authors, however, also show a deep loathing for the goddess, waffling between reverence for a divinity who controls the universe and a distaste for feminine power in any form. Earlier attitudes about Middle Eastern and Old European variations of the archetype clearly persist in tension with classical ones. In *The Meaning of Aphrodite* Paul Friedrich defines the origins of the archetype both in terms of "what it came from," or her historical roots in the Sumerian Inanna, Semitic Ishtar, Phoenician Astarte, Old European bird goddesses, and proto-Indo-European goddess of dawn; and also in terms of "its internal organization at a given time, and the interaction between these two realities"; arguing for a multiple origin of Aphrodite, making her appearance in Greek mythology a combination of many factors, a complex network of attributes he likens to a "paradigm, braid, taxonomy, chain" and even a many-faceted "snow crystal" (5–6). Thus although the "internal organization" of her Greek archetype is dualistic, combining respect for femininity with profound gynophobia, earlier "multi-faceted" attributes remain embedded in classical as in later European variations.

Friedrich notes that one of Aphrodite's most interesting characteristics in Greek mythology is her "liminality," or crisscrossings back and forth between categories which the Greeks took as mutually exclusive. Thus although in Greek culture "sexuality in violation of the code of honor was as polluting as filth or death," Aphrodite engages in "sexual intercourse without pollution"; although mortals and goddesses derive from separate orders of being, she encourages and participates in sexual relationships between them: in a culture that considered feminine beauty suspect she is admired as "the naked goddess" and the "patroness of courtesans"; where marital love was taken merely as a duty to the state, she encourages passionate sexual relations within marriage (134). Where rape is presumed a reward of war and sex is more apt to take this form than that of heterosexual seduction, Aphrodite takes the initiative, retains control, is never raped, and "presents an image of relative sexual equality and an active female role that dynamically contradicts the sexual double standard of the early texts." Friedrich concludes that "in a male-dominated culture like that reflected in Homer and Hesiod, even a relatively active woman defies and threatens and crosses over fundamental categories" (141).

Friedrich's theory of Aphrodite's liminality, her bridging of categories, is important to the literary critic because this process of "crossing over between emotional antitheses or a simultaneous affirmation of them" characterizes many poems about Aphrodite (7). The Aphrodite archetype endures as an explosive force within European culture because it fuses "nature and culture," perceived as opposites in classical as in European philosophy, and "interbraids" qualities which culture attempts to rigidly separate in both masculine and feminine character. She perennially appeals to our need as human beings to affirm bodily pleasure and to our instinctive memory of the holistic feminine paradigms which are part of the Greek Aphrodite's and the Roman Venus's complex roots. The waffling between reverence and loathing for Aphrodite that we find in classical texts can serve as a prototype for the ambivalence underlying points of view, tones, and attitudes taken toward the archetype in more recent poetry. Friedrich, for example, calls attention to the differences between the respectful sixth Homeric Hymn, addressed to "Revered, golden-crowned, and beautiful Aphrodite," and the fifth book of the Iliad, in which she is mocked by the gods for interfering on the battlefield. Recognizing that Aphrodite's appearance in the conflict may be a residue of "warlike Ishtar," Friedrich attributes the episode to "symbolic role inversion," a "further documentation of the deeper fact that Aphrodite is the most potent goddess. The author of the hymn asserts both that she is the most potent and that is why Zeus wants to humiliate her" (62).

The interweaving of magical, political, and sexual powers in Aphrodite both interested and terrified classical authors, who revered her as a cosmic force at the same time as they dreaded her effect on them as men. The first thing that occurs to Anchises, for example, when he discovers in Homer's fifth hymn that he is making love to Aphrodite, is that she will castrate him. Aphrodite's cosmic attributes nonetheless impress writers such as the fifth-century Parmenides and his student Empedocles. Their visions of Aphrodite as the metaphysical binding principle of the universe influenced Lucretius's *De Rerum*

Natura, which in turn affects Dante's principle of "the love that moves the sun and other stars" (canto xxxiii, v. 145) in *The Divine Comedy.*

Aphrodite's role in classical philosophy as a creative force who sustains the universe by keeping destructive drives in "equipoise" is far less familiar than her role as initiator of love of all kinds. The cult of Aphrodite suggests reverence for feminine sexuality which would be wholly alien to Christian culture, a reverence we can find in the few surviving fragments of Sappho's lyrics and which suggests that women's worship of Aphrodite was an expression of their desire to model themselves upon her. Citing a number of other classical scholars, Friedrich asserts that "there is excellent textual and ceramic evidence from many parts of Greece for the existence of groups of young women who were instructed in dance, music, singing, and the care and adornment of the body, and probably the lore and knowledge of sex and motherhood as well" (109). As we shall see in the third part of this book, on Artemis, scholars hypothesize similar cadres of young women in out-of-the-way retreats or "schools" typified by the cult of Artemis at Brauron. Young women under the tutelage of Sappho may have celebrated Aphrodite in the manner Artemis was celebrated at Brauron, removing themselves for a period (some for life) from the demands of early marriage and childbearing. Friedrich's hypothesis is that Sappho was a teacher or leader of such a school who traveled throughout the Mediterranean as a popular lyric poet of the sixth century B.C.E, He concludes that during this period the island of Lesbos "may have been the most distinguished in what I think was an early pan-Hellenic 'women's culture' of colloquial poetry" (110). Within this unusually feminist setting Sappho created her direct, personal, passionate, sometimes angry or mocking lyrics, spoken colloquially and without grandiose attention to literary conventions or metaphysical preoccupations.

Friedrich finds Sappho unique among other classical poets in the way she "restructured and deepened the first-person mode by combining it with her intense emotionality" (120); Sappho's direct address to Aphrodite differs markedly from the reverential and often distrustful distance male classical poets maintain. In Sappho, Aphrodite is a model for conducting one's love affairs, the agent of passion and force who overwhelms lovers with longing, whether of women for men, men for men, or women for women. Sappho's direct, friendly address to the goddess marks an attitude of an apprentice to an acknowledged practitioner of the art and emotional complexities of love, at the same time as she is a familiar and personally loved feminine friend concerned with the same entanglements of passion as the poet who seeks her help. Sappho eagerly acknowledges physical details of lovemaking and feminine sensuality; there is none of the disgust for the female body and the emotions it arouses in men that we find in male classical poets.

One would hope that, fragmentary as the lyrics are, Sappho's poetry would provide a prototype for women poets' approach to Aphrodite. Although there would be no way to prove the connection, it is interesting that the women troubadour poets who flourished in the twelfth century wrote of love with a similar directness, and that these women poets of the Middle Ages were targets, along with Sappho, of the French and German Crusaders against the Cathars in 1204 C.E. The Greeks and later the Christians did everything they could to destroy Sappho's record of happy feminine sexuality; Friedrich notes that 95 per cent, or nine thousand lines, of her poetry was destroyed between 1 C.E. and 1500, "notably as a consequence of Christianity." "This compulsion to burn Sappho," he concludes (in a way that would also apply to the women troubadours), "indicates that her vision threatened the Christian foundations of patriarchy, hypocrisy, and puritanism" (126).

Still, the archetype persisted in the classical Roman Venus. Linked to the Etruscan goddess Turan, this Venus was originally a goddess of vegetation and of the market; she acquired most of the features by which she is known, however, from the imported Greek Aphrodite. Known in 295 B.C.E. as Venus Obsequens, or Venus "who gratifies," by 241 a temple at Mount Eryx which had previously been sacred to Aphrodite (and, before Aphrodite, to Astarte) was renamed for her. Like the Greeks, the Roman poets and philosophers veer between worshipping Venus as the astrological and metaphysical force binding the universe together and degrading her as the worst possible example of female prurience. Lucretius, as we have seen, understands that Venus balances the planets in their courses, and he appeals to her at the beginning of *De Rerum Natura* as the only hope for peace, asking her to "grant that this brutal business of war by sea and land may everywhere be lulled to rest. For you alone have power to bestow upon mortals the blessing of quiet peace." Venus's effectiveness for peace consists in her sensuality as a counter to aggression: "Mars himself, supreme commander in this brutal business, flings himself down at times, laid low by the irremediable wound of love." Like Aphrodite, Venus commands the renewal of the earth and regeneration of its seasons: "since you alone are the uniting power of the universe and without you nothing emerges into the shining sunlight world to grow in joy and loveliness, yours is the partnership I seek in striving to compose these lines On The Nature of the Universe" (26–28). As in the case of Homer, however, the cosmic Venus Lucretius invokes in his first book becomes an object of satire later on, in his fourth, where Venus stands for the evils of feminine sexuality. Lucretius's diction blends the amatory and the military in his description of Venus's effects as "shafts" or arrows, weapons with which she "wounds" men who, "pierced by the shafts of Venus," are drawn to their doom. Nor is this some kind of sadomasochistic amatory play. "This, then," he concludes (meaning all sensual behavior provoked in men by women) "is what we term Venus. This is the origin of the thing called love" (162–63).

Men are mistaken if they think that making love to the woman they desire will quench this destructive passion; it will only infect them with greater and greater desire. The only cure, according to Lucretius, is to avoid being "passionately enamored of an individual at all," to practice masturbation ("vent your seed of love upon other objects") or to use a whore rather than be weakened under the spell of the relentless goddess (163). Another way to avoid Venus is to remember that even the loveliest woman is loathsome in "her physical nature," "driven to use foul-smelling fumigants" when she menstruates and tricking her lover into ignoring this loathsomeness by hiding all of her backstage activities from men she wants "to keep fast bound in the bonds of love" (167).

Although one should discourage one's wife from moving about beneath one when one is trying to impregnate her, which is only deceit on her part (or perhaps an attempt to keep from getting pregnant), Lucretius admits that women feel genuine sexual pleasure: "Sometimes, like the birds and cows and mares, both tame and wild, they are simply in heat—and joyfully copulate with the mounting males" (167–68).

De Rerum Natura, which had a considerable influence on later philosophers, finds its way into the classical wisdom of the Renaissance and into European literature, where Venus's association with feminine sexuality is presumed to be a dire threat to the male population. This unnatural (indeed neurotic) attitude toward sexual generativity and pleasure thus antedates Augustine's prejudice against the body and nature. It is important to note, however, that sexuality is considered feminine, in contrast to more recent attitudes, such as those of the nineteenth century, which took sexuality in a woman as an unwomanly attribute. Although the Greeks and Romans may have been uncomfortable with feminine sexuality, they considered it typical; Venus's and Aphrodite's sexual exuberance, which derives from the deep background of the archetype, is still an important feature in classical mythology.

My hypothesis is that the dialectic between reverence for Aphrodite/Venus as the binding force underlying the cosmos and loathing for feminine sexuality will persist as contradictory attitudes in poems based upon the archetype, because the classical rift between cultural norms and natural desires persists in European culture, enhanced by Christian distrust of everyone's body, with destructive effects upon both male and female psyches. I would argue that it is impossible for cultural codes unnatural to human development to direct men's sensuality entirely into gynophobia or to repress women's sexual delight altogether; the subversive force of normal sensuality accounts for the persistence of the deeper background of the archetype with its affirmation of Eros.

Although state-supported Roman religion sponsored goddesses of virginity, motherhood, and wifehood which could reinforce patriarchal norms for women, Sarah Pomeroy has noted that the cult of Isis, a Middle Eastern import dating back to the Egypt of 2500 B.C.E. which arrived in Italy around 200 B.C.E., was still flourishing among high government officials during the second century C.E. Cleopatra considered herself an incarnation of Isis, and her effect on Augustus was precisely that against which Lucretius had warned. "Unlike Roman cults," Pomeroy writes, "in which the details of worship and the categories of worshippers were rigidly prescribed, that of Isis was capable of unlimited flexibility. The goddess readily encompassed inconsistencies and mutually contradictory qualities. Thus she was identified with many other Mediterranean goddesses ranging from Astarte of Phoenicia, to Fortuna, Athena, Aphrodite, Hestia, Hera,

Demeter, and Artemis" (217–18). Isis had accumulated not only the power of healing the sick and resurrecting the dead but also many "powers associated in the classical world with male divinities," the power of the Indo-European sky gods over "lightning, thunder, and the winds," for example, making her simultaneously omnipotent and nurturant or mothering (218–19). Pomeroy feels that there is a corollary between the development of the cult in the late Roman Republic and the "growing emancipation of women," "since such a goddess would appeal to the freedom to get rid of the inhibitions of traditional gender norms" (225). The cult of Isis was spread throughout the Roman Empire; in the summer of 1988, for example, a temple of Isis was unearthed just outside London.

For at least four hundred crucial years in Roman culture, from 200 B.C.E. until 200 C.E. and later, the vastly popular Isis cult seems to have served as a synthesizing conduit for peoples' needs for a maternal, sexual, politically powerful and wise goddess. Apuleius, writing his humorous *Metamorphoses* in the second century C.E., draws upon this rich accumulation of powers in the Isis archetype. His hero, Lucius, has been turned into an ass, and as a last straw he is expected to pretend to have intercourse with an actress in a dramatic performance of ritual intercourse. He runs away from the scene, which fills him with disgust and terror, and finds himself praying to the goddess for help. He falls into an exhausted sleep and dreams that the goddess comes to him and speaks: "You see me here, Lucius, in answer to your prayer. I am Nature, the universal Mother, mistress of all the elements, primordial child of time, sovereign of all things spiritual, queen of the dead, queen also of the immortals, the single manifestation of all gods and goddesses that are." She says she is Pessinunctica, Cecropian Artemis, Stygian Proserpine, and the Eleusinian Mother of the Corn, as well as Juno, Bellona, Hecate, but, principally, Isis (264–65). Although Apuleius is clearly poking fun at the goddess cults of the late Roman Empire, his parody is based upon knowledge of the many names of a single goddess oddly prophetic of the unitary "Great Mother" concept by means of which nineteenth-century mythographers conflated the many and diverse goddess archetypes of the ancient world.

Citing Aphrodite's prayer to Isis in *The White Goddess*, Robert Graves remarks about its similarity to this Latin prayer from a twelfth-century English book of herbal lore:

Earth, divine goddess, Mother Nature, who dost generate all things and bringest forth even anew the sun which thou has given to the nations; Guardian of sky and sea and of all Gods and powers; through thy influence all nature is hushed and sinks to sleep. . . . Again, when it pleases thee, thou sendest forth the glad daylight and nurturest life with thine eternal surety; and when the spirit of man passes, to thee it returns. Thou indeed art rightly named Great Mother of the Gods; Victory is thy divine name. (64)

Here we have the combined amatory and military facets of Inanna and Ishtar, holistically interbraided with political and cosmic powers. This particular prayer is for the healing secrets of the earth goddess: "Now also I make intercession to you, all ye powers and herbs, and to your majesty." The powers in question are virtues immanent in nature which, if properly approached, may yield her secrets to the petitioner. The "pagan" Latin prayer suggests that in medieval England Christianity may have been more of an ideological superstructure than a widely internalized belief system, undermined by considerable popular allegiance to paganism.

One might speculate that human beings cannot be long starved of natural religion, with its affirmation of bodily realities and celebrations of natural cycles, and that the desire to affirm these values is so instinctive as to continuously undermine antisensual ideologies. From the evidence of the many motifs from Inanna/Aphrodite/Venus/Isis imageries retained both in religion and in popular culture, one might speculate that the love goddess archetype was never entirely eradicated from human consciousness, surviving in encoded and disguised forms not only within the oral subculture but also in literary discourse. I would also suggest that Aphrodite's interbraiding of immanence, spirituality, and sensual and political powers in a holistic paradigm of feminine possibility endows her archetype with an integrative feminist empowerment, which called forth as backlash the minimizations, degradations, and dualistic splits characterizing Greek, Roman, and medieval European attitudes toward feminine sensuality, while the subversive force of normal sensuality nonetheless persists, accounting for the archetype's perennial appeal as a subject of lyric poetry.

5.

Aphrodite in Medieval through Nineteenth-Century Poetry

*I*n *The Mythic Image* Joseph Campbell provides a photograph of a painted tray from the School of Verona in the early fourteenth century. Entitled *The Triumph of Venus*, the twelve-sided tray shows the goddess as a lovely, beckoning, naked woman, encapsulated in an ovular shape, through which beams of light radiate outward and downward. She is flanked on each side by two winged adult cupids, who hold bows and arrows and have bird feet. Although short rays of light in the fashion of a halo spring from Venus's head, the longest shafts of radiance emanate from her vulva to enter the eyes of the six men who look up at her from below. These men, whose attitudes are prayerful, stand buried to their waists in vegetation—grasses and flowers similar in design to those woven in fifteenth-century tapestries—and hovering between the green garden and Venus's feet is a tall tree full of fruit. Campbell (whose analysis has to do with analogues between the worship of Mary and the Buddhist Tara and a comparison of the "maya" they emit) accompanies the illustration with a quotation from Erich Neumann's *Great Mother:*

> The nude Venus within the *mandorla* symbolizing the female genitals appears to a group of men of different periods who are known as great lovers. The ambivalence of the whole . . . is made evident by the

The Triumph of Venus. *Veronese painted tray, early fourteenth century, School of Verona, Italy. Courtesy of the Musée du Louvre, Paris. P. Giraudon (BSXLVII).*

strange genii that accompany the Goddess. These winged creatures, late forms of the bird-shaped souls over which the Goddess rules, are Cupids, but they have ugly birds' claws. These feet, which were formerly a natural part of the birds' body, now produce the effect of an archaic vestige whose significance is evil. Birds' menacing claws are among the rending attributes of the Archetypal Feminine as siren and harpy; here, as is frequently the case, they have been transferred to

121

the male companion figures. In the Renaissance picture the genii
bearing weapons and birds' claws are symbols of the voracious impulses
revolving around the Golden Aphrodite, who enchants and ruins the
men ensnared in her earthly paradise. (145–46)

Facing the Veronese tray, and again without a comment of his own,
Campbell has provided a photograph of Franz Stuck's painting *Sin*.
The subject is a lovely, dark-haired woman, her clothes open from
vulva to neck, outlining an oval, lighted shape of flesh, over half of
which hangs an enormous snake with its head draped menacingly.

In Neumann's book the image facing the Veronese tray is of an
incubus overpowering a prone male victim. Neumann uses the Re-
naissance Venus to illustrate the survival of ambivalent attitudes to
the "Great Goddess" from archaic times to early modern Europe. He
acknowledges that the "birdlike character of woman" has something to
do with her "correlation with the heavens," but "this archetypal
symbol," he posits, "possesses a positive life-giving and a negative
death-dealing aspect," the latter represented by birds' claws as "vora-
cious impulses" used to entrap men in an "earthly paradise" (145–46).
Although these archetypes are included as illustrations of "the positive
elementary character" of the Great Mother, they clearly contain a
threat to men. Neumann feels disgust with aspects of the painted tray
which I find positive and entrancing. The lovers' attitude of rever-
ence, for example, crossing their hands over their breasts or holding
one hand over their hearts, and the worshipper directly below Venus
holding both hands slightly lifted as if to receive the rays pouring
down from her, suggest to me a harmonious ritual of worship elicited
by the goddess figure. Neumann's interpretation depends upon his
perception of bird claws as ugly, although they look like perfectly
ordinary bird feet to me. He also associates cupids with harpies and
sirens, perhaps put off by the spectacle of a naked female holding a
group in thrall through the power of her vulva. We have to ask for
whom the nakedness of woman is an appalling phenomenon, since the
tray itself depicts what could be seen as a survival of the bird goddesses
of Old Europe, Aphrodite the Golden, and Aphrodite astride her
goose.

Distaste for such artifacts is by no means limited to male scholars.
Some feminist historians who comprehend culture as a repository of
male projection would argue that these are male worshippers and,

most probably, a male painter; what we have on the tray could be one more instance of the elevation of "woman" or "love" to an abstract symbol of use to patriarchy. Joan Ferrante, for example, might assert that this is an illustration of the way medieval and Renaissance thinking displaced " 'real people' with human problems," substituting "symbols, aspects of philosophical and psychological problems that trouble the male world" (1). In such a reading the tray does not depict an archetype in the sense of a viable and empowering image which awakens the appreciation of both men and women for feminine sensuality but a stereotype which fails to express any useful truths about our sensuality or about men's relationships to us. This approach defines women and love as abstract symbols which service men but have nothing to do with women's real lives.

A world in which women and love have become abstract symbols is a world of estrangement from nature as well as from our own bodies. We arrive at this estrangement by rejecting our feminine subjectivity out of a belief in an overwhelming masculine dominance. When I began my research on Aphrodite I thought that I would find the archetype entirely colored by a gynophobic patriarchal signature passed down from the Greeks, Romans, and Christian Church fathers to the Victorians. When I examined the texts about Venus and Aphrodite for tone and attitude, however, I began to suspect that the devaluation of Aphrodite's feminine sensuality occurred much more recently than I supposed.

In this chapter I shall survey the way poets from the Middle Ages to the end of the nineteenth century respond to the Aphrodite archetype. We shall see that attitudes celebrating women's sensuality seem to be retained from the archetype's deep background and that there are more celebrations of feminine sexuality the earlier we look in literary history. We shall see that although the historical signatures of the medieval period, the Renaissance, and the seventeenth, eighteenth, and nineteenth centuries mark a poet's perspective on the archetype, it is useful in the case of Aphrodite as of Medusa to develop a continuum based on a scale of attitudes from celebration to loathing which is not entirely historical. My hypothesis is that Aphrodite, like Medusa, retains significant elements of her preclassical background which create a dialectical tension within a given poem between emotions natural to human beings and norms militating against sexual pleasure. Both male and female poets are frustrated by European

123

distrust of sexuality, but again the frustrations follow divergent patterns according to gender. Given the much greater number of poems about Aphrodite than about Medusa, I find it helpful to analyze poems by men and women in separate sections, since the poems by women raise special questions. What, for example, is the relationship between an historical culture's distrust of feminine sensuality and a woman poet's quest for authenticity? To what extent are women's declarations of their frustrated suits marked by cultural prohibitions, and what unique textual strategies do they develop to disguise or encode their desire? Since it is most often male expectations about women that frustrate women poets, it is helpful to deal first with male Aphrodite poems and then examine how women's poems differ from them.

Celebrations of the Love Goddess

Not only is the content of poems about Aphrodite and Venus similar over vast stretches of time, but the conventions for approaching her—the point of view taken by the speaker, the rhetorical forms used to address her, even motifs and images associated with her—remain strikingly constant. The rhetorical forms of apostrophe and invocation, petition and promise of personal sacrifice in return for favors to be received, persist from hymns and prayers to Inanna to nineteenth-century celebrations and petitions to a goddess of love. An examination of the "Hymns to Inanna" which appear at the end of Wolkstein and Kramer's edition reveals characteristics which we will see throughout this category.

In the first of these hymns a speaker addresses Inanna in the first person, apostrophizing her as "the Holy One who appears in the heavens!" and then cataloguing her attributes:

> You shine brilliantly in the evening,
> You brighten the day at dawn,
> You stand in the heaven like the sun and the moon,
> Your wonders are known both above and below,
> To the greatness of the holy priestesses of heaven,
> To you, Inanna, I sing! (93)

The reverential address, the listing of attributes, and the tone of joyous celebration rounding out with the declarative "I sing!" can be recognized as a mode of addressing gods or goddesses with which we are familiar from the Homeric Hymns. Like the hymns of the European Middle Ages and, more familiarly, of Victorian England, the convention often includes the propitiation of a divinity by song, petitions for favors, and promises that the worshipper will demonstrate gratitude by further service and sacrifice. The Inanna hymns are remarkable for celebrating holistic feminine qualities and for their descriptions of the way worshippers conduct themselves during processions and at Inanna's temple during the rites dedicated to her. These hymns celebrate Inanna's prowess not only in love, generativity, and agricultural fecundity but also in statehood and in deeds of war. In other hymns of the same period she is addressed as a war goddess, and in Inanna the apparently opposite facets of love and war are united. We shall see how the aggressive and military aspect of the love goddess becomes split in later lyrics when love is taken as a feminine quality while war is allocated to a male divinity. Her more dangerous, destructive aspect nonetheless lingers in the archetype to stir up attitudes of fright and avoidance.

It is less surprising to recognize in Homer's cosmic Aphrodite elements of Inanna's astronomical powers than to find in hymns to Venus of the supposedly ascetic Middle Ages many analogues to the Inanna texts. The identification of a cosmic principle binding the universe together is the most frequent attitude carrying over from Inanna through Lucretius to medieval materials. Chaucer, for example, blends ideas from the sixth-century philosopher Boethius with Boccaccio's *Filostrato* in a hymn to Venus opening the third book of his *Troilus and Criseyde* (1385/6), addressing love as a feminine cosmic figure:

> O blisful light, of which the bemes clere
> Adorneth al the thridde hevene faire;
> O sonnes lief, O Joves doughter deere,
> Plesaunce of love, O goodly debonaire,
> In gentil hertes ay redy to repaire;
> O verray cause of heele and of gladnesse,
> Iheryed be thy myght and thi goodnesse.

Chaucer conflates sexual love with Boethius's more abstract principle:

> In hevene and helle, in erthe and salte see,
> Is felt thi myght, if that I wel descerne;

125

> As man, brid, best, fisshe, herbe, and grene tree
> The fele in tymes with vapour eterne.

All of nature feels the emanations of the love divinity, moving in due seasons according to her empowerment; these characteristics, which we can recognize as similar to those of Inanna, are then put to the service of "God":

> God loveth, and to love wel nat werne;
> And in this world no lyves creature,
> Withouten love, is worth, or may endure. (143)

It is the goddess of love, Chaucer insists, who makes Jove "amourex . . . On mortal thyng," in love with creation in the neo-Platonic manner of the creator pouring out being into nature.

Medieval attitudes toward sexuality were influenced by a rigorously antisensual church doctrine, which originated with Paul and was imposed upon Europe by Saint Augustine. It was Augustine who interpreted Adam's fall as the result of Eve's lust rather than of disobedience, and official Christian doctrine continued to associate feminine lust with evil. Elaine Pagels remarks that "by the fifth century, the male leaders and theologians of Christianity had accepted and restated the most denigrating traditional views of women. All that was inferior or evil they associated with the female, all that was good and superior with the male," with Eve seen as the bringer of evil in the form of sexuality, the "temptress of man, and the embodiment of all women" (79). Although, as we shall see, this misogynist view represented only one extreme in church doctrine about feminine sexuality, it was a powerful view.

Medieval theologians did not all follow Saint Augustine in considering human bodies and nature itself as "fallen" or ontologically corrupt but (like Meister Eckhart, Julian of Norwich, and Hildegarde of Bingen) accepted nature as the dwelling place of spirit. For these Christians, Eden is not lost but renewed here and now by Christ's incarnation, the divinity embodied in human flesh. Human beings are thus a part of and in balance with nature, not antagonistic to it. It is important for our understanding of the Aphrodite/Venus archetype in medieval times to recognize that living rightly within sensuality could be valued while lust, understood as a wrong relationship to nature, was forbidden.

Aphrodite in Medieval through Nineteenth-Century Poetry

George Economou writes about the two natures of Venus not as a split between the transcendent and the physical but as alternate sensual paths, one to satisfaction and one to perdition. "It is dangerous," he warns, "to regard the two Venuses of medieval mythography and poetry as being aligned within an opposition of *caritas* and *cupiditas* when the mythographic moralizations and poetic uses concentrate upon a single context. That context is earthly love and the two Venuses represent two different dispositions within it: the one, legitimate, sacramental, natural, and in harmony with cosmic law; the other, illegitimate, perverted, selfish, and sinful." It is very important for an understanding of the Aphrodite archetype to recognize that for medieval poets an earthly sensuality is accepted as "legitimate, natural, and in harmony with cosmic law" (20).

Venus appears in courtly love poetry as a focus for prayer, presiding over decisions about love, available for help with one's problems in conducting amorous (and not necessarily sublimated) affairs, often sitting over a court where plaintiffs and love advocates hear special cases brought to her for judgment. Chaucer's proem, in which he prepares himself to tell "to Venus heryinge" (praise) the love story of Troilus and Criseyde, is thus a prayer to the love goddess in her aspect as judge in difficult amatory cases, a role closer to the concept of the immanence of divinity in sexual matters than might be expected without taking into account medieval theology's acceptance of "good" sensuality. Chaucer's court of love was part of a continuum of literary convention going back several centuries. Although it was violently attacked by papal decree, the school of love poetry which flourished in the eleventh and twelfth centuries in southern France (former Roman Gaul) remains a dominant strain in love poetry to the present day and provides a good case of the survival of the love goddess archetype. Various factors, including Occitanian inheritance laws favorable to women, the absence of men on the crusades, and Albigensian theology (which recognized both male and female aspects of divinity), seem to have engendered a love poetry which celebrated women's sexuality. Although some critics might suggest, as does Joan Ferrante, that in the courtly love system women are merely vehicles expressive of men's emotions, containers for masculine preoccupations (1), it is also possible that the act of elevating "the lady" or "midon" and declaring that one can be "ennobled" by revering her contains some traces of the worship of pagan goddesses. Also, the fact that courtly love was not necessarily consummated did not mean that the women addressed in the love poetry were sexless; on the contrary, petitions to the lady for the gift of her love presumed that she was a potentially active sexual partner. Finally, the women who were addressed were powerful, ruling their fiefs in their husbands' absence and, as we shall see, writing love poetry themselves.

There are similarities between conventions and topoi of Provençal love poetry and modes of address and facets of praise found in Sumerian paeans to Inanna. The link between these historically distant modes could be the Roman cult of Isis, which survived in Europe. Not only are the structures of petition and rituals of prayer to the goddess uniform over thousands of years, but specific epithets and apostrophic imageries remain constant as well. Although the Christian Church, for example, found it ideologically necessary to stamp out a vision of life that valued feminine sensuality, it retained in hymns to Mary sublimated versions of earlier pagan conventions. Careful not to swing so far to the ascetic extreme as to lose potential converts, the Provençal "midon," or lady, admired for her potential as a secular love partner, was transformed into the figure of the Virgin Mary, admired for her spiritualized purity.

One principal method of medieval theologians was quite similar to that of Lucretius: undermining the sexual and political powers Provençal poetry invested in women by turning against the sexual content of the archetype. Thus Ferrante traces a gradual degradation inflicted upon Venus

> from her role in Martianus [*De Philogieae et Mercurii Nuptiis*, fourth to fifth century c.e.] as essential to marriage and life, to the corrupted aide of Nature in the De Planctu [Alanus de Insulis *De Planctu Naturae*, twelfth century] and the cohort of evil in the Anticlaudian [Alain de Lille, c. 1128–1202]. In the *Roman de la Rose* [Guillaume de Lorris, 1230, completed by Jean de Meung, 1275], she becomes a powerful figure of lust, who uses Nature and Genius to do *her* will. (61 n. 38)

In the Middle Ages, according to Ferrante, Venus becomes the principle of lust, the spark that sets off corruption in men.

I do not intend to underestimate the impact of medieval clerical asceticism on sexual norms. This "tendency" of "corruption" defines the human body itself as suspect spiritually, both for men and women. The striking point, however, is that although women's greater lack of control can cause trouble for men, even medieval theologians accepted feminine sexuality as a natural, if dangerous, phenomenon.

Unable (and perhaps unwilling) to extirpate either indigenous or imported goddess worship from the church, the theologians perpetuated the archetype in a paradoxically sexless form as a focus of the reverence that had been given to the more sensual Provençal lady. It is hardly coincidental that so many European cathedrals of the period were built over ancient shrines to goddesses of springs and fountains. Joseph Campbell (*Occidental Mythology* 43) and Marina Warner (passim) have amply documented the theory that Mariology retained many elements carried over from the worship of Middle Eastern and classical goddesses. In an era of rigid masculine control and an authoritarian father god with a scarcely less judgmental son, Mary provided relief and perhaps even some role modeling, a way for people to transfer their allegiance from her pagan prototypes to a female divinity who could be addressed in familiar epithets, such as "Our Lady of the Barley" and "Our Lady of the Vine." Pamela Berger has analyzed the development of the figure of the Virgin Mary from earlier European grain goddesses and the creation of saints associated with agricultural miracles, documenting a syncretism extremely useful to medieval Christianity in that it provided an easy adjustment from pagan folk practices to acceptable Christian rituals (89–104).

Bernard of Cluny addresses a hymn to Mary (c. 1140) not only containing hymn and prayer conventions which we observed in prayers to Inanna and classical Aphrodite but listing specific qualities which are traditional epithets for various pagan goddesses. Bernard addresses Mary as "salutaris Virgo" (savior Virgin) under the name of "Stella Maris," star of the sea, Venus's title as morning star as it was Ishtar's and Aphrodite's; he also uses "Celi Regina," Queen of Heaven, analogous to Inanna as cosmic queen; and, also, "Lucis auctorem," the author of light or the sun herself, "Mundo/Lux coelestis," the light of heaven radiating out from herself as its center (454–56). Elements of Awis, proto-European goddess of the sun and of dawn whom Friedrich proposed as one of Aphrodite's interbraided strands, seems evident in Bernard's Mary, who in courtly manner presides over heaven, hearing the vows, prayers, and problems of her worshippers. Secular lyrics such as those composed in praise of one's "fayre Lady" also sound remarkably like spiritual hymns, with Venus's and Mary's titles used interchangeably. Thus in a lyric accompanied by a chorus of "Blow, Nortern wynd, / send thou me my suetung" the poet's epithets for his mistress sound remarkably like qualities ordinarily attributed to the Virgin:

> Heo is coral of godnesse,
> Heo is rubie of ryhtfulnesse,
> Heo is cristal of clannesse
> And baner of bealty. (Carleton Brown 149)

Another poet of the same period addresses his lover as "O excelent suffereigne, mosst semly to see," and after cataloguing similar epithets he prays for her favor much as Sappho prayed to Venus, except that now the recipient of his petition is not the goddess of love but the loved woman herself, to whom he sends along his "lytel balade" as a humble prayer for her favor.

During the Renaissance as well as in the medieval period, secular lyrics both mimicked liturgical hymns and embodied much earlier forms of address to love goddesses. Delight over a communal agreement on how sensuality is to be conducted, leading to social harmony about the way sexuality can be integrated into the ongoing life of a culture, also informed the marriage hymn, or epithalamium, which was popular in the period following the Renaissance. It seems to me that it is not only the poetic convention that links poems of early modern Europe to the third millenium B.C.E., but even more markedly the attitudes which the materials express about love and sensuality. Thus the mood of "The Joy of Sumer," a description of "the sacred marriage rite" celebrated by the ritual intercourse of Inanna and Dumuzi, is strikingly similar to the mood of sixteenth- and seventeenth-century epithalamia. The ancient Sumerians described the delightful preparations of the marriage bed in ways that make them seem similar to English marriage preparations:

> The people cleanse the rushes with sweet-smelling
>   cedar oil
> They arrange the rushes for the bed.
> They spread a bridal sheet over the bed.
> A bridal sheet to rejoice the heart,

A bridal sheet to sweeten the loins,
A bridal sheet for Inanna and Dumuzi.
(Wollstein and Kramer 108)

John Donne, like other seventeenth-century poets, often compared epithalamia and marriage songs. In "Epithalamion made at Lincolnes Inne," for example, he urges a bride to bed under the aegis of the "amorous evening starre," which he describes as "loves altar," where she will be a "pleasing sacrifice" to sexual pleasure. Although one suspects that by the seventeenth century the bride may be "sacrificing" her chances for authentic sensuality upon the marital altar, the mood and the conventions are similar to the rites of Inanna.

As Lise Papetti-Esch has suggested, the popular Renaissance masques, which were skits inserted as musical entertainments or spectacles in plays, represent another survival of secular sensuality. Masques used mythological characters and plots, and often included masked audience members who joined the actors in a general revel at the end. As Northrop Frye has noted, many Renaissance masques depicted ideal worlds, "arcadias and visions of earthly paradise," which permitted the audiences to pretend to be members of a society whose "ideal" quality consisted in a joyous sensuality (*Anatomy* 288). Since gods and goddesses often played roles depicting bodily pleasure as a good, these masques became vehicles for archetypal empowerment in that they enabled the audience to participate in celebrations enhancing everyone's natural sexuality.

Ben Jonson's *Celebration of Charis* (1640) includes an Aphroditian hymn, "Her Triumph." "See the chariot at hand here of Love!" declares an excited onlooker,

Wherein my Lady rideth!
Each that draws is a swan or a dove
And well the car Love guideth. (313)

Like Aphrodite in many Greek vase decorations, the "Lady" goddess of love rides in a chariot drawn by swans and doves; she retains the cosmic imagery of eyes which "delight / as Love's star," the planet Venus; and in a courtly conceit reminiscent of the eye of wisdom archetype, a glance from her eye becomes a beam of beneficent grace. Like Chaucer's "blisful light" of love with its "bemes clere," Jonson's Charis pours radiance out to enliven creation in an empowerment of nature by feminine sensuality and good will analogous to the Veronese tray. His love goddess also retains the Empedoclean balance of the warring elements, controlling "All the gain, all the good, of the elements' strife."

Although A *Celebration of Charis* contains positive affirmations of feminine sensuality, it takes a Puritanical turn when Jonson praises the chastity of the goddess, like "a bright lily . . . before rude hands have touched it" and "the fall of the snow, / Before the soil hath smutched it." Dryden similarly tends to set Venus off against a contrastingly "chaste" Diana in his *Secular Masque* (1700), while in his *King Arthur* (1691), which contains an interesting variety of Celtic as well as classical archetypal materials, he includes a running debate about the right and wrong ways to conduct one's sensual life. From the point of view of archetypal psychology, the masque clarifies wrong (rapacious) from right kinds of sensuality and concludes in a celebration of a "pure" love which is not yet synonymous with asexuality.

The Split Venus

Before a period which began, roughly speaking, in the middle of the eighteenth century, a "good Venus" (to use Economou's term) was cosmic and sensual, legitimizing sexuality for both men and women within cultural constraints that did not consider a sensual woman unwomanly. Chastity corresponded to legitimate sensuality, understood as sexual restraint before marriage but conjugal intercourse enjoyed by both men and women. Bodily sensuality was thus acceptable within certain limits, and not an evil; lust was inappropriate or illegitimate sensuality. Although, as we have seen, a healthy reverence for Venus presiding over a good sensuality was widespread, male poets were often quite ambivalent about the archetype. This was a result partially of clerical asceticism, with its valuation of celibacy (although celibacy itself connoted redirection of powerful sensual forces rather than asexuality), partially of the valuation of premarital chastity. It may also have derived from reverence for the asexual Virgin Mary, which rendered people more in awe of virgins than of sexually active women. I would suggest, however, that male poets' ambivalences about Venus sprang mainly from a fear of the power inherent in women's sensuality, which was considered a natural but dangerous feminine property. Even Saint Augustine did not deny that sexuality was a natural aspect of women, all too likely to over-power the will.

One strategy for expressing ambivalence about the powerful and sensual Venus was to set her off against another deity, often Mars or Diana, whose qualities were projected as contrary to hers and who pitted themselves against her. That Mars had once been part of Inanna as her war goddess attribute and that Diana had incorporated Inanna's rule over nature was unknown to these poets, who nonethe-less expressed recognition, fear, and rejection of these powers latent in the Venus archetype. A second poetic strategy which enabled poets to praise Venus while retaining allegiance to patriarchal norms was to subordinate her to a male divinity. A third was to satirize her for the feminine sensuality which is the distinctive mark of her archetype.

Palamon's visit to the Temple of Venus in Chaucer's "Knight's Tale" provides an interesting example of the way a poet can simulta-neously pray to the goddess of love and undermine her authority. Having declared that Emelye, a young woman he has seen from his prison window, is Venus in human form, Palamon visits the Temple of Venus set up in the lists where he will battle Arcite for her favors. Arcite simultaneously goes to the Temple of Mars to pray for success, while Emelye goes to the Temple of Diana. Palamon's prayer to Venus, "the blisful Citerea benigne" and "Doughter to Jove and spouse of Vulcanus," is entirely respectful, while he assumes Venus's intimate familiarity with and interest in his desires, which include the dis-tinctly non-Aphroditian wish to dominate Emelye, to "have fully possesion" of her. Palamon's suit is confounded by Arcite's death, so that neither Venus nor Mars but (temporarily) Diana wins the day; after further suffering on Palamon's part, Theseus, presiding over a court of love, decides to let him marry Emelye under the aegis not of Venus nor of Diana but of a male metaphysical abstraction, a cosmic "First Moevere," creator of "the faire cheyne of love." It is important to note that Chaucer's chain no longer extends from the cosmic Aphrodite but from a defeminized abstract principle, enabling male dominance over the outcome of his narration.

In Edmund Spenser's poetry adventurers encounter enchantresses in a manner strikingly similar both to pre-Norman Celtic lore and to Arthurian narratives popularized after the Norman Conquest. One cannot help but wonder whether the English audience's enjoyment of stories about knights questing for romance and venturing over the countryside in hopes of encountering enchantingly seductive women awaiting them on magical islands has a lot to do with the Celtic mythologies repopularized by Breton minstrels accompanying the Normans after the 1066 conquest. The layer of classical mythology in English narrative verse sometimes seems thinly stretched over pagan Celtic bases. Jean Markale has demonstrated the sexual freedom Celtic queens and other women enjoyed as a result of a communal (and thus nonpatrilinear) property system; the assumption that a wife might quite naturally take on lovers was only gradually eroded by Christian and patrilinear concepts (30–40). The popular Arthurian materials derive from these same Breton narrative sources, which retain some of the powerful feminine sensuality found in earlier Celtic materials, such as the seventh-century Irish narrative "The Voyage of Bran."

Thus in *The Faerie Queene* (1590) Spenser may be incorporating Celtic archetypes of sexually active queens and divinities into his description of a Venus presiding over her court of love, an archetype which retains elements of Inanna as Queen of Heaven and Aphrodite as cosmic harmonizer. Spenser's Venus sits between young men allegorically representing love and hate, and Spenser praises her for subduing strife and war while maintaining the heavens in their course. The knight Scudamour describes a temple blending pagan with Christian elements, including fumes of incense and sacrifices which steam away to represent the vows of true lovers who "bath in joy and amorous desire." Venus is attended by junior priestesses, and the whole atmosphere suggests Aphrodite's love temples at Corinth, the Roman cult of Isis, and Sumerian temples where feminine sexuality was celebrated.

Spenser's use of these archetypal elements lurking in the deep background of the Venus figure raises some interesting questions about the interaction of the poetic unconscious and the latent content of an archetype. Negative elements which Spenser perceives as horrific also characterize his Venus, who has "both her feete and legs together twyned . . . with a snake, whose head and tail were fast combyned." Although, as we saw with regard to Medusa, the snake with its tail in its mouth is an emblem of regeneration and immortality, Spenser clearly intends to evoke both horror at the anomalous mixture of the animal and the human and the Christian association of snakes with women as sexual temptresses. Spenser's attitude here is interestingly similar to Neumann's assessment of the Renaissance tray: on one hand his patriarchal perspective reads the goddess as repulsive, but on the other the bird and reptile attributes carry survivals of more positive connotations. He is ambivalent about Venus, whom he depicts as both frightening and admirable. Scudamour petitions her as "Great Venus, queene of Beautie and of grace," in a manner which I do not read as deliberately hypocritical. He acknowledges her as world creator and Empedoclean pacifier of the raging elements, with power over savage beasts as well as a deep well of healing merriment:

> Great God of men and women, Queene of th'ayre,
> Mother of laughter, and well spring of blisse,
> Graunt that of my loue at last I may not misse. (504)

Like Palamon, Scudamour wants power over his object, Amoret, who is sitting on Venus's lap. He declares that he is not going to spend his life like Venus's other permanent plaintiffs, these "Great sorts of lovers piteously complayning," and appeals around Venus to the leader of the angel boys who hover about her throne. He holds up his shield to them to declare his allegiance to Cupid, "the God of Love," at the sight of which Venus "was with terror queld," forced to give up the extremely reluctant Amoret, whom Scudamour leads away from Venus's temple and from "her wished freedom," subordinating her to a masculine Eros principle.

In his "Hymn in Honor of Love" (1596), very much in the manner of Chaucer's final hymn in "The Knight's Tale," Spenser apostrophizes a "Great God of might," a male love god emerging out of the fat little cupids on Venus's lap, and constructs a dichotomy between "loose desyre," or mere base lust, and a male "lord of truth and loialtie, / Lifting himselfe out of the lowly dust / On golden plumes up to the purest skie" of sublimated heavenly beauty (744). And in his "Hymne of Heavenly Love," this personified love divinity gives way to a pregnant masculine abstraction, a deity Spenser describes as "pregnant still with powrefull grace / And full of fruitfull love, that lovs to get / Things like himselfe, and to enlarge his race" (751). Here, in the Greek manner of a male god taking over the powers of birth, feminine generativity as well as feminine sensuality is first subordinated, then abstracted, and finally usurped.

Like Jonson and Dryden, Spenser is wrestling with the question of acceptable sensuality, but his historical signature of Puritanical moderation is undermined by the deep background of the archetypes he chooses to employ in his allegory. The classical Venus and the pseudo-Celtic enchantress Acrasia lurking in her Edenic bower of bliss cannot be entirely explained in terms of materials immediately available to Spenser. In the historical realm, Spenser is consciously mediating between normative sensuality and chaotic lust; his personal delight in sensuality and in nature is enhanced by the valuation of feminine sensuality latent in the archetype. I would suggest that when a male poet writes about Venus the impact of his depiction cannot be entirely explained as the projection of his personal state of mind on the subject of feminine sensual power; rather, personal and historical signatures interbraid with the archetype's earlier content.

Spenser and his contemporaries had reason to fear feminine sensuality embodied in a real and powerful woman, a combination of forces which Queen Elizabeth I used to assert her power. Shakespeare too, in "Venus and Adonis" (1593), combines fear of what a powerful woman who intends to follow through on her sexual desires can do with an attempt to subordinate her to a male divinity. Choosing to depict Venus as a powerful older woman trying to seduce a reluctant young Adonis serves both of these ends; it also allows him to mock her sexual importunities. Shakespeare's simultaneously sympathetic and mocking portrait of Venus, expressing a contemporary ambivalence, established his early poetic reputation. Instead of a lover praying to Venus, he uses the Venus and Adonis convention to depict Venus as a "lovesick queen" whose amorous wiles fail to arouse Adonis in the slightest, satirizing the older woman who begs the young lover to respond to her seductions. With a kind of genial acceptance undercut by mockery, Shakespeare nonetheless acknowledges as given the enormously powerful sexual drives from which women as well as men can suffer.

Venus's lament for her dead lover is a conventional archetypal ritual reminiscent of the laments of Isis for Osiris and Inanna for Dumuzi. The Queen of Heaven, in these narrations, is not merely mourning personally but presiding over a cycle of the death and rebirth of a lover who represents the changing seasons and the survival of her kingdom. Robert Graves postulates rituals based on this archetype as the basis for the dying god myths resurrected by G. S. Frazer in the later nineteenth century. To Frazer and Graves the young consort lover of the goddess must be discarded yearly when the frightening queen tires of him, making her even more of a focus for masculine terror.

In the seventeenth century the ritual power of Inanna's lament to restore the seasons is transformed to a pathetic dependence upon her lover for her own survival. Thus William Cartwright's song "Venus for her Belov'd Adonis" in his play *The Lady Errant* (1651) shows Venus trying to bring her lover back to life because without him she is nothing: he is her "Deity," without whom "Venus in Venus there is none / In vain a Goddess now am I" (155–56). These laments suggest simultaneously the powerful passion of women and their lack of identity without a male lover. In his 1616 lyric "The Pourtrait of Mars and Venus," similarly, William Drummond tells the audience of a painting to look at Venus's back as she turns, but then goes on to remark that she wouldn't dare stir in her bed "For feare to wake the angrie God of Warre" (74). Venus must not dare even turn over in bed for fear of her husband, who has usurped her military power. In a poem attributed to Sir Thomas Wyatt, Venus is shown trying on "the helm of mighty Mars the red" as a joke or sport to titillate the god of war by dressing like him, only to be reproved by Priapus (a stand-in for the phallus) to lay aside these great big weapons, since only "I for you am weapon fit and trim" (230). I read these associations of Venus with Mars, which mock her for dressing up as the war god as if she were a little girl playing, as denigrations of the military powers associated with Aphrodite, Inanna, and Ishtar, a kind of sabotage from within the archetype itself—as if, at some level of consciousness, male poets recognized the necessity to defuse it.

The Virtuous Venus

Shakespeare's reader would feel both recognition and discomfort at the spectacle of the importunate Venus trying to seduce her reluctant young lover because he is portraying the phenomenon of a woman taking the initiative in love with someone she is not married to. This action disrupts the norm of chastity, a woman's preservation of her virginity until marriage and her monogamous loyalty to her husband afterward. From the point of view of the male courting under this system, a woman's chief duty was to preserve her "honor" by premarital sexual purity and by marital fidelity. This is not, as we have seen, a sexual prudery but a correct sensuality, the kind of chastity that Spenser understood as the corner-stone for his ethic of moderation, balance, and temperance. As time went on, the sexual content of the Venus archetype was valued less and less until, by the nineteenth century, sexual passion was forbidden for women even in marriage. It is within the context of the evolution of a sexless Victorian chastity that we can understand the strategy adopted by many English poets of conflating Venus and Diana, mixing their attributes into a "Virtuous Venus."

Nancy Cotton Pearse has developed a religious and social context for John Fletcher's "chastity plays," which reflect the more tolerant point of view that the seventeenth century took about feminine sensuality. Pearse suggests that even Fletcher, who was criticized for licentiousness, wrote plays such as *The Triumph of Death* (1611) not to promulgate norms denying women their natural sensuality but to satirize the excessive lechery to which women were subjected at court. Casta, the young heroine of *Triumph,* refuses to go to court because, as Pearse puts it, the Jacobean court was "the very quintessence of iniquity," a place where a virgin could expect to be accosted upon arrival. Casta protests subjection to a sexual compulsion which will destroy her independence. If she goes to court, she insists, she "must be no more my self" but become a mistress to some courtier and grow "so gret and glorious / With prostitution of my burning beauties / That great Lords kneel, and Princes beg for favors." In spite of all this glory, however, she will not be "herself" (34–35).

This debate is about good and bad sex; as Pearse puts it, "the opposing forces which contend for the soul are chastity and lechery" (33). Women have less control over their emotions than men, and are more likely to give in to sensuality. In this context, Fletcher's Casta as a heroine of chastity provides an example of heroic will power and of self-determination, but not of prudery. This recognition of women as sexual beings with dubious control over our sexuality may account for the survival of the Venus archetype, however paradoxical, throughout seventeenth- and eighteenth-century poetry. The popularity of class-ical mythology enabled poets to express their sensuality in spite of the emergent Puritanism, under the guise of employing conventional literary tropes.

In the eighteenth century, poets continued to address Venus in prayers and hymns, adding descriptions of temples which wealthy landowners constructed on their grounds, semihumorous loci for statues of Venus which often became the focus of elaborately landscaped gardens. Carole Fabricant, Douglas Brooks-Davies, and James Turner have described these Augustan gardens as embodiments of the period's profound ambivalence about feminine sexuality. In Fabricant's thesis these gardens "tell the story of a society which demanded contradictory things from its women and its landscapes alike; of men who wanted to be gratified by the full sensual and boisterous reality existing beyond the fence while yet keeping the reality within clearly defined boundaries so that it could be desired and possessed" (131). By shaping their lawns and trees and little rivers, these gentlemen gardeners sought to control both nature and women. "Nature was to reveal her full charms and give of herself generously to her husbandlike viewers," Fabricant writes, "while remaining a discreet, modest maiden who conceals her bountiful endowments from the vulgar, prying eyes of other suitors" (12). This concealment took the form of temples hidden away within private gardens, and also of the Venus statue modestly concealing her pudendum beneath her hands, giving rise to the expression "Venus Pudica," or the sexually modest and hence virtuous Venus.

Male poets construct texts upon a ritual of approaching these temples and praying to the "captured" archetype upon the landowner's altar. Fabricant describes Alexander Pope adapting the persona of a magician to enter Bathurst's "enchanted forest," seeing the "male owner's 'penetration' into the 'inner spaces' of his garden" as his sexual control over a female landscape. In the Vale of Venus at Rousham, the Temple of Flora at Stourhead, among other loci, Fabricant finds "included . . . numerous statues of women, often in varying states of disarray or of undress. There were, as might be expected, a number of representations of Venus" (122). From one perspective, these Venus-centered gardens could be seen as an extreme example of the objectification of women, with feminine sexuality rigidified into statues owned by men. The poet's attitudes, however, do not suggest that by creating and privatizing gardens men have gotten feminine sexuality under any real control. In "The Sexual Politics of Landscape: Images of Venus in the Eighteenth-Century English Poetry and Landscape Gardening," James G. Turner provides an example of one of these poems, written by William Shenstone to the statue of Venus standing in a "Vale of Venus" in the garden at Leasowes, a garden well known to Alexander Pope for its "Semi-reducta Venus." *Reducta,* which has the connotation of "withdrawn," translates from classical Latin as applied by the Stoics to objects which "though not evils were to be regarded as inferiors" (*Cassell's Latin-English Dictionary*, 474). Shenstone's prayer to Venus is a typical example of the metrical dialectic by which eighteenth-century poets expressed not so much an objectification of Venus as a profound ambivalence about the powerful feminine sensuality she represents. Like so much of eighteenth-century poetry, Shenstone's lyric is structured out of paradoxical sentiments contradicting each other:

"To Venus, Venus here retir'd / My sober vows I pay," he insists, only to decry the Aphroditian content underlying his virtuous Venus:

> Not *her*, on *Paphian* plains admir'd
> The bold! The pert! the gay!
>
> Not her, whose am'rous leer prevail'd
> To bribe the *Phrygian* boy;
> Not her, whose martial efforts fail'd
> To save disastrous Troy.

Before praising the Venus Pudica for her "coy reserve," "sweet concealment," and "bashful beauty," the poet protests the immodest sexual content latent in the archetype while fully acknowledging its potency. Her sensuality is only half denied, however, as in his third stanza, where she is seen

> Fresh rising from the foamy tide,
> She every bosom warms;
> While half-withdrawn she seems to hide,
> And half reveals, her charms. (370–71)

Turner concludes that "images like Shenstone's Venus are a compendium of contemporary intellectual processes," in which I would include the need to reduce the classical Venus archetype to the point where she can exemplify contemporary norms for feminine sexuality. The poetic strategy of retaining Venus in full cultural view while reducing the power of her sexuality typifies an historical period in which a transition is taking place between acknowledgment of women's sexual powers and denial that any sexuality is appropriate for women.[1]

Pope seems to have felt a lifelong need to degrade Venus, but the signature of what may be personal frustration imprinted upon his Venus imagery also suggests the procrustean heterosexual norms becoming increasingly problematic for eighteenth-century men. That women had not been significantly weakened is suggested by Pope's diatribes against them, in that he emphasizes their strengths rather than their weaknesses. In his *Moral Essay II* (1735), for example, he criticizes "The Love of Pleasure" as one of women's "Ruling Passions" and "the Love of Sway," equally terrifying. His portrayal of Venus as a kind of sensual mugwump, half modest and half alluring, has a lot to do with men's desire to control women; however, before the nineteenth century this desire did not yet include the need to consider the ideal woman asexual.

The Loathsome Venus

Although in the nineteenth century wilder romantic gardens replaced the Augustan land-scaped enclosures, poets continued to be fascinated by statues of Venus, to which they addressed prayers and hymns. The Venus archetype became a popular subject of poetry after the unearthing of two statues of Venus in the mid-nineteenth century: the Venus of Milo in 1820 and the Venus of Medici in 1830. Many English poets viewed the statues, which were put on display in the Louvre and the Vatican. Although a number of male poets produced celebrations of Venus inspired by these statues,[2] they moved others to condemn feminine sexuality as intrinsically evil.

The Venus of Milo is an Aphrodite figure facing forward, naked to just above her pudendum, beneath which she is modestly clad in a kind of loose drapery. Although this work is considered by many art historians to be one of the most beautiful of classical sculptures, for a number of nineteenth-century British poets it elicits profound distaste. Wilfred S. Blunt, Edward Rowland Sill, and Madison Cawein, for example, were profoundly disturbed by the statue. Blunt's sonnet "The Venus of Milo" (1881) is a perplexed and ambivalent prayer asking her "What art thou? Woman? Goddess? Aphrodite?" and insisting that "never such as thou from the cold foam / Of ocean, nor from cloudy heaven might come." He postulates an alternative Aphrodite as the statue's prototype, one whose sensuality is subordinate to male desire,

The Venus of Milo *Courtesy of the Musée du Louvre, Paris.*

> Who was begotten on her bridal night
> In passionate Earth's womb by Man's delight,
> When Man was young

and in whom he "cannot trace Time's handiwork," namely the features of the Venus of Milo which he sees as "ravished, broken, and thy face / Writ with ancient passions." He dislikes this older passion, preferring a Venus who would be "dumb / To my new love" (54). Sill displays a similar split between an idealized Aphrodite and a maligned one. In "The Venus of Milo" (1883) he contrasts Praxiteles' vision of an "unsullied" "great Aphrodite" in the Venus of Milo to another "form that / Cnidos gave / To senile Rome, no longer free or brave—" (1–2), namely, the Venus of Medici. To my eye, the Medici Venus is a lovely naked figure of a woman slightly inclined forward and covering her pudendum with her hand, but Sill declares her sullied by "Persia's touch," "unclean." Sill's distinction between lust and ennobled love may derive in part from the ambiguity of eighteenth-century poetic conventions about Venus, but I do not think that he is either as ambivalent as his predecessors or as accepting of feminine sensuality as the writers of the medieval period. Rather, the nineteenth-century condemnation of all feminine sexuality as unnatural in and of itself revives the medieval dichotomy between love and lust in a much less healthy fashion: all sexual love is to be feared; only asexual women can be trusted. I see this not merely as a symptom of ill will toward women but also as a psychologically destructive internalization of new sexual norms which deny the authenticity of sensual pleasure for anyone.

The impact of this split between normal sexual pleasure and Victorian prohibition against sensuality for both men and women can be seen in George Henry Boker's sonnet sequence "On Profane Love" (1861–77). In this series of painful love poems the normally lusty poet condemns himself for "The satyr nature [which] riots in my blood," a perfectly normal passion, which he believes sullies "the whiteness of my darling's love," in that it makes her, if she responds, like him, which will "my darker self reprove / Beneath the eyes of her calm purity" (363). In Boker's anguish we can see what happens when a male poet accepts the norm of purity, an absolute sexlessness or "guiltlessness," for the woman he desires: the result is a double bind or no-win concept of love which is inherently destructive for both partners.

Where Blunt, Sill, and Boker feel personally ashamed of their desire, other poets project their shame onto the archetype itself, blaming Venus for her own nature. In these poems the loathing that underlay Oppenheimer's and St. John Rivers's poems about Medusa emerges, with sensual women accused of intrinsic depravity. In Madison Cawein's diatribe against "The Paphian Venus" (1887), for example, a Juvenalian gynophobia marks the extreme negative range of the scale of attitudes toward the archetype: he exudes disgust for "The Paphian goddess on her obscene throne," "Venus Mylitta born of filth and flame," on her boat belonging to a "Chaldean Mylidoth" who conflates Aphrodite, the whore of Babylon, and Medusa, "Whose feet take hold on darkness and despair / Hissing destruction in her heart and hair" (256, 257). Cawein reduces Eros to either spiritualized and disembodied asexual love, on one hand, or pure filth, on the other, much more in the manner of the church fathers than of the less destructive understanding of good and bad sensuality which had only recently been widespread in Europe.

Dante Gabriel Rossetti provides a good example of the kind of angel/demon polarity which Auerbach posited, worshipping a "Blessed Damozel," who leans over the porch of heaven and incorporates many aspects of the Virgin Mary, and expressing his loathing, in contrast, for Liliths and Sibyls, who are seductresses and tempters. Thus in "Venus Verticordia" (which means Venus of Chastity, Venus as the angelic Mary who is supposed to protect women's purity), written in 1881, Rossetti first tells his reader that this Venus "has the apple in her hand for thee," associating her with Eve the temptress, then insists:

> But if she give the fruit that works her spell,
> Those eyes shall flame as for her Phrygian boy.
> Then shall her bird's strained throat the woe foretell,
> And her far seas moan as a single shell,
>
> And through her dark grove strike the light of Troy.
> (*Rossetti's Poems*, 143)

The apple associates this temptress with Eve, with Helen (whose sensuality led to the fall of Troy), and, implicitly, with the wicked queen who tries to kill Snow White. Her flaming eyes suggest a conflation of Venus's potent glance with Medusa's deadly eye, and the reference to bird anatomy seems to be a negative fragment of the Aphrodite/Old European bird goddess, with Rossetti's disgust and terror similar to Neumann's over the bird-clawed Venus.

Thus at the gynophobic extreme of my scale of attitudes we find poets loathing Aphrodite, an attitude most vividly exemplified by Algernon Swinburne's "Laus Veneris," written in 1850, which reflects the popular Wagnerian opera of the 1840s. At the head of his poem Swinburne cites a sixteenth-century version of the Tannhäuser Venusberg narratives (a variation on a widespread European myth also found in the folklore of Italy, Greece, France, Denmark, Norway, Iceland, Sweden, and Wales), immediately derived from Thuringian legends of the end of the fourteenth century. Medieval legend located a pagan shrine, or Venusberg, in a magical mountain, the Horselberg (as well as in several other German towns) and recounted the way the courtly love poet Tannhäuser was lured to his doom there by a love goddess. When Tannhäuser becomes disgusted with sexual pleasure he leaves Venus's underground cavern to go on a pilgrimage to Rome to pray for forgiveness, but the pope refuses to pardon him and he has to return to be enslaved by Venus for all eternity.

Tannhäuser's Venus is undoubtedly a variation on underground and underwater goddesses (like the Lorelei), who remained in folklore long after the Christianization of Europe. The word *Hörsel*, for example, is a variation on Urcel or Ercel, a pagan European moon goddess (perhaps Christianized as Saint Ursula in German hagiography). In *The Wild Man Within*, Edward Dudley and Maximillian Novak talk about European legends of a wild woman "covered with hair except for her gross pendant breasts which she threw over her shoulders when she ran. This wild woman, however, was supposed to be obsessed by a desire for ordinary men. In order to seduce the unwary knight or shepherd, she would appear as the most enticing of women, revealing her abiding ugliness only during sexual intercourse" (21).

As I shall demonstrate in part three, these legendary wild women conflated with Diana or Artemis played an important, and by no means always negative, role in poetry by both men and women; in Swinburne, however, the natural sensuality of the archetype is terrifying to the male hero, threatening Tannhäuser with an engulfing and voracious feminine sexual appetite. Swinburne's Venus nonetheless retains many of her Aphroditian characteristics, being as "Fair stil," for example, "as when she came out of the naked sea," and it is this "beauty of her" that is most threatening.

Although "Laus Veneris" was written before Darwin's ideas had engendered religious doubts among intellectuals, archaeological evidences of goddess worship were beginning to instill male poets with alarm at the idea of overpowering pagan female divinities very much like Swinburne's Venus. With archaeologists and myth scholars reporting not only a monotheistic "Great Goddess" but also male consorts she ritually and periodically puts to death, male poets found the "Great Goddess" terrifying; their fears were inevitably intensified by nineteenth-century culture's insistence that female sensuality was intrinsically anomalous, so that men approaching any but the most sexless of women would become frightened not only of their own "lustful tendencies" but of feminine desires considered monstrous. As we shall see in the next chapter, twentieth-century male poets were influenced by this terror of powerful and sexual goddess archetypes.

Feminist scholars, confronted by loathsome Venuses, "Beautiful/ Terrible Goddesses," and angel/demon polarities, quite naturally see them as stereotypes, targets for deconstruction, rather than empowering archetypes. I hope to have demonstrated that fear and loathing represent only the extreme of a scale which includes far more ambivalent portraits of Venus as well as celebrations of her. I would hypothesize that the Venus/Aphrodite archetype does not have its origin in the male brain or in European patriarchy but originates in perennial human instincts or drives responsive to a Golden Aphrodite whose power to bring about a normal human sensuality, both heterosexual and homosexual, is hard for us, divided from history by Victorian miasmas, to comprehend.

| The Women Poets: Subversive Strategies |

The idea that literary archetypes are masculine products owes a lot to the paucity of women's texts available for study until recently, an absence which led Virginia Woolf to conclude that if we want to know what women wrote about in the Renaissance we will have to invent an imaginary "Shakespeare's Sister." Even before Shakespeare, however, as recent feminist scholarship has disclosed, there were a number of women poets. The women troubadours, for example, developed a school of poetry of their own, celebrating themselves and their sexual potential in a manner reminiscent of Inanna. Meg Bogin, in her *Women Troubadours,* demonstrates the way women poets took advantage of their legal rights of inheritance and their husbands' absence on crusades to develop a school of love poetry less metaphysical and abstract than men's, and more personal, subjective, and direct about their feelings for their lovers. The situations they select, as well as their manner, Bogin comments, are "strikingly different from their male counterparts. Their verse is rhymed, but there is less word play and less interest in the exercise of craft than in the men's poems; the women prefer the straightforward speech of conversation. Perhaps this is because the women write about the relationships that are immediately recognizable to us; they do not worship men, nor do they seem to want to be adored themselves" (13). Bogin points out that the troubadours, like the Catharist sect which also flourished in the region, "considered women and men equals" and enjoyed debating about the impact of sexual equality in "tensons," a form of dialogue poem.

In *Eleanor of Aquitaine: A Biography* Marion Meade points to factors that may account for the survival of earlier attitudes about female sexuality in the Middle Ages. Not only could women in Aquitaine inherit land and in many cases control its use; many of these women differed from "their counterparts in the northern countries" by refusing "to be segregated among themselves or secluded in convents and, if discovered with a lover, they were neither shut up nor killed. . . . In sex, sex roles, and religion, there was to be found a greater degree of tolerance in Aquitaine, a greater respect for the individual" (6). The popularity of love poetry in the region was fostered by Eleanor's grandfather William, whose attitude toward love was entirely secular, without a strain of Platonism. Although patriarchal backlash against women increased markedly during her time, Eleanor managed to ride on a crusade, administer England and large parts of France, and establish in Aquitaine a court of love where women, in Meade's words, might "reign as goddesses or at the least mistresses of their own destinies." Eleanor spent many years in prison at her second husband's behest; later periods read her legendary sexual adventures as reprehensible. The backlash against the sensuality and political acumen of such women, who attempted to act as agents of their own desires and to achieve political as well as sexual sway, was intense and swift; it came from the northern and more patriarchal fiefs in combination with papal edicts calling for the Fourth Crusade, which occurred in the same year as Eleanor's death, 1204, and led to the extermination not only of the Albigensians but also of the sensual school of Provençal poetry, partially through the measure of forcing the wives and women of the vanquished to marry northern husbands. It is interesting that it is this same group of crusaders who, according to Paul Friedrich, were responsible for the public burning of many of Sappho's manuscripts, which demonstrated the same kind of direct, joyous worship of Aphrodite as the poems of the women troubadours.

In the Renaissance, Shakespeare had "sisters" who felt free not only to write about but to celebrate love, even to address poems directly to Venus. In *The Paradise of Women* Betty Travitsky describes this period as one in which the education of women and women's writing activities increased markedly in Britain (4), largely under the influence of the humanistic philosophy of education brought to England by Catherine of Aragon, the first wife of Henry VIII. Catherine was concerned with the education of her daughter, Mary Tudor, who became queen of England in 1553. Ironically, Henry VIII's frantic efforts to produce a male heir led not only to Mary's succession but also to Elizabeth I's in 1558, and contributed to a humanistic reformation which valued education for women.

In the British Museum there is a manuscript of Christine de Pisan's *Oeuvres poetiques*, filled with marginalia depicting women warriors, goddesses, queens, and wives dashing about the countryside doing odd things, like hitting their husbands over the head with distaffs and playing with snakes. The similarly comic feminine marginalia of the Bayeux tapestry suggest that women used the edges of patriarchal artifacts to play about with anarchic possibilities, but Christine de Pisan's manuscript centers on the goddess archetype. One illustrated page is filled with an illuminated Venus sitting on a cloud that looms hugely over a crowd of awed worshippers. Little red hearts are arranged in a circle on her ample lap, and a group of men are receiving similar hearts and offering more up to her. The illustration thus is very similar to the Veronese tray depicting Venus's worshippers, and involves a syncretism of Mary, the sacred heart of Jesus (now located in Venus's lap), prayer, and petition, all for the secular end of a religion of love.

Aphrodite in Medieval through Nineteenth-Century Poetry

Christine de Pisan authored many poems in the courtly manner, some from a woman's perspective, some from a male point of view, and many tensons or debate poems in which both sexes engage in dialogues about secret love, adulterous affairs, and how men and women are to achieve equity in their devotion to each other. Although she is sometimes taken as an isolated example of an active woman poet of the Renaissance, she is not the only poet whose humanistic education and aristocratic status permitted her to compose in this genre. Queen Elizabeth of York (1465–1503) wrote a startlingly forthright prayer to Venus in which she seems to be celebrating the successful consummation of a love affair:

> My heart is set upon a lusty pin.
> I Pray to Venus of good continuance,
> For I rejoice the case that I am in,
> Delivered from sorrow, annexed to plesance

Elizabeth addresses Venus as "a very lantern to all other light" and "Very mirror and star of womanhead," using the archetypal imagery of the sun and the morning star, as well as Venus's mirror, in the courtly mode of thanks for a petition granted and continuing fealty pledged: "My hearty service with my attendance / So to continue it ever I may please" (Stanford, *Women Poets* 16–17).

Mary, Queen of Scots, was well known as a composer of both devotional and courtly love lyrics. Queen Elizabeth I not only wrote courtly love poems but also skillfully applied archetypal imagery to herself in order to enhance her powerful image. She conducted royal tours about the countryside costumed as a "faery queen," using feminine imagery from Celtic sources; she had her portrait painted as a cosmic goddess, standing on a map of Europe with lightning striking on one side of her and sun shining on the other; and she had herself portrayed playing with snakes. Her clothing was embroidered solidly with snakes, lions, tigers, butterflies, birds, even little insects, as if she were trying to empower herself by absorbing the Lady of the Wild Things, or Artemis, into her personality. She declared herself married to her country, and poems of praise written to her sometimes read like prayers to Inanna.

Thus Diana Primrose identifies herself as "Thy Emperiall Majesties etern Votary" and addresses her 1630 hymn of praise to

Great ELIZA, England's brightest Sun,
The Worlds Renowne and everlasting Lampe. . . .
Thou English Goddesse, Emprese of our Sex,

whom she endows with the source of life-enhancing "bemes" in the
same manner as Chaucer's "Joves daughter dere":

So did Eliza cast Her Golden Rayes
Of Clemency, on those which many wayes
Transgrest Her Laes.

Primrose also compares Elizabeth to God, who, in the Neoplatonic
manner, "exceeds," or overflows from, his being, forgiving "His very
Rebells" by "Lending them the light / Of Sunne and Moone, and all
those Diamonds bright" (Travitsky 111–12). Aristocratic women's
participation in culture included writing poetry during a period when
knowledge of the classics as well as individualized reading of the Bible
was encouraged for both sexes. This positive situation existed only for
women of the upper class, but in English culture as a whole feminine
sexuality was far more valued in earlier than in later periods. Marilyn
Williamson, introducing her facsimile edition of Frederick Rowton's
1853 *Female Poets of Great Britain,* cites Ruth M. Bloch's analysis of
the evolution of modern sex roles to argue that between 1550 and
1850 there was a redefinition of sex roles for the "evolving English
middle classes."

In the sixteenth and seventeenth century Protestantism encouraged
the conception that women are similar, if inferior to men; previously
accepted qualitative distinctions between the sexes gradually lost
favor to quantitative ones. Human nature then was seen as the same
in both men and women, although women were, theologically and
theoretically, subservient to men. This view persisted. . . . In the late
eighteenth century, however, this assumption gradually gave way to
such concepts of polarity and distinctness of sexual character as
Rowton does in his introduction to *The Female Poets of Great Britain.*
By Rowton's time, society had assigned each sex a qualitatively sepa-
rate sphere, although the spheres were deemed complementary by
many writers—even equal by some. These perceptions of sexual char-
acter had a powerful effect on the audience a woman envisioned for
her poetry, on how she perceived herself as a poet, on the kind of

career she could make as a writer, even on the kind of subjects about which she thought fit to write.

During these centuries, for example, women gradually stopped writing poetry about sexual love. In the seventeenth century it was a permissible theme for Phillips, Killigrew, and Behn, but by the end of the eighteenth century the theme of sexual love had been replaced by mother love and domestic relationships. Most of the poems written about male-female relationships after that time celebrate a transcendence of the physical. (xi–xii)

I have cited Williamson at length because she and Bloch offer a hypothesis about the evolution and variation in sex roles and expectations about feminine sensuality which varies in important ways from the theory of static, timelessly similar norms we often find in critiques of patriarchy. During the earlier periods, when sexuality was not defined as unfeminine, women could be as wary about Venus as men, although their wariness took quite a different form from the split Venuses in male poetry. They tended to satirically parody masculine literary conventions, developing strategies for writing about love which sometimes enabled them to celebrate Venus but more often enabled them to subvert contemporary sexual norms. Among these strategies were making addresses to a god rather than a goddess of love; using the tenson, or love debate, to provide an outlet for resentment; using the persona of the woman "disappointed in love," which gives the poet permission to pour out her passion; and, spiritualizing or sublimating desire, which enables the poet to be simultaneously sensual and acceptably spiritual.

We have seen how male poets sometimes created narratives in which Venus was compelled to submit to a male love god. This divinity was no mere baby Cupid but derived from the pre-Olympian theology described by Hesiod, where he was one of the four Titans—Chaos, Gaea, Tartarus, and Eros (Campbell, *Occidental Mythology* 234–35). He is not immediately derived from Adonis or from the consort of Middle Eastern goddesses, although some of this archetypal content is undoubtedly latent in the figure, but is part of what C. S. Lewis describes as the "love religion of the god Amor," popularized in Ovid's *Ars Amatoria,* an "erotic religion" which "arises as a rival or a parody of the real religion and emphasizes the antagonism of the two ideals" (17–18).

Although women have sometimes used an archetype which elsewhere I have called "the green world lover" (*Archetypal Patterns in Women's Fiction* 22–24)—an archetype that conflates Adonis, Pan, the pagan "horned god," and the Middle Eastern consort/lover—the "God of Love" women poets petition in early modern Europe serves more as an object of complaint than of praise. Thus the God of Love to whom Christine de Pisan addresses "L'Epistre au dieu d'amour" (1399), a letter of complaint about the mistreatment of women by Renaissance male writers, belongs to this category, as does the male figure sitting heartlessly upon his throne who becomes the satiric target of Aphra Behn's "Song, Love Armed" (1684):

> Love in fantastic triumph sat
> Whilst bleeding hearts around him flow'd,
> For whom fresh paines he did create,
> And strange tyrannic power he show'd.
> (Bernikow 69)

Behn takes responsibility, along with her lover, for letting the tyrannical God of Love into their lives, but she insists that she comes off far the worse as a woman:

> Thus thou and I the god have arm'd
> And set him up a deity;
> But my poor heart alone is harm'd
> Whilst thine the victor is, and free. (70)

By marking the difference between women's suffering and men's easier victories in love, Behn subverts the respectful prayer convention in order to accuse the love god of unfairness. In "Song" (1670), similarly, Frances Boothby cries out to "you powerful Gods!" her complaint about being "An injur'd offering to Love's deity," and asks for revenge on the God of love in the form of a "plague on men / That woman n'er may love again." She begs the gods to "Depose that proud insulting boy, / Who most is pleased when he can most destroy," so that the world will no longer be governed by "such a blind and childish Deity!" The final verse is filled with blame and rage:

> But if you'll his divinity maintain,
> O'er men, false men, confine his torturing reign;

And when their hearts love's greatest torments prove,
Let that not pity, but our laughter move.
Thus scorn'd and lost to all their wishes aim,
Let Rage, Despair, and Death, then end their flame.
      (Williamson 78)

Katherine Philips (1631–64) writes a similar poem, "Against Love," in which she exhorts Cupid to go away ("Hence Cupid") in a kind of rite of riddance which will free her from his "cheating toys" and his "pleasure which itself destroys." The kind of love that Philips can do without results from "Men's weakness" which permits them to endow Cupid "power by their fear" (Stanford, *Women Poets* 59). It is much better to get rid of Cupid than for a woman to be mired in his toils. Anne Killegrew's "Complaint of a Lover" (1685) and Philips's "Ode against Pleasure" are in the same tradition (Williamson 83–85, 67–68).

Behn, Boothby, and Philips are "talking back" to a male god with whose behavior they express displeasure, a mode which reaches its most hilariously satiric form in Behn's "Disappointment" (1684), a travesty upon the pastoral convention in which a shepherd makes love to his bucolic female companion. To the archetypalist it is striking that Behn seems to be satirizing a temple of Venus. In an extended metaphor she likens women's private parts to the "altar" in such a temple, with the shepherd's "daring hand" grabbing "that Altar . . . Where Gods of love do sacrifice: / That awful throne, that Paradice / Where Rage is calm'd, and Anger pleas'd" (Bernikow 73). The daring Behn describes woman's pudendum as "That Fountain where Delight still flows, / And gives the Universal World Repose." The parody turns on the shepherd's impotence; he is "Unable to perform the sacrifice" (74). Behn seems to be parodying sacred sexual rites, and as we shall see in the case of Christina Rossetti's "Birthday," some vestige of a lost love ritual seems to go along with the idea of love divinities. Behn completely subverts pastoral sensuality with the unsuccessful male "damn'd to the hell of impotence," while the shepherdess flees from his limp member.

Women poets sometimes talked back in subversive love poetry to real male poets who had displeased them. Mary Oxlie of Morpet, for example, was the muse or subject of many of William Drummond's love lyrics. Drummond was a typically ambivalent seventeenth-century poet of the split Venus tradition who on one hand could write "Idmon to Venus" (1616) using the conventional prayer form to beg the Queen of Love to quench his torch and to promise her garlands in return for this service, and on the other hand could write "The Statue of Venus Sleeping" (1616) in which Venus becomes a kind of comatose horror whose eyes blind the man who awakens her. Oxlie managed to get back at Drummond by accusing him of idealizing her unfairly, having "so far surpast her Feature" in praise of her that others are falling in love with her as a result.

In the eighteenth century both Ann Finch and Lady Mary Wortley Montagu talked back in much stronger terms to Alexander Pope. Finch wrote "The Answer to Pope's Impromptu" (1741) in which she warns him that if he does not stop criticizing women he will meet the fate of Orpheus:

> Yet venturing then with scoffing rhimes
> The women to incense,
> Resenting Heroines of those times
> Soon punished his offence. (Bernikow 84–85)

Montagu, similarly, attacks Pope's *First Satire on the Second Book of Horace* (1733), characterizing his wit as "an oyster-knife that hacks and hews; / The rage but not the talent to abuse" (Bernikow 93). Using the same kind of chiasmas, or rhetorical crisscrossing of antithetical elements, popularized by Pope, Montagu likens his rage to the debased lust of the brothel. Like Behn, Montagu is using laughter to burst the bubble of male erotic pretensions. Her hilarious "Virtue in Danger: A Lamentable Story How a Vertyous Lady had like to have been Ravished by her Sister's Footman" (1721), to be sung "To the Tune of the Children in the Wood," provides an apt reply to Pope's satire of Belinda's behavior in *The Rape of the Lock* (see Stanford, *Women Poets* 216–21).

Finch and Montagu were not always negative on the subject of love—Finch wrote a poem in imitation of Sappho, and Montagu used the persona of Catullus in a love poem to Lesbia—but they were clearly angered by unfair standards in sexuality. They were probably responding to the residue of clerical distaste for feminine sexuality reinforced by Puritanism. By the nineteenth century, however, radically reduced permission for women's sensuality accompanied the ascendancy of the middle classes, whose women now had to present themselves on the marriage/property market hitherto experienced only by the landowning aristocracy. The concept of "qualitatively different sexual spheres" documented by Williamson was reinforced by the weight of revived religious seriousness, to make it dangerous for women to write about their sensuality at all.

In this atmosphere, women who declared themselves "disappointed in love," survivors of relationships terminated by the death or desertion of their suitors, had a corner on sensual expression. Cheryl Walker suggests that nineteenth-century women poets used "the theme of the forbidden lover," a lost or dead or otherwise inaccessible suitor. It is "out of this experience of deprivation, this secret sorrow, this desire for the forbidden" that "they construct—though not necessarily consciously—a value system that applauds displacement of appetite" (93). Walker concludes that poems about "forbidden lovers" express the woman poet's desire for "worldly power" sublimated into lyrics passionately addressed to the departed suitor.

Since in the period following the Renaissance there are few poems by women celebrating sensuality outright, it is especially surprising to find Christina Rossetti writing a love celebration analogous to the Sumerian songs about intercourse and to seventeenth-century epithalamia, though with no reference whatsoever to marriage. Although her most frequent persona was the disappointed lover, in "A Birthday" (1861) she orders her bed/throne prepared with a delight as imperious as Inanna's:

> Raise me a dais of silk and down;
> Hang it with vair and purple dyes,
> Carve it with doves and pomegranates,
> And peacocks with a hundred eyes;
> Work it in gold and silver grapes,
> In leaves and silver fleur-de-lys;
> Because the birthday of my life
> Is come, my love is come to me.
> (*Complete Poems*, vol. 1, 36–37)

This is not an isolated case of Aphroditian celebration in Rossetti's work. In "Venus's Looking-Glass" (1875) she describes the goddess of love in positive terms, using masquelike imagery of "lovely Venus and her court" who "With song and dance and merry laugh went by" in a procession.

With Rossetti we arrive at a level of consciousness about the normal sensuality inherent in Aphrodite that we will find marking the archetypal signature of twentieth-century poets who achieve a poetry of sexual delight. This consciousness, I would suggest, intensifies the tone of Rossetti's "talking back" sonnet sequence, "Donna Innominata: A Sonnet of Sonnets," in which she uses the personas of the "unnamed ladies" addressed by poets from "that land and that period which gave simultaneous birth to Catholics, to Albigenses, and to Troubadours," where "one can imagine many a lady as sharing her lover's poetic aptitude." In an enigmatic declaration (perhaps designed to obscure the strength of her conviction) she goes on to declare: "Or had the Great Poetess of our own day and nation [Browning] only been unhappy instead of happy, her circumstances would have invited her to bequeath to us, in lieu of the 'Portuguese Sonnets,' an inimitable 'donna innominata' drawn not from fancy but from feeling, and worthy to occupy a niche beside Beatrice and Laura" (Bernikow 126–27). Since she herself is "unhappy," or disappointed in love, and since her "imaginary persona" is distant historically from the nineteenth century, Rossetti can strongly enunciate women's desire for equity in love:

> "Love me, for I love you"—and answer me,
> "Love me, for I love you": so shall we stand
> As happy equals in the flowering land
> Of love, that knows not a dividing sea.
> (*Complete Poems*, vol. 2, 89)

From sitting as a model for Dante Gabriel Rossetti's Virgin Mary, Rossetti must have been acutely aware of how the revival of the medieval Virgin Mary felt to real women. Bernikow suggests that she "observed the actualization of the Pre-Raphaelite idealization of haunted, ethereal female beauty, and saw how it destroyed, disembodied, laid waste both the woman Elizabeth [Siddons] who was its object and the brother Dante who was its victim" (32). The position of single woman in the family who is "disappointed in love" enabled Christina Rossetti to write more passionately and directly than many other women poets of her century.

Like Rossetti, Emily Dickinson constructed the public persona of recluse, then subverted the evangelical Calvinism of western Massachusetts revivals in much the same way that Rossetti undercut neo-medieval Anglo-Catholicism. Dickinson perfected both the talking back and the disappointed lover modes in poetry. She gains permission to be intensely passionate in poems such as "Wild Nights—Wild Nights" (c. 1861), while in "He fumbles at your Soul" (c. 1862) she talks back as a disgruntled lover of God himself, whom she satirizes as a brutal, ineffective rapist whose attempts to "scalp your naked Soul" must be resisted. In "Title Divine" (c. 1862) she boldly claims "as mine!" an entitlement to revere nature through the ruse of being "married" to a God she renounces for the minute particulars of the earth. Her only authentic conversion is to her own vocation as poet, which occurred as a "Conversion of the Mind" when she first read "that Foreign Lady," her fellow woman poet Elizabeth Barrett Browning. It is important to note that in spite of her passionate allegiance to wildness and nature, Dickinson addresses no poems to Venus.

Among the few Venus poems by nineteenth-century women are a few about the Venus of Milo, as ambivalent as those by male poets but marked by gender difference. Sarah Helen Whitman (who incidentally was rescued at the last minute from marrying Edgar Allen Poe) apostrophizes the Venus of Milo as "Goddess of dreams" but conflates her with the Virgin Mary as "mother of love and sorrow" ("The Venus of Milo," 1868). Whereas male poets of the period were either ashamed of the statue's sensuality or denounced it as monstrous, Whitman replaces the Venus who presided over medieval courts of love with a figure who rules only over love's pain, giving the gift of calm in the face of "Such love as from love's martyrdom doth borrow / That conquering calm which only sorrow knows," implying that by the later nineteenth century passionate love has become an entirely negative experience. The deep background cannot be entirely eradicated, however. Whitman acknowledges the lost glory of Aphrodite beneath the spiritualized "Venus, Madonna!":

More fair than when of old thy sea-born splendor
Surprised the senses of Olympian Jove!

Not these the lips, that kindling into kisses,
    Poured subtle heats through Adon's languid frame,
Rained on his sullen lips their warm caresses,
    Thrilled to his heart and turned its frost to flame. (198–200)

157

Like Sills, Blunt, and Cawein, Whitman insists that Aphrodite be neutered of ancient associations. There is no blaming here and certainly no loathing, rather a muted grief that thrilling "warm caresses" now only lead to pain and that the only thing a woman can do is transcend "passion's wild illusion."

Emma Lazarus, whose fondness for statuary of powerful women led to her composition of "The New Colossus," the poem hailing the Statue of Liberty ("Give me your tired, your poor . . ."), wrote "Venus of the Louvre" (the Venus of Milo) in positive terms but felt it necessary to address Venus using the persona of Heinrich Heine, a male poet. By yoking her grief about Venus with Heine's, she is able to lament the goddess's diminished status: once a "foam-born mother of love" but "maimed" now by "Time's brutal hand." Lazarus nonetheless acknowledges the Venus as an enthralling enchantress,

> Serenely poised on her world-worshipped throne,
> As when she guided once her dove-drawn car,—
> But at her feet a pale, death-stricken Jew,
> Her life adorer, sobbed farewell to love.
> Here Heine wept! Here still he weeps anew. (Bernikow, 214)

It is, however, the male poet who is doing the grieving while Lazarus encodes her feminine identity as "one ardent heart" left to weep "For vanished Hellas and Hebraic pain" (219). One suspects that she is also encoding resistance to anti-Semitism, which was intensifying during this period.

It is important that Emma Lazarus feels that she must yoke herself with Heine before she can write a poem about Venus, as if Venus were a suitable subject only for male poetry. If a woman poet was successful, other women assumed that it was because she was not really a woman, but had a "masculine" mind. Thus in a sonnet addressed to George Sand, Elizabeth Barrett Browning, unable to conceive of genius and sexuality as feminine, apostrophizes Sand as "Thou large-brained woman, and large-hearted man" in one sonnet, while in another sonnet she declares that the price for being "true genius" and "true woman" simultaneously is an uncomfortable transvestism which will only be resolved when "God unsex thee on the heavenly shore / Where unincarnate spirits purely aspire" (103). Although Browning has a popular reputation as a successful woman love poet, her attitude to Aphrodite and to romantic love is riven with contradiction. In her

1844 poetry collection she denounces the pagan qualities in Greek gods and goddesses, concluding the volume with "The Dead Pan," in which she exults in the overthrow of the Olympian divinities and in their subordination to Christ and to Christian values. She happily describes Aphrodite as defeated along with her fellow gods and goddesses, "dead and driven / As thy native foam thou art!" (189).

By eloping with Robert Browning from her unwilling father's house, Browning, like George Eliot, put herself in an extremely questionable social position, from which she extricated herself in 1847 by writing "Sonnets from the Portuguese," in which she substitutes spiritual for physical passion and tries to demonstrate that Robert and not she took all of the initiative. Although acutely aware of the period's double standard (which she satirized in 1846 in "Lord Walker's Wife" and "A Man's Requirements," which Thackeray rejected for publication as too risqué), she created in her sonnets a persona sufficiently subordinate to Robert and self-effacing in love to allow for their publication. First, she declares that "Love" first appeared to her as "a mystic Shape" which came up "Behind me, and drew me backward by the hair" (Sonnet I, 214–15) while she "strove" against him. This combines the archetype of Eros as a masculine God and her helpless feminine submission to him, and establishes Browning as suitably modest, and by no means taking the initiative in courtship. It is Robert who is set up as master, with Browning as "a poor, tired, wandering singer" rescued by his "Princely heart" (Sonnet III, 215). She resists his advances, pleading her own unworthiness, for nine more sonnets. Finally, in the tenth, she accepts the passionate love between them, only to insist in the sestet that their romance is part of a "great work of Love" that really belongs to God. Subordinate to Robert and to God, Browning demures that "I should not love withal, unless that thou / Hadst set me an example, shown me how" (Sonnet XII, 217), clearing herself of the crime of being sexually "forward." Thus in the thirteenth sonnet she refuses Robert's request to write about love (this declaration, ironically enough, consisting of a love sonnet), using the excuse that gender norms prohibit her as a woman from expressing erotic sentiment: "Nay, let the silence of my womanhood / Commend my woman love to thy belief,—" (217). Even for this "happy love poet," "womanhood" requires poetic silence, a silence which she breaks only by constant apologies for doing so. As Gilbert and Gubar have pointed out, she "was praised for her blameless sexual life" by a culture convinced that "sexuality and female genius" were a dangerous combination which might set off uncontrollable explosions of female power: "That genius and sexuality *are* diseases in women, diseases akin to madness" (569). Although Browning's later judgment on the double standard in *Aurora Leigh* shows a growth in critical consciousness about the inequity of gender roles in courtship, she has been remembered popularly as a poet of the kind of inequitable heterosexual love her sonnets display.

With major women poets like Browning delighted that Venus is dead and apologizing for their sexual authenticity, it seems clear that the Aphrodite archetype had fallen on very bad times during the nineteenth century. The daring and triumphant Inanna, Queen of Heaven and celebrant of intercourse, seems to have been degraded not only by male but also by female poets into either a sexless and angelic maternal figure or a monster of feminine depravity.

The degradation and spiritualization of the Aphrodite archetype was destructive to men as well as to women. A few weeks before Shelley died, he wrote to Elizabeth Hitchener: "I think one is always in love with something or other; the error, and I confess it, consists in seeking in a mortal image the likeness of what is perhaps eternal. . . . Nor do I risk the supposition that the lump of organized matter which enshrines thy soul excites the love which the soul alone dare claim." He is writing to a woman who, as Nina Epton recounts it, "went to live in the Shelley household for four painful months—after which she was ignominiously dismissed" (278). Here we have the same kind of sublimation of Eros into a transcendent abstraction we saw in Chaucer and Spenser: although Hitchener is clearly the principal victim of Shelley's spiritualization of sensuality, characterized as a mere "lump of matter" which provides the occasion for his entirely bodiless and idealized "love," Shelley degrades his psyche by conceiving of himself and his own body, as well as Elizabeth's, as unworthy. The denial of nature, of one's own body, of the immanence of sensuality, is psychologically destructive (albeit in different ways) for both men and women.

The Aphrodite archetype, in my hypothesis, derives from a normal and pleasureful experience of sex. When a culture degrades it, damage affects both genders, though women are apt to come off worse for the experience. There are male blackbirds in our pie, nonetheless, and not even the king and his male guests are exempt from the sticky, inhibiting crust of patriarchal prescription. In my next chapter I will show how the unhealthy sexual norms of the nineteenth century have a deep impact on male poets of the twentieth century, who continue to be terrified of the polarized "Good/Terrible" stereotype, engulfed by a feminine sexuality they cannot handle, and alienated from their own bodies.

Since the majority of poems about the Aphrodite archetype are by men, the hypothesis that they represent masculine projections rather than any respect for the sensuality of real women is not entirely unwarranted. This postulate, however, depends upon a definition of archetype as a product of the individual psyche, which internalizes a contemporary historical signature without reference either to what is going on in women's minds or to elements of a deeper archetypal background. What if we define archetypes not as intrasubjective or "collective" in the sense of internalized cultural responses but as interpersonal phenomena, the products of relationships *between* persons who are not entirely determined by contemporary culture but responsive to natural instincts? Could we define Aphrodite archetypes as interactions among persons in a field, adapting Fritz Perls's concept of a *mitwelt*, "the common world which you have and the other person has" (6)? Our assumption that the isolated individual represents the pinnacle of psychological health and that autonomy is the ultimate good is, after all, a culturally determined one, quite recent in origin; archetypes were originally shared communally, elements celebrated in stories told around the fire and in ritual enactments. Jean Bolen defines Jung's collective unconscious in terms of synchronicity: "For Synchronicity to happen, the space between individuals and things, rather than being empty, must somehow 'contain' a connecting link or be a transmission medium. Jung calls this the collective unconscious" (*The Tao of Psychology* 36). Using this interactive model of the archetypal process, we could define the Aphrodite archetype as an occurrence between lovers or a communal celebration of sensuality, as in the case of Shakespeare's festive denouements with multiple marriages, for example, or of epithalamia and masques. This common valuation of sexuality is in a constantly dialectical tension with gender norms limiting the instinctive needs of lovers, so that, on one hand, we find premarital chastity limiting Renaissance masques and, on the other, even the sexual prohibitions of the Victorian era modified by a natural delight in sensuality.

161

6.

Aphrodite in Twentieth-Century Poetry by Men

Whether as incidental allusions or narratives shaping poetic structure, archetypes have provided subject matter for generations of male and female poets. Far from being merely decorative or academic conventions, they convey states of mind or psychological attitudes—in the case of Medusa, one's feelings about one's mother and other powerful and authoritative women; in the case of Aphrodite, one's deepest responses to sexuality. Even in the absence of any concrete historical knowledge of the roots of these archetypes in pre-European cultures, poets respond in ways more consonant with non-European attitudes than I expected. I have accounted for these responses by suggesting that the archetypes contain a stimulus which arouses instinctive feelings about them, and that these feelings are not subjective, inherent merely in the individual psyche, but interpersonal, elements in an archetypal field between persons.

In 1894, having blamed Aphrodite's centuries of absence on an "implacable, lean / Horde of ascetics," Grant Allen numbers himself with the "tenderer singers" celebrating her return:

> Under the depth of the wave,
>> Hearing their passionate numbers,
> Piercing her innermost cave,
>> Waken her out of her slumbers,

> Soothed with the sound of their strain,
> Beautiful, merciful, mighty,
> Back to the nations again
> Comes Aphrodite. (13–14)

By the turn of the century a combination of historical, archaeological, and psychoanalytic discoveries had brought the pre-European content of Aphrodite and other goddess archetypes into focus. The combination of sensuality, intellectual acumen, political authority, and reproductive generativity which male poets responded to from Spenser's *Fairie Queene* to the nineteenth-century discovery of Venus statues were now posited as historical realities. This aroused both celebration and terror among male poets who had assimilated the Victorian attitudes to women. The idea that modern consciousness constituted but a thin layer over a substratum of feminine erotic power was not necessarily comforting.

Perhaps the most influential studies of the role of powerful goddess archetypes in ancient history were conducted by J. J. Bachofen, a Swiss scholar who in the 1840s became fascinated by the role of feminine elements in the worship practices of the Etruscans. Although the archaeological evidence was too fragmentary to support his sweeping historical theory, he posited in *Mother Right* (1861) that not only had goddesses been worshipped widely at one time but that an entire stage of human history which he termed "matriarchal" had been characterized by an absolute feminine hegemony. First there had been the stateless Tellurian phase, motherhood without marriage, and no agriculture, a phase of sex and lust he called "hetaerist Aphroditic"; then a Lunar stage of conjugal motherhood, agriculture, and settled communities where "mother right" ruled; and, finally, arising out of a clash of opposites, the Solar or conjugal fatherhood stage, with ownership of property and the development of landless laborers. Although he valued the matriarchal phase and found elements of the anarchical Aphroditian phase admirable, Bachofen described history as progressing from promiscuity through matriarchy to patriarchy. He praised both femininity in general and the chthonic or the earthly features of agricultural and preagricultural societies for the communal virtues which became central to Marx and Engels's similarly dialectical systems. Bachofen's *Ancient Society* (1877) was an important influence on Engels's *Family, Private Property, and the State* (1884).

163

Other myth scholars and archaeologists also were conducting research in the mid- to late nineteenth century who influenced twentieth-century poets' attitudes to matriarchy. In 1882 Sir Arthur Evans arrived to work on Mycenaean archaeological sites first discovered by Heinrich Schliemann, who had been lionized in London in 1877 for his discoveries of artifacts, including many goddess figures. Evans, attracted to Myceanaean history as more vital and interesting than the classical materials dominating Oxford studies at that time, was to modernize the Ashmolean Museum after years of struggle with its more conservative members, who were loath to see their vision of masculine reason and Augustan moderation undermined by the chthonic feminine Evans admired so much. In 1899 Evans discovered on Crete an entire pre-Achaean civilization, and spent the years 1901–30 in excavation and description. His contemporary, J. G. Frazer, kept these materials in the public, and especially the poetic, eye by his popular series *The Golden Bough* (the first two volumes of which were published in 1890), in which he gathered material as evidence of matriarchal systems he documented on a worldwide basis. In Frazer (as implicitly in Bachofen) there is only one monolithic "maternal system," a "matriarchy" of mother right deriving from a figure to whom Frazer and many after him were to refer as "The Mother Goddess." The singular and capitalized title suggests that, seen through late-nineteenth-century patriarchal perspective, the multivariant feminine divinities of polytheistic religions were conflated into one all-powerful, dominant figure, whose orders were carried out hierarchically, in the monotheistic, authoritarian manner of masculine religious systems. This interpretation of religions that had been oriented around gods as well as goddesses overlooks the special impact of polytheism on archetypes and on archetypal responses. It constitutes an anachronistic reading back of Victorian and modern perspectives in a way which distorts the contents of the original archetypes.

Responses to this "Great Mother Goddess," whether in the group form of ritual or the more individualized form of internalized psychological patterns, were the concern of the Cambridge School of classicists, on one hand, and of the new field of psychoanalysis, on the other. At Cambridge, under Jane Ellen Harrison, Gilbert Murray, A. B. Cook, and F. M. Cornford, the ritual basis of myth was studied up to about 1930, fostering Jessie Weston's *From Ritual to Romance* (1920), Maud Bodkin's *Archetypal Patterns in Poetry* (1934), and Emile Durkheim's pioneering sociological studies. U.S. myth scholars such as Joseph Campbell derived their theories directly from the Cambridge School, while U.S. poets drew upon both Frazer and the mytholinguistic theories of Ernst Cassirer.

The mythic work of poets such as Robert Graves, D. H. Lawrence, and Dylan Thomas in England, as of poets such as Conrad Aiken, the Agrarians, and, later in the century, Robert Bly and Gary Snyder in the United States, thus occurred within a context of archaeological studies, myth and art history, new literary theory, and psychoanalysis which emphasized goddess archetypes. Emotional responses to feminine archetypes were the special focus of Jung's theory of the collective unconscious, which was influenced by the work of Bachofen and the revelations of Evans and other archaeological researchers. As I have suggested in the preface, Jung assimilated from his Swiss Victorian upbringing and European academic training a tendency to dualize phenomena and to emphasize their conflictual interactions. On one hand, he arranged phenomena into bipolar categories, while, on the other, he diagnosed polarism as a major symptom of social and psychological dysfunction. In his theory of androgyny as a blend of masculinity and femininity, he posited a postdualistic synthesis in the manner of the historical dialecticians, while undermining his own theory of synthesis because of a terror of powerful femininity inherent in his upbringing and historical period. Thus he described women as not only "other" but terrifyingly different while, paradoxically, he urged the cultivation of "femininity" within the male psyche and of research on the psychology of women.

Jung's disciple Erich Neumann also became known as an authority on the psychology of "the Feminine," and his theories, especially his 1955 study *The Great Mother*, found their way into the prose and poetry of twentieth-century men. His popularity with poets such as Robert Bly seems to have resulted from his articulation of current attitudes about feminine archetypes. I will suggest that his theories reflect the context within which twentieth-century male poets in both England and America develop their responses to the Aphrodite archetype.

Like Jung, Neumann is deeply ambivalent about femininity, an ambivalence embodied in his dichotomous categories of "the good Feminine" and "the bad/terrible Feminine," and in a dialectical theory of history based on antagonism between the earlier "Feminine" and later "Masculine" civilizations: "What Bachofen described as the death character of the material-maternal," he explains, "is an expression of this archetypal domination of nature and the unconscious over life, and likewise over the undeveloped childlike, or youthfully helpless, ego consciousness" (30). We can sense here Neumann's conviction that "Mother Right" involves power/over or one up/one down relationships, and that dominance is a necessary element in social as in mother/son relationships. Although the goal of Neumann's therapy is to integrate the conscious and the unconscious, his historical and personal conditioning leads him to stress their polar and hierarchical relationship. He warns his patients of the peril of having their Egos sucked back "into its womb of origination and death," and insists that a successful psychoanalysis fosters a dialectical working through "positive or negative fascination," "attraction or repulsion" toward assimilation of one's "feminine" tendencies. It is always possible that the patient will be damaged by the unconscious (feminine) forces if he does not succeed in transcending them by the achievement of consciousness.

These simultaneous attractions to and repulsions from "femininity" similarly characterize the approach of many twentieth-century male poets to the Aphrodite figure. It is important to note Neumann's recognition that archetypes such as the "Great Mother" are "psychological realities whose fateful power is still alive in the psychic depths of present-day man" and that "the health and creativity of every man depends largely on whether his consciousness can live at peace with this stratum of the unconscious or consumes itself in strife with it" (43–44). We shall see in this chapter how the "Rebirth of Aphrodite," in Grant Allen's terms, and the advent of the "It girl" (as he termed her), or the free-loving woman, combined with the terror of women, nature, sexuality, and the earth itself to produce twentieth-century poets every bit as gynophobic as Swinburne. I hope to suggest, however, that Jung's and Neumann's identification of gynophobia as a pathology men need to transcend fosters male poets' desire to overcome the intensely destructive gender norms they have internalized.

Fear and loathing of women, especially of women who combine sensuality and intellect, characterizes twentieth-century attitudes as it had Victorian ones. Still convinced that a "good" woman is "pure" or sexless and that a woman demonstrating sexual appetite is a degendered monster, and perhaps in backlash against the insistence of feminists such as Emma Goldman and Margaret Sanger that women should enjoy full autonomy in their sexual relationships, male poets sometimes responded with profound hatred. In a speech in 1971 to the Modern Language Association, Adrienne Rich characterized the world of male poets as infected by gynophobia: "To the eye of the feminist, the work of Western male poets now writing reveals a deep, fatalistic pessimism as to the possibilities of change, whether societal or personal, along with a familiar and threadbare use of women (and nature) as redemptive on the one hand, threatening on the other; and a new tide of phallocentric sadism and overt woman-hating which matches the sexual brutality of recent films" ("When We Dead Awaken" 49).

In my sample of male poets in the twentieth century I do not find this attitude as pervasive as Rich suggests, but it does characterize the works of several poets at the far end of a scale from loathing to reverence for Aphrodite. These poets, who approach the archetype with loathing and horror, are locked in a paralysis which, as I shall demonstrate, other male poets transcend. At this negative end of the spectrum of attitudes toward Aphrodite we find poets whose approach resembles Perseus's toward Medusa, their fear of the love goddess resulting from the same kind of psychological response I described in the first part of this book, in which the male poet seems to be frozen in horror at the conflation of the maternal and the sexual, and writes poems about a fearsome Aphrodite with Medusan attributes.

In "Ode," for example, John Peale Bishop is petrified before the statue of three "sisters," "great women / Who sit / Peering at me with parrot eyes." Although Aphrodite is not specifically identified, the third goddess with "idiot teeth" presides over simultaneously boring and horrific acts of copulation. Bishop suggests that the body, or at least sexuality, is "other," alien to the human consciousness, and he especially loathes the third goddess' message that virgins do not bear sons and that, implicitly, the poet's mother was not a virgin. Horror of intercourse and of powerful women makes Bishop despair that Christ is dead and can no longer save anyone from these powerful archetypes which conflate the sexual and the maternal.

In his description of the digging of these goddesses out of "red Cretan clay" Bishop demonstrates that the turn-of-the-century fascination with the "Great Mother" could (in Neumann's sense) lead to terror as well as to reverence. In "To My Son" George Barker displays a similar fear of the "doom" embodied in the knowledge that one's own mother could engage in intercourse. He informs the poor child of his conception on a May evening, describing sexuality as an awful but inevitable property of the boy's mother, a bloodsucking Venus who "Toys her prey back into life" while he reciprocates: "He rules her with the sexual knife / That kills him" (27). Setting to one side the question of what kind of a father would choose to introduce his child to the facts of life in this way, it is clear that Barker conceives of women as Venuses in the Swinburnian manner and of sexuality as a relentless force dragging him into scenes he would rather avoid.

These two poems only represent single instances in Bishop's and Barker's works, of course; Conrad Aiken spends much more of his opus describing his quest for understanding of women. When he was eleven years old Aiken heard his father and mother quarrel all night long about her fidelity, and in the morning his father killed both his mother and himself. This childhood trauma permanently affected the poet's attitude to women and to his own self and sexuality. In "The Divine Pilgrim," for example, he seeks a "She" who retains much of the cosmic and natural warmth of Aphrodite: "A Woman of fire, a woman of earth, / Dreamed of in every birth." She is also deathly. His solution is to victimize her: "I would tear you petal from petal with slow murder," and although his text, like Swinburne's, is delicately lyric, his intentions are equally sadistic. He assumes the persona of one "who had loved a Lamia," fascinated by this "sea girl" but simultaneously characterizing all women as vampires. As "Divine Pilgrim," similarly, he seeks an "implacable sorceress," who is a "Dancer among bats and serpents" (234–35). Aiken may be responding to the archaeological findings of Middle Eastern goddesses with loathing; it is not surprising that in a poem directly addressed to "Venus Anadyomene" in part IV of "John Deth" (written in 1922) the old magician who is his persona sadistically crucifies Venus.

Although as a feminist critic I might define Aiken's stance as one of unmitigated sexism, I also define his gynophobia as a painful projection onto Venus of a childhood trauma turned into a tragic self-hatred and distaste for his own sexuality. In his autobiographical novel *Ushant* (1952) Aiken expresses his total estrangement from women: "the men *were* oneself," he insists, "the women, no matter how deeply loved, nor with what all-givingness or agony or ecstasy, were not; they paralleled, they accompanied, they counterpointed, but they did not, in the same sense, become intimately the alphabet of one's soul" (14). Neumann conceives of the anima or male feminine character as creating conflict at a time when the personality is undergoing transformation: "Even when the anima is seemingly negative and 'intends,' for example, to poison the male consciousness, to endanger it by intoxication, and so on—even then a positive reversal is possible, for the anima figure is always subject to defeat" (35). This, "defeat" involves a successful assimilation of the personal "Feminine" by the healing male consciousness. For Aiken, however, consciousness and unconsciousness remain antagonistic, "as if the conscious and the unconscious were engaged, had always been engaged, in a dance, the most intricate and surprising and involved and contrapuntal of dances, and this dance, in which light and darkness were the partners, was one's life" (*Ushant* 243). For Neumann, however horrifically he may characterize the interaction of male and anima, male and "Great Mother," the goal is victorious assimilation, but Aiken remains entrapped in antagonism between himself and his unconscious, projected onto gender conflict.

Aiken's British contemporary D. H. Lawrence also experienced a lifelong struggle to come to terms with "the feminine" as personal lover or goddess archetype, so that the majority of his Aphroditian poetry remains close to the gynophobic end of my attitudinal scale. In *Psychoanalysis and the Unconscious* (1921) Lawrence rejects Freud's characterization of the unconscious as a horrible cave filled (in Lawrence's words) with "a huge slimy serpent of sex, and heaps of excrement, and a myriad repulsive little horrors spawned between sex and excrement" (5), defining it instead as "that essential unique nature of every individual creature, which is, by its very nature, unanalyzable, undefinable, inconceivable." "There is a whole science of the creative unconscious," Lawrence reminds us, "the unconscious in its law-abiding activities" (16). In spite of his quest for a healthy unconscious,

Lawrence, like Aiken, becomes mired in terror of an overpowering female archetype whose power derives not from a monotheistic matriarchy but from more recent deviance. Until the twentieth century, in Lawrence's theory, there had been a golden wisdom enabling men to control both women and the unconscious. It is from his conviction that the unconscious was ontologically a male gift, recently usurped by women, that Eros is a bright male "germ" which modern men have allowed women to steal, that Lawrence's attitudes toward feminine sexuality arise.

Thus, in spite of his recognition that psychological health depends upon men's assimilation of the unconscious, Lawrence retains both Victorian disdain for its feminine content and authoritarian methods of overpowering it, insisting on an absolute victory rather than any kind of synthesis. He rejects androgyny out of a conviction that gender is ontologically absolute; one of the greatest defects in modern life, for Lawrence, is the attempt on the part of either sex to incorporate characteristics belonging to the other. In *Fantasia of the Unconscious* (1921) he decries women who attempt self-completion (especially those who try to achieve a sexuality insubordinate to men) as monsters, with special hatred for lesbian Eros. His goal is for men to create a new world by colonizing the unconscious, "the desire of the human male to build a world: not to 'build a world for you, dear' but to build up out of his own self and his own belief and his own effort something wonderful" (this something, in Lawrence's argument, being peculiarly exemplified in "the Panama Canal" [60]). When a woman takes sexual initiative she is unfeminine, since, as he insists in "Education and Sex in Man, Woman and Child," every "cell in a woman is feminine" and every cell in man masculine, and nature decrees that men remain in control. Should a woman deviate from subordination she becomes a "Queen of the Earth" who "tears man to bits," suggesting that not only fear of personal engulfment by the maternal/sexual characteristics of the Aphrodite archetype but also distaste for the idea that a period of feminine power and sexuality had historical reality lurks beneath his theory.

As one might expect, Lawrence's tone toward Venus or Aphrodite in his poetry is infected by terror and sadism. In his earliest poems he seems confused about the difference between intercourse and rape. In "Love on the Farm," to give one of many examples, he thinks that sex is necessarily violent, equating women's sexual drives to the rabbit's desire for the trapper's noose and conflating strangulation and intercourse. The idea that women want to be abused may result from Lawrence's early frustrations with women who (not surprisingly) resisted his advances, their reluctance to make love with him providing his principal target. Thus in "Repulsed" he declares "How we hate one another" because "Helen," though "close by!" will not enter "the fur of the world" with him. When, in "Release," their love is finally consummated, she becomes "earth of my atmosphere," "Substance of my inconstant breath," a kind of introjected anima subordinate to him as primary, essential being. Although Lawrence is never entirely comfortable with women whose sexuality is not controlled by some man, as he matures sexually he transcends this phase of introjection. In "Wedlock," for example, he realizes that his lover is not himself but an "other": "beyond my scope . . . / Something I shall never be" (248).

When Aphrodite or Venus appears toward the end of his life, she is still an inadequate, overly self-conscious modern (sexually autonomous) woman, as in "Spiral Flame," where she is "that poor late makeshift, Aphrodite emerging in a bathing suit from our modern sea-side foam" who "has successfully killed all desire in us whatsoever" or, even more terrifying, Venus as Vesuvius in "Volcanic Venus" and associated poems, where Lawrence coyly finds it "very unnerving, moving in a world of smoldering volcanoes / All more or less in eruption" (539).

His tone is as often anxious as jocular, however. In "What Does She Want" he insists that it is not another lover "she" wants but to bite "him in the neck," and in several poems on "Ego-Found" men and women, he satirizes women who are sexually emancipated or, as in "Wonderful Spiritual Women," both sexual and "thoughtful" while "sitting tight on the craters of their volcano." Lawrence is terrified by the volcanoes he perceives lurking in women (540).

When Lawrence writes about the sexuality of animals he manages to transcend the coy satire and rage of his poems about humans. His healthiest treatments of intercourse, celebrating something like gender reciprocity, occur when he is writing about birds or turtles doing it. Two poems in particular consummate his use of the Aphrodite archetype: "Swan," which celebrates male Eros, and "Whales Weep Not," in which he treats pre-European Aphrodite as fairly as anywhere in his works. In the former poem he embeds his conviction that Eros is an originally masculine cosmic power in the figure of the paternal, sexual water bird, whom we can recognize as a masculine version of the swan which was Aphrodite's familiar and, in preclassical Europe, an important representation of the water goddess herself (see chapter 3). In "Whales Weep Not" Lawrence celebrates the huge matings of whales, "like great fierce Seraphim,"

> And all this happens in the sea, in the salt
> where God is also love, but without words:
> and Aphrodite is the wife of whales
> most happy, happy she!
>
> and Venus among the fishes skips and is a she-dolphin
> she is the gay, delighted porpoise sporting with love and the sea
> she is the female tunny-fish, round and happy among the males
> and dense with happy blood, dark rainbow bliss in the sea.
> (695)

Here the free-flowing generativity of the ocean combines with a prelapsarian, pagan celebration of the immanence of divinity within nature, which is one of Lawrence's more admirable themes. True, sexual happiness seems to depend on compulsive heterosexuality for fishes, but the poem belongs to a period when Lawrence, dying, turns from Venus to Artemis in his imageries, leaving "Far and forgotten . . . the Villa of Venus glowing" to enter into the "heavenly mansion" of "Moon, great lady of the heavenly few" (695). As we shall see in part three, Artemis of the wild things empowers poets to celebrate all of nature, while in her Hecate aspect she helps poets accept death. In his poem about whales, as in this late "Invocation to the Moon," Lawrence approaches an attitude to nature and to women which is more positive than what he wrote before. It is too bad that only in poems about animals, and only when he was dying, was he able to name Aphrodite as a joyous natural power, a power which he could never accept when it was under the control of real and living women.

Like Aiken and Lawrence, from his earliest to most recent collections Ted Hughes is locked into a lifelong antagonism toward women, his poems suffused by the threat we pose. Like Lawrence, Hughes is at his best when writing about animals, and he has produced charming children's literature as well as books of nature poetry which attest to his love for the world of Artemis. When it comes to Aphrodite, however (with the single exception of a courtly love poem;

"Song," apparently addressed to Sylvia Plath), from his earliest collections Hughes conflates the Aphrodite archetype with the threat of feminine sexuality. "Dark Women" (retitled "The Green Wolf" in *Wodwo*), for example, has no women in it, only the archetypal imageries which Robert Graves associates with Celtic goddesses: hawthorn flowers and beanflowers. Where, as we shall see, Graves's approach to Banshees, or Beanshes, Blodeuwedd or Olwen of the Hawthorn, and the May Queen of the Hawthorn or May tree is ambivalent, Hughes emphasizes the destructive qualities of the Celtic archetypes. *Lupercalia* is full of associations between feminine sexuality and a brutish violence, a mood which has not changed ten years later when, in "Crow's First Lesson," he reenvisions the creation scene: trying to utter the word "love," crow gags and vomits, while "woman's vulva dropped over man's neck and tightened" (1277).

Violence as a basic factor in heterosexual love is a constant in Hughes, who conflates gender violence with bird imagery eight years later in *Cave Birds*, a series of poems accompanied by Leonard Baskin's drawings. These poems are structured according to the quest of the male hero into the (feminine) underworld, with an Agon in the depths of the descent suggestive of sacred marriage rites, though savagely undermined by Hughes's conviction that all heterosexual intercourse involves violence. It seems too simplistic to attribute Hughes's attitude to the Aphrodite archetype to a specifically masculine violence. Although it is true that as a young poet Hughes had already shown more consciousness of the destructive than the creative aspects of the white goddess archetypes he adapted from Graves, his personal experience with Sylvia Plath may have reinforced his conviction that heterosexual love is necessarily violent. Linda Wagner-Martin recounts how on the night Plath met him she wrote in her journal that "when he kissed my neck I bit him long and hard on the cheek, and when we came out of the room, blood was running down his face" (130). Plath admired Hughes's violent propensities as something she desired in a lover, writing her mother that she had found him "a large, hulking, healthy Adam," and to her brother that he was "the only man in the world who is my match. . . . He is a violent Adam" (133). Our access to these insights into the personal life of Plath and Hughes reminds us of how important the individual signature can be. As in the case of Aiken, who was affected by the violent death of both his parents when he was eleven years old, Hughes's personal psychology imprints his Aphrodite archetypes with an especially violent sexual tension. Hughes apparently did not transcend this kind of transaction, at least in his poetry, although one senses far beneath the destructiveness of his bird and love archetypes a passage toward some kind of synthesis or healing.

<table>
<tr><td>Terror and
Celebration</td></tr>
</table>

Terror and Celebration

This faint suggestion of a positive outcome for sexual antagonism in Hughes's poetry is far more pronounced in the works of two groups of mythologically self-conscious twentieth-century male poets: Robert Graves and Dylan Thomas as Celtic-influenced British writers of the earlier period and, more recently, Robert Duncan, Gary Snyder, and Robert Bly. The profound ambivalence with which they approach Aphrodite parallels the "split Venus" imagery of earlier male poets. Following the lead of Evans and Frazer, they see Aphrodite as a monotheistic, dominating figure with power over men, who respond ambivalently, with both fear and reverence. In an interesting fashion, however, they are more negative in prose than in poetry, where their appreciation of her qualities and reverence for her powers often overbalances their fear and loathing. When invoking the Aphrodite archetype or an equivalent figure, these poets understand her "evil" aspect as part of a trial which they must endure and transcend. It is thus too simplistic to characterize them as gynophobic; unlike Aiken and Hughes, they are not so much paralyzed by terror as galvanized by fear into a quest for the psychological synthesis that is Neumann's goal, namely a masculine self-acceptance that involves respect both for their inner femininity and for real women.

Graves was introduced to the psychology of the unconscious by W. H. R. Rivers, a therapist who helped him recover from shell shock following the First World War. By teaching his patients the healing values of their own dreams and by insisting that they work their way through the negative as well as the positive dream experiences, Rivers established the kind of psychoanalytic quest that characterizes Jungian therapy. Graves was also fascinated by the theories of matriarchal monotheism popular during his early education, and, ignoring the polytheistic nature of both Old European and preclassical theology like so many of his contemporaries, he insisted in his mythological treatise *The White Goddess* (1948) that "in Europe there were at first no male gods contemporary with the Goddess." Like Jung, Neumann, and Bachofen, he acknowledges the multiple powers of his goddess but nevertheless dualizes them: "As goddess of the Underworld she was concerned with Birth, Procreation and Death. As Goddess of the Earth she was concerned with the three seasons of Spring, Summer and Winter: she animated trees and plants and ruled all living creatures. As Goddess of the Sky she was the moon, in her three phases of New Moon, Full Moon, and Waning Moon. This explains why from a triad she was so often enlarged to an ennead." To this point multiplicity is certainly key. Graves goes on to assert, however, that "it must never be forgotten that the Triple Goddess, as worshipped for example at Stymphalus, was a personification of primitive woman—woman the creatress and destructress. As the New Moon or Spring she was girl; as the Full Moon or Summer she was woman; as the Old Moon or Winter she was hag" (386). As his capitalizations suggest, Graves sees the goddess as a monotheistic, dominating deity; her triads, similarly, have a way of resolving into the poles of creation and destruction. Especially as a muse of English poets has she been fearsome: "Shakespeare knew and feared her," and "Donne worshipped the White Goddess blindly in the person of the woman whom he made his Muse" (426). She is never satisfied with the poet who can never conquer her, and she has a most unfortunate tendency to think that she is a poet herself: "However woman is not a poet: she is either a Muse or she is nothing." What he means by this is not that women shouldn't write poetry but that when they write it, it should be "as a woman, not as if she were an honorary man." To Graves "as a woman" means as his definition of the fearsome White Goddess: "She should be in turn Arianrhod, Blodeuwedd and the Old Sow of Maenawr Penardd who eats her farrow, and should write in each of these capacities with antique authority" (447).

This rather muddied and self-contradictory explanation about the relationship between the poet's muse, the woman poet, and her own vocation inevitably leads women poets to despair over Graves as a man trying to impose his masculine definitions not only upon his own wives and lovers but also upon all women poets. Here, for example, is Margaret Atwood's reaction as a young poet reading *The White Goddess* for the first time:

Graves did not dismiss women. In fact he placed them right at the center of his poetic theory; but they were to be inspirations rather than creators, and a funny sort of inspiration at that. They were to be incarnations of the White Goddess herself, alternately loving and destructive, and men who got involved with them ran the risk of disembowelment or worse. A woman just might . . . have a chance of becoming a decent poet, but only if she too took on the attributes of the White Goddess and spent her time seducing men and then doing them in. All this sounded a bit strenuous, and appeared to rule out domestic bliss. ("Great Unexpectations" 79)

Fortunately for her career as a writer, Atwood recognizes that "Robert Graves didn't have the last word on women writers." I would argue that Graves no more controls the White Goddess archetype than he controls women poets, and that even in his own poetry he transcends the sexual antagonism his prose promotes. Starting from my hypothesis that an archetype carries a deep background often at odds with its nineteenth- and twentieth-century personal signatures, I would define Graves's prose description of the White Goddess as dependent upon a personal and historical signature he imposes upon her, while in his poetry he celebrates less patriarchal aspects of the archetype.

Although I can certainly understand how Atwood came to her conclusions from reading *The White Goddess*, I find Graves's poems at variance with the attitude that the goddess archetype is merely an aspect of man's psyche. Especially in poems that focus on the White Goddess and other female mythological figures, but also in his love poems, Graves perceives women as having real existence separate from his preoccupations about them and writes about goddesses not as merely metaphoric but as archetypes enduring through history which poets must approach with reverence.

The point of "The Succubus" thus is not a horrific portrait of a hated female monster but a description of the wrong way to approach powerful feminine archetypes. It is "despair / In ecstasy of nightmare" that brings the "devil-woman through the air" to you, when you have betrayed the true goddess by approaching love in the wrong way. Graves attributes horrid physical femininity to his own (or his reader's own) "fancy" or "lustful" imagination, in the medieval sense of the wrong kind of sensuality: the results of the "right" kind of natural sensuality are depicted in the second and central stanza, which poses the rhetorical question of why the woman never comes to people who misconceive her "as longed-for beauty" (*New Collected Poems* 42). One becomes a victim of "the succubus" when one has pursued an unnatural, lesser kind of sensuality; the natural Aphrodite arrives when you learn to transcend "grosser" tendencies.

Graves is responding to a Celtic understanding of the relationship between life and death which does not perceive these as opposites locked in dichotomy but as parts of each other. As we shall see in my treatment of the Hecate aspect of the Artemis archetype, this goddess presides over a natural and acceptable death, as well as over birth and rebirth. This both/and approach to mortality and immortality resulted from the Celtic conviction that there had only been one death, Cythraul, the darkness out of which creation arose at the beginning of the earth, and that, as Dylan Thomas was to put it, "after the first death there is no other." The death of the individual merely frees him or her to membership in that part of the tribe which, although dead, remains close (as at the Halloween of Samhain new year holidays) to the land of the living. This kind of tribal unity with the dead has parallels, as we shall see in chapter 10, to many Native American belief systems. Here it is important to note that Graves's studies of Celtic theology allowed him to approach goddesses presiding over death/life in a more positive way than many of his contemporaries, who were more under the influence both of Christian body/spirit and rationalistic mind/matter dichotomies.

In Graves's "Black Goddess" we can see the influence of the Celtic view that nature and the dead remain closely allied. Graves approaches the "black agate eyes" of the archetype as an initiate into her mysteries, one who can get behind the apparently horrific mask to her more beneficient being:

> And your black agate eyes, wide open, mirror
> The released firebird beating his way
> Down a whirled avenue of blues and yellows.
>
> Should I not weep? Profuse the berries of love,
> The speckled fish, the filberts and white ivy
> Which you, with a half-smile, bestow
> On your delectable broad land of promise
> For me, who never before went gay in plumes.
>   (*New Collected Poems* 209)

Berries, fish, nuts, and ivy, while "sacred to" Celtic goddesses, also express the delight of the natural world earned by the quester who is able to plunge through his fears to the happy land beneath nightmare. In "The White Goddess" Graves recognizes that men often mistake her: "All saints revile her, and all sober men / Ruled by the God Apollo's golden mean," but he wants to journey through perils toward a better understanding of her essence, "Beyond the cavern of the seven sleepers" to a place where she lives

> Whose eyes were blue, with rowan-berry lips,
> With hair curled honey-coloured to white hips.

> Green sap of Spring in the young wood a-stir
> Will celebrate the Mountain Mother,
> And every song-bird shout awhile for her.
> (*New Collected Poems* 118)

Here the Artemisian or nature goddess imageries blend with the Aphroditian in a quest through and out of fear of the "terrible female" toward an outcome Hughes's poetry only hints at, but which he failed to achieve because he was locked into terror of the feminine. We find the same kind of progression through fear to reverence for a goddess archetype in "Return of the Goddess" and "The Ambrosia of Dionysus and Semele," where Graves approaches the "tall Queen of the earth" through "halls of fear ceilinged with incubi." Nor do I find Graves's attitude to real women in his love poetry exploitative. When a lover embodies Venus he approaches her with respect, as in "A Measure of Casualness," where (with interesting echoes of Sir Thomas Wyatt) he begs his lover to "Teach me a measure of casualness / Though you stalk into my room like Venus naked."

Thus, although elements of the myth theory he presents in *The White Goddess* certainly seem to derive from an antagonistic definition of heterosexual relations and of the goddess as a creative/destructive archetype, Graves's poetry suggests quite a different attitude. As his own concept that poetry is "a magical language" which endures as a manner of honoring feminine archetypes since the "Old Stone Age" suggests, Graves's poetry may simply be a clearer vehicle for the psyche than his prose. Poetry, in my definition, antedates prose as a theological vehicle and may offer a conduit to the apatriarchal signature of archetypes.

However eccentric Graves's pseudohistorical myth theory may be, he makes two important contributions to modern poetry: he reenvisions powerful feminine archetypes, specifically Celtic ones, and he warns poets against the modern tendency, especially in "European schools and universities" to study myth "only as quaint relics of the nursery age of mankind" (*The White Goddess* 10). He understands that archetypal symbols and quest narratives describe psychological processes and helps erase some of the dualistic tendencies and Victorian gynophobia from the myth materials available to other modern poets. How those poets use these materials, as we have seen most vividly in the case of Ted Hughes, who was profoundly influenced by *The White Goddess,* depends upon the personal signature they bring to them: unlike the works of Aiken, Lawrence, or Hughes, Graves's poems provide an alternate approach to the frightening content of the love goddess archetype, demonstrating that a male poet is not necessarily paralyzed by its fearsome features, which he must learn to work through in his quest for true sexual maturity and for an understanding of real women.

One of the most engaging of the Celtic goddesses Graves resurrects is Olwen, "the laughing Aphrodite of Welsh legend [who] is always connected with the wild-apple" (*The White Goddess* 42). This apple-Aphrodite also appears frequently in both the prose and the poetry of Dylan Thomas, who often wrote about the quest of a male hero for a love affair with a magical and powerful goddess. Although Thomas acknowledges some frightening or "Terrible Mother" aspects of the figure, resulting in some gynophobic poems, her "good" and "evil" aspects rupture dualistic, Christian containers to whirl in a more cyclical fashion and, sometimes, to achieve synthesis. Like Graves, the Welsh Thomas was profoundly influenced by Celtic materials, and his Welsh upbringing exposed him to some interesting variations of Celtic theology. His father, a Welsh speaker who was fond of legend and folklore, named his son for Dylan Ail Mor, who appears in Welsh folklore as Merdin, Mer-Dain, or Merlin, who, as I have detailed in my earlier volume on Thomas's prose *(Dylan Thomas' Early Prose: A Study in Creative Mythology)* was called the "comely one of the sea" to whom God gave the island of Britain (78). Thomas often adapts the persona of the Welsh Noah, Dwyvan, who was reputed to have escaped the flood with his consort Dwyvach to repeople the islands of Britain (63). Thomas's attitude toward sensuality began with his

179

boyish revolt against chapel puritanism, but it was the theology of Welsh unitarian immanentism, promulgated by R. J. Campbell and embraced by a number of Thomas's relatives, which provided justification for affirming the "Immanence of God instead of the Transcendency of God—i.e., that God was not a person, standing outside the creation and looking down from heaven upon man, but was, in fact, in the universe and part of it, to be found in all things animate and inanimate" (7–8). Finally, the pre-Christian Welsh creation stories affirmed the origins of the universe in a kind of poetic act, when light, song, and language erupted all at once, which Thomas blends with his sense of the power of sensuality and the natural world to create a feminine archetype conflating Aphrodite and muse imageries in the poetry that seemed so bizarre to the world of the 1930s and 1940s.

Thomas sometimes creates a horrific Venus image. In "Shall Gods Be Said to Thump the Clouds," for example, he asks

> Shall it be said that, venuswise
> An old god's dugs are pressed and pricked,
> The wet night scolds me like a nurse?

This query, however, is part of a rhetorical question followed by an affirmation that "it shall be said that Gods are stone" and a declaration "Let the stones speak / with tongues that talk all tongues" (*Poems* 68). Thomas's sometimes hostile conflations of the sexual and the maternal and his frequent association of wombs with tombs have less to do with a desire to "doublecross my mother's womb," as he expresses it in an earlier poem (72), than with the copresence of love and death in sexuality. In the first part of "I See the Boys of Summer" his boys mistakenly "Lay the gold tithings [of sensuality] barren"; but in the second part he describes both the boys and himself as "the dark deniers" who, like Graves, must learn not to fear or to waste their sensuality but to "summon / Death from a summer woman," facing up to the mortality implicit in intercourse.

The deathly element in Thomas's Aphrodite figures derives from Welsh attitudes to death as much as from a Christian or rational distaste for mortality. As I mentioned in relationship to Graves's Celtic researches, Welsh theology considered human beings a union of opposite natures, a conjunction of matter and spirit, but accepted these opposites as necessary components of a physical world impregnated with divinity. As in most pagan theologies, this acceptance of life mixed with death as part of a cycling but holy physical universe persisted beneath an overlayer of Christianity in Wales, finding expression in the nineteenth century in a unitarian natural immanentism.

Although Thomas's young heroes are frightened of the sensual women and goddesses they encounter on their quests, he urges them to accept a mixture of creation and destruction inherent in sexuality. Even when he is being most hostile to a specific woman, as in "Into her lying down head" (about his wife, Caitlin), Thomas acknowledges a feminine sensual power whose infidelities attest to sexual autonomy, and he concludes the poem by transcending sexual antagonism. The poet may be "a man torn up" mourning her infidelity, but her "faithless sleep" is the rich dark of immanent sensual power which he nonetheless celebrates. Elements of the "Golden Aphrodite" of natural and delightful sensuality and of the old European and Celtic bird goddess enter into the poem in the hawk imagery, while "carrion" and "paradise" are yoked in a particularly Welsh synthesis (see *Poems* 162–63).

In two of his longest and most important poems, "Ballad of the Long-Legged Bait" (which may also be a response to Caitlin's supposed betrayals) and "A Winter's Tale," we find a more negative and a more positive version of the sensual goddess whose creativity and destructiveness fuse in two of Thomas's unique blends of Welsh archetypes and surrealist symbols. In "Ballad," his hero is a fisherman who uses a "girl alive with his hooks through her lips" as a sadistic "bait," which he trails behind him to lure fishes into raping her. Here, like Hughes, Thomas conflates sexuality with violence, his persona hearing "his bait buck in the wake / And tussle in a shoal of loves" as if this were titillating for her. Specifically identified as the archetypal Venus ("Venus lies star-struck in her wound"), the bait's experience of rape makes the seas dry up and the land reappear until, with the sea, she goes underground, beneath both land and the unconscious, leaving the fisherman standing "alone at the door of his home, / With his long-legged heart in his hand." Clearly, a mistaken idea that women enjoy rape creates a definitely gynophobic attitude toward Venus, who winds up both as victim and as mere facet (anima) of the hero's unconscious, locating "Ballad" somewhere near the Swinburnian end of our attitudinal scale.

As we have seen, however, Thomas's poems are balanced between terror and celebration rather than being consistently paralyzed or sadistic, and "A Winter's Tale" provides a stunning conflation of Welsh, Old European, and classical Aphrodite archetypes. Here the hero is fearful but much less cruel toward a bird goddess, whom he approaches with prayer, awe, and respect: "He knelt, he wept, he prayed. . . . At the point of love, forsaken and afraid"

> Deliver him, he cried,
> By losing him all in love, and cast his need
> Alone and naked in the engulfing bride,
> Never to flourish in the fields of the white seed
> Or flower under the time dying flesh astride. (*Poems* 193)

Unlike the Fisherman, this hero works through the fear of engulfment by the love goddess to an experience of her power that renews not only his sensuality but also language and the natural world:

> Look. And the dancers move
> On the departed, snow bushed green, wanton in moon
> light
> As a dust of pigeons. Exulting, the graved hooved
> Horses, centaur dead, turn and tread the drenched white
> Paddocks in the farms of birds. The dead oak walks for
> love.
>
> The carved limbs in the rock
> Leap, as to trumpets. Calligraphy of the old
> Leaves is dancing. Lines of age on the stones weave in
> a flock.
> And the harp shaped voice of the water's dust plucks in
> a fold
> Of fields. For love, the long ago she bird rises. Look
>
> And the wild wings were raised
> Above her folded head, and the soft feathered voice
> Was flying through the house as though the she bird
> praised
> And all the elements of the snow fall rejoiced
> That a man knelt alone in the cup of the vales. (*Poems* 194)

Thomas's lyric shows his interbraiding of Aphroditian imageries—the dancers celebrating, the pigeons, the horses risen from the dead (Welsh Rhiannon, known to Rome as Eponna, was a horse goddess, nightmare and white mare), the runes coming alive out of the rock as in the Welsh creation stories, the immanence of poetry in matter ("the harp shaped voice of the water's dust,"), and, at the center, the bird goddess binding all of the "elements of the snow fall" together into a celebratory anthem. All are dependent upon the poet's persona kneeling, alone and prayerful, assuming a reverential attitude to the golden bird goddess.

Because of the presence in his work of poems like "Ballad," where terror and sadism overwhelm his reverence and awe, I have placed Thomas in the group of poets who simultaneously fear and celebrate Aphrodite. His poetry reflects two moods about her: one leading him to a path where he can choose psychological health, the other binding him in destructive emotions. Men's poems about Aphrodite seem to be structured upon both their personal projections (based on their experience of patriarchal heterosexuality) and the Aphrodite archetype's sensual, apatriarchal signals. Even though their poems are so often burdened with destructive attitudes toward sexually powerful women, these male poets are trying to transcend gynophobia.

Poets' self-consciousness about myth seems both to aid and obstruct the process of approaching the archetype. We have seen how Grave's researches focus his quest; Thomas, who wrote much less analysis of mythology than Graves, was similarly self-conscious in his dragging up, as he put it, of images "from the nethermost sea of the hidden self," and insisted that once dug up, they should, "before they reach paper . . . go through all the rational processes of the intellect" ("Notes on the Art of Poetry" 152). The generation of American male poets who came of age in the 1940s, when interest in mythology peaked in the university as in the poetic community, were similarly given to mythological theorizing. These poets were especially influenced by Graves's *White Goddess,* which appeared in 1948, and Joseph Campbell's *Hero with a Thousand Faces,* which came out in 1949. Robert Creeley even went to live on Mallorca, Graves's home base, for a period in the late forties and early fifties before joining the Black Mountain School; Robert Duncan wrote an autobiographical work called *The Truth and Life of Myth* (1967); Gary Snyder, in his *Myths and Texts* (1960), describes himself, like Campbell's hero, creating his own life out of myth; and Robert Bly includes a prose myth statement entitled "I came out of the mother naked" in *Sleepers Joining Hands* (1973), a book of poetry. Although on an attitudinal scale these poets often seem more gynophobic that either Thomas or Graves, they also write poems manifesting considerable reverence. In treating their Aphrodite poems as a group I want to focus on the way their texts embody a deadlock between reverential approaches to Aphrodite and horrified abjection.

"Poets must open themselves to mythic reality," Duncan asserts; "the positivistic thought of the last several centuries has thrown a wall up against the deep past and the mythic consciousness found in the Old and New Testaments and in the tradition of visionary poetry dating back to Homer" (*The Truth and Life of Myth* 186). This should warn us that Duncan will try to reenvision values antedating modern European rationalism but that these values will probably be weighted toward the patriarchal. Thus in his two poems about the Aphrodite archetype this "deep past" turns out to be highly colored by a dualistic mindset and by Duncan's personal fear of women. In "The Homecoming" he apostrophizes "great Venus" as "Ishtar, the full-blown rose," but focuses on her relationship to Attis/Adonis, a son or lover figure. The positive rose and shell imagery degenerates by the second stanza into spoiled shadows; by the third and fourth we find Venus shuddering and moaning for her lost consort in the conventional elegy of Venus for Adonis; and in the last two stanzas Duncan gives way to horror at the rebirth of Aphrodite in California as a "whore," intending to engulf a male Attis/Adonis: since "Every man is some woman's son / who mourns and becomes like Venus in her sleep" (*The First Decade* 64–65). Several elements in the text suggest Duncan's conviction that Aphrodite reduces men's stature: the bloody foam is an allusion to the castration of Chronos and suggests women's powerful menstrual and placental fluids; and in his focus on man's role as son to mother, he reduces relationships between the sexes to the boyish/maternal pattern. Like Bishop at the end of "Ode," Duncan's Berkeleyians wind up moaning that "The Lord" (Adonis) has died "and left us less than men." Duncan's approach to Aphrodite is structured on the presumption that if a woman is powerful sexually she must be understood as maternal and dominant over men, whom he reduces to boys cowering before their mothers. Why is this maternal component so pronounced in the Aphrodite imagery of these American male poets, and why are they so unable to transcend the boy/mother into the lover/lover response?

In "The Venus of Lespuges" from the same collection, Duncan transcends boyish terror only to try to assimilate Venus's attributes to enhance his status as poet. He acknowledges the powerful bodily imagery of the prehistoric statue and wants a "return to first things" so that he can play the "female music body" like "the deep strings of the viol / waiting for sound." The problem is that he defines these "first things" in terms of an infant's relation to the mother, while intending to take her over, to play upon her as a passive vehicle of his own poetic ambition. This is not the relationship to the muse that Graves suggested: Duncan's reverence is only to the purpose of sneaking up on Venus, like the wolf on Red Riding Hood's grandmother, in order to swallow her whole, so that her body can be used for his poetic inspiration, while she pours music into the poet, giving him the "forms" and "concrete images" he needs. His approach to Aphrodite is simultaneously rapacious and imperious in his insisting, like a very young child, that his mother give of her body and substance for his narcissistic needs.

Snyder is similarly ambivalent in "Hymn to the Goddess," looking up her skirts and calling her "the wildest cock-blowing / gang-fucking foot-to foul-tongued head chick" (*Mountains and Rivers* 33), but in other poems he approaches "Mother Earth" with gratitude for her multifaceted creation. These more reverential poems often depend upon Native American sources: Snyder adapts the personae of Native American shamans for his personal needs in a manner distasteful to Native Americans, who are not fond of this kind of "white shamanism" because it usurps Native American theology. In *The Black Country* he writes a poem entitled "To Hell with Your Fertility Cult" expressing a childish petulance in his declaration that "this world is just / a goddamn oversize cunt" and displaying his terror of the very feminine attributes he is using for his poetic purposes.

Once again, I do not want to categorize Duncan's and Snyder's approaches to Aphrodite as based merely on the sexism so prevalent in the 1950s and early 1960s. Their waffling about Aphrodite is more psychologically complicated than that. There is a fine line, as Graves had noted, between trying to internalize the muse, swallowing her whole (as Zeus did to Metis, after which he vomited up Athene and Metis's children in a pretense of giving birth to them himself), and remembering that she endures outside the male mind and must be neither degraded nor exploited. It is when the poet tries to reduce Aphrodite to an instrument of his will that he gets into trouble. Thus Richard Wilbur loses touch with Aphrodite by falling down drunk under a table in "A Voice from Under the Table," his behavior foreshadowed by his suggestion in the first line that women are consumables ("How shall the wine be drunk, or the woman known?"). Here Wilbur follows Campbell's argument in *Hero with a Thousand Faces* that woman is something to be known and man always her knower, in contrast to Graves's insistence that the Aphrodite archetype can never be entirely internalized or "known" and that anyone who attempts it will wind up failing both in poetry and in love. In another poem, "She," Wilbur recognizes that he loses Aphrodite when he mistakes her for a personal attribute. Although he seems able to recognize what is wrong with his approach to Aphrodite and might heal himself thereby, these problems do not reach a level of consciousness in poems such as Creeley's "Door" (dedicated to Robert Duncan), in which a "lovely lady" represents an opening in a door that "brings a scent of wildflowers in the wood" (338). Because he is unable to assume a mature posture before her, he remains a *puer aeternus*. Creeley assumes a tone of resignation in the penultimate stanza, declaring that he "will sell / myself in hell" though "in heaven also I will be," sounding much like Swinburne's Tannhäuser, locked forever in the embrace of a Venus he loathes.

I would suggest that an excessive preoccupation with the maternal element in the archetype keeps these poets from getting beyond their fear of Aphrodite. Their failure to arrive at a place where they can participate in a reciprocal relationship while acknowledging the power of feminine sensuality does not entirely erase these poets' recognition that Aphrodite demands an adult rather than an infantile response. The process that Neumann posited as the goal of a successful therapy was precisely this dialectical working through the negative aspects of femininity. Bly, both in his poetry and in his myth theory, articulates the difficulty of transcending dualities in feminine archetypes so that one does not become engulfed or infantile. While one might take "The Teeth Mother Naked at Last" (1970) as the worst kind of sexist response to women, this long poem details the horrors of the Vietnam War, which Bly blames on masculine destructive forces, including a love of death leading to the Vietnam atrocities. In locating the cause of war not in feminine archetypes but in the masculine pathology of refusing to come to terms with the anima, Bly agrees with Jung's and Neumann's theory that men's repression of their emotional and intuitive nature is the cause of twentieth-century wars. I would agree that the splitting off of reason from the body, begun in the Enlightenment and compounded by the Victorian denial of feminine sexuality as good and normal, has contributed to the deadliest violence ever known to the human race. The excessively maternal component of contemporary male Aphrodite archetypes may arise from the way the Victorian placed the maternal and the sexual in separate and irreconcilable feminine categories, prescribing sexlessness even for mothers and sexuality only for whores. Although this was obviously an extreme ideology which could hardly have percolated down to most people's lives, the burgeoning of mass communications in the nineteenth century as well as the growing middle class adoption of such prescriptions made it a widespread and deadly formula which spilled over into violence and war.

The 1950s were a period when Victorian prescriptions for women were resurrected through every educational and journalistic device society could marshal. The resulting repression of authentic feminine power led young men of the 1960s to search for the "Good Mother," not only by wearing long hair and necklaces but by undertaking quests into their psyches. There they encountered the "Death Mother," whom Bly posits as the "Good Mother's" destructive underside. Like Neumann, Bly recognizes that earlier civilizations were much less alienated from this darker side of feminine power, which he exemplifies in the archetypes of Lilith in the Old Testament and Kali in India. "The Death Mother's job," Bly asserts, "is to end everything the Good Mother has brought to birth." Although this sounds negative, Bly does not posit this dark principle as evil in and of itself; rather, he blames the repression of this side of femininity on "father consciousness that is terrified of death," recognizing that "mother consciousness is more confident that the thread of sparks will remain unbroken," that death is part of the regenerative life cycle.

Bly adapts Neumann's dualism in his emphasis on a magnetic feminine energy ranging from the "ecstatic mother" on the positive pole to her destructive aspect, the "stone" mother, on the other. Bly thus sees Medusa, like his "tooth mother," as a "concentration of Great Mother energy . . . so great that it stopped the developing masculine consciousness in its tracks" (41). This is the paralysis that petrifies poets who approach Medusa, as I suggested in the first part of this book. I have described how this deadlock arrests poets Aiken, Lawrence, Bishop, and Hughes. Bly warns his readers that this feminine energy becomes destructive when one reacts to it in fear, when one is unable to deal with death or, for that matter, the body and its sexual demands—as in the dramatic case of alcoholics and drug addicts. Bly recognizes that "death imagery" associated with danger in women "began to surface in America about two decades ago," that is, in the 1950s. He recognizes the terror of the maternal component of the archetype not only in contemporary but also in historical instances, and he notes that "Western literature since Socrates basically describes men's escape from the Mother." From this literature, he acknowledges, women get little help, since "most of the literature written in the last two thousand years has been written by men about their growth." In his recognition in *Iron John* of men's need to come to terms both with their personal fathers and with a wild and apatriarchal masculinity, Bly's attitude toward women shows little change. Nevertheless, Bly's theory that the terror of women manifested in male poetry springs from men's inability to handle the holistic energy of feminine archetypes helps us to understand the attitudes of his contemporaries Duncan, Creeley, and Snyder toward Aphrodite.

The African American Aphrodite

If white male poems about Aphrodite display nineteenth-century ambiguities about the maternal and the sexual, poems by African American men internalize prohibitions against being in love with white women. We have seen in chapter 3, on Medusa in Canadian poetry, that even slight differences in cultural signatures can create striking variations in the Medusa archetype; in poetry by African American male writers we find an Aphrodite who interbraids complex strands of white sexual prohibition, the experiences of African American men, and attempts to reenvision a nonwhite goddess archetype.

When the punishment for even looking at a white woman was often torture, castration, and hanging, African American poets inevitably warned each other against being fatally tempted. In "The Temptress" and "The White Witch" (both published in 1917) James

Weldon Johnson creates a frightening white archetype in order to warn other African American men away from her. In the first poem, the poet is able to put off "Old Devil" as mere "Bogey-man," but when "you take your horns from off your head, / And soft and fragrant hair is in their place," he knows he is really in trouble, that "my chance is slim to win the fight" (41). Here the temptress figure is feminine sexuality but not specifically a white woman, but in "The White Witch" Johnson creates a dangerously Caucasian temptress:

> O, brothers mine, take care! Take care!
> The great white witch rides out to-night,
> Trust not your prowess nor your strength;
> Your only safety lies in flight;
> For in her glance there is a snare,
> And in her smile there is a blight. (19)

She is not an "ancient hag" with "snaggled tooth" but alluringly Aphroditian, with "eyes like ocean waters blue" and golden hair, cosmically powerful ("the infant planets saw her birth"). The poet takes the persona of a Tannhäuser who has barely escaped with his life:

> For I have seen the great white witch,
> And she has led me to her lair
> And I have kissed her red, red lips
> And cruel face so white and fair. (20)

There is a special racial twist to this portrait of the Aphrodite as evil seductress, however: white women are hungry for the young black men's "strong young limbs" because they sense

> The echo of a far-off day
> When man was closer to the earth;
> And she has marked you for her prey.
>
> She feels the old Antaean strength
> In you, the great dynamic beat
> Of primal passions, and she sees
> In you the last besieged retreat
> Of love relentless, lusty, fierce,
> Love pain-ecstatic, cruel-sweet. (21)

Johnson is warning against white women's projections of passions they feel unable to express with white men, so that African American men become vehicles for white women's repressed Eros. Johnson recognizes the temptation which making love to such women must have posed: thus as a "great white witch" who "rides out to-night," Johnson's powerful sexual archetype conflates the Ku Klux Klan imagery with Medusan propensities to snare men "in her glance" and the blighted attractions of an extremely dangerous Aphrodite.

Although Johnson's two poems might belong closer to a gynophobic than to a celebratory place on my scale of attitudes, it is important for me to deal with African American poetry about Aphrodite as a unity in order to examine the unique content of the African American archetype. Johnson's "Beware the white witch" approach recurs frequently in African American poetry, but always interacting with racial as well as with individual and cultural signatures. Implicitly the evil white woman sets off the better black or brown one, a contrast African American poets often make explicit. Thus Johnson writes a traditional poem in praise of "Venus in a Garden," subverting it only in a very encoded manner by valuing her "blood-red roses" from disappointed or heartbroken lovers more than her "snow-white" ones; but in a companion poem he addresses his true love to "Vashti," an imaginary white princess whose Indian name belies her identification. African American poets often reenvision non-European goddess archetypes in order to endow their love poems with negritude; here Johnson gives an apparently non-European, Asian name to a fantasy white woman he desires to serve in the courtly manner.

Countee Cullen is much more explicit in positing a brown versus a white woman in "The Ballad of the Brown Girl," in which the hero, "Lord Thomas," is forced to marry a woman called "Fair London," who is "white as almond milk," rather than his intended bride, who has a "nut-brown throat" and "wild blood" (179). With Cullen we are introduced to the special flavor of the African American Aphrodite, who should be more properly called Oya, a comparable African goddess who conflates warlike virtues with sexuality in a manner reminiscent of Inanna and Ishtar. Cullen describes Lord Thomas's true love not as sweet or lily white but as Afrocentric. Rather than put up with the insults of the white rival, she takes the "dagger serpentine" she wears in her hair and commits suicide, after which Lord Thomas strangles the white woman in a noose of the brown girl's hair before he kills himself too. In a less gruesome poem on the same theme, "A Song of Praise," Cullen addresses himself to a friend who has a much "fairer" or whiter lover whose walk suggests "the soul of Africa" (4).

In both of these poems Cullen's distaste for the white woman is a foil helping him to establish an appreciation of African American women endowed with African archetypal qualities. For example, he invokes a "soul of Africa" for women which includes pride, even arrogance, and wildness which are quite different qualities than those white men value in white women. As we shall see in the next chapter, these qualities belong to African goddesses valued for their anger, their pride, even their destructiveness as necessary variations on their feminine sexuality.

It is this deeper layer of African archetypes, sometimes imagined by the African American male poet without much explicit knowledge of African religious practice, that differentiates the Aphrodite in their poems from her appearances in white male poetry. Deeply affected by nineteenth-century sexual prohibitions, these African American poets nonetheless value the feminine anger, pride, and sensuality that so often horrifies white men. Fenton Johnson, for example, creates "The Scarlet Woman" out of a Negro girl who started out "good like the Virgin Mary and the Minister's wife," but who had only "a white girl's education and a face that enchanted the men of both races" and preferred living as a whore to the life of virtue (24). This might seem like a fairly typical "good whore" stereotype except that the scarlet woman's badness is valued as such. The same theme occurs in Langston Hughes's "Ruby Brown," where Ruby, "because she was colored" and "Mayville had no place to offer her," stopped working in "a white woman's kitchen" and sought out "the sinister shuttered houses of the bottoms" to become a whore to white men. Hughes is singing the blues, I would assume, rather than really believing that being a whore will provide the "fuel for the clean flame of joy / That tried to burn within her soul" (*Fine Clothes to the Jew*, 30). However negligent of the horrors of prostitution his lyric may sound, he values the choice to live by one's sexuality as implicitly authentic. Not that he is consistently given to romanticizing the fate of African American women in love, which he defines in "Beale Street Love" as "a brown man's fist . . . / Blackening the eyes" of a woman ironically named "Clorinda," whose only reply is "Hit me again" (57).

A kind of blues which simultaneously acknowledges African

American women's suffering and praises their endurance occurs in Lewis Alexander's "Negro Woman," which endows a suffering woman with the attributes of both earth and cosmos: "The earth trembles tonight / Like the quiver of a Negro woman's eye-lids cupping tears" (58). This sad mood about the fate of African American women conveys the sense that their bodies and the earth itself are vital parts of each other, derived from conventional European imagery but perhaps also reflecting African goddesses' embodiment of natural forces, and not only the milder attributes of star and stream but also the violent ones, like hurricanes.

When African American male poets abandon poetic conventions derived from white lyrics for their own music and language, they become more celebratory than grief stricken. Thus in the middle of a 1944 collection soberly entitled *Lament for Dark Peoples and Other Poems*, Langston Hughes bursts out in "To Midnight Nan at Leroy's" in praise of a "Shameless gal" men rightly fear ("Wouldn't no good fellow / be your pal") but whose "strut and wiggle" express qualities he admires. The point of the poem is that Hughes celebrates "Shameless Nan" for her shamelessness, as he also does in "Song for a Banjo Dance" when he urges a woman to "Shake your brown feet, honey" and in "Harlem Sweeties," where he makes up a delicious food name for every color of African American woman, from "Brown sugar lassie" and "Caramel treat" to "Chocolate darling / Out of a dream" (*Shakespeare in Harlem* 18–19). Hughes is celebrating negritude in its "rainbow" diversity, along with the richness of African American music and dance. As with Richard Wilbur's desire to drink women down like wine, one wonders about the association of variously complected African American women with different flavors of sweets that the poet would like to eat. I do not read his mood, however, as one of making consumable or edible objects out of Harlem women but of enjoying their diversity and vivacity, affirming his love of colored as opposed to monochromatic white women in a celebration of African American feminine sexuality.

The attempt to call up lost African goddesses to compensate for the emasculations inflicted on African American men by white culture is sometimes only a surface palliative. Robert Earl Hayden's "Idol," for example, only substitutes a cruel Aztec goddess for destructive white women, and Hayden doesn't seem particularly empowered by resurrecting Nefert-iti in "Two Egyptian Portrait Masks." In

"Homage to the Empress of the Blues," he works through his distaste for white culture toward reverence for a powerful African American woman, who "came out on the stage in yards of pearls . . . flashed her golden smile and sang," even though what she was singing about was failure in love, "Faithless Love / Twotiming Love Oh Love Oh Careless Aggravating Love" (44). Such moments of clarity and reverence for a black Aphrodite only occur in the blues, in a context of racial oppression that renders reciprocal Eros problematic.

Johnson's and Hayden's attempts to reach some level of positive affirmation of African American women through reenvisioning African archetypes may enable them to write positively about the real women whose feminine power they admire. The poems which Jean Toomer included in *Cane* express a similar quest for negritude in rural Georgia. In this lyrical novel, Toomer's Fern is a woman who conflates Aphrodite and Artemis: she attracts men but remains a virgin, suggesting the archetype of the virgin as a powerfully sexual woman whose autonomy remains intact. Toomer presents Fern as a kind of priestess of sexual mysteries, although her temple is the open canefield rather than a shrine. In spite of a powerful and reciprocal Eros as displayed in "Her Lips Are Copper Wire," however, *Cane* remains suspended between black culture and the white attitudes which Toomer internalizes.

Forty years later, the poems of Imamu Amiri Baraka display a similarly ruptured celebration of African American culture, with Baraka's reverence for African American women and African goddesses undermined by the overpowering racist viciousness of American culture. Baraka's quest for a holistic black consciousness is also subverted by his internalization of a Sartrean existentialism that led him to overvalue reason and undervalue the world of the body and nature. As a product of the 1950s and early 1960s he also brought not only loathing for white women but a generalized condescension about women in general to his writing of poetry. Baraka's personal life went in the opposite direction from that of Toomer, who eventually downplayed his negritude in a quest for higher consciousness. Baraka started out married to a white woman and affirming a body-devaluing European existentialism but later became a champion of black consciousness. Both poets, however, create a body of work that remains suspended between African identity and internalized white attitudes.

Baraka's writing contains examples of most of the attitudes toward

Aphrodite that I have outlined here. Poems such as "Babylon Revisited" (1969) are warnings against destructive white women quite similar to James Weldon Johnson's "White Witch" if more flagrant in imagery: "she will be the great witch of euro-american legend / who sucked the life / from some unknown nigger" (1322). In "Sex, like desire," he equates young boys' rape of women with desire, if not with love, and sees their actions as part of a quest he also participates in, to find out "Where the life is, all the flesh, to make / more than a silhouette, a breathless shadow. . . ." Here we can sense an erosion of Baraka's sense of his own bodiliness; his alienation as a self he accepts as mere consciousness, a "shadow" or "silhouette," but his dissatisfaction with this state of mind leads to intense questionings in the last stanza:

> What is there? Where is it? Who is she? What can I
> give myself, trade myself, to make me understand
> myself? Nothing is ever finished. Nothing past. Each
> act of my life, with me now, till death. Themselves,
> the reasons for it. They are stones, in my mouth
> and ears. Whole forests on my shoulders. (*The Dead Lecturer* 36)

The (undoubtedly intentional) ambiguity of the pronoun "they" leaves the question open as to whether he is referring to the raping boys or to white culture, but "they" could also be the women themselves in whom he seeks meaning, or his acts of seeking meaning through women, in Campbell's sense. Whatever the case, the poem opens out into a quest for meaning through women, and although the context is rape, I see Baraka's attempts as at least partially authentic, in that his condescension toward women gives way, even in as early a collection as this 1964 one, to an understanding of the sufferings and the power of African American women.

Baraka's "Crow Jane" sequence is addressed to a representative African American woman, whom he first addresses as "Old lady / of flaking eyes. Moon lady / of useless thighs" (49) and describes in "Crow Jane's Manner" as the "mama death" or burial ground for dead young Afro-American men. In "Crow Jane in High Society" he characterizes her as a woman who "fondles another man's / life," but also as his muse ("I am her teller") forced by white society to be criminal ("Crow Jane the Crook"). This woman nonetheless contains the meaning African American poets seek. She is thus elevated to the position of Jesus or, more precisely, of the resurrected Inanna. By the final poem, "The dead lady canonized," she lives in the realm of the gods.

Baraka takes a blues attitude toward a goddess who is subsumed into the masculine Damballah, the powerful female archetype that might empower Baraka subverted into a subordinate position because of his internalization of existentialism and masculinism from white culture. However, like Langston Hughes and other African American male poets, he writes powerful appreciations of specific African American women, as in "20th-Century Fox" where he celebrates a "Dynamite black girl / fucking in the halls . . . outside the shaky mansions of whiteladies" (*Black Magic* 84). In "The woman thing" from the same collection he still displays the damage done to him by existentialism, however, in that he cannot accept his own body as real. It seems to me that Baraka sees himself as "pure impression," a being from the "world of essences" who can only achieve bodily reality through a woman, a poet who is not "seen" unless he is endowed with flesh by the woman he addresses. This modernist attitude of bodily alienation conflates with internalized sexism and with racial oppression to render his approaches to Aphrodite especially problematic. I would suggest that his sense of the overwhelming dominance of the white race derives at least partially from his internalization of the modern European idea that human beings are mere essences alienated from nature as from our own bodies. Thus "Beautiful Black Women . . ." starts out as a powerful affirmation of women like Ruby Dee but turns into a lament that these "Beautiful black women" can do nothing for him in "this terrible land," "the lost heat, and the grey cold buildings of our entrapment" (148). Overwhelmed by the white world and by castrating white women ("these hundred sailing vampires [who] settle their ears to the black man's balls"), he seems entirely dependent upon women's "bodysouls" to unite his mind with his natural being, and his prayer seems hopeless. He is caught in a position analogous to that of Countee Cullen, who intersperses powerful stanzas about "Strong bronzed men, or regal black / Women from whose loins I sprang" with the sad chorus, "*What is Africa to me?*" His heritage is rendered problematic by his conformity to white values.

As we shall see when we look at African American women's poems about goddesses, women poets seem able to transcend the presumption that God and culture are either male or white, but for African American men, who suffer terribly from having been denied sexual and economic masculinity as American culture defines them, European values remain alluring. Thus we find Bob Kaufman, in "African Dream," fantasizing about "Strange forest songs" and rituals presided over "By a scarlet god, / Caressed by ebony maidens," only to dismiss these empowering archetypes as something to be fought off, merely dreams (19). Don L. Lee, similarly, writes a poem in the manner of Margaret Walker's "For my People" for "The negro," but subtitles it "a pure product of Americanism" and subverts the power of African Americans "Swinging, Swinging, / with power to define" both white power and white history in a final verse where the only swinging black people do is by the neck (158). In "Move Un-noticed to the Noticed: A Nationhood Poem," Lee resolves the contradiction between slave history and "civilization" by calling upon his people to "move, into our own, not theirs," to become "worldmakers": "if u can't stop a hurricane, be one . . . be the baddddest hurricane that ever came, a black hurricane named Beulah" (168). It is this female hurricane, worshipped by the Yoruba as Oya, which African American women poets successfully reenvision from the rich material of African archetypes in an especially pugnacious and empowered poetry.

If white male poets internalize a terror of "the feminine" which results from a conflation of maternal and sexual attributes of Aphrodite, African American male poets have special reasons for fearing white women and for wanting to keep their own women subordinate. At the same time, their quest both for an authentic African goddess archetype and for an authentic sexuality endows many of their poems about African American women with a positive tone, as in the case of Don L. Lee's "Poem Looking for a Reader" (subtitled "to be read with a love consciousness"), which he writes as "a fifty minute call to / blackwomanworld" (92). Lee clearly is trying to keep his "blackwomanworld" under his control while working toward reciprocity. His calling up a hurricane Beulah, embodying the full force of an African feminine archetypal power beyond the control of one man, is an act of special courage. Because of the desperate necessity for African American males to assimilate themselves into white culture, the price for their paying attention to African religions and myths is much higher.

than the price paid by white poets who adapt archetypal materials from Celtic or classical mythology. During the back to Africa movement and the later revival of black culture in the 1960s, the act of affirming the African past was especially threatening to conventional ways of surviving by a pretended accommodation to white standards. When white critics comment on this heady rediscovery of a rich and powerful past, moreover, we can be accused of encouraging black people to remain outside the mainstream of white culture. I would argue, however, that (as with Robert Graves's revival of Celtic archetypes) African American poets' reenvisionings of African archetypal materials are more empowering than regressive, part of a drive to transcend the sexual malaise and racism of contemporary life.

Celebration
From the earliest years of the twentieth century many male poets address the Aphrodite/Venus archetype with reverence. Arthur Davidson Ficke's "Cytherea" (1901), Laurence Binyon's "Queen Venus" (1904), A. E.'s (George William Russell) "Aphrodite" (1913), R. P. Blackmur's "Alma Venus" (1926), Ronald Ross's "To Aphrodite in Cyprus" (1928), Denis Devlin's "Venus of the Salty Shell" (1940), Brewster Ghiselin's "Bath of Aphrodite" (1946), Paul Engle's "Venus and the Lute Player" (1962), and Daniel Hoffman's "Aphrodite" (1970) are just a few examples. I want to end this chapter by looking at the way three male poets work through inappropriate approaches to Aphrodite to achieve healthier attitudes, in a manner which illustrates my hypothesis that psychological health for men results from facing up to and absorbing their fear of women's sexuality and then moving beyond gynophobia toward an adult sensuality.

In "To Judith Asleep," John Ciardi achieves balance between a generalized Aphrodite archetype and a specific woman he loves, recognizing the mythic power of her sexuality without subordinating her either as his muse or as a mere vehicle of his desire. At one level the poem is addressed to his real, mortal lover who is lying in bed asleep, "abandoned and naked, all let down / in ferny streams of sleep and petaled thighs / rippling into my flesh's buzzing garden." At another level she expresses forces as "far" as they are "familiar":

> Far and familiar your body's myth-map lights,
> traveled by moon and dapple. Sagas were curved
> like scimitars to your hips. The raider's ships
> all sailed to your one port. And watchfires burned
> your image on the hills. Sweetly you drown
> male centuries in your chiaroscuro tide
> of breast and breath. And all my memory's shores
> you frighten perfectly, washed familiar and far. (208)

There is plenty of fearsome content in Ciardi's Judith: "ritual wars" fought over her and spiritual battles by "desert monks" who "fought your image back / in a hysteria of mad skeletons," content which Ciardi acknowledges in his stance both "of wish and dread" when he thinks about their life together:

> and your white shell
> spiraled in moonlight on the bed's white beach;
> thinking, I might press you to my ear
> and all your coils fall out in sounds of surf
> washing a mystery sudden as you are
> a light on light in light beyond the light. (209)

In the manner of Chaucer in his hymn to love as light and prime mover, Ciardi reveres Judith's cosmic mystery without trying to appropriate it. Although in his final stanza he tries to reduce her to the status of "Child," he recognizes that this stance would trap him in "fear and miser's panic."

Like Ciardi, W. S. Merwin can only arrive at a stance of reverence before Aphrodite once he has recognized and overcome his fear of her destructive capacities. It is as if these poets were bringing back into the archetype the warlike content of Inanna and Ishtar, the aggression and resulting fear that was originally interwoven into one fabric much as life and death were interbraided in Celtic goddess archetypes. Once they recognize her conflation of creation and destruction as part of one unitary archetype, the poets transcend standard attitudes about feminine sensuality to achieve a personal sexual maturity. Thus in "December: Of Aphrodite" Merwin asserts that "In her name I acted" in spite of "Whatever the books may say," then fills his second stanza with instances of men who did not fare as well in the

face of Aphrodite, crazed like Hercules "by that jealous goddess."
Merwin asserts that the destruction wrought in Aphrodite's name is
not her responsibility and that she is ultimately a beneficent goddess.
Fully recognizing the terror inherent in Aphrodite's destructive
capacities, Merwin nevertheless realizes that approaching her is a
matter of perspective, and he chooses to see her not as "a name of
winter" but in her capacity as mistress of the green world and of golden
sensuality.

Like Ciardi with Judith, Wendell Berry, in "The Country of
Marriage," feels most comfortable approaching his lover in the world
of dream. In this poem, however, it is he (not his lover) who sleeps,
moving to a fuller archetypal understanding of Aphrodite. Berry rec-
ognizes the world of archetypes and the unconscious as a locus of
healed relationships between the sexes. He acknowledges the necessi-
ty of danger and risk in the quest for love. In order finally to approach
his lover he needs to replace his reason and self-sufficiency with a trust
in her that is neither boyish nor exploitative:

> How many times have I come into you out of my head
> With joy, if ever a man was,
> for to approach you I have given up the light
> and all directions. I come to you
> lost, wholly trusting as a man who goes
> into the forest unarmed. It is as though I descend
> slowly earthward out of the air. I rest in peace
> in you, when I arrive at last. (7)

It is this giving up of ego, reason, consciousness, and domination that
endows Berry with authentic sensuality:

> What I am learning to give you is my death
> to set you free of me, and me from myself
> into the dark and the new light. Like the water
> of a deep stream, love is always too much. We
> did not make it. Though we drink till we burst
> we cannot have it all, or want it all.
> In its abundance it survives our thirst.
> In the evening we come down to the shore
> to drink our fill, and sleep, while it
> flows through the regions of the dark.

> It does not hold us, except we keep returning
> to its rich waters thirsty. We enter,
> willing to die, into the commonwealth of its joy. (9)

The death Berry mentions is not a mere pun on sexual intercourse; nor is it the utter destruction by Venus experienced by Tannhäuser or the frightening losses of ego feared by many male poets. It describes, rather, the way men must let go of the self, as of dominance and excessive consciousness, to become participants in (rather than conquerors of) the natural world of sensuality. When men reach a healing and reciprocal sensuality, no longer desiring power over women, they attain a new empowerment both within nature and in their own bodies, an empowerment in which neither nature nor body is alien, and the ego does not cower in fear of women or of death. The Aphrodite archetype, rightly approached, gives men entry into a natural world which reason cannot dominate nor the mind assimilate, which is also the realm of Artemis. As I demonstrate in the third part of this book, Artemis, like Aphrodite, provides an entry into the natural world which is the ground of being of all archetypal materials, extending between lovers and between human beings and the earth.

7.

Aphrodite in Twentieth-Century Poetry by Women

*I*n her pioneering study, *Archetypal Patterns in Poetry*, Maud Bodkin remarks that male poets tend to be preoccupied by the maternal content of feminine archetypes, as in the case of Dante's feelings about Beatrice. "Within my own experience," Bodkin declares, "it is only as I related the dialogue and the description of the vision to the movement of the poem in its completeness that I can pass beyond the feeling of revulsion against what seems the dominance in the mind of Dante of the Mother-Imago" (178). "The attempt to trace the form assumed in poetry by the archetypal images of man and woman suggested the inquiry whether one could find in the poetry of woman writers any imaginative representation of man, related to the distinctive inner life of a woman in the same manner as an image of woman appearing in poetry shows relation to the emotional life of man" (290–91). In my early quest for archetypal patterns in women's fiction I followed Bodkin's lead, assuming that a male lover would emerge from women's fiction as the Beatrice equivalent for women, and I did sometimes run into an apatriarchal archetype (like Emily Bronte's Heathcliff, for example) whom I dubbed "the green world lover." In my study of women's poetry, however, I have found that women love poets are often as preoccupied with Aphrodite as are men, although with a special twist of our own: what men fear about our sexuality—engulfment in an uncontrolled Eros, giving up of the

Ego to let one's sensual urges have their way, and the association of these feelings with death itself—we fear in ourselves. While male poets focus on Aphrodite as "other," she can evoke self-doubt and self-loathing in us. Thus while twentieth-century male poets continue to express Victorian horror of Aphrodite, a conventionally beautiful woman poet like Kathleen Raine is horrified by the Venus she sees in her mirror. Men's sexuality *as such* is not a problem for them, but a natural, delightful facet of their personalities; women poets' sensuality continues to make them suspect not only to men but also to themselves. Nineteenth-century distaste for women's sexuality continues to threaten women poets who set out to celebrate Aphrodite; nor does evolution from Victorian gynophobia to sexual enlightenment occur. Although celebrations of feminine Eros occupied feminists and women poets in two high points of the period—the turn of the century and the 1960–70 decade—these years produced many negative as well as positive poems about Aphrodite.

Some of women's most revolutionary erotic manifestos were written between 1900 and 1918. In 1902 Amy Lowell (inspired by seeing Eleonora Duse dance) decided to become a poet, and she published her first collection in 1914; in 1910 Elinor Wylie left her first husband to run away with her lover, and she published her first collection in 1912; both Sara Teasdale and Mina Loy published volumes entitled *Love Songs* in 1917 and were hailed as modern Aphrodites. These women were aware of the new free love doctrines as they came of age, as were younger poets like Edna St. Vincent Millay and Muriel Rukeyser, who joined them in Greenwich Village and were also dubbed poet-priestesses of a free love religion.

I will demonstrate in this chapter's discussion of Aphrodite in pain how hatred of one's own sensuality is as likely to infect these "modern women" as their Victorian predecessors: like women poets in more recent decades of supposed sexual "liberation," they endured the perils of making themselves "free" for men, without being, consequently, at home with themselves, an ironic discrepancy which structured many of their poems. Sadly, I find a similar irony characterizing the experience of women poets during the "sexual liberation" in the 1960s and 1970s. Erica Jong, a contemporary prototype of the great woman lover of the turn of the century, sadly points out that "the eroticism that had ultimately been accepted from Henry Miller and D. H. Lawrence and Joyce has *never* been accepted when it came from a woman writer. . . .

Sexuality was not permitted for women—and to this day, it still is not permitted in many quarters" (273).

In considering poets' use of the Aphrodite archetype, we thus need to remember that "sexual liberation" was not an invention of the 1960s but had its beginnings as early as 1872, when Victoria Woodhull ran for president of the United States on the free love ticket. Woodhull inspired regional poets like Wisconsin's Ella Wheeler Wilcox to conflate the Communist with the sexual revolution: in *Poems of Passion* (1883) Wilcox declares that "My fierce emotions roam out of their lair," hating "King Reason," planning against him an erotic "insurrection of uncontrol" (15). Woodhull was precursor of a revolutionary sexual trend which inspired Olive Schreiner, Margaret Sanger, and Emma Goldman, who believed that "free love" was necessary for social change. Sanger urges recognition of a wife's sensuality and blames organized religion both for women's civil death and for killing an Eros which is woman's natural right: "They shut from her heart and her mind the knowledge of her love life and her reproductive functions" (175). Goldman, an early proponent of the idea that the personal is political, declares that "whether love last but one brief span of time or for an eternity, it is the only creative, inspiring, elevating basis for a new race, a new world" (78); and Mina Loy, in her 1914 "Feminist Manifesto," declares herself "in defiance of superstitition," asserting "that there is nothing impure in sex except the mental attitude toward it. The eventual acceptance of this fact will constitute an incalculably wider social regeneration than it is possible for our generation to acquire" (271). Like Goldman's assertion, Loy's manifesto reminds us that "free love" was part of the revolutionary ideology of the period and that these women believed that an overthrow of society would enable them to establish a saner and more sexually authentic role for women in a new system. These revolutionary declarations led to a backlash which combined post-Victorian gynophobia with capitalist hatred of revolutionaries: the vilification of Sanger, the deportation of Goldman, and Loy's ending of her life creating trash montages on themes of homelessness testify to the punishments which awaited such overt rebellions against feminine sexlessness.

A further complication in twentieth-century women's poetry about Aphrodite arises from a lack of correlation between attitudes to the archetype and a woman poet's stage of life. Though one might expect Aphrodite to concern young women or women in our prime, with older women renouncing her joys for the austerer aegis of Demeter or Artemis, this is not at all the case. A young woman horrified by the impact of her beauty on men often chooses an Artemisian solitude in her twenties; an older woman, able at last to transcend societal stereotypes, can suddenly find sexual fulfillment for the first time in her sixties and seventies. The turn of the century also produced an upsurge of lesbian self-consciousness, which, as Susan Gubar has documented, was accompanied by an interest in Sappho's poetry. "Through the dynamics of their collaboration with Sappho," Gubar suggests, "modernists like Renée Vivien and H. D. present themselves as breaking not only with patriarchal literary tradition, but also with nineteenth-century female literary history" (47). Lesbian women are able to create a love poetry with an energy fueled by distance from the desire for or the possibility of acceptance within patriarchy. In reading lesbian poetry along my scale of attitudes from pain to celebration I am not assuming a "just people" stereotype of lesbianism—the idea that with insignificant differences women who love women are really just like heterosexuals. As my examples of lesbian poetry will suggest, woman/woman Eros has a markedly different quality than heterosexual love, in that it is characterized by a special dynamic of love between individuals of the same gender and its intensity is enhanced by its patriarchal marginality. Andrea Lowenstein and I suggest in *Archetypal Patterns in Women's Fiction* that there is something radically different about the new space created when women love women.

Although I have included blues poems by African American women in the next section, on Aphrodite in pain, and although African American women's love poetry occurs at every point in the continuum of attitudes, I have devoted a separate section to a discussion of the regenerating force African American women poets draw upon to celebrate African goddess archetypes. When we get a combination of racial and sexual marginality in a lesbian poet like Audre Lorde, the poetry that emerges turns out to be the most powerful, celebratory, and apatriarchal of our entire sample. I have thus included Lorde in the transformation category of women who achieve their celebrations through a conscious reenvisioning of the deep content of Aphrodite, working through the shadow and destructive content of recent signatures toward a fully articulated praise for the non-European content of the archetype.

<table>
<tr><td>

Aphrodite
in Pain

</td><td>

Women poets' distrust of Aphrodite derives from distortions of the archetype promulgated by culture. Their approach to Aphrodite is ruptured

</td></tr>
</table>

by men's loathing for feminine sensuality which they internalize from dominant Victorian and twentieth-century sexual ideology. Three vignettes will illustrate this problem: Cleanth Brooks's comment on meeting Elinor Wylie, Randall Jarrell's description of Muriel Rukeyser, and Kathleen Raine's encounter with Venus in her own mirror.

Judith Farr cites Brooks as narrating in his autobiography how "at our Westport house I met the author of *Black Armour,* a phrase that evoked for me an image of herself; for there was something metallic about her and, if not reptilian, glittering and hard, as of some creature living in an iridescent shell. She enters a room with clanking scales, full panoplied for war like Boudicca or an elegantly slim Valkryie" (Farr 10). Although he associates Wylie with powerful Celtic and Nordic archetypes, he perceives her as rigid and reptilian, capable of an evil that consists in hardening herself against men. Wylie's reputation both as a poet and as a lover leads Brooks to project upon her a combination of power and threat, the whole thing delivered in a kind of comradely tone that assumes that others will easily empathize with the way he felt at the Westport cocktail party.

In a dissertation about Rukeyser, Jane Curtis analyzes Jarrell's comments on this left-wing political poet who, like Wylie, had the reputation of a woman determined to stick by her own erotic choices. Here are Jarrell's comments:

> Muriel Rukeyser is a forcible writer with a considerable talent for emotional rhetoric; but she works with a random melodramatic hand, and with rather unfortunate models and standards. One feels about most of her poems almost as one feels about the girl on last year's calender, and prefers to think of Miss Rukeyser only as the poet who wrote Ajanta . . . one feels, with dismay and delight, that one is listening to the Common Woman of our century, a siren photographed in a sequin bathing-suit, on rocks like boiled potatoes, for the weekend edition of *PM,* in order to bring sex to the deserving poor. When you think of yourself as that terrible thing, a public figure—and

Miss Rukeyser does to some extent—it is hard to decide what you do feel, what the reasons are . . . all the time the poem keeps repeating, keeps remembering to repeat, that it is a *good* girl—that it is, after all, dying for the people. (16 n. 46)

As Curtis aptly points out, Rukeyser celebrates physicality in her poetry in much the same manner as Whitman, "yet is it difficult to imagine Jarrell referring to Whitman's sometimes flawed lines by the circuitous route of the poet's body (perhaps 'almost as one feels about the boy in last year's tank suit'). Jarrell does no such cross-referencing between poet and teasing physicality when he discusses male poets . . . when the male critic patronizes the female artist by calling her poem 'a *good* girl' . . . he attempts to reassert his own tradition and leave the woman, again, on the outside, with a different and 'unfortunate' set of standards" (17–18). Like Brooks, Jarrell describes a sensually assertive Rukeyser as "hard" and military (Boudicca, Valkyrie, Siren), emphasizing the fearsome or destructive side of an Aphrodite archetype he projects onto her. Elements of Medusa, of the bird-footed sirens and snake-loving goddesses lurk in the aura Brooks and Jarrell project upon Wylie and Rukeyser. Having made them into satirically exaggerated female stereotypes, they try to degrade them by caricature (Ruykeyser as a girl on a calender, her poem as a girl who is trying to assert her goodness). From the previous chapter we are aware of the psychosexual reasons that male poets need to cut women down; what is important to note here is the impact of being perceived this way on women poets who are determined to write love poetry and to give Aphrodite her due worship.

Our third vignette shows what happens to the psyche of a woman poet victimized by these kinds of projections, when she is unable to internalize anything but an Aphrodite archetype distorted by male attitudes. In "Seen in a Glass" Kathleen Raine summarizes her feelings about how men's attitudes to her beauty have destroyed her capabilities for sensuality: "The Venus in my mirror sighs / . . . / I see in non-existent eyes / The incommunicable selfish pain" (53). Raine uses goddess archetypes in her poetry as demons that get into her psyche to cause destruction rather than empowerment, an attitude toward archetypes that results from the impact of her beauty on men. As a girl still at home in a Wesleyan Methodist household, Raine fell in love with a young man named Roland. Her father greeted the possibility of their engagement with anger, grief, and blame for enticing the young man. During a supposedly educational trip to the Continent after she was separated from Roland, Raine was sexually harassed by her older tutor, only to be told that his attraction to her youthful beauty was "her fault."

Intelligent as well as beautiful, Raine arrived at Cambridge filled with terror at her capacity to elicit sexuality in men. She recalls in her autobiography that

> I had brought with me to Cambridge the strongest possible sense that to attract a man sexually must imply guilt on my part. . . . To awaken such love, such tragic possibilities, must indeed be a grave matter. Twice I had brought sorrow upon myself and upon others by the inadvertent exercise of my power to evoke erotic love; and in Cambridge that power was all the more beyond my conscious control because I had become quite frigid; for not only was I pursued by my own heartbreak, by Roland's battles between desire and asceticism, but by my father's religious grief and anger, and my mother's tears—all caused by my fault.
>
> So that, if other young women might enjoy the play of "laughter-loving Aphrodite," to me it did not seem like play, but deadly earnest, guilt and misery. (*The Land Unknown* 62)

Although she gloried for a brief time in her popularity—being asked to take an important role in a play, for example—she learned "that it is hard, at eighteen, to grasp the truth that to be loved for our beauty is not to be loved at all. We expect to be treated as the goddess whose reflected image we bear; we think we are ourselves that goddess" (*The Land Unknown* 61–62).

Raine is a painful example of a poet educated in the classics in the heart of European culture who is unable to get beyond the male stereotypes of Aphrodite to her own sexual authenticity. The young Raine considers the idea that she is herself "that goddess" a painful delusion; her only solution is to become frigid. Her very closeness to patriarchal culture makes her fatally vulnerable to engulfment in men's ideas about Aphrodite and unable to empower herself through an authentic assimilation of the archetype. This introjection of self-loathing for embodying an Aphrodite archetype does not always come to women poets as young as the eighteen-year-old Raine; some of the women love poets of the early decades of the twentieth century first overtly celebrate Aphrodite and only later, when the scorn of the public for sensual women falls heavily upon them, modify their attitudes to disappointment, renunciation, or anger.

Whereas women poets of earlier periods, such as Aphra Behn, Frances Boothby, and Katherine Phillips, talked back to a male god of love about their frustrations, we find Lady Sackville, disappointed when her husband became unfaithful and abusive, taking out her feelings by attacking Aphrodite. In "Songs to Aphrodite" she laments her exile from being one of "Aphrodite's rose-crowned votaries" to a "colder place, on the chill surface of this passionless sea," and cannot forget in her "Wild heart, insatiate still and still the same" her experiences of Aphrodite in that other "dwelling-place," which had contained the "Altars of some lost ritual of love." Sackville's use of positive Aphrodite imagery reveals her sense of the deep background of the archetype in rituals celebrating women's sensuality; however, she turns against the love goddess in her "Ode to Aphrodite," angrily denouncing her for concealing beneath "calm waters" and the "swing of somnolent tides" much stormier forces, "angry tempests [which] roam along the borders of distracted lands." Lady Sackville is lamenting the transformation of a mellower Aphroditian landscape into "some dangerous shore" (31). We find the same kind of lashing out against Aphrodite in the poetry of Adelaide Crapsey, whose early illness made her approach the goddess elegiacally, and of Edith Sitwell, who, though she transcends her disappointments, writes elegies about Venus as a "dead trull," a moribund old female she wants to kill. The intensity of these renunciations derives, I would suggest, from poets' recognition of the empowering attributes of an Aphrodite whose potency is ruptured by twentieth-century masculine attitudes.

Sara Teasdale, a well-brought-up only child of a Baptist couple in St. Louis, found herself in a double bind very similar to Raine's. As William Drake has noted, she depicted her conflict as being between a modern woman lover and a frightened girl whose conscience was still "a little old Victorian Lady." Drake describes Teasdale torn between an "intimidating inner voice counseling her to be unassertive, obedient, humble, forbearing—traits that were considered to be feminine virtues" and a power "rising against this voice . . . the unsettling power of the 'Aphrodite' she had tried to follow on a road to freedom, love, and achievement. These two antagonists were too evenly matched for either to win a decisive victory" (xxxiii). Drake blames Teasdale's inability to overcome her Victorian conscience on her lack of "spiritual resources," but I diagnose the source of her paralysis as the disjunction between the deeper background of the Aphrodite archetype and a contemporary culture which could not accept a woman poet's articulation of erotic desire.

Although Teasdale began as a poet of women's erotic awakening (as Drake recounts, setting "up a little shrine to Aphrodite in her study and [declaring to a friend] 'She is more real to me than the Virgin' " [xxviii]), she spurned the romantic relationships proffered by John Hall Wheelock and by Vachel Lindsay for a marriage which she felt was financially prudent but which blocked her erotic development. Even before her sensually self-destructive decision, however, she filled her first volume, *Helen of Troy and Other Poems* (1911), with portrayals of women disappointed in love: Helen, Beatrice, Marianna Alcoforando, Guenevere, and Sappho's lover Erinna. All of these women suffered for Aphroditian qualities—Helen for her beauty, Alcoforando and Guenevere for their passionate natures, Beatrice for wanting to experience sensual love rather than being elevated to a spiritual abstraction. Highly conscious of the psychological impact of Victorian gender norms, Teasdale writes "talking back" poems quite similar to Rossetti's Donna Innominata sequence, and it is hardly surprising that she entitled her 1917 edition of women's poems *An Answering Voice* and filled it with poems about erotic awakenings followed by loss or death, by women poets who were disappointed in love.

Throughout her work Teasdale presents herself as a quester after love who is almost always thwarted because she is too passionate and too articulate. As early as 1911 she wrote a poem structured upon this painful ambiguity. She is out walking with a disinterested lover, listening to him talk and allowing him to ignore her feelings. While they stroll in Union Square, a red-light district of the period, she notices the prostitutes walking by, ending her poem with the ambiguous declaration:

> With the man I love who loves me not
> I walked in the street-lamps' flare—
> But oh, the girls who ask for love
> In the lights of Union Square. (32)

Perhaps naively deluded by the idea that it is "love" rather than a crass financial transaction that the girls seek, Teasdale momentarily identifies with the prostitutes. William Drake interprets the poem in terms of her Victorian double bind: "Believing that men were free of the inhibitions that imprisoned women, she could not understand their mysterious reluctance to take the initiative a woman waited for, and she tended to attribute it to shortcomings in herself. The poem reveals the prurient notion, in which Sara had been reared, that sex was essentially pornographic. Any woman who dared to assert herself sexually was automatically branded a whore" (69).

Teasdale's volumes of poetry are, nonetheless, filled with quests for love. In *Rivers to the Sea* she includes a dramatic monologue spoken by Sappho which contains one of her fullest assessments of the Aphrodite archetype. Sappho addresses her prayers to an Aphrodite she simultaneously reveres and deplores, and whom she acknowledges as a source of pain: "I was a sister of the stars, and yet / Shaken with pain; sister of birds and yet / The wings that bore my soul were very tired" (91). Although Teasdale's Sappho affirms her unity with the stars and birds associated with the Aphrodite archetype, she addresses "Love" as a male figure throughout the poem. Vivian Gornick's assessment of Jean Rhys's experiences in love holds true for Teasdale: "She had known from the time she was young that men and women, especially men, fear their own sensuality, that this fear cuts deep, slicing through intelligence and ordinary decency. If you were passionate, and you aroused passion in a man, he hated you; hated and abandoned and punished you" (9).

Teasdale's Sappho seems to be about to commit suicide, while this popular "love poet," torn between a puritan conscience and an authentic passion she could not realize with any of the partners available to her, suffered a lifetime of stress-related illnesses before finally killing herself. One of the striking elements in the biographies of twentieth-century women poets is the recurrence of psychosomatic illnesses. Whether, like Millay and Wylie, they try to live out Aphrodite's desires or whether, like Teasdale and Sitwell, they try to repress them, women's poems about Aphrodite crystallize into a painful combination of their instinctive recognition of the feminine sensuality she promises and their experience of the punishment heaped upon women who celebrate her.

Wylie was a contemporary of Teasdale's who was never allowed to forget that she ran away from her insane husband with an older married man, leaving her young son behind. Although the two were legally married in 1916, both her own social class and the literary world she joined tended to neglect the real person behind the "love poet" persona. Like Teasdale's, Wylie's poems are chiefly about the pain of being too passionate. Some of them are outright laments against the "curse" of being beautiful ("Beauty"); others, like "Confession of Faith," express her genuine terror of her lovers, all of whom she fears "to the bone" (*Collected Poems* 116). Love, in "Incantation," becomes for Wylie "A white door / In a dark lane; / A bright core / To bitter black pain" (35). Her experience of an intrusive and psychologically crippling Eros forces her to develop a "defense," so that from her earliest love poetry she uses images of hardness and opacity, as if she were erecting a barrier between her wounded sensuality and the lovers who have traumatized her. Thus in "The Tortoise in Eternity" she describes herself as a turtle sleeping "Within my house of patterned horn," her soft inner being existing only before birth and after death. In between, whenever she ventures into the world of twentieth-century heterosexual love, she needs a "darling roof" which will be "Tougher than hide or lozenged bark" (34).

The imagery of self-armament and rigidification as protection against what happens when opening herself to love reaches its fullest expression in the hard surfaces, metal shields, and military defenses of *Black Armour*, the collection which Brooks took as characterizing her "reptilian, glittering and even hard" personality. These poems, in groups entitled "Breastplate," "Gauntlet," "Helmet," "Beaver Up," and "Plumes," are talking-back poems written against the modern world's attitude toward her quest for feminine Eros. She includes, nonetheless, a perfectly straightforward and reverential hymn, "To Aphrodite, with a Talisman." We have seen that Medusa in her stony aspect is sometimes conflated with Aphrodite in poems by both men and women; for Wylie, Medusa's petrifaction springs from the poet's inability to incarnate Aphrodite without social prejudice. "Let No Charitable Hope," in the "Gauntlet" section of *Black Armour*, is her lament at society's denigration of her feminine sensuality: "I am, being woman, hard beset; / I live by squeezing from a stone / The little nourishment I get" (35). She herself is the stone she is squeezing, her fist "compact as stone," so that it "preserves a shape / Too utterly its own."

Although Louise Bogan once refused to edit an anthology of women lyric poets out of distaste for what she called the "Oh-God-the-Pain-Girls" school of women poets who, as Elizabeth Frank reminds us, "plaintively descanted on the self-destructive elements common to their erotic lives as women" (63), her own poetry shares Teasdale's and Wylie's entrapment within patriarchal attitudes, a situation about which she is conscious enough to protest but seems unable to escape. The source of Bogan's trauma about her own eroticism seems to have been her passionate mother's love affairs, and she entered an early, disastrous marriage to get away from home. Like Wylie, Bogan soon realized that marriage was not the only way to seek love, and after her divorce threw herself into the Greenwich Village world of "free love," supposedly friendly to freewheeling women like her. As Gloria Bowles describes them, many of her "love poems" of this period are about "the betrayals and confusions of love," which did not prevent Bogan from a lifelong quest for Eros, to the extent that her "happiest times were in her affairs outside marriage, including one with an electrician that lasted eight years, until she was forty-five" (8). "Evening Star," set among any number of pained love poems, nonetheless represents the conventionally reverential prayer to Aphrodite, much like Wylie's hymn.

In spite of her positive attitude toward Aphrodite, Bogan's poems develop a self-protective carapace like Wylie's, characterized, as Deborah Pope has noted, by imageries of hardening, stiffness, and rigidity. In the aptly entitled "Alchemist," she decides to transform her passion into a harder substance: "I burned my life, that I might find / A passion wholly of the mind" (Dark Summer 40). This is not a successful alchemical transformation in the sense of burning through love's pain to a new synthesis; rather, the burning process hardens her psyche without transmuting it, so that her "unmysterious flesh" maintains itself "passionate beyond the will," alienated from "the mind's avid substance." Even her attempt to renounce love of men for love of nature petrifies the green world: in "Men Loved Wholly Beyond Wisdom" she feels that men do not reciprocate women's love and that women must turn away from them into solitude: "To be quiet in the fern / Like a thing gone dead and still" (41). As in her "Medusa,"

Bogan's stone imagery represents a static goddess whose natural sensuality she experiences as rigidity.

Another way in which women poets develop negative images of Aphrodite is through accepting themselves as male projections, subordinating their being to the being of their lovers, and allowing themselves to be subsumed in roles which males (especially male poets) project upon them. The quest for self natural to the development of the male poet involves a search through a variety of love affairs for a true Eros and for the muse; when the woman poet is supposed to *be* that muse her own poetic development can be destroyed. That is the case with Laura Riding, who became part of a *ménage à trois* with Robert Graves and his wife. In an autobiographical poem "My Father and My Childhood" Riding describes changing allegiance early in her life from her mother to her father, who could better instruct her in the ways of the (implicitly masculine) world. As a result Riding falls into the fatal trap of seeing herself only through men's eyes, much in the way that Kathleen Raine internalized men's ideas about her destructive beauty. In "Divestment of Beauty," for example, Riding writes about "She, she and she and she," lovely and glamourous women, but addresses the poem to a male "you" who knows such lovely women are deathly, asking them to get rid of their inauthentically "worshipping eye," "To pluck the loathsome eye" (as in "if thine eye offend thee, pluck it out") of masculine perspective on women's beauty, to "Forswear the imbecile / Theology of loveliness" (74). In an encoded and recondite manner, Riding articulates her consciousness of being turned into something hard (even if a jewel) by somebody else's projections. In "Auspice of Jewels" she criticizes those who "have connived at those jewelled fascinations" women have become. If a woman is hypnotized by men's projections about her, she can be tempted to let her own poetic powers atrophy: in 1939 she simultaneously renounced Graves as a lover and her own vocation as poet.

The impact of associating oneself with a patriarchally degraded Aphrodite is painfully clear not only in Kathleen Raine's biography but in her poetry as well, where she often uses goddess archetypes to describe psychologically destructive forces, demonic powers that cause havoc rather than empowerment: "God in me the four elements of storm / Raging in the shelterless landscape of the mind / Outside the barred doors of my Goneril heart" ("Storm," Bernikow, 179–80). This archetypal self-loathing, in which the woman poet denounces goddesses with whom she identifies but who are hated by men, reaches its devastating expression in "The Pythoness," where we find Neumann's archetype of the goddess as "Terrible Mother" internalized by a woman poet who agrees with the masculine idea that women, herself included, are "polluted." As we can see, the difference between male and female poets' difficulties with Aphrodite has to do with women's internalizing patriarchal distaste for their sensuality. Although both pathologies are debilitating, hatred for the self creates a distinct kind of anguish, quite different from hatred for the "other." I would speculate that the persistence of the "Oh-God-the-Pain" school of women poets throughout the twentieth century can be attributed to this kind of alienation from their own sexuality because of the way men degrade feminine Eros.

There are women poets who (like Conrad Aiken and D. H. Lawrence) write a love poetry hardened into deadlock between their desires and a conviction that love can only produce suffering and pain. Louise Glück, who was born in 1943 and thus writes long after the period of Wylie, Teasdale, and Bogan, creates poetry similarly devoted to a vision of Eros as something which pertains to men and victimizes women. Glück's "Epithalamium" subverts its conventional celebration of happy sensuality to excoriate "the terrible clarity of marriage" and "the formless / grief of the body, whose language / is hunger—" (*Descending Figure* 17). To Glück, Eros is something masculine: "To be male, always / to go to woman," and when writing about caves (which are often genitalic references for women celebrating Eros) experiences only disgust with the smells of love: "So the rot- / scent of its pussy-foot- / ing fingers lingers, when it's over" (*First Born* 33). Like Bogan, Teasdale, and Wylie, Glück refers to early childhood traumas which have a petrifying effect on her psyche. In "Palais des Arts" she writes about "stationary" and "paralyzed" gods, and one "God" in particular seems associated with a father remembered as an agent of terror. In "Bridal Piece," describing "our honeymoon," she recalls this father having "had to have his own way," and in "The Deviation" she talks about the "fear of death" which comes upon "certain female children," "because a woman's body / *is* a grave, it will accept / anything" (*Descending Figure* 32). Glück sees both men and women victimized by love. In "The Fear of Love," from "The Garden," both she and her lover are turned into rock, "That body lying beside me like obedient stone." Although, as we shall see in the next two chapters, this kind of petrifaction often becomes part of an alchemical transformation of the personality through suffering, for Glück there is no synthesis, only a frozen stasis, as if she were a Medusa turning herself to stone.

Some women poets go so far as to describe Aphrodite herself as turned into stone by the trauma of patriarchal heterosexuality. That must be the explanation for Olga Broumas's puzzlingly negative poem about Aphrodite in *Beginning with O*, a collection which otherwise affirms this lesbian poet's empowerment by goddesses. Broumas's Aphrodite is "The one with the stone cups / and the stone face" (18–19). Although many other lesbian poets follow Sappho in celebrating Aphrodite as their special goddess, Broumas associates her with a destructive and phallic heterosexuality.

There is a very fine line, which many women poets cross and recross throughout their life, between a poetry of pained Eros and lyrics affirming Aphrodite. The blues tradition in African American women's poetry (Ma Rainey's "Sweet Rough Man," for example, and Bessie Smith's "Dirty No Gooder Blues") often pointedly satirizes men while seeming to accept pain as part of loving them. Gwendolyn Brooks, in *The Anniad*, creates Annie Allen as a similarly victimized woman, waiting for a "paladin" or hero only to be seduced and betrayed, even the little room she has made into a temple of Aphrodite becoming the place where her "doomer" does her wrong. Deadlocked in love's pain, Annie is left waiting, "Paralyzed and paranoid," for her lover to return and betray her all over again.

Does the blues' expression of pain raise African American women's consciousness of their victimization so that they can do something about it? Isn't their assertion of the difficulty of heterosexual love in its own way a protest? It could be argued that the blues represent women's communicating to each other a simultaneous strength and lament for what has happened to them, cleansing themselves through anger at a cultural situation they are powerless to change. The encapsulating patriarchy is especially painful for African American women, whose men feel demasculinized by economic and social discrimination and often lash out against the women in frustration. Many African American women poets, however, angrily name love's pain in order to transcend both patriarchal and white constrictions. Where Raine is unable to see herself rather than culture's reflection of her in her mirror, Lucille Clifton (like Mary Elizabeth Coleridge) perceives herself as something besides what men see, as a "city / of a woman" endowed with her own "geography." Any man who gets his hands on her, she insists, has "got his hands on / some damn body!" (7).

The difference between these African American poets and the "Oh-God-the-Pain" school of white poets has to do with a weakening of the cultural signature about women's sexuality. Thus Ida Cox, in "Wild Women Blues," suggests "a different system" for when men get violent, reminding women that "you never get nothing / by being an angel child." "Civilization" is useless, patriarchy to be outwitted, the only possibility for women our apatriarchal wildness. I do not want to get into a facile comparison of African American and white women's pain; both groups tend to take patriarchy so seriously that they internalize its destructive aspects. We have seen in the case of Kathleen Raine, however, that there may be a correlation between a woman poet's acceptance of patriarchal values and her entrapment in cycles of painful romance, a factor which characterizes much of the work of two American poets of different generations, lyrical styles, and sexual choices, May Sarton and Diane Wakoski, both of whom try to work through internalized cultural values toward empowerment by goddess archetypes.

Throughout her poetic opus, from the 1930s until the present, Sarton depicts love as intrinsically painful, even violent, while using figures like Eve, Medusa, and Kali as archetypal vehicles for envisioning women's experience. In her sonnet sequence "A Divorce of Lovers" she describes herself and her lover as "these two warring halves" and addresses her partner as "Dear fellow-sufferer, dear cruelty" (Collected Poems 201, 203). In the sequence of love poems entitled Letters from Maine she is again splitting up with a lover (whom she identifies with her muse), who comes to visit only to present the "icy visage" of a "Medusa who has frozen herself into a trance." Although Sarton uses Aphrodite to refer to her lover's arrival out of the sea "Like Aphrodite on her shell" (Letters from Maine no. 9, 26). Sarton depicts the goddess as disinterested in her, the Botticellian imagery mere allusion, while the archetype of a cruel Medusa embodies Sarton's real feeling about her lover. Sarton's love poetry describes a pain and divisiveness which she takes as intrinsic to Eros: in "Myself to Me" she celebrates her solitude until "Love all unasked broke down the door, / To bring me pain as it did before," pain which she feels is necessary for poetic inspiration (CP 365).

Perhaps Sarton's closeting her lesbianism through most of her writing career makes passion a perennially painful experience; moreover, like several other women poets, she seems to have identified more with her father than with her mother, so that her pain may derive, at least in part, from an unconsciously internalized patriarchal attitude which may undermine her attempts at empowerment. Two poems, "My Sisters, O My Sisters" and "The Invocation to Kali," hold the key to Sarton's use of archetypes. Having declared that women poets like Dickinson, Rossetti, and even Sappho have lived "lost, strained, unforgiven" lives and "we who are writing women" are "strange monsters," Sarton bursts forth in the marvelous prayer "To come to the deep place where poet becomes woman" (CP 75), a great hymn to feminine empowerment which is, paradoxically, sandwiched between an announcement that creative women are monstrous (to culture) and Sarton's identification of the deepest wellsprings of poetry with masculinity, "The masculine and violent joy of pure creation." Not only does Sarton identify both birthing and creation with a masculine archetype; she also insists that women will be grounded in nature until "we let this stranger / Plough deep into our hearts his joy and anger," as if only in submission to male violence will we be able to "match men's greatness with our own" (CP 77). If we cannot achieve feminine poetic empowerment without submitting to a rapacious male God, will the ends be worth the means? Sarton seems to accept masculinity and violence as necessary to both love and creation, an attitude which may contribute to the sense of victimization we find in so many of her love poems.

As we saw in her poem about Medusa, Sarton perceives the apatriarchal possibilities underlying the cultural signature, acknowledging beneficence within an archetypal figure whom others take as destructive. This approach to the darker qualities of feminine archetypes characterizes her poem to Kali, whom she introduces, in Joseph Campbell's words, as "the terrible one of many names." We have seen how male poets must approach and assimilate this "Terrible Mother" archetype before being able to experience a true Aphrodite; in this poem Sarton also insists that the only way to creation is "out of destruction" by staying "open-eyed" in Kali's "terrible place" (CP

217

317). "We," Sarton insists, are the Kalis who "gassed God in the ovens" of the concentration camps and, in the sixties (a "time of burning"), must accept rage and fury (319). Sarton conflates the genocidal destructiveness of European civilization with her own rage, envisioning Kali's "dreadful empire" as a passage leading down "to her dark mystery" and to purgation through acknowledging that we all are personally and socially violent. Although Sarton is hopeful that feminine archetypal darkness will renew life, she considers violence and destruction as components of Eros. I find Sarton's opus deadlocked by her excessive valuation of violence and masculinity. There is no permanent arrival of the golden, happy Aphrodite in Sarton's poetry. Like Elinor Wylie and Sara Teasdale, Sarton is enmeshed in a socially unacceptable feminine Eros, and keeps renouncing Aphrodite for a more Artemisian solitude.

Diane Wakoski, who was born in 1937 (when Sarton was publishing her first collection of poems), provides a more recent example of the woman poet struggling with patriarchal attitudes embodied in cruel male archetypes which she has internalized. Like Aphra Behn, Wakoski finds the god of love cruel and creates "the motorcycle betrayer" and "George Washington" to represent him, while her "King of Spain," whom she posits as her ideal lover, is less patriarchal, with some aspects of the green world lover archetype. Although in a number of her early poems, including "Belly Dancer" and "The Priestess No. 1," Wakoski celebrates women empowered by Aphrodite, many of her poems of the 1970s and 1980s focus upon disappointments in love. Dedicating *The Motorcycle Betrayal Poems* to "all those men who betrayed me at one time or another, in hopes they will fall off their motorcycles and break their necks," Wakoski is clearly in the "talking-back" school of women love poets. At this stage in her life, her feelings about her "homeliness" within the context of male ideas about "beauty" prevent her from transcending the pained phase of love poetry. In "I Have Had to Learn to Live with My Face," which is similar to Kathleen Raine's "Seen in a Glass," Wakoski looks in a mirror and sees "My face," which "I have hated for so many years," and which she feels deserves attack: "my face that I wish you would bruise and batter." Wakoski does not achieve self-acceptance easily: nine years later, in *Dancing on the Grave of a Son of a Bitch,* we find the same painful self-hatred in "I Am the Daughter of the Sun," where her mirror once again reflects a face she cannot assimilate: "The truth is my face. / I do not want to look in the mirror" (43–44). In a 1981 interview Wakoski says that when she looks in her mirror she sees "the image of myself as Medea and an image of myself, again, as a murderer."

In *Waiting for the King of Spain*, Wakoski conjures up an archetypal lover while identifying with Artemis/Diana rather than with Aphrodite. She develops a self-empowering image of herself in "Daughter Moon" by assimilating Artemis in both her beneficent and her destructive (Hecate) aspects, synthesizing these facets into a self who can partner the archetypal "King of Spain." Although she cannot assimilate the Aphrodite archetype as part of her psyche, she calls upon Diana/Artemis to help her move toward a feminine archetypal journey into her unconscious.

Perhaps as a result of this process, we find Wakoski in *The Collected Greed* confronting Sylvia Plath, whom she introduces as "a beautiful poet," recognizing that Plath died even though she had the very "beauty" Wakoski thinks she lacks, and refusing to take the path of suicide for herself. Nor will Wakoski die "for a man who betrays me," by falling "into that / weeping well" of the "Oh-God-the-Pain" women; rather, she will celebrate the sense of immanence inherited from her farming grandparents while learning to transcend pain through learning to "be compassionate to others" (117). This decision to move through and beyond pain empowers Wakoski to transcend her tormenters, so that in "Fantasies of Power" she reintroduces the motorcyclist and the King of Spain as unsuccessful opponents who have not succeeded in stealing her heart or paralyzing her with fear. At the end of this collection she assimilates the Artemis archetype, declaring herself "I, moon," an admirer of both men and women.

In accepting the archetypal implications of her own name and thus acknowledging feminine empowerment, Wakoski transcends the masculine power she previously internalized. To be fully transformational, such an inner journey must be a personal exploration, and this she undertakes in "Little Tricks of Linear B," in which she uses fairy tale figures rather than classical ones. The poem is an archetypal descent journey structured upon a series of dreams in which she perceives herself as "the marsh king's daughter" (still male-defined) while acknowledging her role as Persephone, carried away from Demeter's kingdom. She recognizes herself as a "graceless" adolescent girl, accompanied on a picnic by her father, mother, and a friend of theirs she is flirting with. Her mother has baked her feet into a loaf of "pumpernickel bread," and she has been banished to a marsh for her disobedience. It is there that Wakoski addresses the little girl as herself.

The key to such an internal journey can be to rescue one's own inner lost child, but Wakoski's quest is inconclusive, hesitating between her mother's rage and the painful power of her father. Although she asserts that it is up to her to heal herself, Wakoski at the end of the poem is still asking questions about male approval from George Washington and the Marsh King, whose acknowledgment she still requires. In *Medea, the Sorceress* she still thinks that men, not women, possess "secret lives" far more "precious" and empowering than any special knowledge women may have. By the time of her 1986 volume, *The Rings of Saturn*, however, she has taken the crucial step of asking for help from the archetypal Queen of Wands and declares herself ready for a true change, hoping for an alchemical transformation like a "chameleon in the heart of that fire" (62). The change still seems to involve resolving her discomfort with unacceptable body parts and a longing to be made "pure," which, in this context, suggests sublimation rather than synthesis, transcendence away from rather than a celebration of bodily immanence.

In these poems Wakoski hesitates on the edge of transformation, between what men think about her and what she thinks about herself. Like other women poets I have looked at in this chapter, she is engulfed in the patriarchal pie, although she begins to get her head out of the sticky crust. As for male poets, the key to such an emergence lies in a change of attitude toward what is feminine. Men must transcend distaste for the "otherness" of women in order to heal the psychic damage of inauthentic sexuality; women poets struggle with an alienation from their own bodily selves fostered by patriarchy. African American women's blues poetry provides another clue to personal transformation; it combines anger with ridicule, the anger arising from self-worth and the ridicule from a refusal to lie down and take what men deal out. White women poets tend to consider themselves part of patriarchal culture and thus become more engulfed in the patriarchal pie, so that by taking men too seriously we inflict the kind of psychological damage upon ourselves that arises from low self-worth. In the next section I will present more cheerful examples, in which women poets learn to laugh at masculine ideas about feminine sexuality and to reenvision apatriarchal archetypes in a process of self-celebration.

Aphrodite and the Transformation of Personality

In Tarot, the Queen of Wands is associated with the healing power of fire, with the salamander as a creature that transforms itself through alchemy, and with a specifically feminine energy vibrating in nature. She is also linked to Artemis. Although Wakoski's use of the term *pure* could refer to the alchemically purifying aspects of the archetypal Queen rather than to a puritanical denial of the body, her prayer to transcend the roles of daughter and victimized lover remains unanswered. To focus on the turning point where a poet transcends patriarchal signatures to assimilate an empowering feminine archetype, let us consider Judy Grahn's "The Queen of Wands." In this title poem to a 1982 collection, Grahn identifies with both the formal or historical signatures of the Queen of Wands (particularly Helen of Troy) and her immanent natural powers. Her powerful archetypal self-assertion is embedded within a series of poems tracing Helen's power to El-Ana and to "Anael," the "Muhammedan Venus," and archetypes like Helga, Helle, Hlin, Yelana, and El-Inna. In her preface to *The Queen of Wands* Grahn writes that "I first met the Queen of Wands in a 1913 translation of a clay tablet of ancient Babylonian writing" where the story is told "of a queen who has been stolen from her temple and carried away by ship." Although this is a tale of victimization, Grahn identifies with the archetype's enduring powers, her survival as the "weaving spider," or webster; and assimilates her "spider/spirit" weaving words in poetry: "For language is a form of weaving too, a clothing our ideas wear, a glowing flesh they are made of, a heart that beats in them" (xii–xiii). So how does Grahn learn to affirm the spider and the goddess, a natural immanence and a glory transcending "civilization," when other poets accept victimization more easily? The answer can be found in "The land that I grew up on is a rock," in the same collection, where Grahn acknowledges her mother as "a rock," not an obdurate Medusa or petrifyingly terrible mother figure but "a slow, slow / cooled-off flame, and a cradle, both"

(5). Although Grahn wavers between her intellectual father and her tearful mother, her naming of the mother as a core of strength is the turning point in her psychological development, enabling her to assimilate feminine archetypes to heal herself.

As we saw in the case of poets coming to terms with Medusa, each woman needs to accept the sexual content of her mother's life before she herself can achieve a mature sensuality. This does not mean a sharing of intimate details between mother and daughter; nor does it involve a daughter's taking on her mother's sexual identity, which would lead to a dangerous fusion. Just as male poets are often paralyzed by the maternal element in their lovers, women poets can become deadlocked not only by an overvaluation of the father and his world but, even more destructively, by a denial of maternal sexuality. At the personal as at the cultural level, women poets have had to restore value to an Aphrodite archetype which both their educations and their families tempt them to repudiate.

As she would be the first to acknowledge, Grahn's affirmation of feminine archetypes occurs within the context of women poets who for several centuries have been digging underneath classical materials to cleanse them of patriarchal attitudes and restore their original attributes. Her renunciation of allegiance to her father and lovers and naming the aspects of a victimization she repudiates places her in the "talking-back" mode characterizing poets such as H. D., Muriel Rukeyser, and Edna St. Vincent Millay, three very different women who spent years working through the "shadow" of degrading attitudes toward archetypal empowerment.

As Susan Friedman has illustrated, one of the most striking aspects of H. D.'s opus is her self-consciousness about the intricate ways men have encoded distaste for Helen and goddesses and her determination to reaffirm the original value of these archetypes. In "Helen," for example, H. D. first declares that "All Greece hates" Helen, and only then can move toward a reaffirmation of her as "God's daughter, born of love." This poem, Friedman asserts, "takes as its subject the woman who has been the literary and mythic symbol of sexual beauty and illicit love in western culture" but "does something new: it implicitly attacks the traditional imagery of Helen and implies that such perspectives have silenced Helen's own voice" (232–33). H. D.'s anger at Helen's degradation becomes, in Friedman's analysis, a vehicle for transcending the negative content of men's attitudes: "The *Trilogy* carries woman's anger one step forward into the processes of transformation. Recognition of traditional forms of misogyny leads not to despair, but to an affirmation of the poet's power to purify patriarchal images of woman and to resurrect the Goddess as the spirit of regenerative love in the modernist nightmare" (243). Thus in "Tribute to Angels" H. D. describes "Venus as desire" experienced by women as "venerous, lascivious" in men's perception, but she refuses to accept men's degradation of Venus until "the very root of the word shrieks" and "is full, they say, of poison." The key phrase here is the simple "they say," implying that H. D. does not say any such thing, a phrase whose talking-back anger is the vehicle that enables H. D. to venereate Aphrodite, Astarte, and Venus as a unified archetype which will empower her. The key elements in H. D.'s ability to reenvision the Helen stereotype in terms of her deeper archetypal background are naming and anger, a consciousness about the early roots of Greek myth and distaste for devaluation of feminine archetypes. In her idiosyncratic way, H. D. bases her entire poetic work on a dialectical process in which she works through repudiation of feminine archetypes toward a modern reenvisioning of the archetype's deep background.

Several other women poets of the twentieth century undergo a similar lifelong transformation of the personality through facing up to sexual self-disgust, naming it as an externally imposed stereotype and revaluing Aphrodite. In a popular poetry quite different from the scholarly lyrics of H. D., Millay uses a colloquial "talking back" to her male lovers as part of a lifelong allegiance to Aphrodite. Like her contemporaries Teasdale and Wylie, Millay established herself as a "modern woman love poet." Her love sonnets and the lyrics she produced throughout her life are conventional only in form. She achieves a self-sufficient feminine Eros by ridiculing her male lovers' devious tricks and by utilizing the deeper background of the Aphrodite archetype. In A Few Figs from Thistles she affirms the short-term love affair as her natural right ("Whether or not we find what we are seeking / Is idle, biologically speaking"), repudiating the "heavy prince" Eros and announcing herself much too strong for the "puny rain" of his arrows (sonnet viii); at the same time, she transmutes her erotic experiences "Into the golden vessel of great song" in a poetry of passion. Although in this sonnet she is ostensibly taking the high or sublimated courtly love posture of one whose longing remains unfulfilled, she transparently embeds her sexual climax as the source of her poetic empowerment. She transcends her culture's detractions of women's sensuality through ridicule. Her recognition of the way men try to dominate her, her ability to articulate and satirize these attempts, and her allegiance to independent feminine heroes of history and mythology enable her to affirm sexuality without becoming victimized by it. She identifies herself with such great women lovers as Lilith, Lesbia, Lucrece, and Helen but does not merely protest their victimization, as Christina Rossetti did. Like H. D., Millay derives her poetic inspiration from a renewed vision of Aphrodite. "My worship from this hour the Sparrow-Drawn / Alone will cherish, and her arrowy child," she asserts in sonnet xv, while, in the same sequence, she identifies with women throughout history who have loved deeply, "treacherous queens" who, "Heedless and wilful, took their knights to bed" (95).

The older she gets, the more erotically explicit Millay becomes. In 1939 she declares that "I too beneath your moon, almighty Sex, / Go forth at nightfall crying like a cat," living a life built out of "honest bone . . . and anguish; pride; and burning thought; / And lust is there, and nights not spent alone" (125). Although Millay frequently announces that she is going to abandon her lovers for solitude in some little "shanty by the shore" and identifies herself as often with Artemis as with Aphrodite, she combines both archetypes in a lifetime of erotic self-sufficiency and self-determination.

Rukeyser, like Millay, was influenced by Margaret Sanger and the Greenwich Village free love movement early in the twentieth century. But her style of political and epic poetry is very different from Millay's or H. D.'s lyrics, and she uses it to work through the temptation to internalize masculine attitudes about her to a free lover's allegiance to Aphrodite. In 1976 Rukeyser appeared on a panel with Cynthia Ozick, and one of those depressing interchanges occurred in which a woman writer says that she is not a woman writer. In this case, it was Ozick who made this declaration, with Rukeyser replying that "you, Cynthia, write from the mind but I write from the body, a female body"—which is exactly what she had been doing from her earliest days as a poet of both politics and passion (Molly Friedrich 97). As early as "Theory of Flight," the poem which established her reputation, Rukeyser opposed lovemaking to war, calling for an "answer" to "the men walking toward death" to be found in sexuality, "the bones / easing, the flesh slipping perfume upon the air." As Jane Curtis puts it, Rukeyser insists upon the power of sexual energy to redeem humanity, even in times of war, and "One means by which Rukeyser attempts to establish a female identity is through sexual communication" (274). In "Private Life of the Sphinx," in which she talks back to "shaky king" Oedipus in the persona of the sphinx, she asserts that "My questions are my body," antedating the method of writing from the female body which French feminist critics would greet as an innovation later in the century.

Rukeyser did not easily arrive at a position where she could overcome male attitudes to assert sexual self-determination (which included her decision to give birth to a son by her married lover); in the archetypal realm, correspondingly, her work unfolds as a process of transcending identification with male gods. In "Orpheus" she seems to identify with the male god of poetry who is torn apart (by women) and must be reborn, presuming, like Sarton, that poetry springs from a masculine muse. In *Beast in View,* in contrast, Rukeyser structures "Ajanta" upon a rebirth journey like Inanna's descent into the underworld, Ajanta's quest taking her down to a dark cave where she finds the archetypes Rukeyser needs to regenerate her poetry: "Came to Ajanta cave, the painted space of the breast, / The real world where everything is complete" (210). There is a certain violence in Rukeyser's heterosexuality: in the next poem in this same collection Leda is portrayed as "Mortal Girl," "singing at last alone naked and proud" after making love to the god disguised as a swan, praying to him to make her more naturally human as a result of their intercourse. She is not submitting to victimization but asks him to "leave me free / In all my own shapes, deep in the spirit's cave / To sing again the entrance of the god" (212). Overbearing as the traditionally rapacious god may be, the girl's power derives from her celebration of her own passionate mortality. I do not read Rukeyser's "Mortal Girl" as I read Sarton's prayer to be ploughed by the great god of poetry in "My Sisters, O My Sisters," however. Whereas Sarton seemed to ask to be overwhelmed and subsumed by a masculine god, Rukeyser sees intercourse as a vehicle for attaining her own "shape" in complement with him.

In her lifetime of political protest Rukeyser repudiated her businessman father's capitalist values, and in a pivotal collection, *Body of Waking,* she comes to terms with the death of her mother, who had lived only in fear of "the wordless king" who "went isolate and cruel," "His armies all that entered." Whether this refers to her father or to the patriarchal culture her mother feared, in the second stanza of the elegy Rukeyser turns a corner into a compassionate acceptance of her mother through the experience of being a mother herself, which empowers her own rebirth: "You are here, Mother, and you are / Dead, and here is your gift: my life which is my home" (407). There are submerged Aphroditian imageries in the dawning "starflash" (with reference to Venus as the morning star) and in the foam out of which the embryo is born; this is a poem of a holistic initiation into a new feminine identity in which body and mind, spirit ("cloud-companions"), and immanence become intermeshed. In the panel debate Rukeyser acknowledges that "I am a violent person, and I try each day, like the alcoholic, to be non-violent." We can see her sense of violence in two key poems about Venus in *Body of Waking:* "The Birth of Venus" and "The Place at Alert Bay." In the first poem Rukeyser renounces Botticelli's prettification of Venus's origin in her father's castration, "Not as he [Botticelli] saw her . . . But born in a / tidal wave of the father's overthrow, / the old rule killed and its mutilated sex." Although the birth of Rukeyser's Venus is far from nonviolent, she describes a dialectical process in which the goddess has moved through these horrors toward beauty, a beauty achieved by the poet's facing up to the destructive capabilities which are the key to her own and the goddesses' rebirth.

As Jane Curtis has noted, "Rukeyser reeducates us to the masculine aggression which the Hesiod myth perpetuates before allowing for a positive 'translation' of Venus into the goddess of love. The key to a translation from origins in 'the mutilated sex' is the idea of the myth 'being used,' being confronted in its savagery and, like the meanings in Rukeyser's other translations of myth and ritual, changed" (274). I agree that the aggression is not merely masculine and thus outside the poet's feminine experience; I would further suggest that it is a feminine violence experienced both in her own personality and in the warlike element of the Venus archetype and thus a quality that Rukeyser must confront, absorb, and transcend in her life.

Rukeyser was a student of myth and archetypal psychology. As in the case of H. D., her considerable scholarship brings her to a consciousness of the way classical myths degraded women that she puts to use in cleansing her self of stereotypical attitudes. She describes this process in "Long Enough," where she declares herself ready to "Walk out of the pudorweb / and into a lifetime" (413). It is the virtuous/shameful Venus that I examined in chapter 2 that Rukeyser wishes to transcend, breaking through the web of shame, shyness, and decency, which are all connotations of the Latin *pudor*.

The classical myths underlying European culture are far more problematic for poets than are archetypes derived from less divisive non-European sources. In 1949 Rukeyser had taken her baby son with her to explore Vancouver Island, having become interested in Franz Boas's descriptions of the tribes which had lived there. In "The Place at Alert Bay," a poem which comes immediately after "The Birth of Venus," Rukeyser describes an archetypal "Creation pole" which she assimilates as a "Tree of meanings where the first mothers pour / Their totems." She identifies the divinity that inspired the pole as both male and female, both an "Everfound mother" and a "Father of salmon-clouded seas" merging in the "Weatherbeaten image of us all." Although she finds her being and poetic voice through experiencing feminine bodily powers, Rukeyser reveres both male and female archetypes.

Rukeyser's poetry, like Millay's, retains its sense of sexual empowerment to the end. In her next-to-last volume, *Breaking Open*, she includes "In the Underworld," a poem based on Inanna's descent, and two poems very much in the Inanna-admiring-her-own-vulva mode. In "In Her Burning" Rukeyser describes herself as "The randy old / woman" who "said / Tickle me up / I will be dead very soon." Rukeyser's combination of mythological scholarship, sexual self-sufficiency, and refusal to be deterred by poets like Randall Jarrell and a reading public that hesitated to accept such a holistic combination of the political, intellectual, sexual, and creative in a woman, demonstrates the way a poet can be psychologically empowered by the Aphrodite archetype.

If personal transformation depends upon coming to terms with one's mother by transcending her victimization and assimilating her more positive attitudes, completing the rebirth journey requires that we accept frighteningly powerful feminine forces in our own personalities. Merely facing and naming them does not automatically lead to the kind of transformation which Millay, H. D., Grahn, and

Rukeyser achieve through both repudiating masculine attitudes and assimilating archetypal feminine powers. Not only must the inauthentic degradation of archetypes be brought to consciousness and rejected; the most aggressive and frightening aspects of the feminine archetypes must be accepted as elements of oneself. My hypothesis is that there are two layers of shadow within the Aphrodite archetype which women poets must come to terms with: the layer of patriarchal degradation internalized from culture, which includes European disgust for Aphroditian behavior, and a deeper layer containing the intrinsically dangerous aspects of the archetype which the woman poet must integrate. This deeper layer contains the warlike aspects attributed to Aphrodite's precursor Inanna. In what may be the first woman's poem on record (dating perhaps as far back as the third king of the Amorite Dynasty, between about 2258 and 2237 B.C.E.), Eneduanna prays to Anunna, who terrifies "the great gods" and smites "the heads / that you devour cadavers like a dog" (Hallo and Van Dijk 31). Here we find "the Anunna," or Inanna, petitioned not for favors in love but for empowerment in battle, representing the destructive and aggressive aspects of the archetype.

The feminine rebirth journey takes the hero down into the lower realms of her psyche, where she must accept these powerful and potentially destructive inner qualities along with her own mortality. It is for this purpose that Inanna, in the Sumerian epic, leaves her throne to confront her underground sister Erishkigal, who kills Inanna and hangs her corpse from a meat hook. For Demeter, Hecate brings dread news about what is happening to Persephone, who is being raped by Hades in the underworld. In both of these archetypal narratives the hero must come to terms with the faithlessness of males—Dumuzi's seizing the throne the minute Inanna has gone and neglecting to mourn for her; Zeus's and Hades' collusion against Demeter—but can only achieve rebirth after accepting her own inner destructiveness and descending into the humiliating experiences of bodily death. Unlike the rescue *from* the body and entry into the world of the spirit that is the denouement of the Christian resurrection narrative, the outcome is a reempowerment of the personality through affirmation of a specifically feminine and earthly immanence. Although this process bears some resemblance to the male quests I examined at the end of the preceding chapter, we see once again that the terror of fusion with feminine inner forces has a quality for women

different than that of men's confrontation with the terrifyingly femi-
nine as "other."

The archetypal quest through the underworld involves facing and
absorbing a figure much like the Medusa encountered by poets in part
one of this study. If Erishkigal is Inanna's sister and Hecate the friend
of Demeter, war and death are the shadow elements in the Aphrodite
archetype. Judy Grahn uses the Inanna descent narrative to structure
The Queen of Swords, in which she tells the story of Helen's confronta-
tion with Erishkagel in a lesbian bar. Erishkagel tries to get Helen to
look into her mind and remember that "You were a goddess in Christ's
time," but Helen prefers to repress such knowledge, valuing only her
"pretty house, full of glass bells" and the man she lives with, "who does
everything well." Refusing to confront the dark places of her psyche,
Helen falls "through a hole / in the eye of death" and is reborn as an
authentic Venus only after coming to terms with "the dark side of the
mirror," assimilating the shadow of "The Lady of the Great Below"
into her own personality.

Grahn notes that American racism displaces self-acceptance in a
manner analogous to women's repression of our own power. She
conceives of racism as a stereotypical projection onto "other" racial
groups of blame for negative qualities that we cannot accept in our-
selves. The process of withdrawing negative projections, specifically of
withdrawing racial allegations which are displacements of one's per-
sonal violence, is interestingly illustrated in her "Descent to the Roses
of the Family," one of two poems included in *The Queen of Swords.*
Here Grahn tells her brother that all of his and her father's "talk about
nigger" is a displacement of the dark aspects of their father's violent
temperament, which they must both face up to as personal character-
istics. These dark qualities have made Grahn's mother descend into
permanent madness and have left the poet with the sensation of also
falling into a dark hole, mother and daughter (and, implicitly,
brother) damaged by the men in the family with their constant "nigger
jokes and gun stories, / Indian jokes, queer stories and whore stories."
Grahn has survived by recognizing that "nigger is a strong feeling . . .
the forbidden passion" they themselves don't dare express. She has
been able to transcend the racial and sexual stereotypes her family
believes in not merely by naming them but, more crucially, by "My
own descent to find my violence" until "all my own violences" come
home to her.

The African
American
Aphrodite

Judy Grahn realizes that projecting blame onto the world outside of her own psyche will never help her toward healing; only by withdrawing negative projections and entering, in Audre Lorde's terms, the "black places" which are "those fruitful areas of ourselves" can she achieve psychological rebirth. For Lorde, this is a transformation of the personality that takes place under the aegis of her "Black mother," a radically reenvisioned Aphrodite archetype interbraiding the preclassical attributes of Inanna with the qualities exhibited by African archetypal figures such as Oya, Yemanja, and mother Seboulisa.

As we have seen in the case of the blues, African American women in love can become deadlocked in pain just like white women poets. Even in the most gloomy blues, however, there is an "answering back," a consciousness of the details of one's oppression and a determination to take action in one's own behalf. Lucille Clifton's poem "what the mirror said" makes this turn from mere complaint to true protest, the fulcrum being the woman poet's self-pride. In "homage to my hips," the poem that precedes "what the mirror said" in *two-headed woman*, Clifton celebrates her "big hips," which "don't fit into little / petty places," "free hips" which "have never been enslaved." Talking back to the idea that her big hips are not acceptable, Clifton enjoys their magic: "i have known them / to put a spell on a man and / spin him like a top!" (6). What is it that makes one woman poet able to celebrate an "unacceptable" body while others submit to patriarchal ideas of beauty? Kristen Laine, after surveying a wide variety of poems by black women, suggests a "woman-avenger tradition" which carries talking back into concerted action.[1] In my hypothesis, African-American women poets often achieve this avenger status after the same combination of critiquing patriarchal behavior and affirming the deep background of the goddess archetypes that characterizes white poets like Rukeyser and H. D. The variant flavor of their poetry, its unique power, derives both from a profounder marginality and from their bringing to consciousness emperingly angry African archetypes.

Like their male contemporaries, many African American women poets of the twentieth century have wondered what Africa is to them, speculating about how life would be different in the land of origin. In "to merle," for example, Clifton tells her friend that the "last time i saw you was on the corner of / pyramid and sphinx" and that "ten thousand years have interrupted our conversation"; Clifton is locating her reempowerment in lost Egyptian words which she is planning to use afresh. These retrievals of powerful African archetypes occur even before the 1980s. Gwendolyn Bennett, in "Heritage," wishes that she could go "Before the Sphinx" "hear the chanting / Around a heathen fire / Of a strange black race," a longing which leads her to affirm, in "To a Dark Girl," "Something of the old forgotten queens" which "Lurks in the lithe abandon of your walk" (81). In a more overtly outrageous dialect lyric, Margaret Walker celebrates "Old Molly Means," "a hag and a witch; / Chile of the devil, the dark, and sitch," as an empowering legendary archetype who had scared men with the "evil look in her coal black eyes" (142). Molly Means is in the Eneduanna or avenger mode of African American goddess archetypes, inspiring "holy dread" for "her black-hand arts and her evil powers." What we find in Walker as in Bennett is a combination of bodily self-acceptance—a celebration of one's color and hips and way of walking—and ability to overlook (or at least not to internalize) the reactions such "bad" women are likely to get from the encapsulating culture. In Naomi Long Madgett's "Black Woman" we find a similar assimilation of purportedly "jungle" atrributes into a poem of self-affirmation: "My hair is springy like the forest grasses. . . . My black eyes are coals burning / Like a low, full, jungle moon / through the darkness of being" (183–84). Madgett's self-celebration calls out for a partner, but (as we have seen in dealing with African American male poets) her lovers are likely to be terrified by such a woman or taking more acceptable white or submissive black women as lovers. With the Black Power movement of the 1960s, however, African American women became entranced with the powerful womanhood of African goddesses, and they continued the tradition of contrasting such archetypes with the much more subdued images of womanhood white culture proffered.

As in the case of white women poets, African American women poets are able to assimilate goddess archetypes only when they de-liberately renounce white patriarchy. It is her self-celebration and assimilation of archetypal powers that makes Nikki Giovanni's "Ego Tripping" a striking example of archetypal empowerment. Speaking in the voice of various African and Egyptian goddesses as well as Old

Testament heroes, Giovanni announces that "I designed a pyramid so tough that a star / that only glows every one hundred years falls / into the center giving divine perfect light" (1384), that Hannibal and Noah are her sons, and that she is the creator of the entire planet. Whereas Giovanni internalizes a whole range of traditionally male powers to assert her sense of self, June Jordan, in "For my own," develops a powerful African American female archetype from more specifically American experiences, celebrating woman as worker, as wife, as mother in impossible conditions, such as the jailhouse laundry, but combining nurturance with an avenging spirit. Jordan's Queen does not break down into blues or an "Oh-God-the-Pain" conclusion; rather, this section of the poem ends with praise to herself as a powerful Queen. Although there is a combination of the nurturant maternal and the avenging, powerful woman in Jordan's "Queen" that is markedly different in quality even from poems like Rukeyser's "Ajanta" and Sarton's "Kali," there is Aphrodite imagery interbraided with the African motifs—the rose, for example, as well as the shell. Gwen Thomas has written about the "strong Black woman archetype," a figure which should not be confused with the white stereotype of the "mammy" or "Aunt Jemima," which is a distorted degradation of it.[2] We shall see that these "strong Black women," Jordan's "Queen" among them, occur frequently in African American women's poetry, in descriptions of mothers, friends, and lovers and in reenvisioned African archetypes.

In the previous chapter I suggested that the difference between Baraka's internalization of European existentialism and Don Lee's celebration of "Beulah" as archetypal hurricane marks the dividing point between deadlock and process in African American male poets' approaches to Aphrodite. Whereas Baraka's "Crow Jane" remains a victim and his "Ladies" perennially subordinate to the male, Lee begins to assimilate both male and female African archetypes in order to achieve what Audre Lorde defines as self-actualization: "For it is through the coming together of self-actualized individuals, female and male, that any real advances can be made. The old sexual power relationships based on a dominant/subordinate model between unequals have not served us as a people, nor as individuals" (*Sister Outsider* 46). In "The Uses of the Erotic: The Erotic as Power" Lorde defines Eros in its original, Titanic sense as the force central to all life which, although it "has often been misnamed by men and used against women," nonetheless "offers a well of replenishing and provocative force to the woman who does not fear its revelation, nor succumb to the belief that sensation is enough" (54). Mere sensation or mechanical sex is a travesty of the authentically erotic, which can empower not only creativity but revolution: "The very word *erotic*," Lorde reminds us, "comes from the Greek word *eros*, the personification of love in all its aspects—born of Chaos, and personifying creative power and harmony. When I speak of the erotic, then, I speak of it as an assertion of the lifeforce of women; of that creative energy empowered, the knowledge and use of which we are now reclaiming in our language, our history, our dancing, our loving, our work, our lives" (55). Women who must confront a patriarchal superstructure dead set against it do not easily experience such an authentic Eros: like Millay, H. D., and, in her political praxis, most particularly like Rukeyser, Lorde works through renunciation of white patriarchy toward celebration of the golden, transformative, but specifically African American erotic archetypes.

Lorde assimilates classical materials in "The Maiden," in which she seems to identify her birth with the birth of an Aphrodite-like figure ("Once I was immortal beside an ocean / having the names of night"), although she attributes her birth not to Chronos's sickled testicles but to a moon goddess whom she does not find entirely positive. At this stage she feels that she has lost "my mother sea," an alternative maternal source, and must "nest" in the "dried out bed" of "a moon's crater / mouthing the ocean names of night" (*Coal* 34). In its encoded way, this poem seems to express Lorde's disappointment in a virgin, dried-up, and moonlike mother and her longing for the richer, more nurturant characteristics of the maternal ocean.[3]

In "Black Mother Woman" Lorde names, absorbs, and renounces aspects of her mother's life in order to shape her own personality. Still divided between loyalty to her mother and loyalty to a different kind of self, she is in danger of engulfment, the kind of fusion Sylvia Plath experienced, which is the great danger of this dialectic:

> but once you hid that secret
> in the center of furies
> hanging me

233

> with deep breasts
> and wiry hair
> with your own split flesh and long suffering eyes
> buried in myths of no worth.

Lorde's rejection of "myths of no worth" as archetypes displaying only patriarchal signatures enables her to avert fusion with her biological mother and seek rebirth in goddess archetypes:

> But I have peeled away your anger
> down to its core of love
> and look mother
> I am
> a dark temple where your true spirit rises
> beautiful and tough as a chestnut
> stanchion against your nightmares of weakness
> and if my eyes conceal
> a squadron of conflicting rebellions
> I learned from you
> to define myself
> through your denials. (*Chosen Poems* 53)

The Black Mother Woman for whom the poem is entitled is a maternal power Lorde invokes only after coming to terms with her real mother; through naming her mother's weaknesses and enduring her fury, Lorde constructs her own "dark temple." It is a dialectical process of coming to terms with one's personal mother and rediscovering the empowering energy of goddess archetypes that enables Lorde to achieve an authentic voice.[4]

The goddesses whom Lorde incorporates into her poetry—Oya, Yemanja, and Seboulisa—are non-European in their immanent theology. As Judith Gleason has noted of the Yoruba goddess Oya, such an archetype can take the form of "the river Niger, tornadoes, strong winds generally, fire, lightning, and buffalo," and is "also associated with certain cultural phenomena among the Yoruba people (the first to worship her), notably with masquerades constructed of bulky, billowing cloth—ancestral apparitions—and with funerals" (1). Oya is thus a quality or a psychological state of her worshippers, who, in

Gleason's definition, are patrons "of feminine leadership, of persuasive charm."

> To describe and elaborate upon Oya's various manifestations is inevitably to present an idea not commonly thought of when the word *goddess* is mentioned. Oya's patterns, persisting through many media—from air to the human psyche—suggest something like a unified field theory of a certain type of energy that our culture certainly doesn't think of as feminine. To speak of her thus integrally, it has been necessary to attempt to combine two ways of thinking: African and European. (1)

As energy both contained within the psyche and flowing between people, Oya as goddess and Oya as archetypal gestalt are, in Gleason's definition, one and the same thing. In African American women's poetry, empowerment through identification with goddesses often takes the form of first-person declarations like Giovanni's "I was born in the Congo" and Madgett's "my hair is springy like the forest grass." But it can also be seen in more conventional prayers like Lorde's to Seboulisa, "mother of power" in "October." In this formal petition Lorde's goal is empowerment through identification:

> Seboulisa, mother of power
> keeper of birds
> fat and beautiful
> give me the strength of your eyes
> to remember
> what I have learned
> help me to attend with passion
> these tasks at my hand for doing. (*Chosen Poems* 108)

There is an interesting resemblance between prayers to Inanna, Lorde's prayer to Seboulisa, and Elizabeth of York's to Venus: what these petitions have in common is desire that the goddess endow the poet with her celebratory passion so that both her Eros and her creativity may be renewed. Through the African goddesses (who are also worshipped in Caribbean and South American communities) Lorde has a much more immediate access to an archetypal field of feminine eroticism than do poets who address the Greek Aphrodite, so remote in time. These African goddesses, moreover, are much more holistic than the Greek and Roman ones, who were split up between purportedly opposite qualities of wifely anger (Hera), father-identified celibate intellectuality (Athene), other-woman lust (Aphrodite), celibate cruelty (Artemis), and mortality (Hecate). The traditional Yoruba praises of Oya which Gleason cites demonstrate a combination of revenge, power over death, military violence, sensuality, and motherhood, much in the manner of Inanna/Eneduanna: "She walks alongside violence / Ripeness of the afternoon / Powerful river / Fire burns; so does the sun" (2–5). Within the Yoruba religious system this goddess, whom Neumann would label a "Terrible Mother," is appreciated for her terror, which is an aspect of her power and efficacy.

Orisha, in Gleason's explanation, are "numinous archetypal forces" which dwell within "natural manifestations [such] as water, wind, fire, tree, and so on" but which are not worshipped as external to the worshipper but as internal, psychological events such as illnesses and those mental instabilities which nudge us toward rebirth. They also constitute divinities manifested in particular places, persons, and tribes, all of which interact at the shrines and festivals which structure an archetypal field for their celebration. In "The Winds of Orisha" we can see how these African archetypes provide Lorde with the means of transcending the quite different gender values of the America she grew up in. In the first selection of the poem she asserts:

> This land will not always be foreign.
> How many of its women ache to bear their stories
> robust and screaming like the earth erupting grain,

suggesting that women's anger and outrage not only at white America but also at their "once lovers" contains in itself the energy needed for transcendence. Specifically, women's instinctive recognition of apatriarchal archetypes is the driving force of their outrage:

> Impatient legends speak through my flesh
> changing this earths formation
> spreading
> I will become myself
> an incantation

dark raucous many-shaped characters
leaping back and forth across bland pages
and Mother Yemanja raises her breasts to begin my labor near water
the beautiful Oshun and I lie down together
in the heat of her body truth my voice comes stronger
Shango will be my brother roaring out of the sea
earth shakes our darkness swelling into each other
warming winds will announce us living
as Oya, Oya my sister my daughter
destroys the crust of the tidy beaches
and Eshu's black laughter turns up the neat sleeping sand.
    (*Chosen Poems* 48–49)

It is important to note that Lorde is empowered by male as well as female divinities; the complementarity of polytheistic archetypal systems has its own balance and strength, which will prevent her, even while she delivers her critique of capitalist patriarchy, from becoming deadlocked in antagonism against men.

Through reaching into the deep places of the communal psyche for non-European archetypal energies, Lorde empowers herself both as an African American lesbian woman poet and as a source of healing for the white world she lives in. For Lorde, reenvisioning the deep background of archetypes helps the human race to evolve:

The possible shapes of what has not been before exist only in that black place, where we keep those unnamed, untamed longings for something different and beyond what is now called possible, and to which our understanding can only build roads. But we have been taught to deny those fruitful areas of ourselves. I personally believe that the Black mother exists more in women; yet she is the name for a humanity that men are not without. (*Sister Outsider* 101)

"The Black mother," for Lorde, not only constitutes her racial identity but is a state of self-assurance achieved through accepting a psychological "darkness" which has its roots in revolt against white patriarchy but becomes an affirmation of her self at peace with her destructive as well as her creative powers. Lorde inverts the "blackness" and "darkness" and their cognate regions of feminine fury, fleshy Eros, hell, and death feared by Europeans so that, like Oya's stormy powers as hurri-

237

cane, they empower both personal and social transformation. Eros is the central energizing force in Lorde's revolution, Aphrodite-as-Oya-as-Orisha, the goddess whose anger she praises as an aspect of her healing power. Aphrodite's negative features, often dualized in European mythology, are conflated in Lorde's archetypal "Black mother," whom she defines as psychological possibilities, "fruitful areas of ourselves" which empower not only lesbian lovers but also heterosexual women, and even men.

Lorde suggests that many of the negative stereotypes which people use to defame each other center on a "darkness" identified with negritude. Accepting her own blackness, peeling away the layers of anger not only about her mother's and sister's choices but against white culture, white and black men, and white women (as in "Outlines," where she and her white woman lover battle through racial divisions toward a true Eros), Lorde envisions blackness as a combination of racial identity and a nonracially defined acceptance of the "dark" places of one's psyche. Like Grahn, she realizes that projecting blame onto the world outside our psyches will never help us toward healing; only by withdrawing negative projections and entering, in Lorde's term, the "black places" which are "those fruitful areas of ourselves" can we achieve psychological rebirth.

For all its racial specificity, the archetypal dialectic underlying Lorde's and Grahn's poetry parallels successful male poets' quests for Aphrodite. John Ciardi, in "To Judith Asleep," writes that "And all my memory's shores / you frighten perfectly, washed familiar and far" in the same state of mind as W. S. Merwin and Walter Berry, a surrender of self for a greater erotic state. In Berry's words, the male poet's goal to be set free "from myself / into the dark and the new light" is not unlike the "fruitful areas of ourselves" Lorde finds in the black mother archetype.

In calling attention to similarities between male poets' approaches to Aphrodite and Lorde's quest to express both her negritude and her lesbian identity, there is, I admit, a danger of suggesting too facile an analogy between racially and sexually diverse poets. Although the likenesses between such quests cannot override the special nature of the African American and lesbian Eros which Lorde celebrates in her poetry, it is striking to note similarities in the process through which poets of different groups achieve a successful rebirth.

Ferns,
Flowers,
Caves, and
Jewels:
Genitalic
Celebrations

"We must never," Lorde says to Adrienne Rich, "close our eyes to the terror, to the chaos which is Black which is creative which is female which is dark which is rejected which is messy which is . . ." To which Rich replies, "Sinister," and Lorde continues: "Sinister, smelly, erotic, confused, upsetting" (*Sister Outsider* 101). There is a unique flavor in women's poems about Aphrodite, celebrating the particular delights of sensuality felt with our own bodies. Once our terror of ourselves has been overcome, once we abandon other people's denigrations of what is "smelly and erotic" about us, a precise, raucous, delightfully genitalic imagism transfuses our love poetry.

In "Body Language: Imagery of the Body in Women's Poetry," which covers the years between 1960 and 1980, Alicia Ostriker notices that

> one of the ways we recognize a "poetess"—which is to say a woman poet locked into sentimentality by her inhibitions—is that she steers clear of anatomical references. As womanly inhibition declines, we grow aware of its sources in dualistic ideology, gender polarization, and the dread of female sexuality. One of the ways we recognize a woman poet, these days, is that her muted parts start explaining themselves. (*Stealing the Language* 92)

I would postulate that this recent flowering of a poetry filled with feminine genitalic imagery belongs in the context of a long history of women finding images to encode genitalic pleasure. I first realized that classical goddesses can encode feminist attitudes when I came across a Medusa archetype woven into a fifteenth-century tapestry. Following up on a hunch that women's needlework might contain hidden signals from our secret places, I discovered that embroidery books depicting bed canopies, petticoats, chair cushions, and aprons from the Tudor through the Jacobean and Colonial handiwork traditions are full of tulips and carnations and roses and gilliflowers as well as exotic pomegranates, pineapples, and other fruits sewn in suggestively genitalic, labialate, and clitoroid patterns. Feminist artist Judy Chica-

Genitalia on an apron. Author's line drawing from an early-eighteenth-century apron. Courtesy of the Detroit Institute of the Arts.

go has discovered a "central core imagery" of ovoid and floral forms in which a powerful, dark, often mysterious center flares out into a multifoliate encircling pattern suggestive of genital imagery, a discovery which led to her monumental *Dinner Party* (using the traditionally feminine genres of embroidery and china painting) and her *Birth Project* celebrating in needlework women's birth experiences. In developing my thesis that for generations women have been sewing and tatting erotic images into our needlework, I found many patterns adapted from European ornamental traditions, figures such as female sphinxes with lovely faces, wings, and animal feet, their genitalia depicted in vegetal and floral patterns, which were termed "Grottesques" for their origins in old Roman grottoes.

Women's poetry in which natural images embody feminine genitalia is not a recent phenomenon. The nineteenth century had its share of poetic encoded sexual images—for example, the sensual fruits in Christina Rossetti's "Goblin Market." Emily Dickinson's flowers, bees, and butterflies have a sexual specificity which Judy Grahn has suggested serve to encode a lesbian sensuality. Dickinson modeled her poetry on hymns and valentines, using these terse and apparently innocent little lyric forms to disguise volcanic passions. Women poets of the early years of the twentieth century used fruits, flowers, and jewels in much the same way as Dickinson and Rossetti, in a precise, physically concrete poetry which, although it became known as "imagism," can also be understood as a way for H. D., Amy Lowell, Mina Loy, and others to appear "feminine" in a conventionally "sweet" manner while actually writing about the forbidden grottoes of their

Grottesques. From Franz Sales Meyer,
Handbook of Ornament (New York:
Dover, 1957), p. 103. Reproduced with
permission from Dover Publications.

own bodies. Thus Grahn identifies H. D.'s "Winter Love" as an example of the "hot richness" of lesbian sexual imagery (*The Highest Apple* 28–29), a description which parallels Ostriker's analysis of Denise Levertov's "Song for Ishtar" as a source of "a sacred joy [which] can be found within the self" and "requires an embracing of one's sexuality." Ostriker identifies the use of such imagery as an element of a rebirth journey, a "movement downward or inward, in gender-charged metaphors of water, earth, cave, seed, and moon: such is the burden of these and many other poems by women" ("Thieves of Language" 17). I have discovered that the young Inanna's delight in her vulva survives within the images women choose to celebrate Eros because of nothing more complicated than the natural, instinctive recognition that our bodies are "wondrous to behold." Or, as Rukeyser announced in 1960, "Whoever despises the clitoris despises the penis / Whoever despises the penis despises the cunt. . . . / Resurrection music, silence, and surf" (484).

Not all poets who used genitalic images, especially those growing up like Amy Lowell in turn-of-the-century Boston, could afford to be as overt as Rukeyser in 1960. Lowell's relationship to the Aphrodite archetype follows the pattern which I have outlined for poets who successfully transcend society's loathing of their bodies. Lowell, built large on a short frame, was not conventionally "beautiful." More important, women attracted her from an early age, her first crush being on the actress Eleanora Duse. In her first volume of poetry Lowell describes a degraded Aphrodite as "The Captured Goddess," "Bound and trembling, / Her fluted wings were fastened to her sides with cords," being sold into prostitution. Lowell conflates Aphrodite as goddess with temple prostitutes, and although she could hardly have been aware of the degradation of sacred erotic rites by temple prostitution outlined by recent feminist historians, she recognizes that something originally pleasurable and sensual in Aphrodite has been degraded. In "Sultry" she talks back to a male Eros, a "Vengeful god of smooth, imperishable loveliness," while she walks in a masculine garden full of hostile eyes:

> To those who can see them, there are eyes,
> Leopard eyes of marigolds crouching above red earth,
> Bulging eyes of fruits and rubies in the heavily-hanging trees,
> Broken eyes of queasy cupids staring from the gloom of myrtles.

> I came here for solitude
> And I am plucked at by a host of eyes.

Lowell succeeds in transcending hostile masculine perception by becoming an eye in her own right, taking on the ancient feminine persona of the eye of wisdom and justice:

> I too am become a cunning eye
> Seeking you past your time-gnawed surface,
> Seeking you back to hyacinths upon a dropping hill,
> Where legend drowses in a glaze of sea. (470)

Although Lowell insists that the man's eyes are empty, his flowers and fruits mere coverings, she finds herself in the same position as Coleridge, Raine, and Wakoski—looking in a mirror and seeing only how men perceive her: "So that I stare back at myself / And see myself with loathing." At this early phase Lowell knows that she is looking at "My shadow, tortured out of semblance" by "His shadow," so infected by "the mingled shadow" that she cannot perceive her own self in the mirror.

All of this changed when Lowell fell in love with Ada Russell, with whom she spent the rest of her life. Although she had been active in promulgating the ideas and style of the imagist movement before she met Russell, once she recognized that male Eros was nothing to worry about she transformed the terrifying eyes and masculinate fruits and flowers into emblems of a lesbian Eros. She first welcomes Venus into her life as more lovely than Botticelli's vision ("Venus Transiens") in a poem I read as addressed to Russell ("Tell me, Was Venus more beautiful / Than you are"). Then, in "Madonna of the Evening Flowers," she conflates Russell with the Virgin Mary in a rite of garden worship. While pretending to pray to the Virgin in a conventional manner, she is obviously addressing a specific companion in garden talk filled with erotic implication:

You tell me that the peonies need spraying,
That the columbines have overrun all bounds,
That the pyrus japonica should be cut back and rounded.
You tell me these things.
But I look at you, heart of silver,

243

White heart-flame of polished silver,
Burning beneath the blue steeples of the larkspur,
And I long to kneel instantly at your feet,
While all about us peal the loud, sweet *Te Deums* of the Canterbury bells.
(210).

The images of heat and silver, which seem on the surface to be one of those precious, lapidary emblems favored by imagist poets, becomes more specifically genital when it is read within the context of three other poems in the same collection: "The Weather-Cock Points South," "Opal," and "Decade." In the first she is explicitly erotic: "I put your leaves aside, / One by one: / The stiff, broad, outer leaves; / The smaller ones, / Pleasant to touch, veined with purple," so that the purported object of her attentions, a white flower ("Flower of wax, of jade, of unstreaked agate; / Flower with surfaces of ice, / With shadows faintly crimson") can be read as a genitalic image. "The bud is more than the calyx," she concludes. "There is nothing to equal a white bud, / Of no colour . . ." (211). The conflation of floral and lapidary imagery is similar to the jewels and flowers of "Sultry" but with an entirely different attitude. Whereas male Eros dominated the earlier garden, Lowell's new Eden of delights is beneficent and feminine. These images are not vapidly pleasant, however; the Aphrodite encoded in Lowell's jewels and flowers is dangerous. In "Opal" she writes that "You are ice and fire, / The touch of you burns my hands like snow," once again using the apparently acceptable feminine jewel image to describe the perils of Eros and her sensations of terror and wonder at it. "When I am with you, / My heart is a frozen pond / Gleaming with agitated torches," she continues, using the imagery of ice fishing in winter, with its dangers and combination of fire and frozenness, to embody her own hesitations (214). Finally, in "Decade," Lowell uses food to express her erotic security:

When you came, you were like red wine and honey,
And the taste of you burnt my mouth with its sweetness.
Now you are like morning bread,
Smooth and pleasant.
I hardly taste you at all for I know your savour,
But I am completely nourished. (217)

Writing about Lowell's "long time female marriage" and "robust dykeliness," Judy Grahn tells us that her work was so criticized for its lesbian content in the 1920s that many of her overtly erotic poems were kept out of anthologies (*The Highest Apple* 22–25). Lowell was able to insert genitalic images into poems by subverting tropes considered so traditionally "feminine" as to be innocuous. Moreover, in "The Sisters" Lowell makes it clear that she understood exactly what had been ailing the woman love poets preceding her: a "huge, imperious need of loving, crushed (in Elizabeth Barrett Browning's case) within the body she believes so sick," an erotic longing experienced also by Dickinson, whom she recognizes as intrinsically revolutionary. Lowell blames this repression not so much on Queen Victoria as on Martin Luther,

> And behind him the long line of Church Fathers
> Who draped their prurience like a dirty cloth
> About the naked majesty of God. (461)

Lowell's consciousness of and ability to name exactly what it is in patriarchy that has repressed women's authentic Eros and her acceptance of her own body enable her to recognize the empowering possibilities in the Aphrodite archetype.

In her own way, Lowell was participating in the Anglo-American free love movement which I described at the beginning of this chapter, within which Mina Loy, whose style is much more in the experimental and modern tradition that Lowell's, also found permission for her feminist erotic manifestos. Writing about Loy in "The New Poetry and the New Woman," Carolyn Burke recognizes that "it would have been impossible to find reassuringly old-fashioned poems hidden in Loy's 'Love Songs.' Readers accustomed to the conventions of romantic poetry were totally unprepared for her frank exploration of sexual love from a woman's perspective. Even the ostensibly modern Amy Lowell was so shocked by Loy's poems that she threatened to withdraw her support" (45). Loy's "Love Songs to Joannes" describe "Pig Cupid," "His rosy snout / Rooting erotic garbage . . . Among wild oats / Sown in mucous-membrane," and male genitals as "The skin-sack / In which a wanton duality / Packed / All the completions / Of my infructuous impulses" (91–92). Loy's surreal dislocations of grammar and linguistic innovations only lightly veil her erotic images. The section numbered 9 in "Love Songs to Joannes," for example, starts off with references to a conventional enough cosmic Aphrodite:

> When we lifted
> Our eyelids on Love
> A cosmos
> Of coloured voices
> And laughing honey

but continues:

> And spermatozoa
> At the core of Nothing
> In the milk of the Moon. (95).

Although there are delicate "fireflies" doing an "aerial quadrille," Loy's sexual honesty ruptures lyric conventions to affirm an entirely physical sexuality:

> Let them clash together
> From their incognitoes
> In seismic orgasm
> For far further
> Differentiation
> Rather than watch
> Own-self distortion
> Wince in the alien ego. (105)

Loy's unwillingness to participate in "Own-self distortion," her refusal to give in to conventional ideas about female sexlessness, helps her escape "alien ego," false distortions of female self. In "Virgins Plus Curtains Minus Dots" she reasserts the original meaning of virgin not as sexless but as sexually self-determining. Like Lowell and Teasdale, Loy seems to have recognized a lost feminist erotic religion lurking behind prostitution: after she turned against the Futurists in 1916 she produced a play called "The Sacred Prostitute" which was performed in Florence. In "Satires: 1914–1923" Loy's virgin/prostitutes take the side of "flesh in the world," preferring to "Throb to the night" and be "Bait to the stars" (38). Loy ended her life as she had begun it, becoming once more an artist, creating montages from pieces found in garbage pails on the Bowery, where she went about looking for Christ among the homeless.

As a notorious "beauty" in both England and America, Loy's eccentricity and self-determination helped her transcend the kinds of traps that Raine, Wylie, and Teasdale succumbed to. Edith Sitwell, in a much more encoded manner than Loy, also used flower and jewel imagery to encode her erotic desires, writing in an English mystical style reminiscent of the way William Blake used lapidary processes in his recondite Prophetic Books. While she disguised her disappointments in love with the stance of an "eccentric old maid," Sitwell's is a surreal poetry whose energy and verve encodes an energetic and humorous eroticism. One of the most famous productions she and her brothers created was "Façade," a long poem set to music by William Walton which Sitwell enacted as a performance poem before puzzled audiences in both England and America. In "Hornpipe," the thirty-first variation of the piece, Venus appears in the ridiculous posture of "Lady Venus on the settee of the horsehair sea!" born like Aphrodite from the sea. In nonsense verse Sitwell describes Queen Victoria deploring Venus, who "Is as sharp as any lynx and blacker-deeper than the drinks and quite as / Hot as any hottentot, without remorse!" Although Sitwell's hot hottentot could be read as a racist projection of passion onto a stereotyped African, she is like Audre Lorde in the way she comes down on the side of the "blacker-deeper," "hot," "Minx" elements of the psyche rather than align herself with Queen Victoria. Her declaration of allegiance to a dark Eros, interestingly, is set within a background of jazz music.

Another way in which (like Lady Sackville and a number of other turn-of-the-century poets) Sitwell disguised her allegiance to "Queen Venus" was to write about her elegiacally. In "Elegy on Dead Fashion" Sitwell declares Venus moribund. She thus places an Old Queen Venus's passions well in the past. The poem expresses Sitwell's disappointment in Eros through descriptions of lost Edenic gardens filled with sensual fruit and flowers. Sitwell's medley of classical and lapidary imageries elegizes a lost sensuous Eden which owes something both to Christina Rossetti and to Milton. Even though she declares that "The nymphs are dead," Sitwell expects to be alchemically transformed, reborn through fire. In Sitwell's identification with the erotic feminine impulses encoded in her Venus, bacchantes, and nymphs, there lurks a spark of regeneration, a spark which empowers her survival and transformation under the aegis of Aphrodite.

This rebirth is clearer in the less recondite lyrics of "The Bee Oracles," "Medusa's Love Song," and "A Hymn to Venus," in which Sitwell uses alchemical diction to conquer self-doubt and pledge allegiance to Aphrodite. While "Medusa's Love Song" is a lament for "the warmheart of Aprils and apricots," for "gold within like the heart of the honeycomb" which Medusa thinks she has lost forever, in "The Bee Oracles" Sitwell assumes the persona of an "old woman" who is "Half Sun, half Clod," who is one of the "Priestesses of the Gold Comb" or Bee Priestess, "Shaped by Darkness" and regenerating the elements of the earth which is "the honey of all Beings." The Greek word for bee is Melissa, the name of Aphrodite's priestesses at her honeycomb shrine in Eryx; here Sitwell devotes herself to the sun as "Gold man, lying in the dark like the wingless pupa," a dark inner god who "will clothe us again in gold and a little love" (334–35.) In "A Hymn to Venus" Sitwell takes the stance of Elizabeth of York and earlier poets who pray "To the great Rose of the world," although some of the elegiac mode lingers. Sitwell recognizes that Venus has transcended a hardened Medusa state ("Beyond the seeds of Petrifaction, Gorgon of itself") but, like Blake's tears, which alternately turn into jewels and melt again, Sitwell describes petrifaction turning into sensuality.

One can read her "deep rose" not as sexual but as conventionally romantic or alchemical. I read the poem, however, as describing a specifically sensual and genitalic healing, especially in Sitwell's identification of herself with sensuous plants. Sitwell draws an analogy between revitalization of the rose and alchemical transformation of rubies and garnets under Venus's aegis. As different from each other as they may seem, the imagist Lowell, the surrealist Loy, and the eccentric Sitwell resemble Rukeyser, H. D., and Lorde in an energetic outrageousness which helps them win through cultural restrictions to erotic self-celebration. There is not as much difference as one might think between the white British Sitwell and the African American Lorde. Both use jewels as symbols of women's rebirth through Eros; or, as Lorde puts it in "Coal,"

> Love is a word another kind of pen
> As a diamond comes into a knot of flame
> I am black because I come from the earth's inside
> Take my word for jewel in your open light (95)

What they have in common is a unique metaphoric focus, the ability to suggest a specifically genitalic particularity through conventionally "feminine" lyric tropes of flower and jewel.

The difference between poets of the earlier period, such as Lowell and Loy, and the more recent group has to do with their level of explicitness. Lowell and Sitwell still *sound* slightly conventional, while Loy encodes her sexual imageries in the obscurity of experimental verse. Poets of the past three decades, in contrast, find it less necessary to disguise their erotic assertions.

Lorde starts "Love Poem" with a traditional invocation to the earth ("Speak earth and bless me with what is richest"), but what she asks for is a fusion of her body with the landscape:

> make sky flow honey out of my hips
> rigid as mountains
> spread over a valley
> carved out by the mouth of rain.

Once fused with the earth, Lorde uses specifically genitalic natural images:

> And I knew when I entered her I was
> high wind in her forests hollow
> fingers whispering sound
> honey flowed
> from the split cup
> impaled on a lance of tongues. (*Chosen Poems* 77)

The honey image is both specific, referring to bodily fluids, and archetypal, having to do with the bee priestess and the classical association of honey with the golden sensuality of Aphrodite. Here, similarly, is Marge Piercy, in "Doing it differently":

> I crawl into you, a bee furry with greed
> into the deep trumpeting throat of a crimson lily
> speckled like a newly hatched robin. (*To Be of Use* 53)

A healthy acceptance of one's body's landscape, a marveling (like Inanna) at one's own vulva, endows the woman poet with a pleasurable sensuality which enhances her unity with nature. We thus find women not only using isolated natural images like flowers and shells but identifying with the landscape around them, Eros fueling a sense of oneness with the earth until the woman poet transcends the literary metaphoric into the psychological metamorphic. Thus Colleen McElroy, in "And When My Love Calls," declares that

> I am the ocean
> lost in deserts and canyons
> I am evil and moody
> only in your mind
> Snails smooth my hair
> Fish and witches are friends
> I am dark, first satin
> Then velvet

and describes her lovemaking in oceanic terms:

> I rise to the shadows
> My body arched and laced
> In froth. he brushes
> Seaweed from my legs
> And crash against rocks . . .
>
> When my love cools, I am calm
> and work again to move plankton
> toward Alaska in the night. (*Music from Home* 51)

While McElroy uses the first-person declaration of identity with powerful natural forces common to other African American women poets, her analogy between her lovemaking and oceanic processes ("My body arched and laced / in froth") goes beyond mere simile (our lovemaking is like the ocean) to a metamorphosis of her erotic energy into the ocean's power. Olga Broumas uses ocean imagery in an even more explicitly genitalic fashion in "Amazon Twins." She and her woman lover look at each other to perceive themselves as "crustacean-like. Marine / eyes, marine / odors. Everything live / (tongue, clitoris, lip and lip)" (7).

Although Piercy does not invoke Aphrodite explicitly, in an ode to orgasm entitled "O!" she equates the goddess's birth from the sea with sexual consummation:

Oh, the golden bauble of your rising
wet from the waves rippling,
radiating like orgasm, round
as a singing mouth at full stretch,
round as the vagina when it takes, . . .
    you come to us
riding over the white manes
of the waves. (*The Moon Is Always Female*)

As Grahn has noticed about Rich's poetry, one cannot identify this kind of erotic celebration either as pantheistic (worship of divinity latent in nature) or as specifically addressed to "The Goddess": Rich "has never," Grahn reminds us, "named in the magic of her poetry a female god, or addressed her, or even mentioned her in passing. And yet she names the forces, the female godforces, and takes as her major subjects love and beauty, intelligence and memory—surely Aphrodite or perhaps the Hebrew Asherah—in another form" (*The Highest Apple* 116).

Of the woman poets treated in the two chapter, Rich started her poetic career in a place perhaps most like Raine's, being accepted by the male poetic establishment as a "Yale Younger Poet" and writing a modernist academic verse indistinguishable from the verses of her male contemporaries. From this dead center of patriarchal acceptance, Rich nonetheless painfully works her way into the "new space" of lesbian identification and an erotic poetry which is empowered by feminine rather than by masculine imagery. In "xi" of her "Twenty-one Love Poems" she develops an extended metaphor between a hike she and her lover take up a volcanic mountain and the status of their love affair, in a manner which, like that of other poets in this mode, combines genitalic specificity with empowerment through nature. As they move over the difficult landscape of both the volcano and their love, they notice "the small, jewel-like flower / unfamiliar to us, nameless till we rename her, . . . that detail outside ourselves that brings us to ourselves" (2036). Just as we women have had trouble finding words to celebrate the marvelous sensations of our bodies, the flower has been unnamed. In her act of writing the sequence of love poems in terms of a hike over a volcanic landscape, however, Rich "names" even its tiniest flower as genitalic emblem, containing within it the enormous significance of their lovemaking.

8.

Romancing the Stone: Love
Poetry in Canada

*I*n chapter 3, on Medusa in Canada, we noticed the way that the landscape can be foregrounded in Anglo-Canadian poetry, so that its elements become as essential as the human beings experiencing them. The ubiquitous presence of stone in Canadian lyrics (and again, in this chapter, I limit myself to an Anglophone sample), often acting in its own behalf and only very lightly endowed with human features, establishes a relationship of harmony between poet and nature, at best, and, at worst, a dominance of nature over the poet. We saw how Northrop Frye laid aside his descriptions of the more anthropomorphic relationship between the European poet and nature to define Canadian poetry's residence within the leviathan of the created world. Although one would think that the body of literature resulting from this intrusion of obdurate Canadian nature into poets' psyches might be a gloomy one, this is far from the case: their tone is not often tragic, achieving, rather, a kind of witty acceptance unlike *humeur noir*, a lightness of being which may have to do, as I have suggested, with an animistic attitude to nature more psychologically healthy than the mind-over-matter paradigm.

The intrusion of stones into the poetry of lovemaking which I noted in poems about Medusa in Canada may be a result of the poets' acceptance of an obdurate nature, a response quite different from the traditional fear that if you approach the power of feminine sexuality too closely you will be turned into stone. For a significant number of Canadian poets of both genders, petrifaction seems to be a result of successful Eros, a kind of alchemical transformation as reward for approaching Aphrodite successfully.

My study of male poets in chapter 6 suggested that a renunciation of the ego's identification with mind and "civilization" was necessary for poets like Robert Graves and Dylan Thomas in England and W. S. Merwin, John Ciardi, and Wendell Berry in America to transcend terror of women, the dark, and death. These poets assume that they are entering "another world" when they make this leap into a "dark" Eros which remains alien to consciousness: whether describing the woman at the heart of the descent journey in terms of myth or dream they make it clear that she is a denizen of a realm that they enter only when they are asleep to ordinary self. When they pray to a goddess or muse or make love, they visit a world separate from their real, reasonable lives, to which they return renewed. Although there are many Canadian poems in which the poet seems to think that Europe (often Greece) is where you go in order to make love, and although several poets of both genders project human features onto their Venus figures, a significant number of Canadian poets assume that the landscape of a Venus archetype (which many blend with Medusa, Hecate, and Artemis), with her stones and ice and snow, is itself the primary world, endowed with a being-in-its-own-right which transcends their pronouncements about it. In a manner which resembles that of the African American women poets and of the poets whom I discussed in chapter 7 who conflate the landscape of their lovemaking with their own genitalia, these Canadian poets speak as avatars of a natural world into whose mysteries they have been initiated and whose metamorphic language has become their own.

In his analysis of classical and European examples in *The Secular Scripture*, Northrop Frye, like the American male poets, assumes that accommodating either nature or sensuality is a necessary descent that leads away from the normal world of consciousness. He is troubled by a fearsome female he called "Diana of the Triple Will" blended with Aphrodite:

> But, of course, in the world of Eros we can also have tragedy or frustration, of the kind expressed in all the poems deploring the cruelty of a mistress. The disdainful mistress is, in this phase at least,

253

the incarnation of Robert Graves' white goddess or triple will, the Diana of heaven, earth, and hell whose virginity means only the elusiveness of a nature that remains unreconciled to man. As we contemplate this Diana, the symbol of nature as a closed cycle that man is trapped in, she turns into Venus flanked by her lover Mars and her child Cupid, the presiding deity of the red and white world of sexual love, the hungry desire satisfied only by death, the Eros fulfilled in Thanatos. (154)

Although Frye sometimes associates Dianic virginity with sexual innocence, his goddess clearly conflates Hecate (of the triple will) with Artemis and Aphrodite. All three, however, are in his European sample part of an "other" world of extension which can entrap men. We have seen that when he induces patterns from Canadian literary data, Frye perceives that these goddesses embody a nature that, although still quite frightening, is the immanent and appropriate dwelling place for the human spirit.

In *Survival* Margaret Atwood, who gradually abandons European paradigms of mind and spirit for a more immanent relationship to nature in her own poetry and fiction, describes a Diana as a recurrent theme in Canadian literature. Like Frye's European archetype, Atwood's Diana oddly conflates parturition, Eros, an uninhibited natural wildness and aged wisdom, suggesting that when women are no longer subjects in male writing but are writing about their own lives, this uniquely Canadian "Nature-Woman metaphor" emerges: "not just an Ice-Virgin-Hecate figure, but a Hecate with Venus and Diana trapped inside. And perhaps the 'plots'—the stories that can be told—about the Ice-Virgin-Hecate Nature-Monster are not limited to how one is destroyed by or manages to escape or conquer this figure; the story can also be about the attempts of the buried Venuses and Dianas to get out, to free themselves" (210). In 1972, like Frye in *The Secular Scripture*, Atwood still sees these feminine archetypes as a trap to escape or a pit to climb out of. Canadians, she nonetheless asserts, don't have to grieve that "the real Venus is missing" from their continent, having "departed for Europe, pregnant and taking with her whatever fecundity" she can rescue out of the Canadian bleakness; rather, Atwood concludes, the Hecate-Ice-Goddess is actually "a Woman-as-Land figure, or perhaps it is Land-as-Woman," a "Venus [who] is not necessarily absent but concealed" within Canadian literature (208, 211).

Frye and Atwood are both struggling with the disruption of European archetypal patterns by Canadian archetypes which do not conform to them, like square pegs which they cannot fit into traditional round holes. This skewed fit can be seen by the way they use the classical names—Diana, Venus, Hecate—for Canadian archetypes which are not so much embodiments of human qualities, in the European manner, as features of a nonhuman landscape. Canadian archetypes vary from European ones in more than their general features: the archetypal process itself, the gestalt or interaction between mind and archetype, is also different. Where the most commonly accepted relationship between human beings and nature in Europe and America is one of superior to inferior, Canadian literature often suggests that nature is the dominant element.

Canadian critics have continued to suggest that symbols originate in the mind as products of cognition rather than mediate between mind and a nature which also produces them. In *Butterfly on Rock* D. G. Jones recognizes that "the life of the land has been central to the experience of most Canadians and to the literature which reflects their experience" (33), but principally as symbol or attribute of inner consciousness, so that "it comes to symbolize elements of our inner life. As these elements are ignored or repressed, the land becomes a symbol of the unconscious, the irrational in the lives of the characters" (34). Symbols of nature, in Jones's understanding, embody unassimilated psychic materials projected onto the land in what could be psychoanalytically understood as a delusional system; however distorted these projections may be, nature is understood as mere repository of materials for human symbol formation, a traditionally European valuation of mind over nature.

In *The Wacousta Syndrome*, similarly, Gaile McGregor perceives Canadian nature as "not-self," an "unknown and unknowable wilderness [which] almost by default begins to accumulate increasingly sinister gothic overtones," so that, unable to contain mind or human self, it seems to reflect only human horror at such otherness (5). The idea that a hero can learn from nature, making "a spiritual journey *through* it, enduring its gothic aspect as a kind of 'dark night of the soul' that must be traversed before reconciliation can be achieved with the sources of fertility that it—or 'she'—can offer" is, to McGregor, more typical of American primitivism or romantic noble savage sentiments than of Canadian writing (8). So empty and mindless is Canadian nature, she reasons, so "staunchly resistant to assigned meanings," that "at least for the last half century the Canadian literary landscape, recognized as psycho-setting, has demonstrated a consistent significatory potential," a *tabula rasa* so empty and flexible that human beings can create new codes out of it (74). Although she recognizes the Canadian landscape as existentially "other," McGregor nonetheless sees it, in the European manner, as an object of cognition to be assimilated into an anthropomorphosed "Langscape."

It seems to me that for Jones and McGregor, as for Jung, health is to be achieved by withdrawing human projections from nature back into the psyche. My reading of Canadian poetry suggests, in contrast, that for a significant number of Canadian poets, psychological health is achieved not by colonizing nature or withdrawing from it but by establishing a harmonious relationship between one's human perceptions and a wholly nonhuman landscape which gives tongue in its own language. There is a crucial difference, in my hypothesis, between understanding the feminine archetypes emerging from the Canadian landscape as projections of individual terror—anima as alien "Terrible Mother" which must be assimilated, in the Jungian sense, for the individual to be reborn as hero—and understanding them as attributes of a nature which the Canadian poet approaches as nonhuman being. Although Canadian poetry can be ranged along a scale from a loathing of such nature archetypes to reverential approaches to them, the most negative poems about the loathsome Venus, as I continue to term her, are either derivative from European culture or anthropomorphic projections. There are so many other Canadian poems in which the poet struggles to achieve a balance between human self and nonhuman, unassimilable nature, however, that I will argue for a uniquely Canadian version of an interbraided Medusa-Aphrodite-Artemis archetype.

Canadian Loathsome Venuses

I do not mean to imply that the hated goddesses which haunt British and American poets never raise their heads in Canadian poetry; we saw in chapter 3 how St. John Simmons and Daryl Hine among the men and Susan Musgrave among the women envision Medusa as a dangerous figure. This conventionally European attitude toward a frightening female figure is not limited to male Canadian poets. Elizabeth Brewster, in "Moon," presents Artemis as a vindictive goddess "who destroyed Actaeon in her forests" because, "foolish man," he "looked too close / at the naked moon" (37). Although there is certainly a gender difference between Hine's sympathy with the victim and Brewster's with the goddess, both understand her as the enemy of the male hero.

To Séan Virgo, in a more typically Canadian manner, a female figure lurks within nature with intent to devour. In "Crackwillow" she is a white bird who seduces him under the mountain until he falls into "the feathers of the snowbird / dreaming of sleep." Instead of being reborn from the encounter as Dylan Thomas was in "A Winter's Tale," Virgo is trapped under the ice and water. In "She" this deathly figure is more specifically Dianic and Canadian, a moon goddess who lurks "on a shelf of stones" (39). Although Canadian in her stony attributes, she is a facet of the personality who "waits behind your / memory" with destructive intent; the poet understands himself as "an echo of her boygroom, torn from her" (41). Although Virgo's terror of women and perhaps also of nature radiates from this Artemis, the source of his fear is not nature but his infantile "dreams," "shadows," and projections.

The male poet approaching an Artemis/Aphrodite figure as if expecting to be victimized has a feminine counterpart in Susan Musgrave's witch/Hecate/Aphrodite persona, a stereotypically devouring female. Her "Sea-Witch," as we saw in chapter 3, blends Celtic and Canadian sources; in the same 1970 collection she writes a poem "For Séan" (Virgo) about an Aphrodite-like goddess who is less of a natural divinity than a facet of Musgrave's fusion with her lover. Although in a poem like "Woodcutter, River-God, and I" she moves from classical and Celtic stereotypes toward more indigenous figures, Musgrave persists in colonizing nature and in identifying herself with a stereotypically demonic witch or evil goddess perceived in the European manner. We shall also see that internalization of Canadian nature carries over into Musgrave's use of poetry by Native Americans as vehicles for her own attitudes.

To understand the line between a colonizing and an animistic attitude to nature, two early poems by Margaret Atwood, "The gods avoid revealing themselves" and "River," can be read in contrast to Virgo and Musgrave. These poems are concerned with masculine divinities which, in the first poem, Atwood wants to query, but which avoid her questions by sinking into the Canadian landscape. Atwood can marvel at these gods but she cannot absorb them; they may remain beside her but they do not let themselves "be seen" or internalized. In "River" Atwood approaches an icy, masculine Hecate before whom she fears petrifaction as she would if approaching Medusa; she identifies herself as frozen. She is not swallowed up into his perspective, however, but remains other to him as he is to her, though she fears his "latent/hook/locked in the ice" (*The Animals* 25). This sense of a divinity of the opposite sex as obdurate is quite different from Virgo's and Musgrave's mutually assimilable projections.

| *Naming Your Condition* | Traditional European paradigms assume that women are closer to nature than are men; in Canada, nature is distant from everybody. In *Survival* Atwood describes anthropomorphic |

approaches to nature as beneficent goddess as "Position One" in a scale of attitudes to nature in Canadian literature:

> Pretending that Nature is the all-good Divine Mother when you're being eaten by mosquitoes and falling into bogs is Position One. It can't really stand up very long against the Canadian climate and the Canadian terrain, measured against which Wordsworth's Lake District—Divine Mother country—is merely a smallish lukewarm pimple. So most of our Position One Nature poetry is nineteenth century. (61)

Position Two, in Atwood's scheme, occurs when, simply by describing the Canadian landscape, a poet begins to develop an alternative attitude:

> If it is cold, say so—name your condition out loud. In a lot of early Canadian poetry you find the desire to name struggling against a terminology which is foreign and completely inadequate to describe what is actually being seen. Part of the delight of reading Canadian poetry chronologically is watching the gradual emergence of a language appropriate to its objects. (62)

A look at some poems by the Confederation Group, who were civil servants in Ottawa writing between 1867 and 1914, demonstrates

the transition from classical goddesses to distinctly Canadian arche-
types. In 1888 Archibald Lampman, a post office clerk, wrote in a
flowing, Wordsworthian blank verse about Aphrodite as "The sea-
sprung radiant Cytherean" whom he found embodied in a girl he met
on his journey through Greece, "Dripping with sweat, that merry
dark-eyed girl, / Whose sudden beauty shook us from our dreams"
(102–103). This poem is part of "An Athenian Reverie," a dreamlike
recalling of his travels, written in an elegiac tone suggesting that
Lampman thinks that Eros is located in Greece. "The Land of Pallas"
(1899), similarly, is a lost amarital utopia where the "women through
great ages of bright living . . . Stood equal with the men, calm
counsellors" (205–206). Lampman, who carried on a lifelong passion
for a woman he met just after he had married somebody else, assumes
in these conventional verses that Aphrodite, sexual freedom, and
utopia are glories long lost from the earth.

Even when, in the sonnet "On the Companionship with Nature,"
he is describing Canada, his attitude is conventionally Wordsworth-
ian: "Let us be much with Nature," he suggests. "Let us be with her
wholly at all hours, / With the fond lover's zest," so that "Our
thoughts [can be] as sweet and sumptuous as her flowers" (258–59).
His shift in language when, in "The Lake in the Forest," he addresses
the Manitou (an immanent natural divinity or spirit of the Algon-
kian groups) is striking. Although the Manitou controls "sway-
ing fairies over floors / of luminous water lying strange and bright"
in a European fashion, it also rules "The yells and demon laughter
of the loon," and presides over a nature that, as Lampman goes
through the process of catologuing its objects, infects his tone and
style:

> O Master of the noon; the dusky bass
>   Lurk in the chambers of the rocks—the deep
>   Cool crypts of amber brown and dark—and sleep
> Dim-shadowed, waiting for the day to pass.
> The shy red deer come down by crooked paths,
>   Whom countless flies assail,
> And splash and wallow in the sandy baths
>   And Cry to thee to veil
> Thine eye's exceeding brightness and strike dead
> The hot cicada singing overhead. (314)

This is hardly the Wordsworthian nature of Lampman's sonnets or the idyllic groves of his classical poetry, but a place "Of sombre spruces and black pines that stand, / Ragged, and grim, and eaten through with gold." The Algonkian Manitou brings into Lampman's poetry its own un-Wordsworthian characteristics, modifying (in the manner Atwood suggests) his very language. Thus objects like the fox's fur and "the woodman's shanty" belong not to a beneficent "Divine Mother Nature" but to the "Lord of the hissing winds that plunge and blow," where the Manitou reigns as

> Master of the frost,
> The frost that hath its way,
> The waters are forsaken by the loon,
> And the ice roars beneath the winter moon. (316)

This change in style, tone, and imagery from poems dealing with Greece and the Lake Country to poems about Canada occurs within a single poem by D. C. Scott, "Spring on Mattagami." Scott, who was an Indian agent, describes a canoe trip with two Native American guides which convinces him that love in Europe is one thing and love in Canada quite another:

> There is the land of fraud and fame and fashion,
> Joy is but a gaud and withers in an hour,
> Here is the land of quintessential passion
> Where in a wild throb Spring wells up with
> power. (50)

The objects of the Canadian landscape, "the partridge drumming in the distance," for example, would cure Scott's lover of her European inauthenticities: among "the shy moose fawn" and "the hermit thrush," "the white-throat sparrow" and the "deep couch heaped of balsam fir," they could make love stark naked in the bush, where Scott locates passion's "red core." As if abashed by his departure from convention, he ends the poem praying to be held back from his passionate nature by the deities of civilization: "O Law, that deeper lies than Justice" and "O Light, that stronger burns than Love" (52).

It is interesting to examine the poems of Isabella Valancy Crawford, who also wrote in the late nineteenth century, in relationship to

Scott's and Lampman's attitudes toward nature. We can determine the same shift from conventional to fresher tropes between "A Battle" (1874), where she writes about the Moon, Mars, Titans, and Astarte engaged in battles not specific to the Canadian landscape, and poems like "The Camp of Souls" (1880) and "Said the Canoe" (1883), where she assumes Native American perspectives. In "The Camp of Souls" Crawford uses the voice of an immortal Native American, returning in his canoe to the "forests and camps of earth." The poem is filled with imageries typical of the Bruce County landscape where Crawford pioneered, whether in Manitou's land of the dead with lakes as blue "as the wild dove's breast," filled with yellow lilies and "tall, rustling rice-beds," or the world of the present with its "bitter marshes" and "tangled swamp." "Said the Canoe," in which Crawford takes the persona of the canoe paddled by "My [Native American] masters twain," is even more grounded in Canadian nature imagery, filled with "slaughtered fish like swords / On saplings slender" and the gray frozen eyes of dead deer, as well as "the strong, fierce muskallunge" and "The bittern [which], squaw-like, scolds the air" (21–22). The concrete images, as in the case of Scott and Lampman, ground Crawford's poetic style in Canadian nature. As Leslie Monkman points out in A Native Heritage, Crawford should not be accused of romanticizing the Native Americans in that she did not write "poetic versions of [Native American] legends like so many of her contemporaries, but rather lyric and narrative poems that combine the Indian's imagery and animistic perception of the landscape with her own vision. . . . She 'Indianizes' the landscape by exploiting red mythology and sets up a fusion reconciling landscape, red man, and white man in a vision of natural harmony" (132).

Clearly, in addition to the modification of style and attitude caused by naming objects from Canadian nature, these poets are inspired by the Manitou, influenced not only by the presence of Native Americans but by their theological assumptions. Although I will treat the relationship of the Canadian poet to Native American influences later in this chapter, it is important to note Crawford's, Scott's, and Lampman's location of a non-European attitude within Native American theology.

Naming the conditions of Canadian nature continues to help recent Canadian poets who struggle with discrepancies between European and indigenous realities to find their own voices. As Gwendolyn MacEwen puts it in "Dark Pines under Water," what is seen within Canadian nature is simultaneously psychological and nonhuman: "This land like a mirror turns you inward / And you become a forest in a furtive lake"; but the forest is less mental than natural, invading the mind rather than becoming a symbol of it: "There is something down there [in nature and the unconscious simultaneously] and you want it told" (*Magic Animals* 74). This is the stage where, as Atwood has described it, a Canadian poet can become deadlocked in Position Two, remaining weak and helpless as a victim of nature, or engage in Position Three protests, lashing out in anger against the hostile environment (63). A combination of blockage and protest can be seen when Anne Wilkinson, in "Nature Be Damned," speaks as an angry "witch" or Hecate whose powers have left her, separating her from these natural beings because, even though she still feels that "we're kin in appetite," she cannot find rebirth in a country which spring skips over. Although she thinks that "One hundred singing orioles" and other spring creatures should celebrate with her, European seasons are mere fantasy in the face of Canadian facticity: "Then roused from this reality I saw / Nothing, anywhere, but snow."

Douglas LePan's poetry asks over and over again how a language is to be found to embody such a landscape, to find out "what shall be our word as we return, / What word of this curious country?" ("Canoe Trip" 653). He describes Canada as "A Country without a Mythology" where "No monuments or landmarks guide the stranger," who must nourish himself by foraging in a land where "There is no law—even no atmosphere." There is, nonetheless, plenty of "passion" in the August lightning which splits rocks and sets the forests on fire, a natural Eros making it clear that "This is the land the passionate man must travel." He must put behind him the delusion that "waiting around the bend / Are sanctities of childhood" or a gentle green world Eden and recognize that

> nothing alters.
> Mile after mile of tangled struggling roots,
> Wild-rice, stumps, weeds, that clutch at the canoe,
> Wild birds hysterical in tangled trees.
>
> And not a sign, no emblem in the sky
> Or boughs to friend him as he goes; for who

Will stop here, clumsily constructed, daubed
With war-paint, teeters some lust-red manitou? ("A
Country without a Mythology" 654–55).

As if unable to divorce himself wholly from the Victorian idea that
"passion" is necessarily "lust-red," LePan rejects the Native American
Manitou at the end of the poem. This tension between received
mythologies and Canadian realities continues in his "Image of Sile-
nus," where a great blue heron is far more real to him than Dionysus,
Saint Francis, Apollo, or even "Foam-born Aphrodite." He hears the
"captives" of his country lamenting that they have no city and that the
bird is mere mirage, but finally hears, "out of the silence," an authen-
tic song:

It has no words, it is animal, inarticulate—
A ground swell continually making for the shores of
    speech
And never arriving. (658)

The words LePan seeks as poet remain encoded in the great blue
heron, beyond the reach of language.

We saw in the case of both English and American poets writing
about Aphrodite that when they are at home in their own bodies and
engaging in reciprocal, pyschologically healthy love relationships they
tend to find themselves at home in nature as well. Or, as Atwood puts
it, "attitudes towards Nature inevitably involve man's attitude towards
his own body and towards sexuality, insofar as these too are seen as
part of Nature. It doesn't take much thought to deduce what 'Nature is
dead' and 'Nature is hostile' are going to do to a man's attitudes
towards his own body and towards women" (*Survival* 63). In Canadian
poems that have moved beyond merely utilizing natural objects as
psychic projections, there is still a struggle for the poet who wants to
express Eros in terms of Canadian nature. For example, even when
lovers are in pursuit of each other's warmth they tend to become
frozen into the landscape, as in Atwood's "Pursuit," where she
searches "Through the wilderness of the flesh / across the mind's ice /
expanses" for her lover, afraid she will find him frozen to death in the
snow.

Eros and Thanatos are similarly conflated in a typically Canadian
epithalamium by Joan Finnigan, "All Marriages Are Terminated in

Tundra," where she describes being married in Canada as wandering "in a wilderness of moonless dark and ice" with the love relation terminated "in an easy Arctic death," asleep "in a snow-bank" dreaming of "a sunny road in Spain" (170). Not all lovemaking on the tundra ends in death, however. In Ralph Gustafson's "Of Place" the poet's conviction that we ought to take Aphrodite to a warmer place than Canada doesn't prevent him from pulling a comforter made of gravel up over himself and his lover. Canadian poets use rock, stone, glacial, and ice imageries as elements of passion in a way that reconciles the natural sensuality of the body to the qualities of nature surrounding them. Or, as Irving Layton puts it, "Desolation surrounds us, takes us in, fills our minds and hearts. We live with a white blankness nearly six months of each year. . . . In this vast, empty space, in this white blankness, love defines us, gives us a habitation and a name" (14).

Romancing the stone can be merely an allusion, as a verse from Alden Nowlan's "Canadian Love Song" illustrates:

> To my love's bed, to keep her warm,
> I'll carry wrapped and heated stones.
> That which is comfort to the flesh
> is sometimes torture to the bones.
> (*Love When the Nights* 19)

Even though D. G. Jones's Aphrodite in "Fiat Lux" seems to belong in Greece, Jones focuses on "Sunlight on the Greek / stone" and consummates his passion alchemically when "The light conceives / a red man in the rock" (*Under the Thunder* 21). In "14/12/70" he feels that (after sex) "We have been washed by tides / the glacial waters welling up / to shudder and subside," and in "A Danger of Birds" he associates his lover's breasts with "twin eskers when the glacier has passed." It is not just that she inspires natural imageries but that their passion transforms their bodies into the landscape: "Do not pass this way again / or all my tundra may be cracked / with tiny flowers" (*Under the Thunder* 26). In his tenderly parodic poems about Lampman's love affair, Jones mixes Lampman's characteristic catalogues of natural images with images assuming that stones and love go together and that he and his lover are made both of stones and of flesh.

There is no appropriation of the woman's body, no colonization of her in these poems; rather, both men and women poets seem to accept a metamorphosis into nature as an element of lovemaking. I suspect that Atwood would attribute this to getting beyond the sense of being weak and helpless before nature and beyond anger at nature and lovers to Position Four, where nature is by no means "the Divine Mother" or an "evil monster" but "exists as a living process which includes opposites: life and death, 'gentleness' and 'hostility'." (*Survival* 63). We can recognize that this "new" vision of nature is much like the Old European, Celtic, or holistic understanding of the cyclicity of opposites interbraided with each other. Atwood's Position Four is thus as old as it is new, bringing a response to Canadian nature that interbraids European pagan with Native American archetypes.

The key to this attitude is accepting nature as out there—not human, but also not alien in the existential sense of mindless otherness. Human beings are in nature, participants in its processes; it is a nature that transcends human consciousness without transcending matter. In 1968, several years before she wrote *Survival*, Atwood puzzles over this attitude in a poem entitled "The totems." "Why then is my mind / crowded with hollow totems," she asks, suggesting that the "cast skins" and "faces without motion" she perceives mentally are only shadows. She asserts in the second stanza that these empty masks had once been inhabited by animals who danced "in a warmer place." In my reading, Atwood recognizes that representations of nature which are merely mental, which have no existence outside the mind, are empty; but she does not know how to deal with the "different part of the forest" where they have gone. My conviction is that when Atwood and other Eurocentric Canadian poets become stymied by nature they are aided in making the leap to trust the natural world rather than in the human self through the agency of Native American theology.

*The Native
American
Factor*

In analyzing Anglo-Canadians' use of Native American archetypes we need to be wary of European tendencies to take landscape as mere raw material for image formation and Native Americans as mere symbols of self-development. D. G. Jones's premise that the Canadian land is a symbol of the unconscious seems to reflect this European view of nature, especially in his reading of Canadian poets' use of Native American peoples. His

European perspective is evident in his analysis of the Salteaux woman "Keejigo" in D. C. Scott's "At Gull Lake: August 1810." Jones sees the European lover Nairne providing the Native American woman with a means of transcending her unconscious to achieve consciousness, to escape from her (implicitly) lower tribal status to "find in him her release into the light of consciousness" (*Butterfly* 48). Like Atwood's Venus trying to emerge from inside Hecate, Keejigo, in Jones's interpretation, can achieve the elixir of European acculturation only by escaping Canadian nature.

I interpret Scott's Keejigo as a tragic hero who is killed by the double bind of her half-European and half-Indian origins, which she escapes only in death. We will recall that the Indian agent Scott had located "quintessential passion" in the Mattagami landscape rather than in artificial European culture; in "At Gull Lake" he describes Keejigo, a half-Norman, half-Salteaux Venus ("Star she was named for / Keejigo, star of the morning") dressed in antelope skins embroidered with porcupine quills and "A half-moon of powder-blue / On her brow, her cheeks / Scored with light ochre streaks" (54). Whether or not these are authentically Salteaux body paintings, Scott is establishing Keejigo as strikingly beautiful in a Native American rather than European way, speaking "In the beautiful speech of the Saulteaux" to declare her love for Nairne. She is not raised to civilized consciousness, moreover, but has her beautifully made up face mutilated and blinded by her vengeful husband's orders to his other two wives. She disappears into the wilderness, to be apotheosized into a terrible storm, then takes up residence in the sun and the moon. The terror in Scott's account expresses his empathy with Keejigo rather than with Nairne, his attitude not fear of a seductress but awe at her fate, which results both from her tribe's brutal treatment and Nairne's failure to come to her aid. I read his Salteaux Venus not as a container for Scott's projections but as an inhabitant of a disrupted indigenous culture.

To assess whether the Canadian attitude toward nature varies significantly from the European, it is crucial to come to terms with the relationship between the Canadian poet and Native American Canadians. Both the romantic image of the Native American as a "noble Savage" whom the poet envies for an Edenic life and cultured distaste for "lust-red" primitivism represent imported European perspectives. As Atwood puts it in her introduction to *The New Oxford Book of*

Canadian Verse in English, "the Canadian imagination sought to mythologize the native Indian" as early as Charles Mair's verse-drama *Tecumseh* in 1886; but "by 'mythologize' I do not mean 'falsify': Canadian poets, perhaps even more than American poets, have long been obsessed with the shape and inner meaning of the collision between the transplanted and the aboriginal, and by the quest for a spiritual structure that is authentic, indigenous, and accessible to them" (xxxii). Atwood suggests that the spirituality for which Canadian poets quest represents a blend of the way Native Americans approach nature and the white Canadian's awe of it and of them. Although there are instances in which Canadian poets misappropriate Native Americans as personal projections and colonize indigenous archetypes, I have found such "falsified" Native American archetypes no more frequent in Canadian poetry than those approached with admiration. Many Canadian poems about Native Americans contrast European values to indigenous ones, in favor of the latter. It is within this context of Canadian poets' admiration of Native American spiritual and moral integrity that we must question their ethics in expropriating a Native American woman or shaman or hunter to serve as persona. How can we evaluate the tendency of many Canadian poets to use Native Americans not only as subjects but also as voices, speaking in first-person monologues as if they were Native Americans themselves? Or, as James Reaney puts it in "Local Grains of Sand," "we despise the Indian while eagerly sucking at the symbols he evolved from a life supposedly inferior to ours," to which Leslie Monkman adds that "if the image of writers 'sucking at symbols' seems extreme, we must acknowledge that throughout our literary history, the Indian and his culture are vehicles for the definition of the white man's national, social, or personal identity. . . . There is a delicate balance between exploring what is common to all mankind and exploiting the culture of a vanquished people" (163). Any consideration of the literary use of Native American archetypes must address this question of whether the absorption of Native American spirituality into Anglo-Canadian literature and theology represents a psychological, spiritual, and literary imperialism.

The Indian policy of both Canada and America in the nineteenth century was based on the idea that the tribes were becoming extinct and that the best thing to do was to assimilate them into the dominant culture by erasing their languages, ritual practices, and theologies.

Paradoxically, many facets of the Native American culture being exterminated were valued by nonnative Canadians, so that in place names and in naming high schools and athletic teams the waning tribes were milked for the empowerment latent in their archetypal symbols. In both Canada and the United States Boy Scouts and Girl Scouts were "initiated" into pseudo–Native American ritual lore. At the European end of the scale of attitudes to Native Americans we have early examples like "The Rising Village" (1825), which Oliver Goldsmith wrote to posit an evolutionary development for Canadian settlers through difficulty toward happiness, a happiness which involves civilizing a wilderness containing Native Americans. He already discerns a "Happy Acadia" evolving since fifty years previously, when "savage tribes, with terror in their train / Rushed o'er thy fields, and ravaged all they plain," and celebrates, in contrast, "the peaceful arts of culture skilled" he now finds more characteristic of Canada.

As we have seen, however, observation of the Native Americans' ability to adapt to the wilderness led later nineteenth-century Canadian poets to a much more ambivalent attitude, which was influenced by the enormous popularity of Longfellow's "Song of Hiawatha" (1855) both in Canada and America. Even though agent Scott ostensibly was overseeing the natives' evolutionary extinction, he discerned the tragedy of assimilation in a series of poems in which he admires Native American women. In "Watkwenies" (1893) he describes "The Woman who Conquers," an Iroquois tribal leader, as savage in that "Vengeance was once her nation's lore and law," but regrets that she is reduced to receiving the "interest money" due her tribe. His "Onondaga Madonna" (1893) is a "tragic savage," whose "pagan passion burns and glows" but who "thrills with war and wildness in her veins" (*Selected Poems* 14); and in his description of an old Chippewa woman going off to an island to die after a lifetime of valiant courage in "The Forsaken" (1905) he is even more admiring.

Approaching these Native American women heroes with respectful awe leads to Scott's poetic acquisition of an authentic Canadian voice. As I illustrated earlier in the cases of Crawford and Lampman, not only are Native Americans powerful, but their language is a vehicle which the Canadian poet uses to achieve inspiration. Thus in

"Indian Place-Names" Scott regrets that "The race has waned and left but tales of ghosts" along with "the call / Of their wild names that haunt the lovely glens" (SP 36). Scott is a striking example of an Indian agent whose admiration of tribal cultures makes him regret the policies he is trying to enforce, so that he tries in his poetry to preserve the very values he is instructed to eradicate.

It is important to note that although we might read Scott's poetry as inauthentic grief for a doom of which he is the agent, Scott is not creating a Europeanized "noble savage" or interpreting the Canadian landscape as an idyllic Eden; rather, he regrets the passage of a life-style with whose rigors and difficulties he is fully familiar. I find the same admiration of a non-European life-style in similar nineteenth-century and turn-of-the-twentieth-century poems such as Charles Sangster's sonnet "The Red-Men," Thomas D'Arcy McGee's "Arctic Indian's Faith," and Joseph Howe's "Song of the Micmac." Howe is impressed with the Micmac's knowledge of tracking and hunting, admiring "Free sons of the forest" for abilities which are neither pastoral nor Acadian.

A recognition that Native American attitudes toward nature not only differ from but may be superior to European ones is more characteristic of Anglo-Canadian poetry than anthropomorphic projection. Should a line be drawn between using the Native American as metaphor for European-based subjectivity and an acceptable incorporation of Native American spiritual integrity? In the latter category I place Lionel Kearns's "Magic Indians" and Doug Featherling's "Explorers as Seen by the Natives," to suggest but two examples. In such poems assimilation of Native American ways of approaching the harsh realities of Canadian nature seem to provide a healing element to Anglo-Canadian poets, opening the way to their acceptance of their place in the natural cycle. By this means they learn, also, to relate appropriately to wise old women and to the blended Venus/Hecate/Artemis Canadian crone emerging from the landscape.

Two poems about stones as they are used by Native Americans may give us a clue to nonexploitative use of Native American metaphor. In "Fish: Stone: Song" Victor Coleman describes the way Nanaimo Salish first dreams of and then finds a stone that "enabled him to catch more cod" and thus to become "that wealthy Indian / like unto a white man." In his old age he obeys the stone's request that he return it to the spot where he pulled it out of the sea. The poem describes the Native American's respect for what the stone told him to do, suggesting the usefulness of heeding nature. In Coleman's poem the stone is a stone is a stone, productive of fish and of dream visions but bearing no human projections. Robert Kroetsch, in his more complex "Stone Hammer Poem," seems at first to be appropriating a prehistoric hammer stone as a "paperweight on my desk," but in tracing the finding of the stone by his grandfather (who only "thought" his field "was his") and acknowledging that the land really doesn't belong to anybody, Kroetsch seems to have entered into the same Native American relationship to it as Coleman's Salish fisherman. Even when his poem metamorphoses into stone, the stone as object in nature remains endowed with nonhuman essence. By getting in tune with stone the poet gets in harmony with a cosmos which remains beyond the power of human beings to own or to colonize.

Describing herself and her fellow Canadians as inhabitants of a winter landscape in "The Portage," Gwendolyn MacEwen hears the sound of "subtle drums under / the candid hands of Indians" which "are trying to tell us / why we have come" (564). MacEwen senses that the Native Americans have something to tell other Canadians; many poets, as we have seen, not only listen to what the drums are saying but also incorporate Native American attitudes. One of the principal forms that takes is recognizing the manner in which Native Americans understand myth in relation to nature. Such an approach recognizes the failings of "civilization," which is the case in David McFadden's paean to the "beautiful Micmac children" in "Lennox Island." Admiring their beauty, he recognizes that he cannot adapt to the currents of or the leeches in their water and that he must stand quietly because he may frighten them or taint them with his alien culture. Trying to keep his European frame of mind from "poisoning" the children, McFadden internalizes their values: "and I invite life to flow through my body / but I simply become more and more aware / of my powers of destruction and I quietly leave" (384). In announcing his belief that "these children are my ancestors," part of a people who are about to be destroyed but who "populated the once-sacred earth" before civilization arose, his tone is elegiac for a tribe he considers doomed. Although he certainly attributes "noble savage" elements to an Edenic innocence, McFadden understands that the psyches of the children are related, through the history of the human race, to his own unconscious desires.

Is McFadden engaged in a kind of poetic colonization, like a New Age initiate who claims to have been a Native American in a previous incarnation? In his candid recognition of the shallowness of the "widely held belief in Caucasian superiority," I read a nonexploitative admiration of the Micmac children as well as a serious critique of European culture. I do not want to dismiss Anglo-Canadian poems in which Native Americans and Native American archetypes appear as metaphors or as guides to alternative ethics too quickly, recognizing that poems such as Ken Belford's "Carrier Indians," John Newlove's "Pride," and Erin Mouré's "Siksika" can be read as nondegrading and psychically healthy approaches to Native American culture.

Acknowledging the carrier Indians' reputation as "A band of thieves, and liars" Belford nevertheless admires their legend that "when someone you have loved dies, part of your heart dies too." Although he concludes that these are "Ugly people with large eyes. / Having nowhere to go" he nonetheless concludes that "I am one of them" (438). When a poet claims metamorphosis into a Native American, even through admiration of native values, he or she borders on a usurpation which permits poets to swallow up and digest women and "primitive" peoples to enhance their own psychic development. Although Belford approaches this kind of narcissistic exploitation, his respect for Native Americans places him, I feel, closer to a poem like Mouré's "Siksika," which develops an extended metaphor between the way Blackfoot women weigh down their tepees with "wide circles of medicine stones" and the poet's attempt to come to terms with her own body: "Like Blackfeet women / it is us who own the circle of our bodies / unhunted by men" (233).

Newlove wrestles in a similar way with his relationship to Native Americans in a complex examination of the legends of many tribes in "The Pride." This poem in seven parts starts off listing various "images" of Native Americans, the invading Spanish, and the "desolate country," then describes "this western country crammed / with the ghosts of indians" and with their legends. In the second section Newlove is fleshing out each "legend" or archetype, including the Haida and Tsimshian raven as trickster, and the "thunderbird hilunga" also sacred to the Kwakiutl. The only explicitly feminine figure in the list he characterizes as a bringer of "malevolence,"

> the wild woman of the woods—
> grinning, she wears
> a hummingbird in her hair,
> d'sonoqua, the furious one— (340)

who is one of many legends "strong enough / to be remembered." His attribution of malevolence to the one Native American goddess he mentions suggests a significant gender difference from Emily Carr's attitude of awe of and empowerment by the same figure (see below).

In the third section Newlove speaks less descriptively and more personally, querying "what image, bewildered / son of all men" . . . "do you worship" among these "half understood" tales? As history passes and he surveys more legends, he struggles with the relationship between Native American archetypes and the white Canadian poet, locating "the pride, the grand poem / of our land, of the earth itself" in Native American symbols which white Canadians must incorporate in order to create an indigenous poetry. When he confronts Native American legend not as literary image but as a reality transcending human consciousness, he locates poetic success in succumbing to "the sunlit brilliant image" which "suddenly floods us / with understanding" so that

> we are no longer lonely
> but have roots,
> and the rooted words
> recur in the mind, mirror, so that
> we dwell on nothing else, in nothing else

This does not mean, however, that Newlove expropriates Native American values; language and the creation of words can only take place in harmony with a nonhuman reality:

> the thing made up
> of our desires,
> not of its words, not only
> of them, but of something else
> as well

a "something else" beyond but empowering poetic imagination which is

> the knowledge of
> our origins, and where
> we are in truth,
> whose land this is
> and is to be. (342)

In terms of a colonization of the native theology, Newlove's seventh stanza could be read as a usurpation of Native American archetypal power. He recognizes, however, that what the land contributes is not "this handful / of fragments" (of the first section) and that "the indians / are not composed of / the romantic stories / about them." His internalization of Native American spirituality is nonetheless problematical: the Native Americans, he asserts, "still ride the soil / in us," so that "in our bodies entire, in our minds, . . . / at last / we become them." In one reading, Newlove's poetry exploits Native American culture for his own poetic enhancement, using Native Americans the way European male poets have traditionally swallowed up their female muses. He could be accused of "white shamanism" which, as we shall see in chapter 10, the Hopi/Miwok poet Wendy Rose characterizes as white poets' expropriations of the voice and functions of Native American spiritual leaders. As a poet myself, I have listened to the Native American accusation that mining their culture for metaphors and other kinds of themes constitutes an updated form of exploitation and I have ceased to do so; however, the Anglo-Canadian tendency to seek psychological wholeness through the vehicle of indigenous culture deserves literary scrutiny.

The process of colonization presumes a victor and a victim, the one succeeding in taking over the lands and livelihood of the other. Two aspects of Canadian life—the Canadian landscape and the threatening proximity of the United States—place white Canadians much closer to the victim position than their counterparts in England and the United States. In Canada, not only do both whites and Native Americans confront an unassimilable nature; they also entertain profound distrust of the United States elephant, whose every twitch may squash them. The combination of hostile nature and a frightening national neighbor places the Canadian in a different relationship to the Native Americans than that characterizing citizens of the United States. I will return in chapter 10 to this vexed question of the delicate balance between an authentic respect for Native American culture and poetic colonization.

Stones and Crones

My hypothesis is that, in beginning to appreciate the way Native Americans relate to the Canadian wilderness, Anglo-Canadian poets' memories of cognate archetypes and attitudes from their pagan pasts are stimulated. In human history it is only recently that individualism replaced the kind of tribal consciousness characteristic of European cultures as well as of Native Americans. To put if another way, the shock of exile in a particularly obdurate landscape jolts Canadian poets back through very thin recent signatures to nature-centered archetypes similtaneously alien and familiar. I suggest that Canadian poets experience Native American archetypes as an interactive field which short-circuits the far less gynocentric classical mythology.

The Canadian artist Emily Carr's quest into the rain forests of British Columbia to paint decaying Haida totem poles exemplifies such an archetypal Canadian quest. Deep in a nettle patch in the rain forest, Carr comes face to face with the Native American goddess D'Sonoqua: "She appeared to be neither wooden nor stationary, but a singing spirit, young and fresh, passing through the jungle. No violence coarsened her; no power domineered to wither her. She was graciously feminine." Carr finds this carving on an island inhabited by a dozen delicate Egyptian cats, which sit with her while she sketches: "There we were—D'Sonoqua, the cats and I—the woman who only a few moments ago had forced herself to come behind the houses in trembling fear of the 'wild woman of the woods'—wild in the sense that forest-creatures are wild—shy, untouchable" (40).

I would suspect that the strangely conflated Artemis/Hecate/Aphrodite figure I have noted emerging in some Canadian poetry constitutes a merging of Native American goddesses like D'Sonoqua with the classical figures of Hecate, Artemis, and Aphrodite in a syncretic interbraiding of native with European pagan goddesses. The witch archetype in popular European folklore derives from a similar conflation of sexual prowess and a spiritual power that is immanent rather than transcendent, based upon wise women's access to natural phenomena like herbs and animal familiars. Barbara Walker suggests in *The Crone* that Saxons and Danes as well as Celts worshipped "The Hag," who sometimes took the "form of an aniconic stone idol" (54), like the stone of Scone upon which monarchs of England are still crowned. Anglo-Canadian poets, perhaps influenced by Celtic archetypes, continue to associate wise older women with sacred stones. Rather than (as in Atwood's initial hypothesis) depict Venuses trying to escape entrapment within Hecates, Canadian poets often structure their poems upon finding the right way to absorb empowerment from a crone embedded in the landscape.

In that James Reaney alternately takes the persona of the "leather skinned harridan" who had once been a prostitute and of one of the boys who rape her in a ditch, his "Granny Crack" is a transitional and not very respectful poem in this category. He reminds her that "you played a pigsty Venus / When you were young, old dame," and he and his playmates saw her "as an incredible crone" whom they despise in spite of her association with the natural world. Reaney ends the poem speaking in her voice as "the mother of your sun" (256). Although he speaks as crone, rapist, and onlooker, his crone/Venus retains a natural specific of Artemis and Artemis's wildness, closer to the rank world of nature than to the civilized culture of her tormentors.

This conflated archetype can sometimes be found lurking as a slumbering mythic creature awakening within Canadian poetry, as if what A. J. M. Smith in "The Lonely Land" termed "a beauty / of dissonance, / this resonance / of stony strand" were generating its own variety of archetypes (361). Anne Wilkinson's "Winter Sketch" suggests rebirth through ice and snow once Canadians learn to speak the idiom of Canadian nature. We have seen how, once poets name Canadian objects, new archetypal deities begin to emerge, sometimes with classical names but never wholly European or "civilized." This often occurs as an eccentric embedding of folk and classical archetypes into unlikely landscapes, of which the best-known example is undoubtedly E. J. Pratt's "Witches' Brew," in which he celebrates his fifth wedding anniversary in an epic poem about a "Saturnalian feast" under the ocean when three witches spill their cauldron of extremely potent alcohol. Whereas Pratt's Bacchanalian orgy takes place under the seas, Robert Bringhurst, in "Hachadura," seems to depict a Canadian archetype even when describing the "high west" of El Salvador:

> And the light that lies just under darkness,
> Artemis
>
> grazing the ice
> that is sea-rose under the sunset. (73)

Oddly, this sounds much more like the Canadian landscape of "The Greenland Stone" in this same collection, in which Bringhurst describes how "Gods immersed in the masked / North American Air / vanish like the kayak's / white stone anchor" (14). As we shall see in the next chapter, European Artemis as Lady of the Wild Things is associated with animal familiars and with mountains; here, she is made out of Canadian ice and, like D'Sonoqua, is embedded in the landscape.

This Canadian Artemis/Hecate emerges in poems where there has been a successful quest undertaken, the poet acknowledging a need to come to terms with his or her muse. In Barry McKinnon's "Sex at Thirty-One," for example, the poet first recognizes that he needs to understand both speech and love, that he desires "the whole body of imagination," and that this body is as much outside of him as within. He seeks relationships not shaped by "the / greek gods" or the ancient "chinese" but by his personal lovemaking in the present. He knows that his grail is "the cup or mirror to see in that glance another looking / back" but doesn't know whether it is his lover or a hag goddess offering him the cup of love (221). The poem remains problematic because McKinnon wavers between seeing women as real beings and seeing them as awards in a masculine quest; however, he realizes that he must abandon inauthentic Aphrodite archetypes by paying attention to real women.

The outcome of Earle Birney's quest in "The Mammoth Corridors" is less ambivalent than McKinnon's because it is grounded in the landscape of a trip eastward from the West Coast to the cabin where he was born, a quest in which he acknowledges the maternal element both in nature and in his own past. His road eastward leads him on a journey which reverses his father's westward migration (Collected Poems, vol. 2, 62–63). He is able to leave his "own lusts and neckties and novels" as well as his ulcers and accidia behind as he travels the route over the icy mountains which the first Siberians took when they followed the mammoths down from the north. By associating himself with the prehistoric nomads rather than "the applefoam" of the West

Coast, he moves eastward under the aegis of new archetypes, including "that madcap virgin / mother of ice," a divinity who conflates Artemis in her Dianic aspect as the "virgin" and the maternal content of a "mother" lurking like a glacier under the earth. Aphrodite enters the Anglo-Canadian archetypal figure as an intractable presence; passion is cold but powerful, the quester's goal "her love." Birney sees the Canadian goddess lurking within the tundra and permafrost, preserving the ice age forever, but acknowledges that only when he accepts her in all her cold and ice can passion be reborn.

McKinnon and Birney differ from Virgo and Simmons in their attitude to this cronelike love goddess: they do not hate her or try to dominate her but recognize that they must come to terms with her, working out some kind of relationship with her. Although Birney does not specifically mention his mother, his quest ends near the "dazzle of snow the human mesh / where all began for me," suggesting that, like the British and American poets of both sexes, the successful quester has come to terms with the maternal element.

Several Canadian women poets find an analogous crone/ Aphrodite/Artemis archetype (as in the case of women poets in England and the United States), but in their quests the goal is identification with the same rather than the cautious approach to an "other" that characterizes the male poets. Phyllis Gottlieb, in "Paradigm," and Margaret Atwood, in "A Red Shirt," interbraid old women, mothers, lovers, and children in poems that suggest the empowerment a woman experiences when coming to terms with an archetype that unifies the maternal and the sexual with the acceptance of one's own aging.

In "Paradigm" Gottlieb first describes "an old woman / stout and ungainly who lugs / jars of pickled herring to the least grateful of daughters-in-law" (probably the poet) and realizes that the old woman contains a girl's voice calling out to a childhood friend in a long-ago Polish village. Gottlieb envisions the old woman as the being who holds the generations together and "utters a nameless battle-cry," which is the crone's triumphant assertion of the ongoing generations, "red ribbons braided / into the child's blood" (87). The underlying psychological event here is the feminine rebirth quest, the Eleusinian reconciliation of the mother and daughter, daughter-in-law and mother-in-law, daughter and mother, and their acceptance of the crone as a frightening but potentially empowering element of their own future. In "A Red Shirt" Atwood embeds acknowledgment of the crone figure within the time frame of an afternoon when she and her sister sewed a red shirt for her daughter. They recognize that red is considered passionate or even deathly in some countries but claim it in the second section of the poem: "red is our color by birth- / right, the color of tense joy / & spilled pain that joins us / to each other." She and her sister, sewing the red shirt, lean over the table with "earth's gravity furrowing / our bodies, tugging us down," but accept their place in "the procession / of old leathery mothers" who are "passing the work from hand to hand, / mother to daughter, / a long thread of red blood, not yet broken" (102). At the very center of the poem Atwood embeds "the story / about the Old Woman" who "weaves your body" and "weaves your soul" though "she is hated & feared, / though not by those who know her."

> She is the witch you burned
> by daylight and crept from your home
>
> to consult & bribe at night. The love
> that tortured you blamed on her.
>
> She can change her form,
> and like your mother she is covered with fur.
>
> The black Madonna
> studded with miniature
>
> arms & legs, like tin stars,
> to whom they offer agony
>
> and red candles when there is no other
> help or comfort, is also her. (*Two-Headed Poems* 102–103)

Generations of women heal each other as they sew together. Atwood and her sister finish the shirt and give it to the little girl, who runs away "waving her red arms / in delight, and the air / explodes with banners" (105). The Polish "black madonna" icon, which Atwood associates with the agonized offerings of traditionally guilty Christians, derivative from Black Artemis, and the fur-covered "wild" mother seem to resolve the struggle between Venus and Hecate for Atwood, who, very much like Audre Lorde in her assimilation of African goddesses, empowers herself under the aegis of a "dark mother" archetype.

278

Romancing the Stone: Love Poetry in Canada

Although the difference between Birney's and McKinnon's quests and Gottlieb's and Atwood's crone/Demeter/Aphrodite poems is one of identification versus difference, I do not conclude that these mark significant gender variations in Canadian approaches to the archetype. There are Canadian male poems, such as Edmund Fancott's "I am Isis" and John Heath's "Aphrodite," in which the poet quite sympathetically identifies with the goddess as well as female poems, such as Musgrave's "Anima," in which the woman poet tries to distance herself from the "smell of death" she associates with a feminine archetype she wants to evade. Although there are certainly any number of Canadian poems in which men approach women with both repugnance and intent to dominate, we can find examples, including Helene Rosenthal's "Amazon Amazed," in which a woman poet welcomes the Amazon queen's rape by Achilles as "love," being "made a woman" by "Aphrodite's boy" (89). Nor are all Canadian love poems intercourse with glaciers under granite blankets—a lot of Canadian lovemaking takes place in Paris, in Greece, even in Toronto. Nonetheless, the role that an obdurate, unconquerable landscape plays as both image and archetype in the Canadian imagination suggests that the human mind can adapt its archetypal configurations when a new landscape undermines the impact of a previous culture.

Gottlieb and Atwood in their explicit way and, more implicitly, McKinnon and Birney move toward a place of psychic healing because they are able to complete the cycle from Medusa through Aphrodite to Artemis and her Hecate aspect, trying to absorb the import of each element without becoming frozen in terror. I see this as the same archetypal process which helps American poets succeed in their quests for Aphrodite, differing only in the greater ease with which some Canadian poets transcend European culture.

PART THREE

WHERE
THE
WILD
THINGS
ARE

Wild Men and Animals. *Swiss
tapestry, mid-fifteenth century.* © *The
Board of Trustees of the Victoria and
Albert Museum.*

9.

The Artemis Continuum

*I*n considering the "dark mother" element of the Aphrodite archetype we have seen how Aphrodite overlaps both with Medusa and with Hecate, who is the death/night aspect of Artemis. The poet's quest for Aphrodite leads not only to a mature, authentic Eros in his or her psychological life but also to a reconciliation with the terrifying power of one's mother and one's own inevitable death. Nature's frightening aspect, which I term the Hecate factor, could be understood as a psychological experience which we must face and integrate, a factor interwoven with Medusa as coming to terms with our mothers and Aphrodite as coming to terms with our sexuality. In the previous chapter we saw how Canadian poets often interbraid attributes of Aphrodite, Artemis, Medusa, Hecate, and a specifically Canadian wildness which they often associate with the rocky landscape. It is difficult to unbraid Hecate, Medusa, Aphrodite, and Artemis for the purposes of archetypal analysis because they are not, ultimately, unbraidable; they are interwoven facets of a holistic archetypal quality.

When men and women poets overcome their terror of the powerful femininity of the Medusa and "dark mother"/Aphrodite archetypes they break through into a natural imagery, sharply particular, embodying their sensual participation in the ongoing life of the earth. I would identify the metamorphic conflations of landscape and genital imagery of many women poets as well as the bright and particular natural vision of successfully Aphroditian male poets as elements of the

Artemis archetype, understood as a goddess of the wild who blends a healthy animality with a sense of balance in nature. As Estella Lauter describes natural imagery in such women's poetry, "this is the style that allows earth to brown feet, thicken fingers, and unfurl in both brains and onions as Atwood sets seedlings under her window. . . . It is the style that allows Griffin to interweave the blackbird, the light, perception, inner sight, mother and daughter, the bird's flight and our own, pen, paper, hands, tongue and knowledge into her ecstatic affirmation, 'the light is in us' " (*Women as Mythmakers* 217). As a psychological phenomenon, the Artemis archetype or Artemesian frame of mind forms part of a cyclical continuum with Medusa and Aphrodite, as with its own traditionally yoked Hecate element.

The archetypal elements I treat in this final part are thus in many ways interchangeable, not only with each other but also with the Medusa and Aphrodite symbols previously analyzed. It is easier to think of Medusa, Aphrodite, and Artemis/Hecate as segments of a circle than as separate archetypes. Each component of this part of the book similarly could be placed anywhere within my argument. This cyclicity arises from the way that these archetypal elements form part of a psychological cycle, leading in and out of each other in poets' quests for wholeness.

In *The Hero with a Thousand Faces* Joseph Campbell describes the hero's quest into "the regions of the unknown (desert, jungle, deep sea, alien land, etc.)," which in their emptiness are "free fields for the projection of unconscious content" which the quester populates with "ogres" and "sirens of mysteriously seductive, nostalgic beauty." As an example of such seductresses projected by his "heroes," Campbell recounts Russian legends of wild women in the woods:

> The Russian peasants know, for example, of the "Wild Women" of the woods who have their abode in mountain caverns where they maintain households, like human beings. They are handsome females, with fine square heads, abundant tresses, and hairy bodies. They fling their breasts over their shoulders when they run and when they nurse their children. . . . They like to dance or tickle people to death who wander alone into the forest, and anyone who accidentally chances upon their invisible dancing parties dies. . . . They enjoy human lovers, have frequently married country youths, and are known to make excellent wives. But like all supernatural brides, the minute the

husband offends in the least their whimsical notions of marital propri-
ety, they disappear without a trace. (79)

Independent of men, more animal than human, living with each
other "in groups," knowledgeable about healing, potentially deadly
but sexually hungry although hostile to patriarchal notions of matri-
mony, the wild women of the Russian woods carry traits of Artemis as
Lady of the Wild Things, of Amazon legend, and of indigenous
shamanism. Indeed, it is their origin in peasant lore rather than in
aristocratic culture or church doctrine which is important archetypal-
ly. The wild women inhabit a free zone closely impinging upon
culture, a zone of partially repressed paganism which can easily rupture
the patriarchal pie.

To Campbell, however, the wild women live outside the social
structure, in "deserts" he perceives as empty of culture, a natural realm
useful as a mere proving ground for male adventures. Hayden White,
similarly, understands the wild woman archetype as a "form of wild-
ness" created in the Middle Ages to contain "a projection of repressed
desires and anxieties." She is "surpassingly ugly,"

> covered with hair except for her gross pendant breasts which she
> threw over her shoulders when she ran. This wild woman, however,
> was supposed to be obsessed by a desire for ordinary men. In order to
> seduce the unwary knight or shepherd, she could appear as the most
> enticing of women, revealing her abiding ugliness only during sexual
> intercourse. (Dudley and Novak 21)

In this medieval archetype we can detect elements of Tannhäuser's
seductive and destructive Venus, the alluring and terrible Aphrodite,
and a wild woman who shifts from old to young, hag to beauty, as
Artemis alternates with Hecate.

The wild woman archetype conflates Artemis and Hecate with
women from European folk legend much in the manner that the
Tannhäuser legends created an indigenously powerful goddess. There
are many cognate figures in European folklore, including the "Wilde
Frauen" of Germany who haunt Wunderberg near Salzburg and the
Serbian Vilas, women with "long flying hair," according to Thomas
Keightly, who have voices like woodpeckers though they are young
and beautiful and skilled in archery. Like Diana, the Vilas are friendly
with deer: a Vila "usually rides a seven-year-old hart, with a bridle

made of snakes" (492). The Serbian ballads Keightly cites celebrate the Vilas dancing "their magic roundels" in the "cool shade" of the woods and comforting wounded deer in the forests. The urge to marry (in the case of men) or join the wild women in the woods (in the case of women) is constant in European folklore, where escaping culture for the wild wood and patriarchal matrimony for Diana is as likely to lead to empowerment as to death.

White's account is contained in an anthology of essays, *The Wild Man Within,* in which the editors assume that the wild man and his corollary wild women are projections which compensate men but are not alternatives to culture. Nature, in their readings, is empty; wildness a fanciful state pleasing to the makers and audiences of legend but unreal or imaginary, valuable in providing a release from anxiety about civilization. Everything begins and ends in the human (and implicitly male) mind; nature exists as symbol or emblem of human cognition.

Women have always used nature to subvert culture, and the wild woman archetype has always appealed to us. So persistent is our longing for an apatriarchal land of heart's desire that I have been tempted to posit fundamental gender differences between men and women poets' approaches to Artemis. In "No Dancing. No Acts of Dancing," for example, Phyllis Janik celebrates her identification with Campbell's Russian wild women. Her first stanza is a word-for-word quotation of Campbell about what "Russian peasants know," which she turns into a protest against prohibitions of dancing posted above jukeboxes in Greyhound stations:

> these people would die
> if they could see me fling my breasts
> over my shoulder and run . . . (50)

Janik's empowerment derives from turning herself into a wild woman to dance out her feminine sexuality.

Nor are such celebrations of antipatriarchal wild women only a recent aspect of women's poetry. Even Mary Elizabeth Coleridge, whom we last encountered at age twenty-one looking in her mirror and whispering empathy with a terrifyingly wounded female, celebrated wild women in later life. By the time she was forty (in 1890) she had become sufficiently uninhibited to compose a rollicking poem about "The White Women," legendary wild women exotically pale to the Malaysians, who "never bowed their necks beneath the yoke" of men, tamed "the tiger in his lair," and made the falcons and eagles "quail" before them. They are Amazonian ("And when they fight, the wild white women cry / The war-cry of the storm") and simultaneously "pure" and abandoned:

> Pure are they as the light; they never sinned,
> But when the rays of the eternal fire
> Kindle the West, their tresses they unbind
> And fling their girdles to the Western wind,
>   Swept by desire.

The wild women are entirely outside the patrilinear and patriarchal system ("Lo, maidens to the maidens then are born, / Strong children of the maidens and the breeze"), and Coleridge unabashedly celebrates them for six verses before pointing out that they can be deadly to men:

> And none may find their dwelling. In the shade
> Primeval of the forest oaks they hide.
> One of our race, lost in an awful glade,
> Saw with his human eyes a wild white maid,
>   And gazing, died. (*Collected Poems* 212–13)

In an inversion of the structure of "The Other Side of a Mirror," in which Coleridge identified in her last few lines with an archetype that had terrified her in the rest of the poem, she celebrates her wild women until the very end, when she admits their danger for males. Like Janik, Coleridge is empowered by her apatriarchal and Amazonian archetype.

Estella Lauter has noticed in recent women's poetry "the contours of a story about our relationship with nature that emphasizes not subservience or fear, not husbandry or dominance, but equality arising from acceptance of our similarities to other forms of nature without obliterating our differences from them" (*Women as Mythmakers* 215). Although it might be tempting to identify women poets' approaches to nature as an aspect of gender, in my study of men's poems about Aphrodite and Canadian men's poems about nature I have suggested that respect for nonhuman nature is not limited to women but constitutes an attitude achieved by both sexes as part of our psychosexual maturity.

Keith Thomas has described how, as early as the seventeenth century, geographical explorations disrupted Christian ideas about the sovereignty of the human species over nature. Having pointed out that British poet Margaret Cavendish had rejected "the whole anthropocentric tradition, applying a sort of cultural relativism to the differences between the species and arguing that men had no monopoloy of sense or reason," Thomas goes on to illustrate how geographical explorations made it "increasingly hard to maintain that creation existed for the exclusive benefit of the human denizens of one small planet" (128, 167). Thus, although both Christianity and science gave permission to exploit an inferior natural world, these strains of greater respect for the earth persisted, especially in poetry.

In British poetry, where a proclivity for escaping into the green woods to disport oneself with wild gods and goddesses is a recurrent theme from the Middle Ages to the present, Artemis's pagan, indigenous signature tends to subvert the Greek Artemis or Roman Diana layers of the archetype, which are more acceptable to English letters. My hypothesis is that this poetry expresses women's and men's longing for the tonic of wildness and that the Artemis archetype provides occasions for the interplay of poet and nature. I am also suggesting that once we accept the hypothesis that we did not create the universe but exist as integral components of it, poetic celebrations of natural archetypes can be understood as a dialogue between psyche and nature to which both nature and psyche contribute.

> ## The Artemis Archetype

Although, like Aphrodite, the Artemis archetype contains elements of holistic Middle Eastern goddess figures (such as her association with a double axe), most accounts trace the qualities by which she became known in classical culture to Old European goddesses whose attributes interbraided with Near Eastern and Indo-European prototypes. It was the "Indo-European Artemis," according to Markale,

> whom the Romans likened to Diana, and who tallies on a number of counts with the ancient mother goddess of the gods. Artemis and her Indo-Iranian counterpart Arvi are very obscure in origin, but both

derive from some older, probably pre-Indo-European, word. They are generally taken to be forms of the cruel and ancient Scythian Diana, the sun goddess of the people of the steppes, who was worshipped throughout the periphery of the Mediterranean at the time of the Hellenic migrations. In earliest times, human sacrifices were made to Artemis at Sparta. (105)

Marija Gimbutas traces the classical Artemis back to a "Goddess of Life and Death" of the sixth and fifth millennia B.C., a figure she collates from the archaeological evidence of Old Europe. Evidence from Hacilar and Çatal Hüyük in Turkey suggests that cultures where goddesses of life, death, wild nature, and women's cycles were worshipped and where women achieved status as priestesses can be located at the sites of the legends of the Artemis-worshipping Amazons recounted by Diodorus Siculus and other writers. Artemisian goddesses such as Lilith are found in the Old Testament, while Diana of Ephesus is bitterly condemned by St. Paul in the New Testament. She was worshipped at the "temple at the city of Ephesus (in the province of Lydia)," which was "spoken of by Greeks as a shrine of Artemis, and later by the Romans as a shrine of Diana" and "was described by both Pindar and Callimachus as a holy site first founded by Amazons" (M. Stone 187). Merlin Stone suggests a link between sites in Anatolia and the worship of a goddess in Crete; she also mentions settlements of Celtic peoples in Anatolia in the third century B.C. which "resulted in the area of central Anatolia, including the eastern parts of Lydia, then being known as Galatia" (188). Thus in terms of cultures in which the Artemis archetype occurs, a link between Anatolia, Crete, and the Celts is suggestive; classical historians also traced the Amazons of Anatolia to Libya, an association which has some archaeological evidence from Crete in its favor and which might account for the frequent occurrence of "black virgins" surviving in Mariology even in the present day. Regardless of historical hypotheses about her origins, Artemis seems more indigenous to Asia Minor and Europe than does Aphrodite, more embedded in local landscapes and subsequent folklores. Her "virginal" (chaste) attributes were not consistently split off from her maternal qualities as she was assimilated into European literature. It is important to remember that even in classical myth the sexual, maternal, and wild were all present in Artemis. As Gimbutas describes her,

Lilith. A Sumerian cult plaque in baked clay, circa 2300-2000 B.C.E. From Edward A. Armstrong, The Folklore of Birds (New York: Dover, 1970), p. 49. Reproduced with permission from Dover Publications.

The Lady of free and untamed nature and the Mother, protectress of weaklings, a divinity in whom the contrasting principles of virginity and motherhood are fused into the concept of a single goddess, was venerated in Greece, Lydia, Crete and Italy. She appears as Artemis and under many local names: Diktynna, Pasiphae, Agrotera ("the wild"), and Diana in Rome. She, "the pure and strong one," was surrounded by nymphs, flanked by animals, and as huntress dominated the animal world. . . . Well-bred Athenian girls of marriageable age danced as bears in honour of Artemis of Brauronia, and during rites of cult-initiation girls "became" bears, *arktoi*. (198–99)

Associated with "fertility," Artemis presided over births and everything having to do with women's biological seasons. Although several scholars see her shift from pre-Indo-European sun goddess to classical moon goddess as a demotion (Markale 15, for example), as goddess of the waxing, full, and waning moon she embodies all aspects of women's life cycles.

Most important for my purpose of understanding the way the Artemis archetype structures English and North American poems is her wild femininity, her being at home in nature rather than culture. She frequently turns herself into animals, such as bears and does, that serve not only as her familiars but as her metamorphic substitutes. Also, although she is sexual, maternal, and nurturant in her early appearances, Artemis's most constant trait is her implacable opposition to marriage. She represents amarital feminine sexuality to the Greeks as Lilith did to the Hebrews, virginity in the sense of a feminine Eros which is acultural and markedly antipatriarchal. The virginity of the priestesses who served her and of the adolescent girls attending her shrine at Brauron is that of women who retain the right to choose what to do with our bodies—whether to roam at will or stay at home, whether to practice celibacy or make love. Sarah Pomeroy notices that in classical myth both Athena and Artemis "enjoyed many consorts"; "their failure to marry, however, was misinterpreted as virginity by succeeding generations of men who connected loss of virginity only with conventional marriage. Either way, as mother goddess or as virgin, Artemis retains control over herself; her lack of permanent connection to a male figure in a monogamous relationship is the keystone of her independence" (6). Or, as blues singer Ida Cox cogently put it, "Wild women don't worry, / Wild women don't have the blues."

Nor Hall explains this happy wildness of women in terms of a special relationship to nature: "To be virginal does not mean to be chaste, but rather to be true to nature and instinct. . . . The virgin forest is not barren or unfertilized but rather a place that is especially fruitful and has multiplied because it has taken life into itself and transformed it, giving birth naturally and taking dead things back to be recycled. It is virgin because it is unexploited, not in man's control" (11). This virginal Artemisian nature is understood differently from nature in the Old Testament, which is considered barren and hostile to human beings; it is not a tamed garden, however, but fruitful in its wildness, following its own cycles of birth and death in a manner we can recognize from the nonhuman, self-sufficient, and powerful Canadian landscape.

Recognition of goddesses whose home is the untamed wilderness has a long history in the British Isles, where indigenous goddesses probably account for the continuity of wild woman archetypes in British literature and for the popularity of stories in which women and men escape civilization for the green woods. "The basic Celtic goddess type," Ross reminds us, "was at once mother, warrior, hag, virgin, conveyor of fertility, of strong sexual appetite which led her to seek mates amongst mankind equally with the gods, giver of prosperity to the land, protectress of the flocks and herds. More static and more archaic than the [Celtic] gods, she remained tied to the land for which she was responsible and whose most striking natural features seemed to her worshippers to be manifestations of her power and personality" (233).

The most important type of Celtic goddess, who antedated but blended with the Roman Diana, was a deer goddess named Sadv, who went to live among the immortal Tuatha Dé Danann, or the people of the goddess Dana, who appear as ancestor tribes in many Celtic legends. "This hind goddess," Markale tells us, "also figures in Gallic or Gallo-Roman iconography. There exist several statues representing a woman with deer's antlers, notably the one housed in the British Museum; this portrays a seated goddess, holding on her knee a horn of plenty and on her left shoulder the head of a ram. Her face is entirely human except for the deer's antlers sprouting from her hair" (104). In many medieval legendary hunts, a female deer or hind, usually snow white, becomes the quarry; sometimes she is hunted down, but often she eludes the hunters, leading them to wander forever in the woods.

In *The Stag of Love: The Chase in Medieval Literature*, Marcelle

Thiébaux sees such quests as erotic, the hunter falling madly in love with his quarry, his sufferings in her pursuit often a punishment for not properly worshipping a goddess. Thiébeaux cites Pausanias (c. 174 C.E.), who tells of Artemis sending a stag "to entice a certain hunter" because she is "moved to vengeance by the omission of her rites." Thiébeaux comments that such "malice of the goddess of the chase was familiar enough in the middle ages" (59) and describes medieval stories of a hunter driven on by Diana or "Eros or Aphrodite . . . later it may be Nature, Amours, Lady Venus or Frau Minne" (93), so that "there are vestiges too of a supernatural chase arranged by a willful Diana" in stories like that of "the Lady Niniane's luring her lovers, notably Merlin, across a ford or by a fountain." (105).

Artemis's punishments are more painful and terrifying to men than those of Medusa, who turns you (presumably painlessly) to stone, or of Aphrodite, who only submits you to sexuality. Sometimes Artemis lets her hounds tear the hero apart, as in the story of Diana and Actaeon in which she is angered by his seeing her naked in her bath; wounding and castration also occur frequently. This "willful" and malicious Diana accounts for the "Diana of the Triple Will" who appears in Northrop Frye's accounts of the archetype. The important point is that a frightening goddess who drives you on your quest until you change your attitude about her (or perish) serves the same function as Medusa and Aphrodite.

Venus's home under the mountain, in the Tannhäuser legend, has its Celtic equivalent in kingdoms under the sea or fairy other worlds enchanting to mortals which Markale identifies as patriarchal displacements of previous cultures where women held power, a driving underground and underwater of the Tuatha Dé Danann. The wounding of the hero, as in the twelfth century "Lay of Guigemar," is (in Markale's hypothesis) a displacement for rendering him impotent, "for, in all twelfth- and thirteenth-century courtly literature, a wound in the thigh is a euphemism for a wound in the genitals," as in the case of "the Fisher-King, who, also wounded in the thigh, was rendered impotent, as a punishment for having uncovered the Grail without being entitled to do so" (105). The Artemis archetypal narrative describes a male hero who has approached the goddess in the wrong manner and whose impotence is not necessarily permanent: "the goddess reserving Guigemar exclusively for herself by rendering him impotent until she, the one woman in the world, can cure him" (105).

293

Markale is thus not describing an act of vengeful castration perpetrated out of hatred of masculinity or of heterosexual Eros but an act of sexual instruction and healing which nudges the hero into a better and more appropriate approach to the goddess.

The Artemis archetype, then, contains an attitude toward nature and femininity that we have already come across in those poets who are able to withdraw projections of terror at conflation of the maternal and sexual in order to achieve erotic maturity or who, like a number of Canadian poets, try to live in harmony with a nonhuman nature. Sadv, the elusive hind goddess, has much in common with Medusa, hiding her beauty behind the Gorgon's mask until her initiates approach her properly, and with Aphrodite, who punishes mistaken approaches but awards those who transcend their terror of her. The British and North American poetry which I will briefly survey in this chapter corroborates this conflation, in that however asexual the received Diana archetype is supposed to be, her wild and self-determined sensuality often emerges as her salient feature. Once again, the official asceticism of the Christian church is undermined by poets' natural drive for healthy sensuality; even in the nineteenth century the solace that women poets seek by escaping heterosexual Eros for nature retains this sensual flavor, suggesting that the lure of the green world is not a sexless virginity but a repudiation of sexual restrictions.

We shall see how Artemis's association with deer and with bears permeates Celtic mythology and indigenous folklores to influence European and North American literature, accounting both for British attitudes to the greenwood and for Canadian attitudes to bears which might otherwise seem anomalous in European culture. To put it another way, British educators' attempts to circumvent the wild materials lurking in England's folklore is subverted by the Celtic and pagan background embedded in the Artemis archetype.

Artemis in Poetry

Whatever attitude a poet may take toward Diana, British poets consistently recognize her opposition to matrimony and her dwelling in the wilderness with a band of like-minded maidens. Read positively, Diana or Artemis is always associated with collective feminine independence in the green world, characteristics celebrated by male poets such as Sir Walter Raleigh in "Praisd be Dianas faire and harmless light" (1593) and Ben Jonson in *Cynthia's Revels* (1600). In an anonymous poem from *England's Helicon* (also 1600) Diana sings in "A nimphs disdaine of Love" that "Than love there is no vainer thing, / For maidens most unfitting," mourning for a time before they gave way to men's charms when

> women knew no woe,
> But lived themselves to please,
> Men's feigning guiles they did not know,
> The ground of their disease. (124)

Although Diana is identified with a premarital chastity balanced against Venus in poems which debate the relative virtues of sensuality and celibacy, she is not consistently asexual. One surprising discovery that emerged from my survey of pre-twentieth-century poems about Diana is that she often gives permission for sex and frequently makes love herself. *England's Helicon* provides a rich source not only of Diana archetypes but also of wild wood celebrations which ought to provide material for further analyses of seventeenth-century archetypes.

Another surprising trend in poetry about Diana is the contrast between the way she is degraded by twentieth-century male poets and celebrated by earlier ones. Artemis as frightening temptress and deadly hunter is far more common in twentieth-century than in earlier poetry. An early modern example of this deadly Diana is Ernest Rhys's 1913 "new Diana" who "makes weak men her prey," determined to "Hate, hunt, do murder, and yet love them too" (813). In 1951 Horace Gregory posits a similarly dangerous female in "The Night-Walker," a dreaded "ancient huntress" who "Walks across night" and who has always "deceived / The unwary into an immoderate love of death" (111). Midcentury women poets can portray Diana with similar distaste, so that Jessie Lemont, in her 1946 "Diana Remembers Actaeon," can speak as a Diana who impassively watches her hounds leap at his throat (121). These negative examples of what we might call the Actaeon complex derive from male fear of or female identification with Diana's murderous "otherness," a negative attitude explained by Neumann in his conflation of Artemis with "goddesses whose nature is that of the Terrible Mother: Kali of India, Gorgon of the pre-Hellenic age, and Hecate of Greece, as well as terrible Ishtar,

Isis, Artemis, and innumerable goddesses of the underworld and the dead. To this group belong such negatively demonic figures as the Erinyes, Furies, and lamias, the Empusae, witches, and so on" (80). Neumann's theories are characteristic of midcentury male fears not only of explicitly nightmarish "crones," witches, or wise old woman archetypes, maternal crones who control death as well as birth, but also of any feminine sexuality independent of male control.

This terror of apatriarchal feminine Eros includes fear of Amazons' capacity to reproduce from captive males and give back (or kill) male progeny, a repulsion from the idea of women controlling our own generative powers. Thus Walter James Turner, in "The Seven Days of the Sun," contemptuously asks "Dian, Isis, Artemis, whate'er thy name" whether "thy white stags [can] / Move and beget themselves," and goes on to characterize the moon as "Mere insubstantial light," ruling only over "Chaste negatives, washwhites of chastity!" (301). In Robert Hillyer's 1952 masque "The Garden of Artemis or Apollo's Revels," Artemis's follower Clorinda, whom the goddess tries to protect from "love's too honeyed burning," is overcome by Apollo and by love so that the chorus can happily sing that "The God will summon / Her forth as woman" (49). The masque is based on the midcentury idea that love can only occur under male auspices. Twentieth-century hatred of Artemis probably goes deeper than distaste for feminine chastity, deriving venom from the affirmation of lesbian Eros and feminine solidarity latent in the Artemis/Amazon archetype.

In earlier poetry, Artemis has less to do with "Terrible Mother" projections and is more likely to represent a beneficent alternative to patriarchal sexuality. As such, Diana may preside over a pre-patriarchal phase of a maiden's maturation without violently opposing the girl's eventual growth into (necessarily patriarchal) sensuality. In a more conflictual mode, she is paired with a Venus principle that eventually overthrows her. Even in masques, plays, and poems structured upon debates about the relative worth of Venus and Diana in which such a victory over Diana's devotees is the outcome, her position is valued as worth defending.

An example of Diana helping a maiden move from celibacy to sensuality is her appearance in Chaucer's "Knight's Tale," where Emelye appeals to her to resolve Arcite and Palamon's deadly competition for her hand. With her maidens and the appropriate incense and clothing (wearing a corona of green oak), she appeals to the "chaste goddesse of the wodes grene," petitioning her also in her Hecate aspect as "Queen of the regne of Pluto derk and lowe," to help her in her dilemma. Although she declares that "I / Desire to ben a mayden al my lyf, / Ne nevere wol I be no love ne wyf" in the correct manner, she goes right on to ask Diana for help in choosing which man to marry. Although Chaucer may intend Emelye's simultaneous declarations of chastity and desire to be taken humorously, her ambiguity is nonetheless archetypally suitable in a prayer for help in making a decision about her sexual future. Chaucer's blending of Diana's "chastity" with Venus's love counseling, moreover, typifies a conflation of Eve, Venus, and Diana which occurs frequently in later British poetry. As Douglas Brooks-Davies notes, "Milton's exploration of Eve [in *Paradise Lost*] echoes Spenser's elaborate exploration of the growth to sexual awareness of Britomart." Eve in her Eden, Diana in her green world, and Venus in her sensually blissful rose garden are often conflated in Renaissance and later poetry (51). Queen Elizabeth I exploited the Artemis archetype by associating herself with the idea of virginity as being in control of one's own sensual decision making. Thus in John Lyly's 1591 *Endymion* we find that "The Earl of Leicester, as Endymion, pleads his passion by proxy" to her; and in 1584 George Peele describes Diana who "Bestows the apple of gold on Queen Elizabeth," whom he describes as "As fair and lovely as the Queen of Love, / As chaste as Dian in her chaste desires" (15).

The debates about the relative merits of chastity and marriage nonetheless could represent Venus and Diana competing for a young girl's loyalty. Thus Diana is set up as the opposite principle to Venus and then debated about in Lydgate's *Reason and Sensuality* (Turner 51) in a pattern I discussed earlier in relation to Fletcher's chastity plays. In Robert Greene's 1607 "Radagon in Dianam," Venus takes revenge against a mocking Diana who has been bathing with her virgins, washing their "Golden haire" "And singing all in notes hye / Fie on Venus flattring eye." This is too much for Cupid, who shoots arrows of love at them, so that Calisto falls immediately in love with Jove and the rest of the maidens follow suit, including Diana, who falls head over heels for Endymion (302–303). The idea underlying such narratives is that virginity is all very well, but young maidens should not linger in that state forever before tasting the joys of sensuality. Unfortunately, sensuality becomes increasingly male-controlled as time goes by, making maidens ever more reluctant to abandon Diana for

Venus and endowing the green, apatriarchal woodlands with increasing appeal, not only to women but also to men who prefer to be outlawed from the constraints of culture.

Intense longings for such a wild world were a predominant theme of nineteenth-century romantic poetry by both men and women. There are many poems in praise of chaste Artemis or Diana, just as there had been throughout the centuries, but perhaps the most thoroughly detailed example of romantic use of the Artemis archetype is Keats's *Endymion* (1818), an early poem in which the young poet celebrates nature and sensuality in an adaptation of the myth of Endymion and Semele. The classical story of a mortal who falls fatally in love with the moon only to be rewarded with eternal sleep belongs to the moon-as-fatal-seductress category of Artemis narratives, Endymion led on and on in his quest for an elusive and ultimately punitive goddess. The ambiguities of the overlong, rambling "antique song" serve nonetheless to encode and obscure Keats's attitude toward a feminine sexuality which interbraids Aphrodite and Artemis.

In a letter about *Endymion* written to John Taylor, Keats states that he is describing the gradation of a "Pleasure Thermometer," divided up into steps toward sensual happiness. As the editors of the *Norton Anthology of English Literature* (1979, vol. 2) express Keats's intention, in "the orthodox view," such "felicity" is supposed "to be achieved by a surrender of oneself to God. For Keats the way to happiness lies through a fusion of ourselves, first sensuously, with the lovely objects of nature and art, then on a higher level, with other human beings through 'love and friendship' but in the final degree, only through sexual love." (804 n. 7). The poem is framed in a revel honoring Pan, where Endymion is sitting gloomily on the sidelines until his sister takes him to an island to tell her what is troubling him. Pan was a strictly pre-Olympian and often semianimal nature divinity of perennial fascination to British poets, who found it easy to conflate the archetype with indigenous pagan divinities like the stag god Cernunnos. Endymion's inability to enjoy Pan's revels spring from his confusion over a vision or dream (or real meeting—the ambiguity pervades the poem) of the goddess of the moon; his archetypal quest is to find her once more. It is in Book IV that this task brings him into contact with a Native American maiden, "the Indian Maid," with whom he falls in love, in spite of the fact that she is "dark," whereas the Cynthia or Diana he thought he was looking for is blue-eyed and golden-haired.

Although Jung would interpret this encounter as the hero's coming to terms with the shadow or dark side of his self, understanding Endymion's quest to work through his fear of femininity in order to more authentically encounter the goddess, I read the adventure as the hero's coming to terms with an inhabitant of the green world understood as nature in its own right, a real (not internalized) wild woman. Her being "Indian Maid" makes one wonder whether Canadian poets, who were devoted to romantic poetry, might have derived part of their poet/Native American archetypal narrative from this British prototype. Endymion thinks that he is betraying Artemis for the Native American who initiates him into "mortal love," making him give up his pursuit of disembodied beauty and abstract principles:

> Pan will bid
> Us live in peace, in love and peace among
> His forest wildernesses. I have clung
> To nothing, lov'd a nothing, nothing seen
> Or felt but a great dream! O I have been,
> Presumptuous against love, against the sky,
> Against all elements, against the tie
> Of mortals each to each, against the blooms
> Of flowers, rush of rivers. . . .
> My sweetest Indian, here,
> Here will I kneel, for thou redeemed hast
> My life from too thin breathing. (634–50)

Like the victims of the hunter Diana, Endymion has taken an erroneous approach to the goddess and must work through his mistake. He compounds his error by feeling guilty about his mortal love for the Native American, who, in a variation of the kiss-the-toad-who-turns-into-a-prince motif, turns back into Cynthia at the end, when she and Endymion wander off to "range the forests" forever. We could read this metamorphosis as insulting to Native Americans; in another reading, however, Keats allows his hero to win Cynthia only through accepting the Native American as worthy of love, thus transcending his initial dualism by interbraiding the "dark-eyed stranger" and the golden-haired, blue-eyed lover into a single Artemis archetype. In this reading, Keats protests nineteenth-century devaluations of sensuality and nature.

Endymion and Cynthia wander off into forests which had offered similar solace from patriarchy to poets of earlier centuries. Not only for Shakespeare's refugees to Arden and for Robin Hood and Maid Marian in their green wood but also for a wide variety of later poets, the wild world offered perennial escape. Thus we find Anne Finch, in her 1793 "Nocturnal Reverie," longing to escape where "The waving moon and trembling leaves are seen" and join in the "shortlived jubilee the creatures keep, / Which but endures, whilst tyrant-man does sleep." Although this escape is spiritual rather than sensual, the green wood is the only place in Finch's world of "cares, our toils, our clamours" where the "free soul" can attain "composedness" (112). This Gaelic "land of heart's desire," with its immortal fairy wives and husbands, appealed to some writers, while as the nineteenth century wore on others turned to gypsies, Native Americans, and the ever-popular Pan. The American poet Alice Brown hungers for "the deep wood" where Pan lives, longing to spy "upon him, creeping in the deep / Removed courts, where Dian's self might sleep" (7). Cheryl Walker has noted the intense appeal of what she calls "the sanctuary poem" for nineteenth-century women, citing as an example Felicia Hemans's "Forest Sanctuary," which "she considered her best work, [and which] offers an example of a theme that became standard in the American female canon, a retreat to a 'bower of refuge' in order to escape some violent assault, whether upon the body or the consciousness, and to experience a creative sense of freedom impossible in the world left behind" (26). Such sanctuary poems, according to Walker, represent the world "as not merely irritating but threatening to the self, having caused both physical and emotional torture," and they may end in the poet's choosing celibacy or even the peacefulness of death (52).

Women take sanctuary in the green world to renounce excessive gender demands and to renew and reempower themselves. Jeffrey Steele has described a period in Margaret Fuller's life when she felt estranged from two men—Ralph Waldo Emerson and Samuel Ward—and decided to explore mythology as a way to withdraw "from heterosexual society and to rely on her own resources" (8). Writing sketches based on her study of figures from mythology such as Diana of Ephesus, Artemis, Cybele, and Isis, Fuller found that women could use their studies of goddess archetypes to strengthen their independence from men. In 1841 she held "conversations" to discuss mythology, including one which took place in mixed company where Diana became the specific topic. "Margaret wanted to pass on to Diana," her friend Caroline Healey Dall wrote, "but there were too many clergymen in the company." She brings the discussion to Diana nonetheless, with startling results:

> "When Fuller finally does bring the Conversation around to Diana, 'Her pure and sacred character with the Athenians was compared to that of Diana of Ephesus, whose orgies were not unusual, and who was considered as a bountiful mother.
>
> IDA RUSSELL said that *her* mythology accused Diana of being the mother of fifty sons and fifty daughters!
>
> MARGARET laughed, and said that certainly was Diana of the Ephesus!'" (116, citing Dall)

Fuller clearly understood the sensual subtext of the "pure" Diana archetype of the nineteenth century and drew upon Diana's sensuality as well as her independence as a model for action. Like Keats, moreover, Fuller was given to positing Native Americans as models of natural selfhood, the Native American maiden worshipping the sun alone in her tent being an important image in *Women in the Nineteenth Century* (1845).

The goddess of the moon, as Keats so thoroughly illustrated, cannot be spiritualized away from her celebration of powers immanent in nature and in women's biological cycles. Even though many nineteenth-century poems by both men and women describe Diana or Cynthia or transcendent moon goddess, the archetype pulls them back into appreciation of nature. Thus, although Paul Hayne entitles "The Vengeance of the Goddess Diana" (1875; first version 1859) in a way suggestive of the Diana-as-castrating-huntress narrative, his long poem outlines a variation of the archetypal quest for Diana understood as a psychological journey toward selfhood. His hero, Avolio, sets forth as "a gentleman . . . of gracious air, / And liberal as the summer" to explore some deep forests in Sicily at the time the Normans ruled there. In this neomedieval narrative the hero is an "ardent knight," seeking glory by braving the dangers of the wild forests. He hears the cries of Diana's hounds in pursuit of Actaeon and Actaeon's "bitter shriek of human agony," but it is important to note that Hayne understands the sound of Diana's hunt for Actaeon as a "haunting" of the forest, an obstacle meant to frighten Avolio. He is not turned back from his quest, however, though he does lose his liberal and rational stability: "His reason in a whirling chaos, lost / Compass and chart and headway" (43), plunging into a world of psychological indeterminacy he will have to find nonrational means to negotiate. At the core of the bleak, haunted wood he comes upon a terrifying female snake, which tells him that it is being punished in that form for defying Diana, "the night's immaculate goddess." It can only be turned back into a woman if "some man, large-hearted as a God" kisses it on the mouth, and, while he hesitates, the snake lectures to him about Diana's existence not as "a vague image of the brain" but as a being who "both was and was not," and who remains embodied in "eternal nature." Avolio has overcome terror of Actaeon's fate only to be faced with the vengeance of Diana if he, like the snake/woman, fails to understand her enigma. Our hero is able to transcend such ignorance by kissing the snake, who immediately turns into a sensual and caressing woman with whom he wanders off into the future. As if frightened by the immanent sensualism he is celebrating, Hayne ends the poem with an apologetic coda in which Avolio answers the challenge that his new lady worships Diana by insisting that she worships "Christ the Lord," while his lady gazes into his face as if she "yearned to whisper tenderly: 'O, brave, kind heart! I worship only thee' " (54). Thus the patriarchal ideology is restored at the end of a poem outlining a quest for psychological health which can only be achieved by authentic appreciation both of nature and of feminine power and sensuality.

The desire to flee culture for the green wood seems especially pronounced in later nineteenth-century poetry, when many women poets associate Diana or wild Artemis with escapes from distasteful heterosexual experiences. Emily Dickinson, in an early poem (no. 24, 1858), writes about maids keeping a "Seraphic May," their celebration a Beltaine revel of dancing she longs for among "people upon the mystic green" far removed from "the different dawn" she must suffer (843). Conflating Eden and wildness in a later and even more intense poem (no. 249, 1861), "Wild Nights," she longs for an "Eden" that is both sensual and acultural.

Although the twentieth century was supposed to have liberated women for "free love," even modern love poets such as Edna St.

Vincent Millay, Elinor Wylie, and Sara Teasdale found the constraints of heterosexuality so debilitating that they longed for Artemisian solutions. An escape to nature as a protest against her lover's behavior thus motivates Millay to renounce Eros for "a little shanty on the sand" where she will be "happier than I ever was before" (33) and leads Wylie to declare that "I shall lie hidden in a hut / In the middle of an alder wood," "With the back door blind and bolted shut, / And the front door locked for good" (*Collected Poems* 284). As Teasdale suffers through her love life, similarly, she begins to value the solitary wisdom of older women; in "The Crystal Gazer" she identifies with a wise old crone ("I shall gather myself into myself again, / I shall take my scattered selves and make them one"), and in "The Solitary" she gives up on men, declaring herself "self-complete as a flower or a stone" (179).

It will be recalled that although Edith Sitwell constructs a kind of eccentric spinster persona, her poetry is filled with sensual imagery. Another British woman poet, Ruth Pitter, cultivates a similar stance of a woman poet who renounces Eros for a highly sensual nature. For Pitter, who achieved a significant public reputation (she was awarded the Queen's Gold Medal for Poetry at age fifty-seven), her crafted persona was as important as Sitwell's. She takes the stance of single woman as Christian mystic, declaring early in her career her renunciation of marriage for the sake of poetry.

Even Pitter's allegiance to a solitary and passionless "Dear Perfection" contains elements we can recognize as sensually Artemisian. Her "Dear Perfection," the muse embodied in bud and leaf, is "a spark" in Pitter, "a flame of pure desire." In "The Bad Girl," Pitter recognizes the "woodland" young girl she once declared allegiance to, who "Made the brown gold" and was "A noble thing, a lovely theme, / One that could not be cast away." Although she has cast her away by this stage in her poetic life, "she had better have died," because she has become part of a disturbing inner presence, an angry old/young avatar of "things childish" who is Pitter's inner "bad girl," Aphroditian qualities she has repressed, her wounded inner child whom she needs to integrate into a healthier selfhood. It is as a process of assimilating repressed Aphroditian qualities that I read two of Pitter's poems as prayers to Artemis in her Diana and Hecate aspects. In "The Downward-Pointing Muse," the muse Pitter has chosen appears as remote, never smiling, mirroring heaven, but paradoxically pointing only downward, "to the deep mines, the dreadful core; / To the dark Mother" (55–56). Thus no matter how sublimated her muse, Pitter acknowledges that her only way of achieving selfhood is in questing down, "to the buried Sun," into immanence. Pitter understands that she cannot fulfill her quest until she celebrates her bodily nature and the earth and comes to terms with the dark mother presiding over these facets of existence. Her quest is accomplished in "Tawny Owl in Fir-Tree," which she addresses to "mother Cybele," a nature/moon goddess originating in Phrygia and Lydia. She envisions this goddess as someone locked inside a tree. Like poets approaching Medusa, Pitter sees "Her face" as dangerous, potentially "fatal," that of "a woman in an old dark song, / Mad from hard terror, mad from utter wrong" (189). Pitter approaches the dead, cold, lifeless female face framed with the stony hair of Medusa in much the same manner that Mary Elizabeth Coleridge acknowledges the terrifyingly wounded woman in her mirror as her true self. Pitter turns a corner in her psyche in her last stanza: "But she is mine. I lift the old dark word. . . . Break the old tyranny, release and right her" (166). Pitter's acknowledgment of the angry, solitary, and obdurate bird as part of her self empowers a shift in attitude which releases her from terrified enslavement to her shadow. Like Sitwell, Pitter protects her public reputation by encoding her descent downward from the Christian mysticism and her declaration of allegiance to nature in obscure diction.

The Cybele archetype and her passion for nature empower Pitter to avoid institutional Christianity's distaste for nature. Betty Meador, in an article on the reemergence of the archetypal feminine, theorizes that "deep shadow issues arise between the values of the patriarchal god, Yahweh, who is wholly spirit and completely free of nature, and the values of the goddess who is in and of nature and sanctifies the material world" (29). By "shadow issues" Meador means qualities that culture forces women to repress: Old Testament Judaism and Christian ideology repudiate both nature and women's "body and its functions which are so intimately a part of her development." When women poets like Pitter and Sitwell in England and Dickinson, Millay, Wylie, and Teasdale in the United States turn from patriarchal Eros to nature, they reject culture's sexual restrictions to affirm sensually empowering archetypes.

Both Keats's *Endymion* and Hayne's less famous poem describe Artemis helping the hero come to terms with sexual passion and with nature. Although twentieth-century male poets have less trouble accepting Artemis's immanence, they seem disgusted by her celebration of women's reproductive cycles, especially by the suggestion of any sexual choice which occurs beyond male control, whether for intercourse or for celibacy.

Gary Snyder, in his poems about Artemis, follows a pattern not unlike Keats's Endymion and Hayne's Avolio: he sets out as the type of hero Campbell described in 1949, confronting the horrors of femininity in a kind of initiation trial, but learns to approach women and nature as beings-in-their-own-right. In 1954 he wrote "Praise for Sick Women," which is filled with gynophobic loathing, especially for women's menstrual periods of "gut-cramp" when their "sick eye bleeds the land." By 1956 Snyder realizes that "Occult & witchcraft evils [are] each all true," things "We learn to love, horror accepted," although in 1968 he petulantly declares:

> Artemis
> So I saw you naked—
> Well go and get your goddam'd virginity back
> (*The Back Country* 68)

On one hand, he ridicules Artemis's virginity; on the other, he expresses his terror of her in his identification with Actaeon.

In the same volume, however, Snyder has a poem, "For Plants," which associates the classic Artemis with an old Native American woman, an "ancient virgin," and in a decidely ambivalent ending confronts "Artemis naked" like a "soft white / buried sprout" (81). Although there is something pale and moribund about Snyder's sprout image, it suggests rebirth and regeneration. Snyder has placed himself under the aegis of Native American religion in order to achieve his new stance toward women and nature, sometimes speaking as a "shaman," sometimes translating Native American prayers (as in "Prayer for the Great Family," written "after a Mohawk prayer"). In "Mother Earth: Her Whales," written for a summer solstice celebration in Stockholm in 1972, he calls in a "Native" manner for solidarity of the "Standing Tree People, Flying Bird People," protesting the industrial robots who are destroying nature. Snyder seems to have broken through to an understanding of nature as valuable in its own terms, the whales "like breathing planets / In the sparkling whorls / Of living light" which human beings can destroy but which we had no hand in creating. It is interesting that, like D. H. Lawrence, Snyder seems to be able to approach nature respectfully only by usurping Native American or animal perspectives. Snyder nonetheless pursues the same quest as Keats, Hayne, and Pitter to discard his distrust of the natural world.

We have seen in the cases of Coleridge, Cox, and Janik that when women poets give themselves permission to celebrate the erotic self-sufficiency of the Artemis archetype, they tend to go wild. Artemis and her Amazon maidens are so free of patriarchal restraint that their archetypes empower women poets to revel joyously in their marginality. In earlier periods such literary celebrations often centered on Pan, gypsies, or distinctly apatriarchal wild men of the woods, or the figure I have described as the green world lover. I showed in chapter 7 how recent women poets celebrate entirely apatriarchal experiences of both heterosexual and lesbian Eros. Their outrageous genitalic Eros celebrates not only Aphrodite's beneficent but also her more dangerous aspects, such as the storm goddess archetypes reenvisioned from African mythology by African American poets like Lucille Clifton and Audre Lorde. We saw how the joy of these poems derives from an imploded marginality, the dynamism let loose when women poets free themselves from constraint, discovering themselves far less stuck in the crusts of the patriarchal pie than they had thought, able even to fly right out of the window.

The way to the moon is not easy for women poets, however. In the title poem of *The Moon Is Always Female*, Marge Piercy is able to "tell you / what I have learned lying under the moon / naked as women do" only after excruciating descriptions of clitoridectomy and other patriarchal abuses, and in "O!" (from the same volume) women can worship the "lady of the wild animals" only by escaping to an "island / in the sea where love rules and women / are free" to follow their own erotic impulses (133). There is a marginality inherent in such declarations of allegiance to the moon which Piercy expresses as a need to retreat to an island and which many women poets describe as their desire to escape into a wilderness wholly removed from culture. Although Piercy's overtly Aphroditian Artemis is more characteristic of recent than of pre-twentieth-century poetry, we have seen that women poets have identified with wild women and longed for escape to their forests for a much longer time.

<table>
<tr><td>

The Hecate
Factor

</td><td>

In Roman mythology Hecate appears in triplicate, sometimes as the moon or Luna in the sky, Diana on earth, and Hecate in Hades, or

</td></tr>
</table>

representing three key stages in women's life cycles: maidenhood, motherhood, and maturity or wisdom. The Hecate archetype represents women's content with each of our life stages, our ability to be at one and the same time ten years old, adolescent, and endowed with the wisdom of ninety. Hecate's incorporation of all the feminine ages at once takes the form of a triadic nature exemplified by the three Furies, the three Fates, and other triple deities in classical literature, such as the three Gorgon sisters. Statues from the period when Rome and the Celtic Gauls influenced each other depict triple goddesses presiding over fountains and springs, and Hecate seems to have conflated easily with similar goddess archetypes in Celtic Britain. In British literature Hecate often recurs in these three forms, mentioned as "Triple Hecate's team" in Shakespeare's *Midsummer Night's Dream* and referred to by Herrick in "To Electra" as the "Three Formes of Heccate."

As a goddess of war and death Hecate presides not only over Celtic battle literature but, much earlier, over military history in the Middle East. Sumerian Enheduanna, a high priestess of about 2300 B.C.E., prayed to Inanna as

> Lady of elemental forces . . .
> flood-storm-hurricane adorned . . .
> a whirlwind warrior
> bound on a twister . . .
> fighting is her play
> she never tires of it
> she goes out running
> strapping on her sandals . . . (Meador 24)

Assessing the stormy power of Enheduanna manifest in her translation of this prayer, Meador notes that in such figures "the archetypal feminine announces herself through the elemental forces she controls—wind, storm, flood, hurricane, tornado, earthquake, fire. She destroys the old order, the old church, the old house, the old way of being with a sweep of her powerful hand. These forces of nature and

307

their counterparts in the psyche—furies, rages, passions, intensities of emotion—announce the arrival of the goddess in her primal form" (23–24).

When Audre Lorde peels her mother's anger "down to the core of love" in "Black Mother Woman," the "temple" of her mother's "true spirit" contains the Yoruba goddesses of Lorde's African heritage. Reading poems like Lorde's, white women sometimes feel a lack of similarly powerful archetypal materials in our heritage, which by this point in my study we can recognize as both a false lack and one deliberately fostered by patriarchy. With much the same effect that the Indian policies of Canada and the United States sought to erase Native American archetypes from tribal memories, traditional education in England and the United States has insisted upon classical rather than Celtic or pagan mythology as suitable for the young. But so enormously powerful are our lost archetypes that they endure in our popular celebrations. The traditional Celtic new year of Samhain is still observed on its appropriate date with rituals which are recognizable as rooted in the Hecate archetype. Halloween celebrations of the "dark" side of the psyche, which embodies our experience of death and rebirth, tragedy and continuity, are only one example of the way psychologically healthy archetypes endure despite efforts to repress them.

Most distasteful to patriarchy, as we can see from the murder of so many women as witches, have been old women in our power over the life cycle—birth, abortion, healing, and easeful death—feminine powers which, Barbara Walker suggests in The Crone, represent "that part of pre-Christian religion that was most particularly obliterated because men found it most intimidating: the negative aspect of the all-powerful Mother, who embodied the fearful potential for rejection, abandonment, death" (12). I have described this frightening aspect of goddess archetypes in terms of the warlike proclivities of Inanna, the fear that Medusa brings to the hearts of those still terrified of their mothers, the danger of losing yourself in Aphrodite's pleasures, and Artemis's threatening aspect as erotic hunter.

Hecate in triplicate continued to appear in the folklore of such Gaelic lands as Scotland, Wales, and Ireland and in adjacent areas in England. Celtic war goddesses like Morrigan, Babd, and Macha, writes E. Jan Jacobs, take the form of a raven war goddess in Celtic legend, though "the Raven-War Goddess can be equated with the nurturing Mother Goddess. Carrying the assumption even further it is possible that sometime within the Celtic culture the creator/destroyer of the world was woman and as such held a great deal of power" (4). Ross describes one such incarnation of the Morrigan in a Scottish Gaelic ballad when she comes to the hero in hag form:

> There were two slender spears of battle
> upon either side of the hag;
> her face was blue-black, the lustre of coal
> and her bone tufted tooth was like rusted
>   bone.
>
> In her head was one deep pool-like eye
> swifter than a star in a winter sky;
> upon her head gnarled brushwood
> like the clawed old wood of aspen root!

In the single eye and tooth we can see analogues between this Gaelic hag goddess and Medusa with her Gorgon sisters, degraded in Celtic as in classical legend by men's terror of her. Ross asserts that "the basic Celtic goddess type was at once mother, warrior, hag, virgin, conveyor of fertility, of strong sexual appetite which led her to seek mates amongst mankind equally with the gods, giver of prosperity to the land, protectress of the flocks and herds" (233).

Markale accounts for the degradation of this enormously powerful goddess in terms of changes within oral Celtic traditions reflecting "the reversal of ideas about femininity within new patriarchal social structures" which led to the removal of the goddess "outside of the lawful limits" of culture, her stag goddess form being degraded to the prey of male hunters. "So," Markale concludes, "just as the mother goddess became the father god and the sun goddess became the sun god, the hind goddess naturally became the stag god celebrated in Celtic statues of a man with stag's antlers" (106). However it came about, folklore traditions about witches establish them as priestesses of such a god, whom the Christians could degrade was a "devil" with horns and tail and cloven hooves and who, as we have seen, is easily conflated with Pan and other apatriarchal archetypes.

The witches, in the meantime, along with the goddesses whom they worshipped, were transformed in the crucible of patriarchal gynophobia into grotesque old women. The motivation for this change, according to Barbara Walker, was men's fear of women's sharp tongues, which they thought capable of castration:

> Popes and priests of the Inquisition firmly believed that witches' words could take away men's virility and even their sexual organs without any physical contact at all.
>
> In return for the imagined castration, men sometimes tried to retaliate in kind, symbolically castrating women by denying their sexuality. Thus, women who dared to be defiant were often called ugly—that is, sexually unattractive—even when their appearance was wholly irrelevant to the issue. Therefore the witch became, as a stereotype, both old and ugly. (*The Crone* 138–39)

Whereas witches are said to remain forever old and ugly, hags can change themselves into beautiful women and sometimes alter periodically with nubile maidens, as in the case of Godiva, who rode into town as the spirit of spring to replace the gloomier hag of winter (Burland 50–51, 55). Godiva is an English version of the Irish Cailleach and Scottish Mala Liath (gray mare), who keeps her youthful counterpart imprisoned in a cave on Ben Nevis and bears many of the characteristics of Brigid, goddess of the Brigantes. In these Celtic goddesses the qualities of age and wisdom are separated from the qualities of youth and attractiveness, the hag described as the persecutor of a younger self who is sometimes rescued by a young male sun god. This is the same kind of dualistic process by which the Greeks weakened holistic goddesses in order to degrade them, ensuring that they would no longer be perceived as beneficent agents in the feminine life cycle. Such dividing up of originally powerful archetypes into lovely maidens versus horrible hags and degradations of holy women and wise crones into figures of derision have reinforced the cult of youth dominating norms for femininity in present-day England and the United States (think of the skin cream advertisement in which a lovely forty-year-old woman asserts that she is going to fight aging all the way). That the degradation has not been totally successful can be attested to by the recurrent archetypes of hags, crones, and witches celebrated by women poets.

It is especiallly interesting that women poets should not only identify themselves with the sensual outlaw Artemis and long to join wild women and/or Pan in the woods but also see themselves as witches and hags, affirming their archetypal character as wise and holy women learned in healing skills and in negotiating around the corners of life's phases. "Witchcraft was hung, in history," announces Emily Dickinson in 1883:

> But History and I
> Find all the Witchcraft that we need
> Around us, every Day— (no. 1583, 656)

not exactly denouncing the tradition, and in "I Think I was enchanted" Dickinson describes the conversion she experienced when first reading her fellow woman poet Elizabeth Barrett Browning, likening her poetry to "Tomes of solid Witchcraft" in which she finds not only magic and "Deity" but "Antidote" (no. 593, 291). In "Witch-Woman" Amy Lowell takes on her usual persona of male admirer of a powerful female but puts his terror aside when she switches to a third-person prose-poetry description of their encounter:

> Body touches body. How sweet the spread of loosened
>   bodies in the coil of sleep, but a gold-black
>   thread is between them. An owl calls deep in
>   the wood. . . .
> Naked and white, the matron moon urges the woman.
>   The undulating sea fingers the rocks and
>   winds stealthily over them. She opens the
>   goat-skin wide—it falls.
> The walls of the world are crashing down, she is naked
>   before the naked moon, the Mother Moon, who
>   sits in a courtyard of emerald with six
>   black slaves before her feet. Six—and a white
>   seventh who dances, turning in the moonlight,
>   flinging her arms about the soft air,
>   despairingly lifting herself to her full
>   height, straining tiptoe away from the slope
>   of the hill.
> Witch-breasts turn and turn, witch-thighs burn, and the
>   feet strike always faster upon the grass. Her
>   blue-black hair in the moon-haze blazes like a
>   fire of salt and myrrh. Sweet as branches of
>   cedar, her arms; fairer than heaped grain,

311

> her legs; as grape clusters, her knees and
> ankles; her back as white grapes with smooth
> skins. (276–77)

Although Lowell's witch-woman proves deadly for her male lover, turning into "a skeleton dancing in the moon-green air, with a white, white skull and no hair," she remains lovely even in her death aspect, making him curse his patriarchal god as a "vengeful and cruel Father, / God of Hate." Lowell, who like Margaret Fuller drew inspiration from Native American legends, endows her Diana with qualities strikingly similar to those of Dylan Thomas's apple goddess, while she recognizes as clearly as Dickinson (who described God as a rapist in no. 315, "He fumbles at your Soul") that the Christian father god is the deadly enemy of Eros, of women, and indeed, of the universe.

Thomas's Welsh Arianrhod, as Robert Graves explained her, held power not only over sexuality and generation but also over language itself. Words were her gift, the poet needing to approach her reverently in order to write at all. Witches did not achieve their healing by reciting prose paragraphs while administering their herbal cures; they were known for their rhythmic chants and magically effective verses. The association between chanting holy women and enchantresses is rooted in poetry's imitation of the rhythms of the heart (perhaps as heard from within the womb), and it is no coincidence that one of the powers Perseus usurps when he kills Medusa is poetic creativity, embodied in her horse-child, Pegasus. I would attribute the tremendous opposition which women poets suffer from men, especially from male poets, to male desire to prevent our using the incantatory power of poetry. When women poets write, they become especially threatening to men, and no wonder, when we consider what happens when Anna Hempstead Branch identifies herself with a witch:

> Perched upon straightness I seek a wilder zone.
> My Flying self—on this black steed alone—
> Drives out to God or else to utter death.
> Beware straight lines which do subdue man's pride!
> 'Tis on a broomstick that great witches ride.
> Wild, dangerous and holy are the runes
> Which shift the whirling atoms with their tunes.
> Oh like a witch accursed shall she be burned
> Who having flown on straightness has returned.

Branch as witch-poet has usurped "straightness," the linear logic of patriarchy's arsenal, and turned it into a steed on which she rides into an inspiring wildness. The prize for her daring is language itself, words which she regenerates for her own purposes:

> I say that words are men and when we spell
> In alphabets we deal with living things;
> With feet and thighs and breasts, fierce heads, strong
>   wings;
> Material Powers, great Bridals, heaven and Hell.
> There is a menace in the tales we tell. (Berkinow 245–46)

Branch seems to intend "men" generically here: her achievement is an explosion of marginality, envisioning herself as outlawed witch in order to steal back the power of poetry. In this identification with her "shadow" side, all that culture has pronounced deviant in women, Branch is empowering herself in a process quite similar to that undertaken by Dickinson and Lowell and, for that matter, Keats.

I read Lowell's conflations of gold and black, black and white color imagery as troublingly racist in her acceptance of slavery and in her internalization of blackness as a psychologically empowering quality. She might also be read, however, as assimilating what culture has devalued as "dark" in the same manner that Keats's Endymion learned to worship a Native American/Cynthia conflated goddess and that Lorde was to reaffirm the black mother goddess as an empowering poetic archetype. Lowell and Keats turn to the wild world to escape what white patriarchy has said about women, about the earth, and about sensuality. In this escape they are able to achieve a state of "magical" potency, an archetypal empowerment from which they affirm their stance within the cycling of the natural universe.

I remain troubled, however, by British, American, and Canadian poets' use of Native Americans as vehicles for psychological development. Are they not exploiting Native Americans in the same way that male poets have traditionally exploited female muses, absorbing their potency while failing to acknowledge them as agents in their own right? Before exploring the commonalities of the bear archetype in the Artemis/Callisto narrative, European bear folklore, and Native American bear mythology, I will devote a penultimate chapter to surveying archetypal patterns in Native American poetry and to assessing the vexed question of white poets' literary exploitation of them.

10.

Archetypal Patterns and Native American Poetry

While analyzing Artemis and wild archetypes in Anglo-Canadian, American, and British poetry, I have suggested two ways of evaluating white poets' appropriations of Native American archetypes. On one hand, there is no mistaking the element of exploitation, a kind of literary imperialism, in white nonnative poets' adaptations of Native American spiritual and archetypal material; on the other hand, many white poets use Native American archetypes respectfully, in a quest for personal and planetary healing. Although a number of poets expropriate Native American archetypes (and even individual Native Americans) as mere vehicles for their psychological development, others revere Native Americans and their theologies for keeping pathways open for psychological and ecological harmony. These poets are working along the same lines as Audre Lorde, when she sees the poetic quest as a search for the "dark mother" within all of us.

We need to draw a sharp line, however, between Lorde's quest for the dark mother and the way many white poets exploit Native American archetypes. In this chapter I will first review the European roots of this kind of literary imperialism as it occurs in Jung's theory, then look at Native American critiques of such spiritual and archetypal abuse. My primary purpose, however, is to survey archetypal patterns in Native American poetry in order to review an earth-centered and naturistic archetypal poetry based upon explicit theological premises.

In their detailed, well-defined theological context, Native American archetypes differ from the fragmentary outcrops of pagan images characterizing wild and Artemisian poems in the European tradition, where pagan archetypes are more likely to occur as vaguely encoded bits and pieces, divorced from the theologies in which they were once embedded. I will argue that Native American nature and goddess archetypes are both different from and analogous to European and American ones. My survey of the way Native American archetypes work in Native American poetry will establish the context for my final chapter, where I will test my hypothesis that there is a lode of pagan archetypes indigenous to American, Anglo-Canadian, and British poetry by looking at the way these groups approach the archetype of the bear.

I have demonstrated in this study that there is a tendency in European and American poetry to locate what is "wild" (that is, antithetical to the Christian insistence that one's own sensuality and one's enjoyment of nature constitute "sin") in such archetypes as Artemis, the Lady of the Wild Things, wild men and women in European forests, gypsies, witches, and Native Americans. Jung saw such figures as both "other" to and exploitable by the European psyche. His writings value their culture as pointers for European psychological health. According to Jung, "primitive" peoples have a special relationship to mythology, dwelling within a "preconscious" state in which they experience archetypes with a special immediacy. He does not value their cultures, however, except insofar as they can point the way to psychological health for his European patients. "Primitive" people, like women, are important in Jung's system as factors that can be colonized or internalized by overcivilized Europeans. Nor does Jung value nature in and of itself; he values myth for its "spiritual" transcendence of the very material realm that Native Americans consider the source of spirit (see *Archetypes and the Collective Unconscious* 154). Jung's disciple Neumann, similarly, values the nonphysical, spiritualized property of myths to the extent that he ascribes evolution away from animal to spirit to "the goddess": feminine archetypes, he asserts, were "at first worshipped as an animal-lioness, she-bear, bird, snake," but these evolved into "a human goddess, beside which the animal stands as an attribute . . . thus the transformative character of the feminine rises from the natural to the spiritual plane" (287). As James Hillman explains sublimation of the material factor in Jung's archetypal theory, archetypal images constitute "the inward reflection of an external object" to the extent that psyche ("soul") is superior to nature and myths are more essential phenomena than matter. Only "ego-consciousness," which to Jung is an unhealthy mode of perception, understands nature as real; the healthy self exploits it as the repository of raw material only in order to become more spiritual. Archetypal images, according to Hillman, "give psychic value to the world," rather than the other way around, the world endowing images with value as would occur in Native American theologies: they are "trans-empirical," deriving from and belonging to the realm of "soul" (*Archetypal Psychology* 11–12). The European psyche or soul, in this system, experiences "primitive" peoples (including Native Americans) merely as internalized "shadows," belonging to an inferior inner realm which is to be exploited for psychological healing and then transcended. This process differs from Lorde's quest for the "dark mother" in that it exploits negritude, darkness, maternity, and women as mere rungs on a ladder to personal (and most often white male) improvement. This is, then, the psychoanalytic version of the "noble savage" stereotype; fantasizing a life with noble "primitives," the client empowers "primitive" drives within his own psyche. Perhaps the best example of this phenomenon in the poetry I have studied heretofore is Keats's Indian Maiden, who "stands for" the "dark" or richly sensual element which Keats's hero must incorporate into his own psyche before the Indian "turns into" the white Cynthia.

Jung's theories about "primitive" people are an example of a Euro-chauvinistic mindset, an exploitative hierarchicalization of the world's peoples, that is widespread in both popular culture and literary practice. In the latter realm, for example, pseudo–Native American rituals get incorporated into camp and scouting ceremonies, often under the assumption (deeply offensive to local tribal members) that "all the real Indians have been dead for a hundred years." In poetry, similarly, Native Americans appear not as creative agents of distinct living cultures whose archetypes are embedded in unique theologies and rituals; rather, they appear to "stand for" aspects of heart and body the European and American poets feel they have lost. It is the use of Native American personae and archetypes as a "quick fix" by non–Native Americans who have been conditioned to devalue body and nature that many Native American critics object to so strenuously.

White feminists attracted to New Age exploitations of Native American religious practices are criticized by Cherokee writer Andrea Smith, who says that though these white women's interest in Native American traditional spirituality, "with its respect for nature and the interconnectedness of all things, is often presented as the panacea for all individual and global problems," it is not "based on a respect for Indian spirituality" but upon "a very old story of white racism and genocide against Indian people." Smith (in an article aptly titled "For All Those Who Were Indian in a Former Life") criticizes white women who "seem determined not to look into their own cultures for sources of strength. This is puzzling, since pre-Christian European cultures are also earth-based and contain many of the same elements that white women are ostensibly looking for" (74).

As another Native American woman poet put it, "I am pleased that you admire my lover, but I would hate it if you slept with him. I'm pleased that you admire my religion, but I would hate it if you practiced it." Many whites have adapted a New Age method of psychotherapy, which terms itself "shamanism," whose non-Indian practitioners not only set themselves up as healers but even purport to initiate other non-Indians into their systems. Their activities appall Native Americans like Geary Hobson, a Cherokee, who has coined the term "white shamanism" to describe "the growing number of small-press poets of generally white, Euro-Christian American background, who in their poems assume the persona of the shaman, usually in the guise of an American Indian medicineman. To be a poet is simply not enough; they must claim a power from higher sources" (100–108, as cited in W. Rose.) Hopi-Miwok poet and anthropologist Wendy Rose joins with Hobson and fellow Native American writers Silko, Young Bear, and Sainte-Marie in her conviction that white shamanism constitutes a "cultural imperialism," especially since no self-respecting Indian poet ever set himself or herself up as such a "guru" to heal or bless other people. "The 'whiteshaman',," suggests Rose, "is getting a piece of the action in contemporary manifest destiny and is, in essence and in philosophy, descended from earlier colonists, as well as related to the most brutal modern ones" (13, 16).

Especially insulting to Native Americans is the sacrilegious usurpation of traditional theologies. "Such claims," Rose reminds us, "whether sacred or secular, are without the community acknowledgment and training that are essential to the position. Would it not be absurd to claim one was a Rabbi if one was not even Jewish? Or that one was a jet pilot without having been inside an airplane?" (13). No wonder that

> Native Americans view this phenomenon with some humor and with some anger, wondering sadly why this particular set of symbols, this imagery, this stereotype is used to imply access to spirituality (or, to use the Greek concept, the 'muse'), when, we are quite sure, access to such powers exists in every culture. It is a belief shared by most Native Americans that all cultures were given certain gifts and a certain place by the Spirit People or the Great Mystery. That they differ from one another is not a theological contradiction nor even a 'problem'. What makes the 'whiteshaman' feel compelled to go outside of his or her own culture for spiritual and creative nourishment? And, further, to disregard accuracy? (14)

Both Rose and Smith call attention to the indigenous pagan materials which European and American poets have forgotten about as victims of a process analogous to the deliberate erasure of materials valuing women and nature that has taken place among Native Americans during recent centuries.

White poets' hunger to batten upon other peoples' archetypal systems derives, in my hypothesis, largely from the ignorance in which most Europeans and Americans have been kept by the deletion of pagan materials from our formal education. I have suggested that one reason for the savage repression of Celtic materials, for example (which were widely popular and structured the archetypal narratives of the medieval Arthurian legends and the Renaissance *Faerie Queene* as well as masques and poetry throughout the history of British literature), was their portrait of Celtic women as far more sexually free than the church fathers allowed and in control of considerable legal and economic status as well. Women's far lesser civil and religious status in Greece and Rome, reinforced by classical dualizing of feminine quali-

318

ties into separate and often antagonistic goddesses, was less threatening to Christianity as it tried to consolidate its authority in England. Whereas British, Anglo-Saxon, or Norse pagan mythology might have proved dangerously subversive to both patriarchal and Christian plans, the lands of origin of Greek and Roman mythology were at a convenient distance from England, endowing them with an aura of privilege.

Paula Gunn Allen attributes attempts by American and Canadian authorities to eradicate traditional Native American cultures to an analogous fear of the subversive power of Indian women. "The physical and cultural genocide of American Indian tribes," she reasons,

> is and was mostly about patriarchal fear of gynocracy. The Puritans particularly, but also the Catholic, Quaker, and other Christian missionaries, like their secular counterparts, could not tolerate peoples who allowed women to occupy prominent positions and decision-making capacity at every level of society. Wives telling husbands and brothers whether to buy or sell an item, daughters telling fathers whom they could and could not murder, empresses attending parleys with colonizers and being treated with deference by male leaders did not sit well with the invaders. (3)

Among the tribal examples Allen documents are the systematic undermining of the Cherokee Women's Council; the discrediting of their traditional tribal leader, the Beloved Woman of the Nation; and the whites' setting up of a patriarchal code to be administered to the traditionally matrilinear Iroquois by the renegade Handsome Lake, "who, with the help of devoted followers and the exigencies of social disruption in the aftermath of the war, encouraged the shift from woman-centered society to patriarchal society" (32–33).

Allen explains how these subversions of tribal governance were reinforced by the translation of feminine deities into male gods. With the objective of

> social transformation from egalitarian, gynecentric systems to hierarchical, patriarchal systems . . . the Hopi goddess Spider Woman has become the masculine Maseo or Tawa, referred to in the masculine, and the Zuñi goddess is on her way to malehood. Changing Woman of

the Navajo has contenders for her position, while the Keres Thought
Woman trembles on the brink of displacement by her sister-goddess-
cum-god Utset. Among the Cherokee, the goddess of the river foam is
easily replaced by Thunder in many tales, and the Iroquois divinity
Sky Woman now gets her ideas and powers from her dead father or her
monstrous grandson. (41)

Prohibitions against traditional ritual practice—it was not until 1979
that it was "legal in the United States for Native Americans to
practice their traditional religions" (Ywahoo 1)—were reinforced by
forcible removal of children to "boarding schools," where they were
mixed in with children from other tribes and forbidden to speak their
own languages, as part of a concerted plan for what Allen aptly
identifies as "cultural and spiritual genocide" (42).

During the past three centuries, official government policies
toward Indians in North America have deliberately masculinized
religious and political structures, many of which, like the Celtic ones,
accorded women more civil and religious status than could be toler-
ated. Our ability to historically document these subversions provides
us with an example of a chronologically telescoped disempowerment
of femininity, which is nonetheless analogous to what went on in
classical Greece and Rome and ever since in European attempts to
inhibit memories of earlier and more egalitarian cultures. Allen points
out that what was done recently to the Native Americans not only
devastates their cultures but "reinforces patriarchal socialization
among all Americans, who are thus led to believe that there have
never been any alternative structures" (36).

To an archetypalist, the evidence of the undermining of religious
symbols and deities as part of a recent political and economic attack
against tribal cultures has a haunting similarity to what has been done
to European archetypal systems over thousands of years. However
fascinated we may be by this commonality with Native American
archetypal history, we must not only avoid both the Jungian tendency
to perceive Indians as "shadow" elements of our own psyches and the
New Age imperialism, but, less obviously, we must also watch out for
the temptation to claim that these historical similarities make Native
Americans "just like us," suggesting that the unconscious is so col-
lective that ethnic distinctions are incidental.

Archetypal
Patterns in
Native
American
Poetry

Now we all move, we're moving with this earth,
The earth is moving along, the water is moving
    along,
The grass is moving, the trees are moving, the whole
    earth is moving,
So we all move along with the earth, keeping time
    with the earth.
(Botowatomie song, translated by Alanson Skinner;
Terrell and Terrell 21)

Traditional Native American poems are incantations which enable the poet to get in touch with his or her place in the community and in nature. The poet is not singing about subjective emotion, in the European manner: the audience for poetry and poetry's intention are communal. "The tribes," Allen writes, "do not celebrate the individual's ability to feel emotion, for they assume that all people are able to do so. . . . The tribes seek—through song, ceremony, legend, sacred stories (myths), and tales—to embody, articulate, and share reality, to bring the isolated, private self into harmony and balance with this reality" (*The Sacred Hoop* 55). Individualism would be a symptom of disease to Native Americans, for whom poetry is part of a matrix binding the individual simultaneously to the group and to the cosmos. Their poems often serve what we would term practical purposes (such as to propitiate the object of a hunt, celebrate the seasons while grinding corn, aid in childbirth, or drop hints about good paths for going somewhere), and these poems are valued as much as their "metaphysical" poetry.

Let me shoot a small bird for my younger brother.
Let me spear a small trout for my sister.
    (Tlingit lullaby; Swanton 393)

My words are tied in one
With the great mountains
With the great rocks,
I, one with my body
And my heart.
    (Yokuts; Houston 20)

You are glad, you are glad
You beat my song, you beat my song.
> (Nootka song congratulating a rival; Densmore, *Nootka and Quileute Music* 336)

I follow the river
In quest of a young beaver.
Up the river I go
Through the cut willow path I go
In quest of a young beaver.
> (Navajo; Levitas et al. 105)

I add my breath to your breath
That our days may be long on the Earth;
That the days of our people may be long;
That we shall be one person;
That we may finish our roads together.
May my father bless you with life;
May our Life Paths be fulfilled.
> (Laguna medicine song, cited by Allen in Dexter Fisher 129)

There are poems to accompany every activity in the day, a sacralizing of the ordinary that infuses a playful tone into much Native American poetry, a playfulness which should not be confused with childishness. This kind of joking and humor characterizes elders, healers, and clowns who can make up or recall a good joke or story of song to help the rest of the group cope with the harsh realities of life. "To European eyes," William Brandon notes, American Indian life "appeared to consist overwhelmingly of play taken seriously. If the Pawnees had operated a General Motors, each worker would have had his time-clock punching song, his assembly-line song, and so on, and the management would have been at least as attentive to the songs as to the rate of production, probably more so" (xii).

A song or poem is often a special gift earned or given and treasured for life. Such is the case narrated by Pawnee-Otoe poet Anna Lee Walters in "Hartico," where she is thanking her grandfather for a special song he has given her. She thinks of her beloved grandfather as a "powerful old bear" and herself as a "rabbit," and remembers when

I saw an old bear hold a rabbit
>   ever so gently in one huge hand. I heard him sing bear
>   words
rabbit did not know but could understand.
The bear was sleepy. The rabbit could tell because the
bear would often yawn . . .

Granpa, the bear would then speak. This is what he said.
"Rabbits are fond of songs that sing about frybread!"

>   Old bear gave the song to the rabbit. They held it
>   between them to make it strong with laughter from
>   the rabbit and the bear.

>   There is not another one like it. My children have
>   searched for one. I brought the song here now
>   so you can look at it. We will sing it. (111)

Walters's specially inherited song is not quoted in the poem about it; such a powerful song is unlikely to be divulged to an extratribal audience. The poem is not admired merely as the grandfather's creation but is enhanced by being "held between" the grandfather and granddaughter. They have identified themselves with a bear and a rabbit, not allegorically or metaphorically, making bear and rabbit vehicles for human meaning; rather, the poet and her grandfather are engaging in a totemic metamorphosis, participating in bear and rabbit being.

In explaining Sioux symbology, Lakota shaman Lame Deer remarks that "we Indians live in a world of symbols and images where the spiritual and the commonplace are one. To you symbols are just words, spoken or written in a book. To us they are part of nature, part of ourselves, even little insects like ants and grasshoppers. We try to understand them not with the head but with the heart, and we need more than a hint to give us the meaning" (cited in Allen, *The Sacred Hoop* 69). Like Lame Deer's grasshoppers and ants, Walters's rabbit and bear are "parts of nature" called into relation with her and her grandfather as "parts of themselves," not anthropomorphically but animistically. This animism, as I suggested in part one, extends to objects in nature considered "inanimate" in European thought. Here, for example, is a fragment of an Omaha ritual addressed to a rock:

> unmoved
> from time without
> end
> you rest
> there in the midst of the paths
> in the midst of the winds
> you rest
> covered with the droppings of birds
> grass growing from your feet
> your head decked with the down of birds
> you rest
> in the midst of the winds
> you wait
> Aged one. (Brandon 83)

As archetypal symbols deriving being from a nature which is not human, animals and rocks endow poem and song with unique animal and rock qualities. This kind of poetry moves in an archetypal field linking human beings to nonhuman ones, communicating with each other. Human, animate, and inanimate beings participate in a harmony which it is the goal of Native American poetry to imitate, and thus incorporate into the human culture, by means of incantation, rhythm, and dance.

The animism of Native American belief systems does not consist, then, in humans endowing natural objects with human attributes (anthropomorphism) but in accepting the intrinsic essence of natural objects as of equal worth to and equally as capable of communication as humans. Whereas Europeans would see the act of hearing messages from animals and natural objects as a human "reading in" or perception originating in culture and the cognitive processes, Native Americans would insist that the nonhuman source of the message is its greatest value. This belief derives in many tribes from a feeling that animals and nature in its processes of survival are much wiser and stronger than humans, whom they perceive as among the weakest of beings.

Totemism, in which Walters and her grandfather could be participating by their relationship to bear and rabbit, derives from an Algonquin word denoting a family or clan's association with an animal or natural object, and is thus a kind of animism in which a group traces its origins to and maintains a right relationship with its ancestor. To many contemporary anthropologists and commentators, as to Claude Lévi-Strauss, for example, the bear or rabbit is a "*sign* which explains a natural event or phenomenon by means of an already existent cultural construct" (*Totemism* 125), but to the Native American the bear or rabbit is acultural, its value and appeal resident in its ursine or lapine wisdom and attributes.

Euro-American psychoanalytic theory recognizes animism as a natural human tendency but allocates it to a childhood out of which human beings are expected to evolve toward a "higher" level of conceptualization. Thus Freud associates animism with the uncanny, as a phase in children and "in primitive men [*sic*] that none of us has passed through . . . without preserving certain residues and traces of it which are still capable of manifesting themselves, and that everything which now strikes us as 'uncanny' fulfills the condition of touching those residues of animistic mental activity within us and bringing them to expression" (240–41). Piaget, similarly, understands childhood as a time of spontaneous animism in which we are merged in the general flow of consciousness without awareness of our individuality. Since personal development, or individuality, has more value in his system than being merged in the flow of nature, we must learn to leave animism behind. Children must stop talking to animals and listening to trees in order to develop; friendly interchanges with the nonhuman and the enjoyment of natural objects as responsive companions are childish tendencies which must be outgrown. Freud and Piaget urge a course opposite to Native American psychological systems; in these systems individualism is considered a pathology and health located in listening to and achieving harmony with nature. "This earth is a living being," writes Cherokee spiritual leader Dhyani Ywahoo. "Here on earth we are all connected through the sacred currents of life" (134). A desperate hunger for this healthy Native American naturism, combined with ignorance of our own pagan roots, is what drives non–Native Americans into inappropriate attempts to participate in Native American religion.

One result of growing up and away from such animistic participation in the universe is that the more rational and the more removed from nature we become, the more threatening nature and the universe seem. When the "supernatural" and the "natural" are conceived of as opposites, we get the kind of starkly terrifying and meaningless landscape experienced by some Canadians (see chapter 3) and by European existentialists and modernists. Native American animism does not divide spirit from nature in such a dismaying way; as A. Irving Hallowell puts it with reference to Ojibwa ontology, "the concept of supernatural presupposes a concept of the natural. The latter is not present in Ojibwa thought. It is unfortunate that the natural-supernatural dichotomy has been so persistently invoked by many anthropologists in describing the outlook of peoples in cultures other than our own" (151). Dualities like natural/supernatural and animate/inanimate, which derive from European thought systems, cannot be fitted into Ojibwa metaphysics.

Native American Goddess Archetypes	

In many Native American theological systems, goddesses created the world and have maintained it ever since. There is Thought Woman of the Keres, Tse che nako, for example, who in the beginning of the world "finished everything, thoughts, and the names of all things. She finished also all the languages." (Allen, *The Sacred Hoop* 12). Spider Woman, Corn Woman, Earth Woman, Serpent Woman, First Woman, Coyote Woman are but a few of her tribal names. European anthropology has often demeaned the complex powers of such goddesses by defining them as "fertility" figures in a way which Allen feels "trivializes the tribes and . . . the power of woman. Woman bears, that is true. She also destroys. That is true. She also wars and hexes and mends and breaks. She creates the power of the seeds, and she plants them." As one example, Allen describes the Hopi creator Hard Beings Woman, Huruing Wuhti, who is "is of the earth. But she lives in the worlds above where she 'owns' (empowers) the moon and stars" (*The Sacred Hoop* 14). Huruing Wuhti, like Tse che nako, transcends European dualism; they synthesize war and love, cursing and blessing, birth and death. Although there is a degree of analogy between these Native American goddesses and the Greek Aphrodite in her cosmic and liminal aspects, they have more in common with her Middle Eastern predecesors Ishtar and Inanna in their syntheses of intelligence and passion, world creation, the invention of language, and military prowess.

Archetypal Patterns and Native American Poetry

Obviously an entire library could be written about Native American goddess archetypes, but here I want only to introduce the way feminine and goddess archetypes work in this vast body of material. We need to remember that Native American poets experience the interaction between traditional and white images and poetic attitudes whenever they sit down to write. For example, "love poetry" as a genre in which lovers address each other is a nonnative innovation not widely popular before contact but now mixed in with traditional attitudes to sexuality in much Native American poetry.

The fear of women's powers, and perhaps the special kind of terror that comes from conspiring with whites to undermine it, is undoubtedly enhanced by the otherness accorded to gender by most tribal social systems, in which what is male and what is female are kept separate. It is difficult for whites in patriarchy, and especially for feminists, to understand gender complementarity, which resembles the healthy blending of balanced forces attributed to Old European cultures by Gimbutas and Ochshorn but has little similarity to recent gender arrangements. My graduating senior majors in Women's Studies at the University of Wisconsin, for example, could not quite get their minds around a Winnebago visitor's comfort with the fact that men perform certain social functions and women other ones in her tribe. They automatically assumed that if men customarily did one activity and women another, a masculine domination would be present. It is difficult for young women in patriarchy to understand cultures which dualize gender functions as empowering to the well-being of the community.

Many tribes construct gender in a similarly dialogic manner in an effort to achieve harmony between women's potentially dangerous power and male needs. For example, menstrual taboos can be understood not as "about sin or filth" but "about power": "The truth of the matter as many Indians see it is that women who are at the peak of their fecundity are believed to possess power that throws male power totally out of kilter. They emit such force that, in their presence, any male-owned or -dominated ritual or sacred object cannot do its usual task" (*The Sacred Hoop* 47). Wisconsin activists supporting Ojibwa treaty rights were upset one year when, at the beginning of a round dance, they were reminded that if anyone was menstruating she should stand aside from the circle. Respect for Native American traditions should have stilled the ensuing outcry; the protesters also

327

misunderstood that the point of women standing out of the circle was our enormous power during menstruation. It is hard for whites to understand that these Native American menstrual taboos derive from awe rather than from gynophobia. I vividly remember the gasp of surprise when a group of undergraduates who had spent the class bemoaning the degradation their families had accorded their first menstruation were told by an Ojibwa student about her delight at the joyous community dance celebrating her menarche. An acknowledgment of feminine power rather than expression of disgust for women's bodies underlies such customs, Allen writes:

> The tribes see women variously, but they do not question the power of femininity. Sometimes they see women as fearful, sometimes peaceful, sometimes omnipotent and omniscient, but they never portray women as mindless, helpless, simple, or oppressed. And while the women in a given tribe, clan, or band may be all these things, the individual woman is provided with a variety of images of women from the interconnected supernatural, natural, and social worlds she lives in. (*The Sacred Hoop* 44)

While remaining wary of facile analogies between Native American and European symbols, it is helpful to look at a few examples of such archetypes as Moon Goddess, Love Goddess, Crone, and Healer in Native American poetry. For one thing, Native American women poets do not attribute "Terrible Mother" characteristics to their mothers in the way that white poets do. P. C. Smith, after comparing Native American poets' attitudes toward mothers to a collection of mother and daughter poems edited by Lyn Lifshin, concludes that there is a striking difference between a white poet's tendency to see "a woman relative as an alarmingly alien creature," sometimes "genuinely life-threatening," "usurping, draining in her otherness," and Native American women poets' celebration of their love and sameness:

> The image of the woman relative as an alien being simply does not appear in contemporary Native American women's poetry. I don't mean to say dissent between women is absent from poetry, it is not. . . . If a female relative seems strange, it is not because she is a medusa or a harpy or a killer of her helpless carp-child, but because that woman literally cannot be spoken to, since her tongue and her ways are literally, not just metaphorically, not the ways of her relative. (2)

Whereas white culture considers "family conflict as inevitable, natural, even healthy and to be encouraged in some measure," in the sense of the necessity of individuation and autonomy, Native American mothers and daughter understand each other as links in a powerful intergenerational femininity often ruptured by white values.

Thus the Haida mother sings to her new baby daughter that

> You came to me, you came to me.
> You came walking to me, calling me "mother,"
> Instead of to someone else

and lets her know how she delights in femininity:

Women are better than men, women are better than men.
Women have more property. (Nootka; Densmore, *Nootka and Quileute Music* 336)

There will be special ceremonies for the phases in the girl's life until she is initiated into the full womanhood of the Haida:

> For this you are a woman, a woman,
> For this you are a woman, you are a woman,
> To command the house-poles of Skidegate Inlet,
> You are a woman, a woman. (Haida; Swanton 13–16)

It is in this context of a valued femininity that many Native American goddess archetypes provide celebrations of self in the matrix of tribal gender systems. Here, for example, is part of a traditional Anishnabeg prayer:

> Woman!
> Mother! From your breast
> You fed me.
> With your arms
> You held me.
> To you, my love.
>
> Earth!
> Mother!
> From your bosom

I draw nourishment
In your mantle
I seek shelter.
To you, reverence. (Johnston 24)

Chickasaw poet Linda Hogan includes her mother with her father, uncle, grandfather, and grandmother in "Heritage": "From my mother, the antique mirror . . . [who] left the large white breasts that weigh down my body" (164). Hogan is celebrating an interbraiding of generations and a special heritage from her mother and grandmother, which represents what many white poets as well must painfully achieve after transcending the terror of mothers and of femininity which Europeans consider normal. We have, nonetheless, seen examples of such poetic empowerment in the intergenerational poetry of Atwood and Gottlieb and in the cases of white poets who have been able to see behind the mask of Medusa.

Chicana poetry (which deserves a volume of its own) blends Native, Spanish, and Anglo traditions but, as Tey Diana Rebolledo suggests, finds special solace in the landscape of the desert. Thus she cites Gina Valdes's poem "The Knowing Earth":

In this, my own land, I stand an alien
Mistreated, oppressed, unwanted, at best ignored
But this knowing earth recognizes me. (107)

Rebolledo, noting a "connection between female sexuality and the desert landscape" in Chicana poetry, especially in contrast to their experiences in the cities, cites Pat Mora's poem in which

The desert is no lady.
She screams at the spring sky, . . .
Her unveiled lust fascinates the sun. (117)

To the urbanized Chicana poet, the desert has become the wild place where feminine sexuality can be asserted against the incursions of Anglo and Spanish patriarchal norms. "Nature and the land thus become allies of the woman hero," asserts Rebolledo, "keeping her in touch with her self, they are a kind of talisman that enables her to make her way through the alienations of male society, and also of the received female traditions of a limited society, whether represented by the history of Spain or Mexico" (123).

The sense of alienation from one's own body fostered by Christian patriarchy is foreign to much traditional Native American poetry. As one Ojibwa love-charm spoken by a woman puts it, "I can charm the man / He is completely fascinated by me" (Densmore, *Chippewa Music*, 89–90). Where Euro-Americans might read a romantic submission or making an object of oneself into this charm, Native Americans would understand it as a typical example of women's delight in a feminine sexuality at home in nature. "In both traditional and contemporary literatures," note Patricia Clark Smith and Paula Gunn Allen,

> wilderness often appears not as mere landscape-backdrop, but as a spirit-being with a clearly sexual aura. That being, who always embodies some aspect of the land, may be either male or female. A male being may abduct a human woman, or a female being may seduce a human man, but subjugation is not the dynamic of either event. . . . In such comings-together of persons and spirits, the land and the people engage in a ritual dialogue—though it may take the human participant a while to figure that out. The ultimate purpose of such ritual abductions and seductions is to transfer knowledge from the spirit world to the human sphere, and this transfer is not accomplished in an atmosphere of control or domination. (178)

We shall see, thus, that the relationship between a Native American girl and the bear who abducts or marries her is not a story of sexual domination or human-animal antagonism but a sacred interchange of animal and human spirit. In such stories, which are often origin narratives telling how a particular tribe or clan came by its special wisdom, "spirit" does not have the connotation of masculinity and divine transcendence. Rather it has to do with inspiration, the natural wisdom that humans breathe in from animals and other beings.

Having acknowledged this heritage of empowering sexuality and closeness to nature in traditional Native American women's poetry, we have to recognize that many contemporary Native American women poets are affected by invasion, genocide, and attempts on the part of both government policymakers and Christians to destroy tribal religions and erase any feminine empowerment they foster. When we take into account the mixed blood of many of these poets, we can understand how their internalization of white norms can lead to a psychologically destructive alienation. Thus Joy Harjo, in "The Woman Hanging from the 13th Floor Window," expresses the despair of the urban Native American woman suspended between the urban asphalt and the tall glass houses of Chicago, "crying for / the lost beauty of her own life." In "I Am a Dangerous Woman" Harjo speaks as a Native American woman who has set off an airport's "guncatcher machine" with her traditional power:

> i am a dangerous woman
> but the weapon is not visible . . .
>   inside my head. (129)

In "The Lady in the Pink Mustang" Louise Erdrich describes a traveling prostitute coping with self-division ("The body disposable as cups") by making her Johns replicate her alienation. She gets even by painting "her nipples silver for a show," then tells them that "Kissing these . . . is to kiss yourself away, piece by piece" (89). Erdrich's Lady is a vengeful sex goddess with some similarity to the Middle Eastern archetypes who, like the Yoruba goddesses celebrated by Audre Lorde, combine sensuality and aggression. As in the case of African American women poets, however, Native American women are much closer in time to this powerful feminine archetypal heritage than are Euro-Americans, whose Aphrodites are apt to be more pathetic, encrusted with thousands of years of distrust for feminine sensuality.

Unlike British and American poets, contemporary Native American poets are well aware of the recent history of their people's defeats. One mode of feminist empowerment is the celebration of self-sufficient women from tribal history who have used their sexuality to outwit their conquerors. Cherokee poet Rayna Green's "Coosaponakeesa (Mary Mathews Musgrove Bosomsworth), Leader of the Creeks, 1700–1783," concerns a famous Creek woman whom Green describes as "all woman / part swamp rat / half horse" who cut a swath through a number of white lovers and husbands (including Oglethorpe) to try to save her people and their land. That is not the end of the story to the Creeks, however, who "say Mary came back as Sherman" and lives on today in "The Creek girls in Oklahoma" who "laugh like Mary now / wild and good" who will accept "no deals this time" (115). In "Naneye'hi (Nancy Ward), the Last Beloved Woman of the Cherokees, 1738–1822," similarly, Green asserts that even after the whites "said she wasn't needed anymore" and "said the women might as well go home," they failed to undermine the spirit of Cherokee women bounding back from years of silence to "do their jobs again" (114). These poems interbraid contemporary Native American women with their powerful ancestors in an intergenerational empowerment so that they may transcend all attempts to repress them.

In Native American poetry, ancestors, goddesses, female relatives, and contemporary women participate in an archetypal empowerment which is rarer in poetry by Euro-American and British women. Native American resembles non–Native American poetry, nonetheless, in the way goddess attributes are accorded to the moon, with moon goddesses revered by both men and women. Thus Suqamish poet Agnes Pratt writes about a "love too tenuous for words" in terms of the moon, and promises to keep "the interwoven strands of you / As I keep the enduring moon / And its web of shadow" (85). To the Inuit the moon is "She who will not take a husband," although to the Haida she is Roong, a male god. The close synchronization between the moon's phases and women's menstrual cycles contributes to her role as Changing Woman both of the Lipan Apache and the Navajo. As is the case of the many reverential poems written by white males about the moon, men as well as women seek out her special blessings. Nez Perce poet Phillip William George demonstrates in "Night Blessing" the moon's beneficence to men as well as to women.

> I raise yearning arms
> And stand naked
> Within Her sacred view. (44–45)

The moon as Changing Woman embodies old age as well as maidenhood and the reproductive years. In Native American poetry the crone archetype is a frequent object of praise and reverence, because age is valued: old people or elders have achieved wisdom and know lots of songs about how to heal, help in childbirth, bless, and make the passage from life to death easier. Native American poets of both sexes conflate tribal grandmothers with goddess-creators to construct admirable archetypes. The Keres' Spider Woman and Thought Woman, for example, are simultaneously generators of the universe,

revered divinities, and attributes of present-day Keres women. Paula
Gunn Allen addresses "Grandmother" to Spider Woman:

> Out of her body she extruded
> shining wire, life, and wove the light
> on the void. (3)

Beth Brant also conflates her grandmother with the earth itself,
understood in Mohawk theology as situated on the back of a turtle:

> I lie in Grandmother's bed
> and dream the earth into a turtle.
> She carries us slowly across the universe. (32)

In a prose piece on "Native Origin" Brant conflates turtle, mothers,
grandmothers, and Mohawk goddesses when she recounts how "A
turtle rattle made from a she-turtle who was a companion of the
women's mother" is used in a longhouse ceremony, the turtle having
"died the night she died, both of them ancient and tough. Now the
daughter shakes the rattle, and mother and she-turtle live again" (33).
Reverence for the enduring power of feminine tradition is not limited
to women: male poets such as Mohawk Peter Blue Cloud, in a poem to
his herb doctor aunt, "To-ta Ti-om," Tuscarora R. T. Smith, in
"Yonosa House," and Mesquakie Ray Young Bear, in "Grandmother,"
experience empowerment from older female relatives to whom they
accord respect and love.

Elder women preserve in memory the stories, healing methods,
and tactics for survival for many of the tribes. Often these older
women narrate the dangerous vision quests they endured in order to
receive their shamanic powers, quests which are analogous to rebirth
journey narratives in European and Euro-American archetypal litera-
ture. In a paper on healing songs of Native American women, Helen
Jaskoski collects a variety of healing songs by women healers, whom
she finds "much rarer than men practitioners" (1). The stories and
songs of such tribes as the Seneca, Flathead, Jutenai, Hope, and Taos,
moreover, are rarely divulged, often held closely secret (from men as
well as from outsiders) within the women's medicine societies. Jaskos-
ki writes about Djun of the Tlingit, Snapia of the Comanche, the
Crow shaman Pretty-Shield, and a Papago healer, "Owl woman," as
examples of women doctors who create healing songs. Owl Woman

acquired her healing songs after empowering herself to heal others and to commune with the dead by taking a perilous journey to the spirit land.

I want to conclude my survey of Native American archetypes with Native American healing poems, one by Owl Woman and two by the contemporary Oneida poet Roberta Hill Whiteman. In the 1920s Juana Manuel (Owl Woman of the Papago) permitted twenty-seven of her songs to be recorded. Some of them are "given" by people who have died as messages back to their relatives; other songs, achieved by Owl Woman's heroic vision journeys or trances, help either in recovery or in dying. The purpose is not so much to effect cures as to heal the psychological problems of patient and relatives, to ease grief in some cases, or, as Jaskoski cites an Apache doctor, to see to it that "after these songs everything evil from the heart to the head comes out" (119). In psychoanalytic terms, these healing women are poets who dare to articulate what they have learned during their journeys into the unconscious in quest of power; archetypally, songs of this sort can be understood as narrations about rebirth quests whose goal is not the aggrandizement of the individual poet but the health of the people she is trying to help.

Here, for example, are excerpts from various healing songs in which Owl Woman intrepidly recounts her dangerous quest for healing powers:

> I can not make out what I see.
> In the dark I enter.
> I can not make out what I see.
>
> Yonder lies the spirit land,
> Yonder the spirit land I see.
> Father ahead, in front of me,
> I see a spirit stand.
>
> In the great night my heart will go out,
> Toward me the darkness comes rattling,
> In the great night my heart will go out.
>
> I am going far to see the land,
> I am running far to see the land,
> While back in my house the songs are intermingling.
> (Jaskoski 121–22)

335

Owl Woman is in a trance; though sitting in one place, psychologically she has gone on a quest for the wisdom to help her patient. She has the aid of her owl familiar, the bird for whom she is named. Coming up against a blindingly dark night, she keeps going even though she can't see anything. She visits the "spirit" land where the dead live, encounters the darkness rattling frighteningly from it, but has such courage that she is able to let her "heart" go out into it. Thus her courage, skill, and love enable her to bring back from the unconscious/spirit land what is needed for her community.

This same kind of quest into the unconscious, described often as a dreaming reported back to the tribe, is undertaken by both male and female shamans; the resulting healing songs spring from the individual's ability to encounter the more frightening depths of the unconscious without being so fearful as to become paralyzed there. They are sometimes, as in the case of the Kashia Pomo, called "Dreamers," who, Allen explains, are "responsible for the continued existence of the people as a psychic (that is, tribal) entity" (*The Sacred Hoop* 204). Such healers can be old or young but are often past menopause.

Because of the intergenerational empowerment Native American women expect to derive from each other, grandmothers and other older tribal women are celebrated. Unlike Mary Elizabeth Coleridge, who is horrified by the feminine suffering she sees on the other side of her mirror, or Kathleen Raine, trained to loathe even her own beauty, a poet like Linda Hogan can look in the mirror she has inherited to affirm the wisdom etched in wrinkles which are just like her mother's. In "calling myself home," Hogan is empowered by the grandmother/mother/daughter as well as by the father/uncle/grandfather lineage, celebrating tribal women who "laced the shells of turtles / together, pebbles inside / and they danced / with rattles strong on their legs" (157).

Just because the destruction of their traditional tribal practices and religions is recent, however, doesn't make the quest for rebirth through affirmation of their ancestors easy for Native Americans. In two poems about struggling to take a positive approach to life in spite of internalized oppression, Oneida poet Roberta Hill Whiteman demonstrates the pain involved in rebirth. Both "Star Quilt" and "Dream of Rebirth" are suspended between pain and hope, with the possibility of giving up as strong as the hope for survival. In the first poem the intricate patterns of the quilt, "A star forged from linen thread and patches," is the locus of hope: Beneath it, through Eros, Whiteman and her lover move toward survival, but neither the lovely patterns of the quilt nor the memory of other lands prevent their bitterness. But it is out of such bitterness that healing may come: "anoint us with grass and twilight air, so we may embrace, two bitter roots" (282). In "Dream of Rebirth," similarly, "We stand on the edge of wounds," Whiteman and her fellow Native Americans caught within a culture that has tried to obliterate them. It is only by naming and enduring this pain that rebirth will come: "Groping within us are cries yet unheard," "Yet within this interior, a spirit kindles." Their hope is for a future time when, having transcended white pity, "Some [of us] will rise that clear morning like the swallows" (282). Although "Dream of Rebirth" shares elements with many non–Native American archetypal rebirth narratives, it is also entirely different from many of these I have treated in this study, in that it is based upon the pain of trying to survive attempts of the colonizers to obliterate not only ownership of land but one's tribal culture.

There are, nonetheless, similarities between Native American poets' quests for harmony with both their communities and the earth and archetypal processes which the many non–Native American poets of both genders whom I have analyzed in this book undergo. The result of overcoming one's terror of Medusa, Aphrodite, Artemis, or Hecate (or all four blended into each other) is, for example, a psychological health which includes acceptance of one's place in nature. There are parallels, similarly, between the archetypal quests of Owl Woman and the Sumerian Inanna, who descends into the underworld in a quest which will enhance her people. The quests of women poets like Judy Grahn and Muriel Rukeyser, to cite but two examples of the many I have treated, are analogous to Native American quests both in general structure and in outcome. To the extent that non–Native American poets are open to the pagan content latent in both their European cultures of origin and the deep background of classical mythology, they are able to participate in mythic healing and archetypal empowerment.

Although the quest for psychic wholeness and its outcome of harmony with nature occurs within many poems by British and American men and women without reference to Native American belief systems, we have seen how in both Canadian and American poetry the Native American becomes the agent of healing to mediate between the Europeanized poet and the landscape he or she inhabits. It is not surprising that these poets, whose education neglected their own background in pagan mythologies, should ignore these in favor of the more immediately accessible Native American natural theologies.

How, then, to respond to the just outrage of Native Americans against white poets who use them as personae and exploit their much-persecuted religions in order to aggrandize their literary stature? This conundrum facing white writers is exemplified in the situation of the Canadian poet Anne Cameron, whose Nootka friends urged her to publish *Daughters of Copper Women* and other materials which had once been secret within their medicine societies. She states that her 1981 publication was a response to their mutual feeling that it was time for women to bring

> the pieces of the truth together . . . scattered pieces from the black sisters, from the yellow sisters, from the white sisters, are coming together, trying to form a whole, and it can't form without the pieces we have saved and cherished. Without the truth we have protected, women won't have the weapons of defense they need. If we hold our secret to ourselves any longer, we help the evil ones destroy the Womanspirit. (145)

At the 1987 Third International Feminist Book Fair in Montreal, however, a younger generation of Native Canadians who wished now to speak for themselves asked Cameron to stop using native materials in her books. It seems to me that within the context of Andrea Smith's and Wendy Rose's expositions on how Native American spiritual abuse and white shamanism are painful to Native Americans, this is a perfectly reasonable request. A poem is always an inner journey, a communication of one's spiritual quest to one's audience; therefore, writing poems using Native American rituals and symbols usurped from their vision quest constitutes both disrespect for and exploitation of Native American theology. Or, as Susan Hawthorne aptly puts it in "The Politics of the Exotic: The Paradox of Cultural Voyeurism," such activities are as intrusive as pornography: "Having destroyed the 'other', both in the outer world and in the inner world, the empty dominant culture seeks to locate the secret of the 'other's' vitality" (623).

In response to this situation I have removed from circulation several poems I wrote that used Native American symbols or activities to express my personal quest, and I no longer use Native American ritual materials in group activities with women. I still read Native American literature, write about it, and teach it, however, hoping to introduce students and audiences to the many unique angles on the human experience which knowledge of Native American literature can provide. As should be clear from my comments throughout this book, I also celebrate the pagan cultures in the deep background of American and British archetypal systems.

So successful were the European "counter mythmakers" that the pagan archetypes were forced out of memory. My theory of the acultural authenticity of archetypes derives from the amazing way the lost content (like joy in wildness), whether Old European, Celtic, Germanic, Norse, or even ancient Middle Eastern, persists within recurring archetypes throughout the history of poetry. I am not suggesting a "collective unconscious" that eradicates the sharp differences between cultures, however; my hypothesis that the archetypes of Native Americans and Native American peoples of Canada run parallel to pagan European archetypes does not mean that I consider them "just like" each other. To clarify the relationship between archetypal symbols and narratives in the various cultures I have examined, I will devote the last chapter to an archetype sufficiently recurrent to provide a good sample for archetypal comparison and contrast among British, Canadian, American, and Native American poets.

By concentrating on the bear archetype as it occurs in classical, Native American, American, Canadian, as in Celtic/Germanic/Norse mythological systems, I want to raise the question of whether the common perceptions of the right path to psychological health, a viable human community, and environmental survival which the bear archetype evokes constitute messages which, in our very different ways, we all need to hear.

11.

Bear!

Once you accept that animals and plants and natural objects are endowed with a being different from that of humans, you need to develop good relations with nature. Shifting from anthropomorphic to animistic thinking requires you to discard the assumption that if a bear figures in a story it must be a symbol for something human. Since we are brought up to believe that people are superior to animals, we assume that bears in stories are people dressed up as bears or that even if they really are bears, they exist to tell us about human rather than about bear values. As Margaret Atwood aptly puts it, the traditional European attitude to animals in literature is that they are "Englishmen in furry zippered suits, often with a layer of human clothing added on top." When we come across Native American stories of a girl who marries a bear, we tend to superimpose our European perspective upon them, interpreting the bears as somehow humans clothed in animal skins (*Survival* 73).

Native American Bear Archetypes	Traditional Native American songs and chants approach the bear as other than human, though with human similarities:

A Foot.
A foot with toes.
A foot with toes came.
He came with a foot with toes.
Aging as he came with a foot with toes. (Diné; Levitas 105).

The bear is entirely beyond human control, and deeply feared:

How shall we hide from the bear that is moving
    all around the world?
Let us cover our backs
    with dirt that the terrible great bear from
    the north of the world may not find us. (Kwakiutl; Houston 58).

Only the wisest, most experienced holy men and women dare to declare that

I am like a bear.
I hold up my hands
waiting for the sun to rise. (Northern Ute; Houston 24).

Not all metamorphoses of humans into bears or bears into humans are for the good of the tribe. Among the Ottawa and the Ojibwa, bear-walkers (me-coub-moose) turn into dangerous balls of fire, as do the Bodewadme man-doz-it, traveling "great distances quickly" and bringing "bad luck, disgrace, poverty, sickness and even death on their enemies or on people who they believe have wronged them" (Dobson 82).

In Native American stories which account for totemic tribal origin, the impulse is not toward humanization of the bear but toward bearification of the humans, an interchange in which human beings learn how to revere and respect bear values which they need in order to survive as a people. Here, for example, is the way a bear blessed a Winnebago man:

Human, I said that I blessed you and I really mean it. Earthmaker created me and gave me control of many things. Human, I bless you. As many years as Earthmaker bestowed upon you, that number I also bless you with. You will reach the limit of the years that were granted you. With my body I also bless you. Whenever you are hungry and

Excited Man Forgets His Weapon.
Tudlik (c. 1890-1960), Canadian Inuit
People, 1959. Paper stencil, sealskin
print. © The Detroit Institute of the
Arts, 1990, Founders Society Purchase,
Director's Discretionary Fund.

wish to kill a bear, put a pipeful of tobacco for me. If then you go out
hunting, you will be successful. Don't abuse the bears. I am the chief
of the bears. I bless you. Never before have I blessed a human being,
as long as I have lived here. As long as your descendants live on this
earth, so long will this blessing last. . . . When you put this kettle of
food on the fire and offer me tobacco see to it that you keep away
menstruating women . . . (Winnebago; Levitas 46)

Whereas to the European mind this bear blessing might seem
wishful thinking, a tribe's self-serving account of its special totemistic
endowment, to the Winnebago it is a word-by-word account of what
the bear said to the man. But, argues the European, the human heard
the blessing, either consciously or unconsciously (as in a dream or
trance), and the unconscious, whether individual or collective, is
human. That is what I am no longer sure about; we are, after all,
animals. In delineating the "androcentric bias" which Mircea Eliade
brings to the interpretation of symbols, Carol Christ notes the way

historians consider the written word objective while devaluing physical evidence as only accessible to subjective interpretation: "In so doing they display unacknowledged, but classical, Western bias against the physical. Behind their dismissal of the physical evidence from prehistory lies the Platonic notion that ideas expressed in the written word are more real than physical reality" (78). Native American archetypal reasoning does not limit its definition of the unconscious to the individual or the collective human psyche. Native American archetypes are not transcendent in the orthodox Jungian sense of a suprahuman realm of fixed and numinous figures; rather, to the Native American archetypes spring from an understanding of the unconscious as an interactive field extended between human beings and nature, in this case the bear. Linguistic theories based on the premise that language is more authentic than the material world are alien to Native Americans, who believe that Earth has a language of its own.

The totemic origin stories upon which Native American bear archetypes are based are not about evolution from bears, in the sense of an improvement in humans consequent to their transcendence of animality: humans derive their distinguishing tribal attributes from a powerful and superior animal ancestor who has endowed them with bear blessing. "Indeed," asserts Catharine McClellan, "the major philosophical concern of all the Yukon Indians is how they may best live in harmony with the animals who basically have so much more power than humans, especially since the Indians have to confront and kill the animals if they are to stay alive themselves" (6).

I do not think that we can define Native American attitudes to bears as theriomorphism, in the sense of human beings elevating animals to the status of gods, which would imply a spiritualization of the animals, a sublimation of their natural powers. Although many tribes refer to bear gods as bear "spirits," and although these spirits live in the realm of the dead, they are not separated out from nature but take their place in the generations alongside human ancestors, always accessible to the tribe. Our familiarity with classical and Christian divisions between body and spirit, soul and matter, makes it difficult for us to grasp a theology which reveres bear and human ancestors, the living and the dead, as both eternally immanent and eternally present, or immortal.

The taboo against menstruating women in the Winnebago bear

blessing brings up an association between women and bears that is widespread among Native American tribes. The specific prohibition has to do with women's power when their blood is flowing, which, as we have seen, was so potent that it would disturb any male ceremony. Menstruating women go off into seclusion to keep from rupturing day-to-day life. One of my students, Marla Schneiderman, discovered that in some instances Native American women are thought to turn into bears when menstruating; she cites R. W. Dunning on the Ojibwa, among whom "approaching the time of a girl's first period, she is known as *wemukowe*—literally, 'going to be a bear'—and during her seclusion she is known as *mukowe*—'she is a bear'."[1]

Many tribes trace their origins to a "bear mother," who is sometimes a real bear and sometimes a girl who has taken a bear as a lover. As Atwood has noted, this latter propensity carries over from Native American into white Canadian literature to the extent that "affairs with bears seem to be a peculiarly Canadian interest."[2] Among Native Americans the "girl (or boy) who marries the bear" story often has to do with the origins of the tribal totem. In *The Girl Who Married the Bear*, the definitive work on the subject, McClellan tells about a "favorite story of the Tlingit- and Athabascan-speaking Indians of Southern Yukon Territory" which starts out with a disobedient young girl who, while out gathering blackberries, "repeatedly jumps over grizzly bear excrement and says insulting things to it" (5). Since Native Americans and bears both share berry fields at the same time of year, when it is crucial to store up against the oncoming winter, correct human-bear behavior would require that you sing to warn (nearly blind) bears of your presence (today hikers in bear country often wear bearbells to serve this purpose). For her two serious transgressions of correct human-bear relationships the Yukon girl is kidnapped by the bear people and marries a bear chief.

McClellan details many different versions of this story, attributing some of the variations to the gender of the teller. In many accounts the girl, frightened at first, falls in love and lives happily with the bears, giving birth to two half-bear children. In some accounts she begins to grow fur herself and turns into a bear, and on many totem poles she is depicted as fully bear, the Bear Mother. However, her happy life with the bears is interrupted when her brothers arrive looking for her. The bear husband steps out and allows himself to be shot, but not before he sings the special song his half-bear children will carry back to the tribe, which is now endowed with his totemic powers.

Stories of girls marrying bears are not limited to the Northwest coast but occur among native peoples throughout Canada and the United States. There is a Blackfoot story, for example, about a "young woman with many suitors" who "refused to marry" because "it seems that the young woman had a bear for a lover, and, as she did not want any one to know this, she would meet him when she went out after wood." Her little sister finds out, however, and the brothers go out and kill the bear lover. "Now the older sister was a powerful medicine-woman," and she turns back into a bear when the little sister touches her in the wrong place while they are playing. When the little sister tells the brothers what has happened, they go out to kill the bear sister, but she kills them first and turns them into the Great Dipper. "This is how the seven stars (Ursa major) came to be" (Stith Thompson 164–67).

Here we find a conjunction between the original Blackfoot bear girl story and astronomical lore derived from the European pagan archetypes I will discuss later in this chapter. The two distinct traditions interweave in a way that cannot be attributed merely to European influence, but with the Native American and Europagan threads clearly distinguishable in their interbraiding. We can see this same kind of Native American–European interbraiding of bear girl archetypes in "The Bear Girl" narration told by Ojibwa Delia Oshogay in 1942. In this story, "There was an old man and his wife who had three daughters. One of them looked just like a bear, with fur and everything." Since the parents are poor, the two older daughters go off on a quest for husbands, with the littlest bear/daughter following behind. The bear/daughter, named Mako, saves them from an evil witch (there are maleficent witches in both Ojibwa and European folklore) and earns marriage with two sons of a king through her magical ability to get the sun and the moon back from the witch, who has taken them out of the sky. When the second of the two princes she marries refuses to sleep with her (because she is too ugly and bearlike) she allows him to throw her into the fire, but "suddenly a beautiful woman popped out of the fire and fell onto his bed. He was so happy. They sent for clothes, and he dressed her up. She became a queen, but she had no power any more. She had lost all her power with her bear selfhood. This time, when he used to come near her, she moved away and wrapped herself up in bed away from him. They brought her family to the palace" (Barnouw 195). The incursion of European norms devalues the animality of the bear and imposes a norm of human "beauty" which deprives the bear girl of her sexual power and magic as a medicinewoman. The beauty-and-the-beast motif, in which the beast must be anthropomorphosed in order to be valued, contrasts sharply with the traditional Native American archetype of the bear husband whose virtue is in his bearness.

In the Native American girl-who-married-the-bear stories, the common thread is a right relationship between a hero and a bear, which follows upon making a mistake in her approach to the bear, learning to correct the error and to behave more suitably, then developing an interchange with the bear that can be brought back as a boon to the tribe. This process is like the mistaken approaches to Medusa, Aphrodite, and Artemis which British and American poets must correct in order to get into right relationship with her. I have noted that when such a correct approach is achieved a sense of harmony with nature often characterizes the outcome. In Native American narratives of people approaching bears we thus see a similar archetypal process from error (and disrespect), through correction of the error (and more appropriate reverence for nature).

Perhaps in association with their role as tribal ancestors, bears in Native American stories are often described as nurturant foster parents for human children who wander into their dens. The Onondaga, for example, tell the story of a lost boy who is fostered by a bear. The Chitimacha tell a precontact variation in which "an old couple raised two nephews," caring for them until they could be self-sufficient, after which the two "grandparents" then turn back into bears and go off into the woods (Levitas 9). In a postcontact Tewa story interbraided with "Goldilocks" motifs, a little boy sits at a table in a Bear house and eats from the bowls, and when Bear Woman comes home she tells him he is a little bear brother. Although the little boy is "frightened and ran away from them," in the denouement "his mother was glad that Bear Woman had treated him well. So she said to her husband, 'Whenever you see a bear, do not kill it because Bear Woman was good to our child' " (Levitas 265–66). A variation of these child/bear visits and metamorphoses structures Laguna-Pueblo poet Leslie Marmon Silko's "Story from Bear Country," in which she reminds her readers that if you wander away to the bears, "The problem is / you will never want to return" because "Their beauty will overcome your memory" (*Storyteller* 204–205). There is rarely any doubt in Native American bear poems and stories, whether precontact or after the arrival of Europeans in America, that human beings need to revere and respect the metaphysical beauty of bears. This metaphysical beauty is part of a good in nature which human beings strive to get into harmony with. Thus the Ojibwa achieve their greatest good of "life in the fullest sense, life in the sense of longevity, health and freedom from misfortune," a goal which "cannot be achieved without the effective help and cooperation of both human and other-than-human persons, as well as by one's own personal efforts" (Hallowell 171).

Europagan Bear Archetypes

The folklore of Europe, which arrived in America with the colonists, displays an animism derived from the stratum of pagan archetypes underlying a transparently thin and historically recent suit of patriarchal clothing. Writing about the Old European symbols documented by Gimbutas, Gloria Orenstein points out that "because these symbols translate an animistic vision that perceives the existence of a vital life force inherent in all matter, the 'vitalist' symbol is linked to a more highly energized form of aesthetic expression in order to incorporate the gestural, oral, and ritual dynamics of a language that has nonverbal components indicating ceremony, song, and movement" (75). In our love affair with written language we often block our minds off from the vitality of our oral, gestural, and ceremonial heritage. The repression of our pagan past surfaces in the affinities and expropriations of indigenous American beliefs which Native Americans find so insulting.

My feeling is that the analogues between Native American and European folklore have to do with similar human responses to similar natural phenomena prior to the mind/matter splits fostered by medieval religion and enlightenment science, so that attitudes to bears in European archetypal variations of the child going to live with the bear and the animal bride and groom narratives are comparable. The European equivalent of the Native American boy who goes to live with the bear narrative, for example, is the story of Goldilocks, or the Three Bears, a nursery staple throughout Europe and America even today. We feminist critics have approached "fairy tales" with suspicion about their patriarchal content, only to find our own readings undermined by the vital substratum of paganism latent in their archetypal content. Madonna Kolbenschlag, for example, in her 1979 *Kiss Sleeping Beauty Goodbye*, subtitled *Breaking the Spell of Feminine Myths and Models*, starts out with the hypothesis that fairy tales reflect patriarchal stereotypes of a limited femininity. As she works through her material, including variations of the Goldilocks and Beauty and the Beast stories, she describes female heroes who rebel against patriarchy to empower themselves through alliance with animals and nature.

In a popular English version of the Three Bears story, Goldilocks, like the young Yukon heroes, "was not at all a well-brought-up young girl," and she intrudes into the house of "good Bears, who did nobody any harm," and who have much better manners than she does. When they return she rudely jumps out of the window "and whether she broke her neck in the fall," concludes the Victorian moralist, "or ran into the wood and was lost there, or found her way out of the wood and got whipped for being a bad girl and playing truant, no one can say" (Martignoni 73). Kolbenschlag starts out by analyzing the golden hair motif as symbolizing "the capacity to transform brute nature into 'soul' " (114) but ends up affirming Goldilocks' return to the forest as an act of immersion in nature. She "returns to the essential solitude that is the basis of autonomous relationship, the solitude that is a principle of mediation between intimacy and privacy, role and identity, affiliation and self-actualization, nature and culture." The pagan force latent in the archetypal narrative undermines our patriarchal premises: "Goldilocks is at home in the forest" (117). Like many Victorian women poets, the girl hero becomes empowered by escaping culture for residence in the apatriarchal wildwood. Kolbenschlag also reads the hero of the Beauty and the Beast archetypal narrative as "in command of herself" from the story's outset and empowered by the "beast," to which she offers herself in ransom for the sake of her father. The "beast" treats his bride well and sends her back to her father's house with many gifts. "In allowing her to return to visit her father the Beast gives her ultimate power over himself," Kolbenschlag asserts, "including, in Jean Cocteau's film version of the tale, the empowerment [of] the key to Diana's lodge." In Kolbenschlag's reading, Beauty realizes that the beast is her own instinctual life and a god in nature:

"As Beauty discovers the 'beast' in herself, she discovers the god in the Beast." In linking her erotic maturation to an apatriarchal green world lover, Beauty, like the initiates of Artemis, engages "in the process of exorcising patriarchal images" (161).

In European folklore many stories insist that a young girl accept the animal qualities of a suitor (as in kissing the frog or embracing the beast) so that he can turn back into a human being from an (implicitly) inferior state. In these stories animality is an element we need to come to terms with, but it can be taken off like a fur coat, one's bestial nature put aside when the superior human form beneath is revealed. As in the case of the Russian hero who must learn to be polite to his toad wife, the process is one of correcting an intolerable lack of respect for animals, replacing an anthropomorphic egotism with a more animistic reverence for nature.

There are many European analogues to Native American animal bride and groom stories, especially about women who make love to or marry bears. Snow White and Rose Red, for example, find solace in their loneliness, playing with the big bear that spends the winter in front of their fireplace; and after their cleverness and courage help him to defeat the evil dwarf who has stolen his treasure, he turns back into a prince and marries Snow White, marrying Rose Red, in turn, to his brother. We see the same kind of reciprocal friendliness with animals (as well as improved relationships with dwarfs) in the story of Snow White, whose ability to survive in the forest is also rewarded with marriage to a prince. In European folklore, women's friendship with bears, toads, and other animals focuses on achieving harmony between human beings and nature, even when the denouement seems to subdue her in patriarchal marriage.

Bears in fairy tales are evidence of archetypes which lurked around Europe long before the Grimm brothers started writing down what "old wives" told them. In fact, there is sufficient evidence of bears in Neanderthal hunts and ceremonies to identify them as archetypes which in the depth of their background antedate *Homo sapiens.* "The bones of more than five hundred cave bears killed by hunters were found in a cavern near Erd, Hungary, and radiocarbon-dated to 49,000 B.C.E. Thirteen thousand years ago, thirty thousand bears had been killed at the Swiss cave of Wilden Mannistock, where some forty-two skulls were placed in a line" (Buffie Johnson 338). Gimbutas has documented the widespread occurrence in Old Europe of bear artifacts shaped as vessels which have the same relationship to water as snakes and birds; statues of mothers holding babies, both wearing bear masks, suggest Old European versions of the bear mother with whom Artemis was later associated.

As late as 1697 Europeans were still writing accounts of real bears nursing human children (Dudley and Novak 190–91). Prehistoric bear lore passed into European literature along Celtic as well as more obscure pagan pathways. One of the most important centers of early Celtic culture was at Berne in present-day Switzerland, where, according to Ross, a statue of a seated goddess

> holding fruit for the nourishment of a bear carries the inscription *Deae Artioni Licinia Sabinilla*. Dea Artio, "Bear Goddess," finds a parallel in a second goddess associated, as her name suggests, with the same animal, the goddess Andarta, "Powerful Bear." The name Art, "bear," occurring in names such as Artgenos, "Son of the Bear," occurs widely in Welsh and Irish personal names and in toponymy. (349)

The Celtic bear goddess Dea Artio is also associated with the British warrior Arthur, who never died but lives still on the immortal island of Avalon.

Such indigenous European bear archetypes were sometimes interbraided with bear lore imported from India by Gypsies. Wendy Osterweil has researched the "various beliefs in Gypsy culture in which the bear is endowed with healing and other magical powers," as

> in some Romanian provinces [where] the bear is believed to cure people during a celebration called Martini, in honor of the god Mars. During this period, the sick are brought to lie on their stomachs in front of tame bears. The bears are thought to cure the patient by jumping up and down on her/his back. . . . A bear in one's village is believed to drive away evil spirits and provide general good fortune. If the bear voluntarily enters one's home, this is also a sign of prosperity. . . . Pregnant women wear bear claws and children's teeth as amulets around the bodies to bring them healthy children.[3]

One of these Gypsy groups who revere bears both in life and in death, giving them special burial, is called the Usari.

The Bear Goddess Dea Artio. Switzerland, second century. Bronze statuette. Photograph by Stefan Rebsamen. Courtesy of Bernisches Historisches Museum.

Long before the arrival of the Gypsies in fifteenth-century Europe, indigenous people praised their heroes by associating them with bear metamorphoses. The Norse highly valued warriors who went "berserk," becoming bearlike during battles; and the Anglo-Saxons named an important folk hero "bee-wolf," a bear kenning. In medieval "heraldry the bear denoted the man of power or nobility attacked by underlings." To the church fathers, however, the bear archetype's evocation of admiration for animal power made it

a symbol of evil. Even in the pre-Christian era the bear seems to have been a symbol of male sexuality: tales of bears kidnapping and raping women and of bears becoming secret paramours of willing wives are widely disseminated in European folklore. Angelo de Gubernatis cites Danish and Russian tales of women who were violated by bears and gave birth to half-human, half-ursine monsters. . . . By the end of the twelfth century, the bear had become established as a pictorial motif to signify male sexuality . . . [and] the church made the equivalence clear and saw the bear as a symbol of lust. (Rowland 32)

When Christians failed to eradicate the pagan bear archetype, they sometimes syncretized it, as in the case of the elevation of Urcel, a bear goddess worshipped in Cologne, to the status of St. Ursula, an Artemislike priestess who traveled everywhere with a court of "eleven thousand virgins." Urcel is probably a Saxon variation on the Celtic Artio worshipped at Berne, both analogous to the she-bear worshipped as Artemis, the mother of the animals, at a shrine Herodotus locates on the island of Calliste.

Even when European Renaissance educators chose to substitute elite classical for pagan archetypes as suitable to learning (undoubtedly to deflect what might happen should their students be empowered by the indigenous pagan archetypes), the conjunction of bear goddess and bear mother myths in Artemis of Brauron enabled much of the bear archetype's original deep background to survive in both the oral cultures and poetic history. Archaeologist Lilly Kahil, in "Mythological Repertoire of Brauron," analyzes archaeological findings at a site on the east coast of Attica which was excavated in 1948–63. According to Kahil, the Akropolis at Brauron dates to the Neolithic period but became the site of the worship of the Anatolian Artemis around the eighth century B.C.E. This Artemis is clearly a lady of the wild things, in the sense of presiding over the "fertility" both of animals and of humans, "mistress of the animals in general" as well as a goddess who has an important role in all of the phases of women's biological cycles; from birth to death, from birth's "happy delivery" to a good death under the aegis of a "torch-bearing" Artemis/Hecate, women turned to this goddess for help in our lives.

The bear figures in the *arkteia*, or rites of consecration of young girls to Artemis, emphasize "the importance of the bear in the cult of the Attic Artemis." On some vases little girls are taking off their clothing to begin a footrace with a bear standing in the background who is "very certainly the bear who attends the ritual which is held in its honor." There are also a priestess, apparently supplicating the bear, and a man and woman who "are wearing masks of bears." In her summary of the role of Artemis in these artifacts and in classical literature, Kahil sees a conflation of civic virtues, such as Artemis presiding over young brides, families, and childbirth, and her wild character: "even as a civic goddess, Artemis never loses her essential character of goddess of the outdoors and of nature" (243). The relationship between these apparently opposite functions—civic and wild, marital and natural—is less obscure when we understand European archetypes as mediators within a field which harmonize the social and instinctive lives of human beings. To recall that one's personal instincts are shared with nature, young girls, brides, and mothers turned to Artemis as bear goddess, being required as brides to "make a ceremonial visit to the bride-room at the temple of Artemis at the festival of Artemis" (as one Cyrenean document from the fourth century B.C.E. prescribes) and, when pregnant, to return "to the bride-room in the precinct of Artemis and give the Bear priestess feet and head and skin of the sacrifice" (Kraemer 16).

Artemis of the young girls, the "virgin" (sexually self-determining) Artemis, Artemis of brides, and Artemis presiding over childbirth can be understood as a goddess who ensures that her charges attribute their biological experiences to her and hence to powers specifically feminine, remembering in her ceremonies that sexuality and reproduction belong to women and not to men. As bear mother and bear goddess in shrines like the one at Brauron, Artemis links women's wildness to our social functions. The Artemis cult at Brauron is probably one of many places where women sought to reinforce our instinctive powers in spite of attempts to control our sexuality. Perennially accessible and popular, the bear archetype lurked close to the surface of the European psyche.

When the invading Achaeans needed to enforce more patriarchal control than indigenous Old Europeans might be willing to accept, they used narratives about gods and heroes raping local divinities and their priestesses and worshippers to suggest the kinds of punishment a sexually self-determining woman might expect. It is interesting that when threatened with rape, women heroes often turned themselves (or were helpfully metamorphosed) into natural objects: Daphne turned into a laurel tree to escape Apollo, Syrinx into a reed to avoid Pan, and Arethusa into a spring to elude Alpheus.

Sometimes this metamorphosis is described as a punishment visited upon the hero by a patriarchalized goddess, as in the case of Athena turning Medusa into a snake-haired Gorgon. It is this kind of punitive metamorphosis (in some variations at the behest of Hera and in others at the behest of her own beloved Artemis) that turns Callisto into a bear. Kathleen Wall traces the Callisto archetype as a structural motif in European narratives from medieval to modern literature, analyzing plots as diverse as Milton's *Comus*, Brontë's *Jane Eyre*, and Hawthorne's *Scarlet Letter* in terms of Callisto's degradation from priestess of Artemis, through rape, to bear and eventually the constellation Ursa Major. In the classical narrative, Callisto (who as Artemis Calliste is sometimes conflated with Artemis herself) is approached by Zeus disguised as Artemis and makes love with him (the implications of this for women loving women are fascinating: Callisto only makes love to Zeus because she thinks he is Artemis.) Wall cites a number of authorities who suggest that Callisto is actually Artemis herself, including Pausanias, "whose description of the site of Callisto's grave and Diana's temple strongly suggests that Callisto was a local, Arcadian aspect of the virgin goddess," and William Sherwood Fox, who, using "both internal evidence and information about the cult of Artemis specific to Arcadia, writes that "in Arkadia the bear was an animal sacred to Artemis, one of whose cult-titles was Kalliste, a name which could readily be worked over into Kallisto. Kallisto, then, both maiden and bear, was none other than Artemis herself" (13–14). Wall posits the classical Callisto stories as a degradation of the Hieros Gamos or sacred celebrations of intercourse. Certainly the young huntress and devotee of the sexually self-determining Artemis is degraded by Zeus's seduction.

The final archetypal question which I want to raise in this volume has to do with the way animistic instincts or healthy pagan stirrings toward harmony with nature spring up within Eurocentric poets when they evoke the bear archetype. I also want to query the relationship between bears and goddess archetypes, not only Artemis as bear goddess but also the Hecate factor latent in Artemis, in order to suggest analogies between these powerful feminine bear archetypes and fiery Ishtar, African Oya, and Celtic holy hag. The bear archetype, which in some European folklore traditions is specifically associated with Medusa, brings this volume full circle, back to the frightening but maternal archetype as vehicle of awesome feminine power.

We have seen that although the Aphrodite archetype seems to contain traces of an authentic feminine eroticism which subverts cultural norms forbidding sexuality for women, it often becomes entangled with patriarchal signatures. When poets write about bears, the bears resist similar subversion by Christian or Eurocentric signatures, rarely "standing for" human qualities, almost never approached as humans in bears' clothing. The pagan and pre-Christian content of the bear archetype seems so powerful that it retains its animistic integrity within patriarchy even more easily than do goddess archetypes.

I had originally thought that Canadian poems would approach the bear as bear, while U.S. and British poems (particularly those by men) would differ significantly along gender lines. Surely, I thought, the hostile patriarchal view of women and nature as "other" would infect twentieth-century male poets in England and the United States, subverting the archetype's deep background, so that there would be marked differences between male and female poets' attitudes to bears. That is not what the poems demonstrated. As in the case of each archetype I have studied thus far, poems about bears can be arranged along an attitudinal scale from loathing to reverence. Whether the bear is the object of a traditional hunt or is to be pitied for being caged in a zoo, whether the bear is approached for its erotic, natural, or godlike powers, many poems by men and women in England and the United States as well as in Canada revere bears as animate beings in their own right and not as anthropomorphosed vehicles for human qualities.

The Wrong Way to Go on a Bear Hunt

In the United States, as in Canada, there are enough real bears running around to be threatening and to make the quest to kill them a frequent subject. (Abraham Lincoln wrote a poem, "The Bear Hunt," in which he celebrated "a wild-bear chace" as a source of "glorious glee" [Newman and Suk, inscription]). Sometimes U.S. male poets writing about bears approach them with as much violence and loathing as the most gynophobic of poets disgusted with Medusa or Venus: it is not coincidental that such poems, at the pathological end of the bear archetypal continuum, combine disgust for women and violence against bears. In the first line of "The Poem of the Year of the Bear," Russell Banks calls a bear "the bastard," and goes on to depict it as a disgusting and unreliable deviant who is attracted to "the smell of teen-aged cunt." Having degraded both the bear and women's bodies, Banks identifies with the bear as somebody who has "got to squat and talk about it / with these serious young ladies from Ohio" (94–95). His quest for the bear fails because he associates its bodiliness with aspects of feminine generativity which he cannot handle.

When male poets get wind of Native American bear hunting rituals, they can go in for the white shamanism deplored by Wendy Rose (see chapter 10), appropriating bits and pieces of Native American ritual and lore in poems which some Native Americans consider spiritually abusive. In "The Bear," for example, Galway Kinnell is both self-congratulatory and self-disgusted, using the persona of a shamanistic bear hunter. He does not ask permission of the bear to kill it, survives by eating bear turd, and hacks the bear open to crawl inside it, betraying disrespect for both himself and the bear. No Native American shaman could declare a bear's eyes "petty" or its smell an "ordinary, wretched odor," and if his ritual called for eating the bear he would conduct himself with reverence rather than loathing for both the bear and himself. However dissociated from the bear, Native American practice, and his own instincts Kinnell may be, he seems to be punishing himself for his incorrect approach to the archetype: as in the case of Banks, he conveys self-satire, which admits his unhealthy relationship to nature.

Gary Snyder (whose dissertation on Haida myth ought to have taught him better bear manners) childishly declares his intention in "this poem is for bear" to "sneak up on the bear" so "It will grunt and run," and descends to an insulting levity (*Myths and Texts* 23). His tone and manner are entirely inappropriate to the shamanic persona he expropriates here and in his 1960 "Shaman Songs." As in the case of Banks, disrespect for bears and women make this poem insulting to Snyder's Haida informants. We have seen how, at this period in his poetry, Snyder loathes both young girls (especially menstruating ones) and goddesses. In later poems, such as "The Way West, Underground" (1974), Snyder achieves a more respectful attitude to bears (though not to women). By the time of his 1990 essay collection, *The Practice of the Wild*, however, Snyder has transcended both gynophobia and androcentrism, withdrawn projections from women, and recognized that we are animals that communicate with other natural beings in a linguistic field:

> The world is watching: one cannot walk through a meadow or forest without a ripple of report spreading out from one's passage. The thrush darts back, the jay squalls, a beetle scuttles under the grasses, and the signal is passed along. Every creature knows when a hawk is cruising or a human strolling. The information passed through the system is intelligence. (19)

To the extent that he relies heavily on Native American concepts for this theory, however, Snyder is still practicing white shamanism.

We find the same kind of disrespect for bears in the Canadian poet Séan Virgo's "Shaman's Song" as in Snyder's early poems. Virgo supposedly adapts Kishkatenaw sources, in which he takes the persona of a shaman whose attitude about burrowing into the she bear's den to copulate with her is smug and self-congratulatory: "she cries tears / upon my shoulder / Because it is so good" (96–97). Although Virgo's prurient "translations" are the exception to the way most contemporary Canadian poets approach bears or Native Peoples, it will be recalled that his attitude to Venus was one of Victorian disgust. Daryl Hine provides a similar case of a Canadian male poet who found it hard to cope with Medusa (see chapter 3) and who, in "A Tour in the Forest," approaches bears and other animals with a medieval distaste: he finds their woodlands full of "Desire, an unreflecting dusk" and feels alienated from their "forest loneliness and gloom," where only criminals and "Animals not you and I / Lie beneath the evergreens" (22–23). My hypothesis is that these male poets who fail to respect bears and nature are also unable to deal with their feelings about women.

Using the ending of Snyder's "this poem is for bear" as an example, John Elder has suggested that this kind of disrespect represents "an admission, I believe, of the distance separating Snyder and his society from the sacramental unity of Native American Culture." Elder sees Snyder's attempts at "synthesis in his own life between Native American theology and Buddhism" as a positive factor: "Native American vision, like the Dharma, may be transmitted and developed in cultural contexts different from its origins" (45). He nonetheless reads "this poem is for bear" as unsuccessful because Snyder has not first embedded himself in his own culture, in contrast, for example, to farmer-poet Wendell Berry: "One must become, as

Berry suggests in the title to his most recent book of poems, A Part of the earth, not a calculating consciousness held *apart* by its own individuality" (52). Although Elder reads disparity between Berry and Snyder in terms of the difference "between poets who have fed on a certain kind of destructiveness for their creative glow . . . as against those who have 'composted' themselves to become richer and stronger, like Wendell Berry," I would posit the respect Berry has for women as an important element in this difference. It is also possible that Berry's persona as farmer provides him an authentic natural or pagan self of the kind Snyder must borrow from his Native American sources.

Walking with Bears

Bears figure in many poems in which the poet is trying to come to terms with his or her own instincts. It is as if the animism attributed by Piaget to an immature, precognitive childhood state were recognized by these poets as a quality crucial in adulthood. The popularity of fairy tales throughout European history suggests one way in which adults (for whom they were originally written) could continue to get in touch with animistic feelings. The widespread popularity of fairy tales in the Victorian age certainly suggests some attempt at compensation for its concerted attacks on instinct. Like Keats's Endymion, fairy tale heroes like Snow White and Beauty learn to accept the instinctive side of the human personality, which is clearly conceived of as a good.

In twentieth-century poems, bear archetypes convey instincts which human beings need to get in touch with. These poems are animistic in the sense of taking the world of the unconscious as extended between human beings and nature, a field of energy connecting the human community to its natural habitat. Such a world is not a childish state to be grown out of, in Piaget's sense, but a necessary state of mind for poetic inspiration. I disagree with Bruno Bettelheim, who, even as he notes the value of fairy tales in helping children experience the unconscious and preconscious, defines them as merely internal symbols or subjective projections:

> Both dangerous and helpful animals *stand for* our animal nature, our instinctual drives. The dangerous ones *symbolize* the untamed id, not

yet subjected to ego and superego control, in all its dangerous energy. The helpful animals *represent* our natural energy—again the id—but now made to serve the best interests of the personality. There are also some animals, usually white birds such as doves, which *symbolize* the superego. (76; italics mine)

In light of my study of the erotic content of the Aphrodite archetype, Bettelheim's association of doves with the superego is an especially striking example of the way Christian sublimations (in this case, of the earthy bird goddess into emblems standing in for the "holy spirit" of the trinity) can infect an archetype's pagan content. Although I agree with Bettelheim's theory that fairy tale animals get us in touch with our instincts, I do not interpret bear archetypes as merely subjective; rather, they interact with our instincts as elements in a field of mutually communicating beings.

We have seen that poets do not always achieve a comfortable rapport with bear archetypes. Delmore Schwartz, for example, in "The Heavy Bear Who Goes with Me," deplores "that inescapable animal [that] walks with me, / [which] Has followed me since the black womb held," a "stupid clown" and "swollen shadow." Schwartz's diction demonstrates an instinctual imbalance, a condition which also alienates him from his lover (64). Although he declares himself unable to deal with "The scrimmage of appetite" within himself, the intensity of Schwartz's despair attests to the power of the instincts the bear archetype stirs up.

There are many poems, in contrast, which treat the bear as a being in its own (implicitly nonhuman) right with which the poet tries to get in touch. In Yvor Winters's "Quod Tegit Omnia," for example, "the bear comes forth" in a notion parallel to "the mind, stored with / magnificence," which proceeds "into / the mystery of Time." In such poems the bear is simultaneously "out there" in nature and "in here" within the individual psyche, by no means a mere human projection.

Many poets describe a bear which is caged, trapped, dancing at the end of a chain, or otherwise at odds with its natural state, expressing the poet's rebellion against cultural norms. My hypothesis is that these poets are not merely using bears as metaphors but reaching out to real bears to get in balance with human instincts which society represses. Thus in "Dark Song" Edith Sitwell assumes the persona of "the maid," who sits by the fire, "furry as a bear," and mourns "the brown bear," "Captive to cruel men." Far from reducing the bear to an allegorical emblem, Sitwell recognizes its instinctive vitality lacking in her own life by fantasizing a metamorphosis in which she becomes the rambler in the dark woods.

| *Talking with Bears* | I have described how getting into a right relationship with the Canadian landscape so often endows poets with new inspirations (see chapter 3); once in touch with bears, Canadians |

become linguistically regenerated. Thus John Thompson celebrates animals rising up out of the earth in "The Bread Hot from the Oven," and includes "two bears [that] burn the dawn . . . that I feel as words I do not know, / of immense weight" (345). This sense that the bears contain a verbal tangibility is analogous to the Celtic sense of words as organic and of nature as speaking its own language. Thompson feels the bears and deer as an "immense weight" of words, words not spoken by humans, which are elements in a field of communication shared with animals and trees.

In Margaret Atwood's characterization in "Night Bear Which Frightened Cattle," the bear appears in one of Susanna Moodie's dreams as "real, heavier / than real," its weightiness creating "a mute vibration" (*Journals* 38–39). Atwood depicts Moodie's dream as communicating a reality outside human consciousness which nevertheless produces a resonance available to the poet. Robertson Davies, in his novel *The Rebel Angels*, describes a Gypsy's "Bear Chant" as constructed of both human and ursine elements: this is

the music Gypsy bear-leaders played or sang to their animals. . . . How would one talk to a bear which could kill? How would one ask it for friendship? How would one invite its wisdom, which is so unlike the wisdom of a man, but not impenetrable by a man? This is what the Bear Chant seemed to be—music that moved slowly, with long interrogative pauses, and unusual demands on that low, guttural voice of the fiddle, which is so rarely heard in the kind of music I understand and enjoy. *Croak—croak*; tell me, Brother Martin, how is it with you?

What do you see? What do you hear? And then: *Grunt—grunt*,
Brother Martin (for all Gypsy bears are called Martin) says his pro-
found say. (133)

Given recent discoveries about the love songs that whales sing to each
other and the complex communication of dolphins, Davies's analysis
of the old Gypsy fiddle tunes seems considerably less unlikely.

One of the most complex poems about a quest for the bear which
endows the poet both with its palpable presence and with linguistic
empowerment is Canadian poet Dennis Lee's "The Gods." In an
earlier poem, "The Coming of Teddy Bears," Lee expresses the child-
hood harmony with "teams of fuzzy / Teddy bears" who had helped
him sleep as a child, but in "Gods" he moves into a far more dangerous
and adult realm of ursine empowerment. By "Gods" he understands
the immanent beings more characteristic of native religions than of
transcendent Christian deities: "their strokes and carnal voltage, / old
ripples of presence" which he at first mourns as lost to most of us, for
whom "the tickle of the cosmos is gone." The similarity between Lee's
and Dylan Thomas's concept of the nonhuman universe as palpable
and communicative suggests an interesting link between Celtic and
Canadian naturism. Lee's symbolism is especially Canadian, however,
in his choice of the bear as a "random example" of what a "god" might
be like. Lee recognizes that human beings may be destroyed by the
force latent in the bear archetype but that we can only ignore it at the
price of our instincts and our relationship to nature (371–74).

Bear Lovers

Bruno Bettelheim has noted that the story of
the animal groom or animal bride "is so popular
worldwide that probably no other fairy-tale
theme has so many variations" (283). In these
stories, as we have seen in the case of both Native American and
European archetypal narratives, a young girl takes an animal husband
or a young man takes an animal bride. Many poems show how, by a
right approach to the bear, a poet can achieve sexual maturity. There
are some male poets who retain the medieval association of bears with
lust but learn to accept both lust and bear. William Heyen, in "The
Bear," depicts himself following the "musky, rutting smell" of a bear to

"its spring lair," where it guards a woman he makes love to, while "the enraged bear [stood] guard / beside her bed." While he makes love he turns into a bear himself (58). For Canadian poet bill bissett the bear is also associated with lust and sex, in an orgy held in the bear's mouth: thousands of people "wer fucking endlessly in / side th great mouth uv / th bear," a celebration which has cosmic dimensions, bear and lovers alike "lit by the galaxes" (106). I do not read these raunchy male poems about bears and lovemaking as exploitative of women. When Earl Birney identifies his lover with a bear, as well as with "a sturdy racoon," "a shy bobcat," an "ochre/squirrel," and "an arkfull she is / of undulant creatures," I do not see him degrading her but celebrating their mutual pleasure (*Collected Poems* 176).

Women poets like Edith Sitwell seek instinctual regeneration through the bear. Judith Rose announces, "I would embrace the bear," and even though frightened by "the coldness of his breath" and "his sleep face mask," she insists that she trusts "his roundness" and gets ready for the embrace as "with drowsy fulfillment / he lumbers toward me." (32); and Janet Beeler ponders "this great grey bear / stinking of fish and mud, this enormous longing / feeding on my dreams each night" (46). Like Heyen, Paula Goff finds her bear wandering as a potential lover in the city streets, and, simultaneously, "running loose / In my past." She must "go back" to the place in her life where "the white bear is lost," running cold and afraid through the city. She tells herself, "I know nothing of bears," and "I came here unexpectedly from my bed," wearing a white nightgown and trying to figure out what "can I do for this creature?" (43). These are, in a sense, all "inner bears," the bear archetype calling up bearlike but subjectively human instincts; however, none of these bear poems posits its bears as merely anthropomorphic. I do not read these poems as reducing real bears that walk the earth to vehicles for merely human emotions: when a poet invokes the archetype, its nonhuman and strictly ursine powers awaken with it. Poets who have been exposed to Native American theologies recognize the analogues between Native American bear archetypes and these long-forgotten pagan repositories, which do not lie so very deeply, after all, beneath the surface of the lives of those of us who are of European descent. This is why some poets who start off on their bear quests inspired by Native American archetypes quickly shift to paths more familiar to them and to those in their audience who are not Native American.

The bear poems I have studied in this chapter take a parallel quest to that which Native Americans experience in dreams and on vision quests, which Hallowell describes as the "means by which it was possible to enter into direct social interaction with persons of the other-than-human class" (171). As Paula Gunn Allen puts it, "the American Indian perceives all that exists as symbolic." "An Indian," she asserts, "at the deepest level of being, assumes that the earth is alive in the same sense that human beings are alive," but "this attitude is not anthropomorphic. No Indian would regard personal perception as the basic, or only, unit of universal consciousness" (*Sacred Hoop* 70).

Critics more wed to Enlightenment European thinking than I am will argue that these bear poems are products only of the human mind and that to define the human mind as one among other communicants in a natural field of being is mere wishful thinking. In the last analysis, my readings indeed derive from what I have come to believe about the relationship between human beings and the earth. In the brief conclusion which follows this chapter, I will explain my conviction that a choice between anthropocentric and animistic beliefs structures ethical choices which impact upon the future of the planet.

As environmental degradation increases and the ozone is rent over large sections of the United States, Canada, and Europe, Native American and Europagan ethics, with their reverence for the earth, are direly needed. Writing about women and nature, Susan Griffin captures the fellowship of these two natural theologies:

> And so it is Goldilocks who goes to the home of the three bears, Little Red Riding Hood who converses with the wolf, Dorothy who befriends a lion, Snow White who talks to the birds, Cinderella with mice as her allies, the Mermaid who is half fish, Thumbelina courted by a mole. (And when we hear in the Navaho chant of the mountain that a grown man sits and smokes with bears and follows directions given to him by squirrels, we are surprised. We had thought only little girls spoke with animals). (1)

Like the fairy tales and Navaho chant Griffin cites, poems governed by the bear lover archetype demonstrate how, by a right approach to the bear and a coming to terms with his or her sexuality, a poet can achieve a harmonious relationship to real bears and the real earth.

The Bear Mother

It is striking that Jung called up a bear archetype indigenous to Switzerland, the old Celtic Artio served by priestesses during the high years of Celtic civilization, in order to describe his relationship to his mother. In his recollections of his childhood, he recalls that during the daytime he perceived her as bearlike, in a nurturing and friendly fashion; at night, however, "she seemed uncanny. Then she was like one of those seers who is at the same time a strange animal, like a priestess in a bear's cave. Archaic and ruthless; ruthless as truth and nature. At such moments she was the embodiment of what I have called the 'natural' mind." As Demaris Wehr points out with reference to Jung's "paranormal" feelings about his mother, Jung spend much of his professional life trying to posit the self in balance between the "normal" and the "paranormal," locating the ability to achieve such balance not in a transcendent superego nor even in the rational ego but in a self which could mediate between these "human" qualities and the natural world (Jung, *Memories* 105, as cited in Wehr 30). His anthropomorphic assumption that the objective world could be internalized and transformed into subjective experience never quite overshadowed his sense that people like his mother had access to a world in which human and animal instincts were blended, whose deep background, in my hypothesis, was in pagan eras antedating Swiss-German culture.

For both Eurocentric and Native American poets, the bear remains an unpredictable and dangerous archetype, conveying an uncontrollable force in nature. It will be recalled that poets' ability to deal with childhood memories of the overwhelming power of the mother determines their success in approaching both Medusa and Aphrodite, and that only when their projections of terror and disgust are withdrawn can they celebrate both their own sensuality and nature's power. When poets approach the bear they are in the same kind of psychological peril as when they approach goddesses, and in their frequent quests to the dens of bears, many of the same rules apply. Animal archetypes like the bear seem to contain especially powerful doses of natural energy, undoubtedly because they lack the human associations that accompany even Artemis at her wildest. In their dangerousness they resemble the hurricane and tornado goddess

African American poets invoke, as well as the Hecate attributes of wise women and crones presiding over birth and death.

Poets who associate extremely wild and distinctly nonanthropomorphic bears with their ancestors, more recent relatives, and even with their own mothers, may be inspired by Native American archetypes, but they transcend white shamanism by focusing on Europagan bear archetypes lurking in their own indigenous backgrounds. Thus, for but one example, we find American poet Janet Beeler, in "Considerations on Indo-European Culture," getting in touch with "women whom I remember / without any words at all" by considering the Indo-European roots of "the words for salmon / for birch tree / for willow / for wolf and bear." Through the words for natural phenomena she gets in touch with powerful ancestral women "carrying on your hips / clinging bear babies / leaping salmon babies":

> lying down in the tawny dusk
> salmon babies at the breast
>
> bear babies at the breast
> warm belly beds
> for all the naked babies
>
> nothing but skin between you
> and all your skin the same skin
> all smoky all downy all brown
>
> all your words the same words
> for birch and salmon and bear (53)

As in the case of many Canadian poets, Beeler's bear carries her into a realm of solid physicality and bodily regeneration, an energy field where human and non-human interact.

Beeler's human women nursing bears suggest her acquaintance with cultures (like the modern Ainu) in which sacred bears are suckled by human mothers. A number of poets, both male and female, conflate the archetype of the wild bear with elements of their own feelings about their mothers. These bear mother and bear grandmother poems resemble poems structured upon a poet's fearful approach to an awesome Medusa, but the essential animality of the bear renders them more frightening and, paradoxically, more familiar, as if we were much more closely acquainted with bears than with classical Gorgons. They are "dark mothers" closer to the hearts of poets of European derivation, which, like goddess archetypes, test our psychological maturity.

In "The Bear Sisters" the Canadian poet Rikki writes about her dying grandmother metaphorically in a way that borders on the metamorphic. As the grandmother is dying she orders the poet to find her treasures out in her shed, reminding Rikki of "A great befuddled bear" who "bumped around upstairs" cursing her fatness and telling her how conventionally slender she had been as a girl. Rikki's poem is about a bear grandmother whose physical pride has been undermined by her longing for a slender human image, a woman who is out of touch with her fleshly ursine being: "My grandmother—that great blind bear / Who near the end hid the mirrors / Afraid to see her body gone bad" (27). Although the grandmother is fixated on contemporary norms of feminine beauty, her poet granddaughter metamorphically shape-changes her into a bear to affirm her power.

Judith McCombs, similarly, perceives her mother as a bear victimized by patriarchy in "The Man," in which she witnesses a maternal bear killed by men who are following the principle of "dominion over every living thing." Their victim is "the black furry mass of the bear" who "sits on her haunches, back to a stump, / an ancient, massive, dog-nosed brute / pawing the dogs / who yap & skitter away" while McCombs remembers

> (My mother's mother, huge in her dress
> sits in the creek, swatting the water & laughing)
> She is warm, stupid; she smells of bear
> an abundance of flesh, stumpy limbs
> stone of a head & little pig ears
> teats where she rears, in the black close fur
> She smells like my mother
> my mother's mother
> she does not understand
> she won't get away.

McCombs conflates her mother-as-bear and grandmother-as-bear, presenting the latter as much more positive about her animality than Rikki's self-hating grandmother, but nevertheless about to be victimized. As they move in for the kill the bear "rears, paws, shakes her head & its wattles of fur / thinking she's won" but her body is "hung, dressed, weighed on accurate scales" having provided "the thrill of a lifetime" to the hunters (76–77).

Rikki and McCombs are engaged in the naming of their mothers' victimization that we identified as such a crucial step for women poets as they learn to remove projections of fear and loathing from their mothers in the process of maturation. As in the case of poems about Medusa, both men and women engage with the bear mother archetype, though even in respectful approaches there are significant gender differences. Thus James Wright, in "March," writes about the emergence of a mother bear who has been hibernating and giving birth under the snow:

> When the wind opens its doors
> In its own good time,
> The cubs follow that relaxed and beautiful
> woman. (23)

I do not read Wright's maternal bear as turned into a beautiful woman from a beast in the animal bride manner; rather, I think that he is identifying with the cubs for whom she is the protector and all-powerful maternal being. There is a definite distance, nonetheless, between male poet and maternal bear: he witnesses her hibernation, birth giving, and emergence, but he does not participate in it sensually. So, too, W. M. Ransom writes of a dream in which a white woman and four brown bears come forward to where "We bowed in a ritual I did not know I knew" before a figure which interbraids the woman and the bear who "lumbers up the hill, low to the ground. . . . Tonight she comes for me" (31). Although a close, physical engagement is implied at the end, it is implicitly threatening; and although the poet is much closer to the bear and her bear smell than Wright, she is still, whether bear or golden-breasted human woman, "other" to the poet.

Two poems by women with which I want to conclude our bear quest display a much more intimate physical relationship with the maternal bear. The first, by Judith Johnson Sherwin, is about a ritual dance with a bear. The bear is "a great Female Bear" who teaches the poet a dance which empties her out and then lays her "bare to love," if only she will "let the old She Bear lie / down and hold you in Her arms" (115). This immensely threatening bear embodies all the danger of her species simultaneously with all that we are terrified of in our own mothers, and invites us into a dance of life which may involve being flayed alive by the power of our mothers' darkness. The threat of the Medusa and of the maternal terror she embodies in poems by women about their mothers is fully present, but Sherwin faces up to them in adventuring to a bear den, expecting empowerment. The immediacy of such a poem derives from our much greater affinity with the bear than with the Medusa archetype.

In a less terrifying but equally courageous approach to the maternal power of the bear archetype, Mary Oliver, in "Winter Sleep," lies down with a she-bear to hibernate together for the winter, like "Two old sisters familiar to each other" who "begin to breathe together—." Through imagining hibernating with the bear, Oliver is able to enter into a place of instinctual calm, feminine intimacy, and oneness with nature. The outcome of her hibernation is poetic empowerment arising from her archetypal courage. Like so many who achieve this special, calm inner strength through right approach to goddess or bear archetypes, Oliver delves beneath language to a tactile, sensually specific harmony with nature. Or, as she puts it in "Wild Geese,"

> You do not have to be good.
> You do not have to walk on your knees
> for a hundred miles through the desert, repenting.
> You only have to let the soft animal of your body
>   love what it loves. (14)

And it is really a very simple thing—to accept ourselves as animals in harmony with a planet where we are entirely and happily at home.

Conclusion

In the course of studying archetypal patterns in poetry by men and women in the United States, Britain, and Canada, I have redefined archetypes as elements in an interwoven matrix comprising earth, human beings, animals, and other living creatures and plants. Not only in Native American poetry but also in the deep pagan background of European and North American archetypes, the planet's inhabitants seem to be communicating with each other in a way analogous to the "Gaia hypothesis," a recent scientific concept that the earth is an interactive, interdependent gestalt of life forms.

My hypothesis, which is a very old one indeed, deviates from the traditional assumption of many European and North American intellectuals that the human mind can and should "master" nature. Poetry demonstrates how belief in this idea can be unhealthy for human beings and other living things, producing individual suffering, devasting historical conflict, and ecological degradation. Developing this archetypal hypothesis in the 1980s was made difficult for me by academic fashions which promulgated the mind-over-matter view of the earth. Theories about the supremacy of the human mind posited words as not only superior to all objective phenomena but also their source: the words for your life, your gender, and nature took primacy over their actuality, so that it was "subjective" to trust your own experience, "essentialist" to pay attention to gender, and "sentimental" to love nature.

Writing archetypal criticism in the 1980s thus did not win me any academic popularity contests, and my fellow feminist scholars, as well, were wary of the approach I was taking. The mere word *archetype* often aroused strong emotions, as if in using it we feminist literary critics were besmirching our reputations by association with the patriarchal and even defamatory behavior of other archetypalists. I particularly remember one Modern Language Association business meeting, where we were setting up panels for the following year, when a colleague with whom I was on perfectly friendly terms arose to denounce our use of *archetype* in the title of the session we were planning. She assumed that if we used the term, even in a feminist critical argument, we were identifying ourselves as obedient disciples of Carl Gustav Jung, Northrop Frye, or Joseph Campbell. If we incorporated elements of their thinking into our theory, this argument ran, our findings must inevitably be tainted.

This accusation might not have been made had not academic theory making taken on a disturbingly authoritarian flavor during the 1980s. Colleagues willingly subjected themselves as obedient disciples to one or another theorist, and then, having positioned themselves in his camp and learned its secret codes, poured down scorn upon anyone who questioned his "doctrines." My colleagues began to "position themselves" and then to flail away against each other and against rival schools of thought. By the mid-1980s the graduate students trained in these tactics had become tense and wan, and often mute. It seemed to me that the best of them were suffering from shell shock, stunned into silence by fierce combat in seminars and classrooms, and that the worst were full of the passionate intensity required to keep sharpening their intellects as weapons against each other. Even our undergraduate classrooms were becoming judgmental shockboxes which students feared to enter, rather than fields of thought where hypotheses could be tossed about and experimented with in the unconstrained and playful manner necessary for fresh intellectual ideas to flourish. As an alternative to the model of classroom as combat zone and out of my conviction that cognition cannot take place in an interrupt-and-attack classroom where intellectual growth is blocked by the powerful emotions of fright and flight, I developed the method of nonviolent pedagogy which will be the subject of my next book.

Theoretical positions are not value free: at the last trump, whether we go with the hypothesis of anthropocentric determinism or whether we agree that we share our field of dreams with other beings is a matter of personal belief. But have my eco-feminist value system and my pagan theology skewed my results? During our quest through archetypal patterns in poetry we caught sight of a relationship between our selves and the earth markedly different from the presumption that we can and should take power over nature and that our minds are constructed to that end. Though I am certainly vulnerable to accusations of filling out my archetypal theory in colors from my personal paintbox, I hope to have demonstrated that my inductions are not merely subjective deductions from what I had already decided about the universe before I wrote this book, but are viable hypotheses supported by more than four hundred poems.

And what do we know about the human mind, about the brain and the process of cognition? Very little, much less than we know about most of our other bodily functions. Although we have been dreaming for many thousands of years and our mammal ancestors dreamt before us, neither science nor psychoanalysis has revealed much about these complex archetypal landscapes which all of us adventure through every night. Poetry is analogous to controlled dreaming, with poetry like those dreams we enter into and use our intelligence and emotional courage to experience and comprehend. The poet filters archetypal symbols and stories into consciousness and structures them as oral or written forms. Does this literary construction arise only from the individual, or can it be defined as merely the ideological script which the poet has unwittingly internalized? Are there other layers latent in the poetic symbol not derived from the contemporary historical signature? Are elements of premodern and even apatriarchal signatures embedded in archetypes? These are the questions I have addressed as a feminist archetypal theorist concerned with the way poetry works for the human psyche and with the implications of this for the future of the earth.

The word *theory* derives from a Greek term meaning "a speculation, a beholding." We can define theory as a contemplation of material resulting in a description, categorization, and positing of hypotheses about it. In Greek antiquity an alternate connotation associated theory with Theors, celebrants hired by the state to perform a religious ritual. From the first rumblings of what was to come in the late 1970s, I was bemused by the archaic religious vocabulary used by even my most secularized academic colleagues, who proceeded to flail away at each other using such terms as "dogma," "canon," "exegesis," "rubric," and "heresy" as if the Enlightenment had never taken place. Out of a valid concern not to be fooled by cultural norms embedded in literary texts, critics used archaic Theor vocabulary to unmask the tricky Theors whom they suspected of encoding their ideological norms in literature. This activity often took the form of rebellion against authority, while intellectual adrenalin poured out in a fraught atmosphere reminiscent of one's adolescent feuds with one's parents. At the same time a tendency to obey the authority of theoretical fathers become prevalent in an atmosphere hauntingly similar to the outcome of Orwell's *1984*, where the Theor O'Brien says to Winston after torturing him into conformity: "you believe that reality is something objective, external, existing in its own right. . . . But I tell you, Winston, that reality is not external. Reality exists in the human mind, and nowhere else."

By 1990 academic arguments about theory were raging in circles, without any closure or outcome. It was clear that turf was being defended but no lands occupied and that finding new worlds of being was less important than sustaining the battles about the old ones. I could not see the dialectics leading to syntheses nor the deconstructions to constructions of worlds preferable to those under attack.

Pedagogically speaking, it seemed to me that both my colleagues and the graduate students they were training in these methods exhibited a tendency to become stuck in the second stage of cognitive development, the one that usually occurs during the freshman or sophomore year when you realize that there is no single truth which explains everything (see Perry, and Downing and Roush.) At this stage students go in for a jaded kind of relativism, which in my undergraduate days in the 1950s took the form of a world-weary stance of existential cynicism and the wearing of black turtlenecks. As I recall, beneath our turtlenecks beat very anxious hearts indeed, frantic that with our brilliant intellects we had cut the ground out from under our own feet. We scrawled the question WHY? on our dormitory doors, but the anxiety of meaninglessness left us ripe for recruitment by whatever ideological Theors might happen along.

I think that the paradoxically hegemonic relativism which characterized literary theorists in the 1980s sprang from a similar anxiety of meaninglessness, from which it was comfortable to lapse into disciple-Theor obedience. The allure of dogmatic antidogmatism is that you can keep on eating your authoritarian cake while sounding brilliantly iconoclastic too. Authentic intellectual development requires you to transcend both authority and rebellion against it to take the next steps in cognition. Nancy Downing and her colleagues (using a model originally developed by Cross to describe African American students' progress from passive acceptance to ethical commitment) suggest that the stage of revelation when you encounter relativism and critique culture is followed by a period of "immersion" or "embeddedness" when you reconnect with the empowering elements of your ethnic and gender background. Having developed a position from within that particularity, we learn to understand it as one among a variety of possible stances. Accepting our theories and values while empathizing with other peoples' different choices, we move on to seek coalitions to work together for the common good.

The idea that it is intellectually unsophisticated to choose values to act upon from among competing truths is enormously helpful to any Theors in the vicinity who seek to control us. This "doctrine" prevented many of the best and brightest feminist intellectuals of the 1980s from organizing in behalf of themselves, other women, or the planet, a situation from which two Republican administrations trying to return us to the economics and social ethics of the nineteenth century benefited enormously.

In this book I have suggested that it is when poets think that they are locked inside their own minds, isolated within their subjectivity, that their poetry displays a deterioration in their relationships to other people and to nature. From my study of Aphrodite I concluded that archetypes are not subjective, resident only in the individual brain, but transactive elements interrelating in a field. When poets accept that other people are endowed with equal being as themselves and that the earth is a complex, stunning reality, both their dysfunctional relationships and their violence against nature diminishes. From the evidence of the hundreds of poems I have studied and the lived experience of the poets who wrote them, it also appears that gender differences are not, in and of themselves, destructive to a poet's psyche; that a woman poet approaches female archetypes like Medusa as same while a male poet approaches them as different is not a problem until one sex attributes lesser being to the other and presumes that a power/over relationship is natural.

From the poems about Artemis I came to my hypothesis that when we define the unconscious as more collective than subjective, more interactive than projective, we arrive at a definition of an archetypal field where earth, human beings, animals, and other living creatures interact in a matrix with archetypes as means of communication.

Conclusion

Poets who perceive archetypes in this way engage the readers' pleasure in aesthetic form, imagery, and music as a way of nudging us toward psychological health and ecological renewal.

In suggesting that archetypes interact in fields and that the archetypal narratives structuring poems are maps of physical and psychological health, am I not indulging in naive assumptions about the inherent value of such symbols? Aren't archetypal symbols often used for evil ends, as in the case of the swastika or of the appeal of Wagnerian narrations to the Nazi movement, not to mention the exploitation of love-goddess stereotypes to promote the objectification and sexual torture of women? It should be evident by this point that archetypes are powerful psychosocial forces capable of unleashing destructive as well as constructive personal and social events. Abjecting oneself before a god or goddess who gives one permission to do violence not only to one's enemies but also to one's individuality is an example of an evil use of archetypes to validate power/over relationships. In a less frightening but insidious way, the advertising industry has devised sophisticated methods for quantifying the instinctive response to archetypes by fastening sensors to the surface of our skin which measure our galvanic reaction to especially appealing images. Whether they are used for commercial, social, military, or religious ends, archetypes can drag us in the opposite direction from personal, social, and environmental renewal. They are nonetheless in and of themselves value free, usable, like dynamite, either for good or ill. We ignore their existence at our peril.

Life, as Aristotle once reminded us, is not a quality but a mode of action. Literature, as I read and teach it, is a means toward ethical choice. Contemporary Theors cannot control our psyches unless we give them permission. We do not read and teach literature in order to escape from the real world any more than we would choose to remain for our whole lives in the world of dreams: poetry and dreams are means to ends we must choose, maps for each of us to determine the path we will walk in our brief time upon the earth.

Poetry, which often knows better than prose, can be read simultaneously backward and forward, backward to cultures which had better ways of relating to each other and to the earth than we have recently valued and forward into alternative paradigms. Those of us who are of European ancestry assume that we must either accept the isolation of consciousness and stoically endure the angst proffered by

374

modernism, existentialism, and "postmodernism" or try to turn our-selves into somebody else by raiding non-European belief systems. But if our education has deprived us of the knowledge of Europagan archetypes, there is nothing to keep us from researching our ancestors' wisdom and reembedding ourselves in it.

What about those of us whose ancestors colonized North America and attempted to eradicate its indigenous cultures? Are we not exiles caught between two worlds—the lands of our ancestral past and the land we inhabit as conquerors? I think that we who live in the United States can learn a valuable lesson from our Canadian neighbors, whose literature demonstrates the way landscape contributes to the archetypal matrix, interbraiding its features with Canadian poets' personal and European signatures. The way the earth is moving along just now, we have much in common with our fellow beings upon it. If we listen to what the earth is trying to say to us, we can dwell in the land, no longer exiles from somewhere else but here at last, attuned, in harmony.

Notes

1. The Other Side of a Mirror

1. Sources noted on the chart in addition to those appearing in Works Cited are George Emmanuel Mylonas, "Religion in Prehistoric Greece," in Vergilius T. A. Ferm, ed., *Forgotten Religions* (Freeport, N.Y.: Philosophical Library, 1950); Sir Arthur Evans, *The Palace of Minos*, 4 vols. (London: Macmillan, 1922–37); James Mellaart, *Earliest Civilizations of the Near East* (London: Thames and Hudson, 1965), and *Çatal Hüyük* (London: Thames and Hudson, 1967); and Stephen S. Langdon, *The Sumerian Epic of Paradise* (Philadelphia: University of Pennsylvania Press, 1915), and *Tammuz and Ishtar* (London: Oxford University Press, 1914).

2. See Sir Arthur Evans, *The Palace of Knossos* (London: Macmillan, 1936); R. W. Hutchinson, *Prehistoric Crete* (Harmondsworth, Middlesex: Penguin Books, 1963); H. E. L. Mellersh, *The Destruction of Knossos: The Rise and Fall of Minoan Crete* (London: Hamish Hamilton, 1970); Leonard Robert Palmer, *Mycenaeans and Minoans: Aegean Prehistory in the Light of the Linear B Tablets* (London: Faber and Faber, 1961); and Mellaart, *Earliest Civilizations* and *Çatal Hüyük*.

5. Aphrodite in Medieval through Nineteenth-Century Poetry

1. In a comprehensive survey, "Venerean and Related Iconography of Pope, Fielding, Cleland and Stern," Douglas Brooks-Davies suggests that Pope conflated Venus not only with Diana (*"Venus Virgo"*) but also with the "Venerean type known to the Renaissance as the armed Venus (possessing the weapons of Minerva or Mars,) the *Venus Armata*" (179). This is interesting archetypally in that it suggests the survival of the military, warlike attributes of Inanna and Ishtar even as late as eighteenth-century versions of Venus. Brooks-Davies illustrates how Pope develops Belinda in *The Rape of the Lock* as a mixture of warlike and sensual Venus attributes which he sets up as targets for satire. I read Pope's paradoxically crafted heroic couplets, with their metrical yoking of contradictions, as a lyric embodiment of the double bind about feminine sexuality in eighteenth-century culture.

2. See, for example, Thomas Hervey's "Illustrations of Modern Sculpture," Thomas Hake's "Venus Urania," Lord de Tabley's "A Hymn to Aphrodite," William Morris's "Epic of Hades" and Grant Allen's "Return of Aphrodite."

7. Aphrodite in Twentieth-Century Poetry by Women

1. Kristen Laine, a graduate assistant, came to these conclusions while doing research and bibliographical work for this volume.

2. I am grateful to Gwendolyn A. Thomas of the University of Denver for this concept, which she developed in a paper, "The Androgynous American: The Strong Black Woman," at the 1977 Popular Culture Association convention.

3. I am grateful to my student Clarinda G. Pettit for calling my attention to this poem in a 1982 paper, "Renewing the Moon: An Analysis of 'The Maiden' by Audre Lorde," which she wrote for a course I teach, Mythology in Women's Literature.

4. I am grateful to Estella Lauter of the University of Wisconsin–Green Bay for calling Lorde's use of the dark mother archetype to my attention in her essay "Eros and Creativity: Audre Lorde's Figure of the Black Mother Within."

11. Bear!

1. Marla Schneiderman, "The Storyteller and Poet in Relation to the Bear," class paper for English 515 at the University of Wisconsin, April 1984. Schneiderman cites Dunning from Victor Barnouw, *Wisconsin Chippewa Myths & Tales*, 248.

2. Margaret Atwood, "Canadian Monsters," 121. See also my essay "Affairs with Bears: Notes towards Feminist Archetypal Hypotheses for Canadian Literature" in Barbara Godard, ed., *Gynocritics/La Gynocritique* (Toronto: ECW Press, 1987), 157–78.

3. Wendy Osterweil, "Ursari and Bears," paper for English 515 at the University of Wisconsin, April 1984, 7. Osterweil cites Jean-Paul Clebert, *The Gypsies*, trans. Charles Duff (London: Penguin, 1967); Charles Duff, *A Mysterious People: An Introduction to the Gypsies of All Countries* (London: Hamish Hamilton, 1965); and Bernice Kohn, *The Gypsies* (Indianapolis: Bobbs-Merrill, 1972).

Works Cited

Abrams, M. H., ed. *The Norton Anthology of English Literature*, 4th ed. 2 vols. New York: Norton, 1979.

Aiken, Conrad. *Collected Poems*. 2nd ed. New York: Oxford UP, 1970.

————. *Ushant*. Cleveland: Meridian, 1952.

Alexander, Lewis. "Negro Woman." In *The Poetry of Black America: Anthology of the Twentieth Century*. Ed. Arnold Adoff. New York: Harper and Row, 1973. 58.

Allen, Grant. *The Lower Slopes: Reminiscences of Excursions Round the Base of Helicon, Undertaken for the Most Part in Early Manhood*. London: Mathews and Lane, 1894.

Allen, Paula Gunn. "Grandmother." In *Songs from This Earth on Turtle's Back: Contemporary American Indian Poetry*. Ed. Joseph Bruchac. Greenfield Center, N.Y.: Greenfield Review Press, 1983. 3.

————. *The Sacred Hoop: Recovering the Feminine in American Indian Traditions*. Boston: Beacon Press, 1986.

————, with Patricia Clark Smith. "Early Relations, Carnal Knowledge: Southwestern Indian Women Writers and Landscape." *The Desert Is No Lady: Southwestern Landscapes in Women's Writing and Art*. New Haven: Yale UP, 1987. 174–96.

Amico, Eleanor B. "The Status of Women at Ugarit." Ph.D. diss., U of Wisconsin, 1990.

Apuleius, Lucius. *The Transformations of Lucius; Otherwise Known as The Golden Ass*. Trans. Robert Graves. New York: Farrar, Straus & Giroux, 1951.

Atwood, Margaret. *The Animals in That Country*. Toronto: University of Toronto Press, 1968.

————. "Canadian Monsters: Some Aspects of the Supernatural in Canadian Fiction." In *The Canadian Imagination*. Ed. David Staines. Cambridge: Harvard University Press, 1977. 97–122.

————. *The Circle Game*. Toronto: Anansi, 1966.

————. "Great Unexpectations." Ms 16 (July–August 1987): 78–79, 195.

————. Introduction. In *The New Oxford Book of Canadian Verse in English*. Ed. Margaret Atwood. Toronto: Oxford UP, 1982. xxvii–xxxix.

————. *The Journals of Susanna Moodie*. Toronto: U of Toronto P, 1970.

————. *Survival: A Thematic Guide to Canadian Literature*. Toronto: Anansi, 1972.

378

————. *Two-Headed Poems*. Toronto: Oxford UP, n.d.

Auerbach, Nina. *Women and the Demon: The Life of a Victorian Myth*. Cambridge, Mass: Harvard UP, 1982.

Auslander, Joseph. *More Than Bread: A Book of Poems*. New York: Macmillan, 1936.

Banks, Russell. "The Poem Of The Year of the Bear." In *Bear Crossings*. Ed. Anne Newman and Julie Suk. Newport Beach, Calif: New South, 1978. 94–95.

Baraka, Imamu Amiri. "Babylon Revisited." In *The Norton Anthology of Modern Poetry*. Ed. Richard Ellmann and Robert O'Clair. New York: Norton, 1973. 1322–23.

————. *Black Magic: Collected Poetry 1961–1967*. Indianapolis: Bobbs-Merrill, 1969.

————. *The Dead Lecturer*. New York: Grove Press, 1964.

Barker, George. "To my son." In *Twentieth-Century Poetry: American and British (1900–1970)*. Ed. John M. Brinnin and Bill Read. New York: McGraw-Hill, 1970. 26–27.

Barnes, Hazel E. "The Look of the Gorgon." *The Meddling Gods: Four Essays on Classical Themes*. Lincoln: U of Nebraska P, 1974.

Barnouw, Victor. *Wisconsin Chippewa Myths & Tales and Their Relation to Chippewa Life*. Madison: U of Wisconsin P, 1977.

Beeler, Janet. "Feeding Time." In *Bear Crossings*. Ed. Anne Newman and Julie Suk. Newport Beach, Calif: New South, 1978. 46.

————. "Considerations on Indo-European Culture." *Dowry*. Columbia, Mo: Breakthrough Books, 1978. 53.

Belford, Ken. "Carrier Indians." In *The New Oxford Book of Canadian Verse in English*. Ed. Margaret Atwood. Toronto: Oxford UP, 1982.

Bennett, Gwendolyn B. "Heritage" and "To a Dark Girl." In *The Poetry of Black America: Anthology of the Twentieth Century*. Ed. Arnold Adoff. New York: Harper and Row, 1973. 81.

Berger, Pamela. *The Goddess Obscured: Transformation of the Grain Protectress from Goddess to Saint*. Boston: Beacon Press, 1985.

Bernardus Morlanensis, Monk of Cluny. In *Analecta Hymnica*. Vol. 50. Leipzig: O. R. Reisland, 1907. 454–56.

Bernikow, Louise, ed. *The World Split Open: Four Centuries of Women Poets in England and America, 1552–1950*. New York: Random House, 1974.

Berry, Wendell. *The Country of Marriage*. New York: Harcourt Brace Jovanovich. 1973.

Bettelheim, Bruno. *The Uses of Enchantment: The Meaning and Importance of Fairy Tales*. New York: Knopf, 1976.

Birney, Earle. *The Collected Poems of Earle Birney*. 2 vols. Toronto: McClelland and Stewart, 1975.

Works Cited

————. "November Walk near False Creek Mouth." In *15 Canadian Poets*. Ed. Gary Geddes and Phyllis Bruce. Toronto: Oxford UP, 1970. 15–23.

Bishop, John Peele. "Ode." In *A Little Treasury of Modern Poetry*. Ed. Oscar Williams. New York: Scribner, 1952. 330–32.

bisset, bill. *Selected Poems: Beyond Even Faithful Legends*. Vancouver: Talonbooks, 1980.

Bloch, Ruth M. "Untangling the Roots of Modern Sex Roles: A Survey of Four Centuries of Change." *Signs* 4 (Winter 1978): 237–52.

Blunt, Wilfred S. *The Poetry of Wilfred Blunt*. Selected and arranged W. E. Henley and George Wyndham. London: Heinemann, 1898.

Bly, Robert. *Selected Poems*. New York: Harper and Row, 1986.

————. *Sleepers Joining Hands*. New York: Harper and Row, 1973.

Bodkin, Maud. *Archetypal Patterns in Poetry*. London: Oxford UP, 1963.

Bogan, Louise. *The Blue Estuaries: Poems 1923–1968*. New York: Farrar, Straus & Giroux, 1968.

————. *The Collected Poems of Louise Bogan*. New York: Noonday Press, 1954.

————. *Dark Summer*. New York: Scribner, 1929.

Bogin, Meg. *The Women Troubadours*. London: Paddington Press, 1976.

Boker, George Henry. "Sonnets: A Sequence of Profane Love." In *The American Poets: 1800–1900*. Ed. Edwin Cady. Glenview, Ill.: Scott, Foresman, 1966. 360–63.

Bolen, Jean Shinoda. *Goddesses in Everywoman*. San Francisco: Harper and Row, 1984.

————. *The Tao of Psychology: Synchronicity and the Self*. San Francisco: Harper and Row, 1979.

Bowering, George. "Desert Elm." In *An Anthology of Canadian Literature in English*. Ed. Donna Bennett and Russell Brown. 2 vols. Toronto: Oxford UP, 1983. 2:378–84.

Bowles, Gloria. "The Pursuit of Perfection." Review of *Critical Essays on Louise Bogan*, ed. Marie Collins; *Louise Bogan*, by Jaqueline Ridgeway; *Louise Bogan: A Portrait*, by Elizabeth Frank; and *A Separate Vision: Isolation in Contemporary Women's Poetry*, by Deborah Pope. *Women's Review of Books* (July 1985): 8–9.

Branch, Anna Hempstead. "Sonnets from a Lock Box: XIV, XXV, XXI." In *The World Split Open: Four Centuries of Women Poets in England and America, 1552–1950*. Ed. Louise Bernikow. New York: Random House, 1974. 245–46.

Brandon, William, ed. *The Magic World: American Indian Songs and Stories*. New York: Morrow, 1971.

Brant, Beth. "Ride the Turtle's Back." In *Songs from This Earth on Turtle's*

Back: Contemporary American Indian Poetry. Ed. Joseph Bruchac. Greenfield Center, N.Y.: Greenfield Review Press, 1983. 32.

Brewster, Elizabeth. "Moon." In *Mountain Moving Day: Poems by Women.* Ed. Elaine Gill. Trumansburg, N.Y.: Crossing Press, 1973. 37.

Bringhurst, Robert. "Hachadura." *Bergschrund.* Victoria, B.C.: Sono Nis, 1973. 67–80.

Brooks-Davies, Douglas. "The Mythology of Love: Venerean (and Related) Iconography in Pope, Fielding, Cleland and Sterne." In *Sexuality in Eighteenth-Century Britain.* Ed. Paul-Gabriel Bouce. Manchester: Manchester UP, 1982. 176–97.

Broumas, Olga. *Beginning with O.* New Haven: Yale UP, 1977.

Brown, Alice. *The Road to Castalay.* Boston: Copeland and Day, 1897.

Brown, Carleton, ed. *English Lyrics of the Thirteenth Century.* Oxford: Clarendon Press, 1932.

Browning, Elizabeth Barrett. *The Complete Poetical Works of Elizabeth Barrett Browning.* Ed. Ruth M. Adams. Boston: Houghton Mifflin, 1974.

Bunting, Basil. *Collected Poems.* Oxford: Oxford UP, 1978.

Burke, Carolyn. "The New Poetry and the New Woman: Mina Loy." In *Coming to Light: American Women Poets in the Twentieth Century.* Ed. Diane Wood Middlebrook and Marilyn Yalom. Ann Arbor: U of Michigan P, 1985. 37–57.

Burland, C. A. *Echoes of Magic: A Study of Seasonal Festivals through the Ages.* Totowa, N.J.: Rowman & Littlefield, 1972.

Cameron, Anne. *Daughters of Copper Woman.* Vancouver: Press Gang Publishers, 1981.

Campbell, Joseph. *The Hero with a Thousand Faces.* Princeton: Princeton UP, 1949.

———. *Occidental Mythology.* Vol. 3, *The Masks of God.* New York: Viking Press, 1952–68.

———. *The Power of Myth.* With Bill Moyers. Ed. Betty Sue Flowers. New York: Doubleday, 1988.

———. *Primitive Mythology.* Vol. 1, *The Masks of God.* 1959.

Carr, Emily. *Klee Wyck.* Centennial ed. Toronto: Clarke, Irwin, 1971.

Cartwright, William. "Venus For Her Belov'd Adonis." In *The Life and Poems of William Cartwright.* Ed. Cullis Goffin. Cambridge: Cambridge UP, 1918. 155–56.

Cassell's Latin-English and English-Latin Dictionary. Ed. J. R. V. Marchant and Joseph F. Charles. New York: Funk & Wagnalls, 1958.

Chaucer, Geoffrey. *The Book of Troilus and Criseyde.* Ed. Robert Kilburn Root. Princeton: Princeton UP, 1954.

Chodorow, Nancy. *The Reproduction of Mothering: Psychoanalysis and the Sociology of Gender.* Berkeley: U of California P, 1978.

Works Cited

Christ, Carol P. "Mircea Eliade and the Feminist Paradigm Shift." *Journal of Feminist Studies in Religion* 7 (Fall 1991): 75–94.

Christine de Pisan. *Book of the City of Ladies.* Trans. Earl Jeffrey Richards. New York: Persea Books, 1982.

Ciardi, John. "To Judith Asleep." In *Today's Poets: American and British Poetry since the 1930s.* Ed. Chad Walsh. New York: Scribner, 1964. 208–209.

Cixous, Hélène. "The Laugh of the Medusa." In *New French Feminisms.* Ed. Elaine Marks and Isabelle de Courtivron. New York: Schocken, 1981: 245–64.

Clifton, Lucille. *two-headed woman.* Amherst: U of Massachusetts P, 1980.

Coldwell, Joan. "The Beauty of the Medusa: Twentieth Century." *English Studies in Canada* 11 (December 1985): 422–37.

Coleman, Victor. "Fish: Stone: Song." In *The Contemporary Canadian Poem Anthology.* Ed. George Bowering. 4 vols. Toronto: Coach House Press, 1983. 1: 69–70.

Coleridge, Mary Elizabeth. *The Collected Poems of Mary Elizabeth Coleridge.* Ed. Theresa Whistler. London: Rupert Hart-Davis, 1954.

———. "The Other Side of a Mirror." In *The World Split Open: Four Centuries of Women Poets in England and America, 1552–1950.* Ed. Louise Bernikow. New York: Random House, 1974. 137.

Cox, Ida. "Wild Women Blues." In *The World Split Open: Four Centuries of Women Poets in England and America, 1552–1950.* Ed. Louise Bernikow. New York: Random House, 1974. 278–79.

Crawford, Isabella Valancy. "Said the Canoe." In *An Anthology of Canadian Literature in English.* Ed. Russell Brown and Donna Bennett. 2 vols. Toronto: Oxford UP, 1983. 1: 19–23.

Creeley, Robert. "The Door." In *Today's Poets: American and British Poetry since the 1930s.* Ed. Chad Walsh. New York: Scribner, 1964. 338–40.

Cross, W. E. "Negro-to-Black Conversion Experience: Toward a Psychology of Black Liberation." *Black World* 20 (1971), no. 9: 13–27.

———. "The Thomas and Cross Models of Psychological Nigrescence: A Review." *Journal of Black Psychology* 1978, no. 5: 13–31.

Cullen, Countee. "Heritage." In *The Norton Anthology of Modern Poetry.* Ed. Richard Ellmann and Robert O'Clair. New York: Norton, 1973. 647–50.

———. *On These I Stand: An Anthology of the Best Poems of Countee Cullen.* New York: Harper and Brothers, 1947.

Culpepper, Emily Erwin. "Ancient Gorgons: A Face for Contemporary Women's Rage." *Woman of Power* 1 (Winter–Spring 1986): 22–24.

Curtis, Jane Elizabeth. "Muriel Rukeyser: The Woman Writer Confronts Traditional Mythology and Psychology." Ph.D. diss., U of Wisconsin, 1981.

Davenport, Doris. "Afracentric Visions." Review of *The Temple of My Familiar* by Alice Walker. *Women's Review of Books* 6 (September 1989): 13–14.

Davies, Robertson. *The Rebel Angels*. New York: Viking, 1981.

Densmore, Frances. *Nootka and Quileute Music*. Bulletin 24. Washington, D.C.: Bureau of American Ethnology, 1939.

———. *Papago Music*. Bulletin 90. Washington, D.C.: Bureau of American Ethnology, 1929.

———. *Chippewa Music*. Bulletin 45. Washington, D.C.: Bureau of American Ethnology, 1910.

Dickinson, Emily. *The Complete Poems of Emily Dickinson*. Ed. Thomas H. Johnson. Boston: Little, Brown, 1960.

Dinesen, Isak. "The Fish." *Winter's Tales*. New York: Vintage, 1951. 225–47.

Diodorus Siculus. *Diodorus of Sicily*. Trans. C. H. Oldfather. 10 vols. Cambridge: Harvard UP, 1935.

Dobson, Pamela J., ed. *The Tree That Never Dies: Oral History of the Michigan Indians*. Grand Rapids, Mich.: Grand Rapids Public Library, 1978.

Doll, Caroline. *Margaret and Her Friends, or Ten Conversations with Margaret Fuller upon the Mythology of the Greeks and Its Expansion in Art* (1895). New York: Arno Press, 1972.

Doolittle, Hilda (H. D.). "Tribute to the Angels." In *Norton Anthology of Literature by Women*. Ed. Sandra M. Gilbert and Susan Gubar. New York: Norton, 1985. 1468–82.

Downes, Gwladys. "The Return." In *Canadian Writers in 1984*. Ed. W. H. New. Vancouver: U of British Columbia P, 1984. 97.

Downing, Christine. *The Goddess: Mythological Images of the Feminine*. New York: Crossroad, 1984.

Downing, Nancy E., and Kristin L. Roush. "From Passive Acceptance to Active Commitment: A Model of Feminist Identity Development for Women." *Counseling Psychologist* (October 1985): 695–708.

Drake, William. *Mirror of the Heart: Poems of Sara Teasdale*. New York: Macmillan, 1984.

———. *Sara Teasdale: Woman and Poet*. San Francisco: Harper and Row, 1979.

Drummond, William, of Hawthorndon. "Idmon to Venus." In Vol. 1 of *The Poems of William Drummond of Hawthornden*. 2 vols. New York: Scribner, 1894. 162.

———. "The Pourtrait of Mars and Venus." *Poems and Prose*. Edinburgh: Scottish Academic P, 1976. 74.

Works Cited

Dryden, John. *Dryden: The Dramatic Works*. Ed. Montague Summers. 6 vols. London: Nonesuch Press, 1932.

Dudley, Edward. "The Wild Man Goes Baroque." In *The Wild Man Within: An Image in Western Thought from the Renaissance to Romanticism*. Ed. Edward Dudley and Maximillian E. Novak. Pittsburgh: Pittsburgh UP, 1972. 115–39.

———, and Maximillian E. Novak, eds. *The Wild Man Within*. Pittsburgh: U of Pittsburgh P, 1972.

Duncan, Robert. *The First Decade: Selected Poems 1940–1950*. London: Fulcrum Press, 1968.

———. *The Truth and Life of Myth: An Essay in Essential Autobiography*. New York: House of Books, 1968.

DuPlessis, Rachel Blau. *Wells*. New York: Montemora Press, 1980.

Economou, George D. "The Two Venuses and Courtly Love." In *In Pursuit of Perfection: Courtly Love in Medieval Literature*. Ed. Joan Ferrante and George D. Economou. Port Washington, N.Y.: Kennikat Press, 1975.

Elder, John. *Imagining the Earth: Poetry and the Vision of Nature*. Urbana: U of Illinois P, 1985.

Elias-Button, Karen. "Athene and Medusa: A Women's Myth." *Anima* 2 (Spring 1979): 118–24.

———. "Journey into an Archetype: The Dark Mother in Contemporary Women's Poetry." *Anima* 4 (Spring 1978): 5–10.

———. "The Muse as Medusa." In *The Lost Tradition: Mothers and Daughters in Literature*. Ed. Cathy N. Davidson and E. M. Broner. New York: Ungar, 1980. 193–206.

Elizabeth of York. "My Heart Is Set Upon a Lusty Pin." In *The Women Poets in English*. Ed. Ann Stanford. New York: McGraw-Hill, 1972. 16–17.

England's Helicon. Ed. Hugh Macdonald. London: Routledge and Kegan Paul, 1949.

Epton, Nina. *Love and the English*. London: Cassell, 1960.

Erdrich, Louise. "The Lady in the Pink Mustang." In *That's What She Said: Contemporary Poetry and Fiction by Native American Women*. Ed. Rayna Green. Bloomington: Indiana UP, 1984. 88–89.

Evans, Mari. *Nightstar: 1973–1978*. Los Angeles: Center for Afro-American Studies, 1981.

Fabricant, Carole. "Binding and Dressing Nature's Loose Tresses: The Ideology of Augustan Landscape Design." In vol. 8, *Studies in Eighteenth-Century Culture*. Ed. Harry C. Payne. Madison: U of Wisconsin P, 1979. 109–35.

Farley, T. E. *Exiles and Pioneers: Two Visions of Canada's Future 1825–1975*. Ottawa: Borealis Press, 1976.

Farr, Judith. *The Life and Art of Elinor Wylie.* Baton Rouge: Louisiana State UP, 1983.

Fawcett, Edgar S. *Fantasy & Passion.* Boston: Roberts Brothers, 1878.

Ferenczi, Sandor. "On the Symbolism of the Head of Medusa." *Further Contributions to the Theory and Technique of Psychoanalysis.* Comp. John Rickman. New York: Boni & Liveright, 1927.

Ferrante, Joan M. *Woman as Image in Medieval Literature, from the Twelfth Century to Dante.* New York: Columbia UP, 1975.

————, and Economou, George D., eds. *In Pursuit of Perfection: Courtly Love in Medieval Literature.* Port Washington, N.Y.: Kennikat Press, 1975.

Finch, Anne. "A Nocturnal Reverie." In *The Norton Anthology of Literature by Women.* Ed. Sandra M. Gilbert and Susan Gubar. New York: Norton, 1985. 111–12.

Finnigan, Joan. "All Marriages Are Terminated in Tundra." In *The Poets of Canada.* Ed. John Robert Colombo. Edmonton: Hurtig, 1978. 170.

Fisher, Dexter, ed. *The Third Woman: Minority Women Writers in the United States.* Boston: Houghton Mifflin, 1980.

Fisher, E. T. "Cultic Prostitution in the Ancient Near East: A Reassessment." *Biblical Theology Bulletin* VI (1976): 225–36.

Fisher, Elizabeth. *Woman's Creation: Sexual Evolution and the Shaping of Society.* Garden City, N.Y.: Anchor, 1979.

Fontenrose, Joseph. *Python: A Study of the Delphic Myth and Its Origins.* Berkeley: U of California P, 1959.

Frank, Elizabeth. *Louise Bogan. A Portrait.* New York: Knopf, 1985.

Freud, Sigmund. "The Uncanny." *The Standard Edition of the Complete Psychological Works of Sigmund Freud.* Ed. and trans. James Strachey. 23 vols. London: Hogarth Press, 1962. 17: 219–52.

Friar, Kimon. "The Stone Eyes of Medusa." *Greek Heritage* 6 (1965): 26–39.

Friedman, Susan Stanford. *Psyche Reborn: The Emergence of H.D.* Bloomington: Indiana UP, 1981.

Friedrich, Molly. "Writing Hath No Sex, BUT . . ." *Majority Report* 5 (April 17–May 1 1976).

Friedrich, Paul. *The Meaning of Aphrodite.* Chicago: U of Chicago P, 1978.

Frye, Northrop. *Anatomy of Criticism.* Princeton: Princeton UP, 1957.

————. *The Bush Garden.* Toronto: Anansi, 1971.

————. Conclusion. In *Literary History of Canada.* Ed. Carl F. Klinck et al. 2d ed. 3 vols. Toronto: U of Toronto P, 1976. 2: 318–61.

————. *The Critical Path: An Essay on the Social Context of Literary Criticism.* Bloomington: Indiana UP, 1971.

————. "Haunted by Lack of Ghosts: Some Patterns in the Imagery of Canadian Poetry." In *The Canadian Imagination.* Ed. David Staines. Cambridge: Harvard UP, 1977. 22–45.

————. "National Consciousness in Canadian Literature." In *Divisions on a Ground: Essays in Canadian Literature*. Ed. James Polk. Toronto: Anansi, 1982. 41–55.

————. *The Secular Scripture: A Study of the Structure of Romance*. Cambridge: Harvard UP, 1976.

Frymer-Kensky, Tikva. "Inanna—the Quintessential Femme Fatale." Review of Wolkstein and Kramer, *Inanna, Queen of Heaven and Earth*. *Biblical Archaeology Review* 10 (September–October 1984): 62–64.

Gawein, Madison. *Intimations of the Beautiful*. New York: Putnam, 1894.

George, Phillip. "Night Blessing." *Voices from Wah'Kon-Tah: Contemporary Poetry of Native Americans*. Ed. Robert K. Dodge and Joseph B. McCullough. New York: International, 1974. 44–45.

Gilbert, Sandra M., and Susan Gubar. *The Madwoman in the Attic: The Woman Writer and the Nineteenth-Century Literary Imagination*. New Haven: Yale UP, 1979.

Gimbutas, Marija. *The Goddesses and Gods of Old Europe, 6500–3500 BC: Myths and Cult Images*. 2d ed. Berkeley: U of California P, 1982.

Giovanni, Nikki. "Ego Tripping." In *The Norton Anthology of Modern Poetry*. New York: Norton, 1973. 1384–85.

Gleason, Judith. *Oya: In Praise of the Goddess*. Boston: Shambhala, 1987.

Glück, Louise. *Descending Figure*. New York: Ecco Press, 1980.

————. *First Born*. New York: Ecco Press, 1968.

Goff, Paula. "The White Bear." In *Bear Crossings*. Ed. Anne Newman and Julie Suk. Newport Beach, Calif.: New South, 1978. 43.

Goldman, Emma. *The Traffic in Women and Other Essays on Feminism*. New York: Times Change Press, 1970.

Goldsmith, Oliver. "The Rising Village." In *The Poets of Canada*. Ed. John Robert Colombo. Edmonton: Hurtig, 1978. 36.

Gornick, Vivian. Review of *The Complete Novels of Jean Rhys*. *Women's Review of Books* (June 1986): 9.

Gottlieb, Phyllis. "Paradigm." In *Canadian Poetry: The Modern Era*. Ed. John Newlove. Toronto: McClelland and Stewart, 1977. 87.

Grahn, Judy. *The Highest Apple: Sappho and the Lesbian Poetic Tradition*. San Francisco: Spinsters, Ink, 1985.

————. *The Queen of Swords*. Boston: Beacon Press, 1987.

————. *The Queen of Wands*. Trumansburg, N.Y.: Crossing Press, 1982.

Graves, Robert. *New Collected Poems*. Garden City, N.Y.: Doubleday, 1977.

————. *The White Goddess: A Historical Grammar of Poetry and Myth*. Amended ed. New York: Farrar, Straus & Giroux, 1966.

Green, Rayna. "Coosaponakeesa (Mary Mathews Musgrove Bosomworth), Leader of the Creeks, 1700–1783." In *That's What She Said: Contem-*

porary Poetry and Fiction by Native American Women. Ed. Rayna Green. Bloomington: Indiana UP, 1984. 114–15.

———. "Naneye'hi (Nancy Ward), the Last Beloved Woman of the Cherokees, 1738–1822." In *That's What She Said.* 112–14.

———, ed. *That's What She Said: Contemporary Poetry by Native American Women.* Bloomington: Indiana UP, 1984.

Greene, Robert. *The Plays and Poems of Robert Greene.* Oxford: Clarendon Press, 1905.

Gregory, Horace. *The Selected Poems of Horace Gregory.* New York: Viking Press, 1951.

Griffin, Susan. *Woman and Nature: The Roaring inside Her.* New York: Harper and Row, 1980.

Grilikhes, Alexandra. *On Woman Artists: Poems 1975–1980.* Minneapolis: Cleis Press, 1981.

Gruber, M. I. "Hebrew Qedesah and Her Canaanite and Akkadian Cognates." *Ugarit Forschungen* 18 (1986): 133–48.

Gubar, Susan. "Sapphistries." *Signs* 10 (Autumn 1984): 43–62.

Gustafson, Ralph. *Selected Poems.* Toronto: McClelland and Stewart, 1972.

Hake, Thomas Gordon. *The Poems of Thomas Gordon Hake.* New York: AMS Press, 1971.

Hall, Nor. *The Moon and the Virgin: Reflections on the Archetypal Feminine.* New York: Harper and Row, 1980.

Hallo, William W., and J. J. A. Van Dijk. *The Exaltation of Inanna.* New Haven: Yale UP, 1968.

Hallowell, A. Irving. "Ojibwa Ontology, Behavior, and World View." In *Teachings from the American Earth.* Ed. Dennis Tedlock and Barbara Tedlock. New York: Liveright, 1975. 141–78.

Harjo, Joy. "I Am a Dangerous Woman." In *That's What She Said: Contemporary Poetry and Fiction by Native American Women.* Ed. Rayna Green. Bloomington: Indiana UP, 1984. 128–29.

Harner, Michael. "Beating the Drum for Shamanism." *New Realities* (July–August 1988): 73–76.

Harrison, Jane Ellen. *Mythology.* Boston: Marshall Jones, 1924.

———. *Prolegomena to the Study of Greek Religion.* London: Merlin Press, 1980.

Hawthorne, Susan. "The Politics of the Exotic: The Paradox of Cultural Voyeurism." *NWSA Journal* 4 (Summer 1989): 617–29.

Hayden, Robert Earl. *Selected Poems.* New York: October House, 1966.

Hayne, Paul Hamilton. *The Mountain of the Lovers.* New York: E. J. Hale and Son, 1875.

Heavysege, Charles. "Sonnet Sequence from Jephthah's Daughter." In *100*

Poems of Nineteenth-Century Canada. Ed. Raymond Souster. Toronto: Macmillan, 1981. 6–15.

Heyen, William. "The Bear." *Bear Crossings.* Ed. Anne Newman and Julie Suk. Newport Beach, Calif.: New South, 1978. 58.

Hillman, James. *Archetypal Psychology.* Dallas: Spring Publications, 1985.

Hillyer, Robert Silliman. "The Garden of Artemis." *The Suburb by the Sea.* New York: Knopf, 1952. 44–50.

Hine, Daryl. *Selected Poems.* New York: Atheneum, 198.

Hobson, Geary. "The Rise of the White Shaman as a New Version of Cultural Imperialism." In *The Remembered Earth: An Anthology of Contemporary Native American Literature.* Ed. Geary Hobson. Albuquerque: Red Earth Press, 1978. Reprinted U of New Mexico P, Albuquerque, 1981. 100–108.

Hogan, Linda. "calling myself home." In *That's What She Said: Contemporary Poetry and Fiction by Native American Women.* Ed. Rayna Green. Bloomington: Indiana UP, 1984. 157–58.

———. "Heritage." In *That's What She Said.* 164–65.

Houston, James, ed. *Songs of the Dream People: Chants and Images from the Indians and Eskimos of America.* Don Mills: Longmans, 1972.

Hughes, Langston. *Fine Clothes to the Jew.* New York: Knopf, 1929.

———. *Lament for Dark People and Other Poems.* Selected ed. by an amateur. 1944. 31.

———. *Shakespeare in Harlem.* New York: Knopf, 1942.

Hughes, Ted. *Cave Birds: An Alchemical Cave Drama.* London: Faber and Faber, 1978.

———. "Crow's First Lesson." In *The New Norton Anthology of Modern Poetry.* Ed. Richard Ellmann and Robert O'Clair. New York: Norton, 1975. 1277.

———. "Dark Women." ("The Green Wolf"). In *Today's Poets: American and British Poetry since the 1930s.* Ed. Chad Walsh. New York: Scribner, 1964. 391–92.

———. *River.* London: Faber and Faber, 1983. 88.

Jacobs, E. Jan. "The Crone: A Brief Study of an Archetype." Undergraduate paper, U of Wisconsin, 1988.

James, E. O. *Myth and Ritual in the Ancient Near East.* London: Thames and Hudson, 1958.

Janik, Phyllis. "No Dancing. No Acts of Dancing." In *A Change in the Weather: Midwest Women Poets.* Ed. Peg Carlson Lauber. Eau Claire, Wisc.: Rhiannon Press, 1978. 49–50.

Jarrell, Randall. "Muriel Rukeyser." *Poetry and the Age.* New York: Farrar, Straus & Giroux/Noonday Press, 1953. 163–66.

Jaskoski, Helen. "My Heart Will Go Out: Healing Songs of Native American Women." *International Journal of Women's Studies* 4 (1980): 118–34.

Johnson, Buffie. *The Lady of the Beasts: Ancient Images of the Goddess and Her Sacred Animals.* San Francisco: Harper and Row, 1988.

Johnson, Fenton. "The Scarlet Woman." In *The Poetry of Black America: Anthology of the Twentieth Century.* Ed. Arnold Adoff. New York: Harper and Row, 1973. 24–25.

Johnson, James Weldon. *Fifty Years & Other Poems.* Boston: Cornhill, 1917.

Johnston, Basil. *Ojibway Heritage.* Toronto: McClelland and Stewart, 1976.

Jones, D. G. *Butterfly on Rock: A Study of Themes and Images in Canadian Literature.* Toronto: U of Toronto P, 1970.

———. "For Eve." In *An Anthology of Canadian Literature.* Ed. Donna Bennett and Russell Brown. 2 vols. Toronto: Oxford University Press, 1983. 2:276–77.

———. *Under the Thunder Flowers Light Up the Earth.* Toronto: Coach House Press, 1977.

Jones, LeRoi. See Baraka, Imamu Amiri.

Jong, Erica. *Here Comes & Other Poems* (originally *Fruits and Vegetables and Half-Lives*). New York: New American Library, 1975.

Jonson, Ben. *A Celebration of Charis.* Ed. Ian Donaldson. Oxford: Oxford UP, 1985.

Jordan, June. *Things That I Do in the Dark.* New York: Random House, 1977.

Jung, C. G. *Archetypes and the Collective Unconscious.* Trans. R. F. C. Hull. 2d ed. Princeton: Princeton UP, 1969.

———. *Memories, Dreams, Reflections.* New York: Random House, 1961.

———. *Psychological Reflections.* Ed. Jolande Jacobi. New York: Harper and Row, 1953.

———. *Symbols of Transformation: An Analysis of the Prelude to a Case of Schizophrenia.* Trans. R. F. C. Hull. 4th ed. New York: Pantheon Books, 1956.

Kahil, Lilly. "Mythological Repertoire of Brauron." In *Ancient Greek Art and Iconography.* Ed. Warren G. Moon. Madison: U of Wisconsin P, 1983. 231–44.

Kaufman, Bob. "African Dream." In *Modern and Contemporary Afro-American Poetry.* Ed. Bernard W. Bell. Boston: Allyn and Bacon, 1972. 129–30.

Keats, John. *Endymion.* In *John Keats: Selected Poetry and Letters.* New York: Holt, Rinehart and Winston, 1965. 29–150.

Keightly, Thomas. *The World Guide to Gnomes, Fairies, Elves and Other Little People.* (Originally published in 1880 as *The Fairy Mythology*). New York: Avenel, 1978.

Works Cited

Kinnell, Galway. "The Bear." In *Bear Crossings*. Ed. Anne Newman and Julie Suk. Newport Beach, Calif.: New South, 1978. 7–9.

Kolbenschlag, Madonna. *Kiss Sleeping Beauty Goodbye: Breaking the Spell of Feminine Myths and Models*. Garden City, N.Y.: Doubleday, 1979.

Kraemer, Ross S., ed. *Maenads, Martyrs, Matrons, Monsters: A Sourcebook on Women's Religions in the Greco-Roman World*. Philadelphia: Fortress Press, 1988.

Kramer, Samuel Noah. "Poets and Psalmists: Goddesses and Theologians." In *The Legacy of Sumer: Invited Lectures on the Middle East at the University of Texas at Austin*. Ed. Denise Schmandt-Besserat. Malibu: Undena, 1976: 3–21.

———. *The Sacred Marriage Rite*. Bloomington: Indiana UP, 1969.

Kroetsch, Robert. "Identification Question." In *The Contemporary Canadian Poem Anthology*. Ed. George Bowering. 4 vols. Toronto: Coach House Press, 1983. 3:166.

———. "Stone Hammer Poem." In *An Anthology of Canadian Literature in English*. Ed. Donna Bennett and Russell Brown. 2 vols. Toronto: Oxford UP. 2: 238–42.

Lampman, Archibald. *The Poems of Archibald Lampman*. Toronto: U of Toronto P, 1974.

Lauter, Estella. "Eros and Creativity: Audre Lorde's Figure of the Black Mother Within." In *Writing the Woman Artist*. Ed. Susan Jones. Philadelphia: U of Pennsylvania P, 1991.

———. *Women as Mythmakers: Poetry and Visual Art by Twentieth-Century Women*. Bloomington: Indiana UP, 1984.

———, ed., with Carol Schreier Rupprecht. *Feminist Archetypal Theory: Interdisciplinary Re-visions of Jungian Thought*. Knoxville: U of Tennessee P, 1985.

Law, Helen Hull. *Bibliography of Greek Myth in English Poetry*. Folcroft, Pa.: Richard West, 1979.

Lawrence, D. H. *The Complete Poems of D. H. Lawrence*. Ed. Vivian de Sola Pinto and Warren Roberts. New York: Viking Press, 1964.

———. *Psychoanalysis and the Unconscious and Fantasia of the Unconscious*. New York: Viking, 1960.

Layton, Irving. "What Canadians Don't Know about Love." In *Love When the Nights Are Long: Canadian Love Poems*. Ed. Irving Layton. Toronto: McClelland and Stewart, 1962.

Lee, Dennis. "The Gods." In *The New Oxford Book of Canadian Verse in English*. Ed. Margaret Atwood. Toronto: Oxford UP, 1982. 371–74.

Lee, Don L. "Move Un-noticed to be Noticed: A Nationhood Poem." In *Modern and Contemporary Afro-American Poetry*. Ed. Bernard W. Bell. Boston: Allyn and Bacon, 1972. 166–68.

————. "The Negro (a Pure Product of Americanism)." In *Modern and Contemporary Afro-American Poetry*. 157–58.

————. "A Poem Looking for a Reader." In *Soulscript: Afro-American Poetry*. Ed. June Jordon. Garden City, N.Y.: Doubleday, 1970. 92–94.

Lemont, Jessie. "Diana Remembers Actaeon." In *The Poetry Society of America Anthology*. New York: Fine Editions Press, 1946. 120–21.

LePan, Douglas Valentine. "Canoe Trip." In *An Anthology of Canadian Literature in English*. Ed. Russell Brown and Donna Bennett. 2 vols. Toronto: Oxford UP, 1983. 1:653–54.

————. "A Country without a Mythology." In *An Anthology of Canadian Literature in English*. 1:654–55.

————. "Images of Silenus." In *An Anthology of Canadian Literature in English*. 1: 655–58.

Lerner, Gerda. "The Origin of Prostitution in Ancient Mesopotamia." *Signs* 11 (Winter 1986): 236–54.

Lévi-Strauss, Claude. *Totemism*. Trans. Rodney Needham. Boston: Beacon Press, 1963.

Levitas, Gloria, Frank R. Vivelo, and Jacqueline J. Vivelo, eds. *American Indian Prose and Poetry: We Wait in the Darkness*. New York: Putnam, 1974.

Lewis, C. S. *The Allegory of Love: A Study in Medieval Tradition*. London: Paddington Press, 1976.

Lindsey, Karen. "Medusa." In *Woman/Poems III*. Ed. Celia Gilbert and Pat Rabby. Lexington, Mass: Woman/Press, 1974.

Littlejohn, Bruce, and Jon Pearce. Introduction. In *Marked by the Wild: An Anthology of Literature Shaped by the Canadian Wilderness*. Ed. Bruce Littlejohn and Jon Pearce. Toronto: McClelland and Stewart, 1973. 9–12.

Livesay, Dorothy. "On Looking into Henry Moore." In *An Anthology of Canadian Literature in English*. 2 vols. Ed. Russell Brown and Donna Bennett. Toronto: Oxford UP, 1982. 1:517–18.

————. "Summer Landscape: Jasper." In *15 Canadian Poets Plus 5*. Ed. Gary Geddes and Phyllis Bruce. Toronto: Oxford UP, 1978. 25.

Lorde, Audre. *Chosen Poems: Old & New*. New York: Norton, 1982.

————. *Coal*. New York: Norton, 1968.

————. *Our Dead behind Us*. New York: Norton, 1986.

————. *Sister Outsider: Essays and Speeches by Audre Lorde*. Trumansburg, N.Y.: Crossing Press, 1984.

Lowell, Amy. *Complete Poetical Works of Amy Lowell*. Cambridge: Riverside Press, 1955.

Lowell, Robert. *Near the Ocean*. Drawings by Sidney Nolan. New York: Farrar, Straus & Giroux, 1967.

Works Cited

Lowther, Pat. "Coast Range." In *15 Canadian Poets Plus 5*. 367–69.
———. "Notes from Furry Creek." In *15 Canadian Poets Plus 5*. 366–67.
———. *A Stone Diary*. Toronto: Oxford UP, 1977. 8–9.
Loy, Mina. *The Last Lunar Baedecker*. Ed. Roger C. Conover. Highlands, N.C.: Jargon Society, 1982.
Lucretius, Titus Carus. *On the Nature of the Universe*. Trans. Ronald Latham. New York: Penguin Books, 1976.
Lyly, John. "The Earl of Leicester, as Endymion, Pleads His Passion by Proxy." In *The Queen's Garland*. Comp. Muriel Clara Bradbrook. London: Oxford UP, 1953. 27.
McClellan, Catharine. *The Girl Who Married the Bear*. Ottawa: National Museums of Canada. Publications in Ethnology no. 2, 1970.
McClure, Michael. *Fragments of Perseus*. New York: New Directions, 1983.
McCombs, Judith. "The Man." In *Bear Crossings*. Ed. Anne Newman and Julie Suk. Newport Beach, Calif.: New South, 1978. 76–77.
McElroy, Colleen. *Music from Home: Selected Poems*. Carbondale: Southern Illinois UP, 1976.
———. *Queen of the Ebony Isles*. Middletown: Wesleyan UP, 1984.
MacEwen, Gwendolyn. *Magic Animals: Selected Poems Old and New*. Toronto: Macmillan, 1974.
———. "The Portage." In *An Anthology of Canadian Literature in English*. Ed. Russell Brown and Donna Bennett. 2 vols. Toronto: Oxford UP, 1983. 2:564.
McFadden, David. "Lennox Island." In *The New Oxford Book of Canadian Verse in English*. Ed. Margaret Atwood. Toronto: Oxford UP, 1982. 384–85.
McGregor, Gaile. *The Wacousta Syndrome: Explorations in the Canadian Langscape*. Toronto: U of Toronto P, 1985.
McKinnon, Barry. "Sex at Thirty-One." In *The Contemporary Canadian Poem Anthology*. Ed. George Bowering. 4 vols. Toronto: Coach House Press, 1983. 3: 219–23.
McMorris, Susan. "Images of Aphrodite." Unpublished paper, U of Wisconsin, 1984.
Madgett, Naomi Long. "Black Woman." In *The Poetry of Black America: Anthology of the Twentieth Century*. Ed. Arnold Adoff. New York: Harper and Row, 1973. 183–84.
Markale, Jean. *Women of the Celts*. Trans. A. Mygind, C. Hauch, and P. Henry. London: Cremonesi Publications, 1975.
Martignoni, Margaret E., ed. *The Illustrated Treasury of Children's Literature*. New York: Grosset & Dunlap, 1955.
Meade, Marion. *Eleanor of Aquitaine: A Biography*. New York: Hawthorne/Dutton, 1977.

Meador, Betty De Shong. "Forward into the Past: Re-emergence of the Archetypal Feminine." Paper presented at the Ghost Ranch Conference for Jungian Analysts and Candidates. May–June 1988.

Mellersh, H. E. L. *The Destruction of Knossos: The Rise and Fall of Minoan Crete.* London: Hamish Hamilton, 1970.

Merrill, James. *From the First Nine Poems 1946–1976.* New York: Atheneum, 1982.

Merwin, William S. *The Dancing Bears.* New Haven: Yale UP, 1954.

———. *A Mask For Janus.* New Haven: Yale UP, 1952.

Millay, Edna St. Vincent. *Collected Sonnets.* New York: Washington Square Press, 1967.

Monkman, Leslie. *A Native Heritage: Images of the Indian in English-Canadian Literature.* Toronto: U of Toronto P, 1981.

Montagu, Lady Mary Wortley. *Essays and Poems.* Ed. Robert Halsbrand and Isobel Gruney. Oxford: Clarendon Press, 1977.

Mora, Pat. "Unrefined." *Chants.* Houston: Arta Publico Press, 1984. 8.

Morris, Sir Lewis. *The Epic of Hades.* London: Kegan Paul, 1879.

Mouré, Erin. "Siksika." In *Canadian Writers in 1984.* Ed. W. H. New. Vancouver: U of British Columbia P, 1984. 233.

Musgrave, Susan. *Grave Dirt and Selected Strawberries.* Toronto: Macmillan, 1973.

———. *Songs of the Sea-Witch.* Vancouver: Sono Nis Press, 1970. 25–37.

Nemerov, Howard. *The Western Approaches: Poems 1973–1975.* Chicago: U of Chicago P, 1975.

Neumann, Erich. *The Great Mother: An Analysis of the Archetype.* Princeton: Princeton UP, 1963.

New, W. H. *Articulating West.* Toronto: New Press, 1972.

Newlove, John. "The Pride." In *The New Book of Canadian Verse in English.* Ed. Margaret Atwood. Toronto: Oxford UP, 1982. 338–44.

Newman, Anne, and Julie Suk. *Bear Crossings: An Anthology of North American Poets.* Newport Beach, Calif.: New South, 1978.

Novak, Maximillian E. "The Wild Man Comes to Tea." In *The Wild Man Within: An Image in Western Thought from the Renaissance to Romanticism.* Ed. Edward Dudley and Maximillian E. Novak. Pittsburgh: Pittsburgh UP, 1972. 183–221.

Nowlan, Alden. "Canadian Love Song." In *Love Where the Nights Are Long: Canadian Love Poems.* Ed. Irving Layton. Toronto: McClelland and Stewart, 1962. 19.

Ochshorn, Judith. *The Female Experience and the Nature of the Divine.* Bloomington: Indiana UP, 1981.

O'Flaherty, Wendy Doniger. *Women, Androgynes, and Other Mythical Beasts.* Chicago: U of Chicago P, 1980.

Works Cited

Oliver, Mary. "Wild Goose." *Dream Work.* New York: Atlantic Monthly Press, 1986.

———. "Winter Sleep." *Twelve Moons.* Boston: Little, Brown, 1979. 53.

Olsen, Tillie. "Silences." *Silences.* New York: Delta, 1989.

Ondaatje, Michael. "Women Like You." In *The Contemporary Canadian Poem Anthology.* Ed. George Bowering. 4 vols. Toronto: Coach House Press, 1983. 2:84–85.

Oppenheimer, Joel. *The Woman Poems.* Indianapolis: Bobbs-Merrill, 1975.

Orenstein, Gloria Feman. *The Reflowering of the Goddess.* Elmsford, N.Y.: Pergamon Press, 1990.

Ostriker, Alicia Suskin. *Stealing the Language: The Emergence of Women's Poetry in America.* Boston: Beacon Press, 1986.

———. "The Thieves of Language: Women Poets and Revisionist Mythmaking." In *Coming to Light: American Women Poets in the Twentieth Century.* Ed. Diane Wood Middlebrook and Marilyn Yalom. Ann Arbor: U of Michigan P, 1985. 10–36.

Outram, Richard. "Tattooed Lady." In *The Poets of Canada.* Ed. John Robert Colombo. Edmonton: Hurtig, 1978. 194.

Page, P. K. "Mineral." In *Canadian Poetry: The Modern Era.* Ed. John Newlove. Toronto: McClelland and Stewart, 1977. 193.

Pagels, Elaine. *Adam, Eve, and the Serpent.* New York: Random House, 1988.

Palmer, Leonard R. *Mycenaeans and Minoans: Aegean Prehistory in the Light of the Linear B Tablets.* 2d rev. ed. London: Faber and Faber, 1965.

Papetti-Esch, Lise. Seminar paper on the masque. U of Wisconsin, 1987.

Pearse, Nancy Cotton. *John Fletcher's Chastity Plays—Mirrors of Modesty.* Lewisburg: Bucknell UP, 1973.

Peele, George. "Diana Bestows the Apple of Gold on Queen Elizabeth." In *The Queen's Garland.* Comp. Muriel Clara Bradbrook. London: Oxford UP, 1953. 15.

Perls, Fritz. *Gestalt Theory Verbatim.* Ed. John O. Stevens. New York: Bantam, 1969.

Perry, William A. "Different Worlds in the Same Classroom: Students' Evolution in Their Vision of Knowledge and Their Expectations of Teachers." *On Teaching and Learning, Journal of the Harvard-Danforth Center,* May 1985, 1–17.

Phillips, Katherine. "Against Love." In *The Women Poets in English.* Ed. Ann Stanford. New York: McGraw-Hill, 1972. 49.

Piercy, Marge. *The Moon Is Always Female.* New York: Knopf, 1980.

———. *To Be of Use.* Garden City, N.Y.: Doubleday, 1973.

Pitter, Ruth. *Poems 1926–1966.* London: Cresset Press, 1968.

Plath, Sylvia. *Ariel.* New York: Harper and Row, 1966.

Pomeroy, Sarah B. *Goddesses, Whores, Wives, and Slaves: Women in Classical Antiquity.* New York: Schocken, 1975.

Pope, Alexander. "Moral Essays: Epistle to Burlington." *The Poems of Alexander Pope.* Ed. John Butt. New Haven: Yale UP, 1963. 586–95.

Pope, Deborah. *A Separate Vision: Isolation in Contemporary Women's Poetry.* Baton Rouge: Louisiana State UP, 1984.

Pratt, Agnes. "Empathy." In *Voices from Wah'Kon-Tah: Contemporary Poetry of Native Americans.* Ed. Robert K. Dodge and Joseph B. McCullough. New York: International, 1974. 85.

Pratt, Annis. "Archetypal Approaches to the New Feminist Criticism." *Bucknell Review* 21 (Spring 1973): 3–14.

———. *Archetypal Patterns in Women's Fiction.* Bloomington: Indiana UP, 1981.

———. "Aunt Jennifer's Tigers: Notes towards a Preliterary History of Women's Archetypes." *Feminist Studies* 4 (February 1978): 163–94.

———. *Dylan Thomas' Early Prose: A Study in Creative Mythology.* Pittsburgh: Pittsburgh UP, 1970.

———. "Spinning among Fields: New Directions in Feminist Archetypal Theory." In Carol Rupprecht and Estella Lauter, eds., *New Directions in Feminist Archetypal Theory.* Knoxville: U of Tennessee P, 1985. 93–136.

Primrose, Diana. "Chain of Pearle. . . ." In Betty Travitsky, *The Paradise of Women.* Westport, Conn.: Greenwood Press, 1987. 111–12.

Quinn, Sister Bernetta. "Medusan Imagery in Sylvia Plath." In *Sylvia Plath: New Views on the Poetry.* Ed. Gary Lane. Baltimore: Johns Hopkins UP, 1979.

Raine, Kathleen. *Collected Poems.* London: Hamish Hamilton, 1956.

———. "Invocation." In *The World Split Open: Four Centuries of Women Poets in England and America, 1552–1950.* Ed. Louise Bernikow. New York: Random House, 1974. 179–80.

———. *The Land Unknown: Chapters of Autobiography.* New York: George Braziller, 1975.

———. "The Pythoness." In *The World Split Open: Four Centuries of Women Poets in England and America, 1552–1950.* Ed. Louise Bernikow. New York: Random House, 1974. 180.

Rainey, Gertrude. "Sweet Rough Man." In *The World Split Open: Four Centuries of Women Poets in England and America, 1552–1950.* Ed. Louise Bernikow. New York: Random House, 1974. 275.

Ransom, W. M. "On the Morning of the Third Night above Nisqually." In *Bear Crossings.* Ed. Anne Newman and Julie Suk. Newport Beach, Calif.: New South, 1978. 31.

Works Cited

Reaney, James. "Granny Crack." In *The New Oxford Book of Canadian Verse in English.* Ed. Margaret Atwood. Toronto: Oxford UP, 1982. 256.

———. "Local Grains of Sand." In *Canada: A Guide to the Peaceable Kingdom.* Ed. William Kilburn. Toronto: Macmillan, 1971. 27.

Rebolledo, Tey Diana. "Tradition and Methodology—Signatures of Landscape in Chicana Literature." In *The Desert Is No Lady: Southwestern Landscapes in Women's Writing and Art.* Ed. Vera Norwood and Janice Monk. New Haven: Yale UP, 1987. 96–124.

Rhys, Ernest. "Diana." In *The Oxford Book of Victorian Verse.* Oxford: Clarendon Press, 1913. 813.

Rich, Adrienne. "From Twenty-one Love Poems." In *Norton Anthology of Literature by Women: The Tradition in English.* Ed. Sandra M. Gilbert and Susan Gubar. New York: Norton, 1985. 2036.

———. "When We Dead Awaken: Writing as Re-Vision." *Lies, Secrets, and Silence: Selected Prose, 1966–1978.* New York: Norton. 33–49.

Ricou, Laurence. Preface and Introduction. *Vertical Man/Horizontal World: Man and Landscape in Canadian Prairie Fiction.* Vancouver: U of British Columbia P, 1973. ix–xii, 1–19.

Riding, Laura. *Selected Poems: In Five Sets.* New York: Norton, 1973.

Rikki (Erika Ducornet). "The Bear Sisters." In *Four Canadian Poets.* Vancouver: Intermedia Press, 1976. 27.

Robbins, Rossell Hope, ed. *Secular Lyrics of the Fourteenth and Fifteenth Centures.* 2d ed. Oxford: Clarendon Press, 1952.

Rose, Judith. "The Bear." In *Bear Crossings.* Ed. Anne Newman and Julie Suk. Newport Beach, Calif.: New South, 1978. 32.

Rose, Wendy. "Just What's All This Fuss about Whiteshamanism Anyway?" In *Coyote Was Here.* Ed. Bo Sehóler. U of Aarhus, Denmark.

Rosenthal, Helene. *Listen to the Old Mother: Poems New and Selected.* Toronto: McClelland and Stewart, 1975.

Ross, Anne. *Pagan Celtic Britain: Studies in Iconography and Tradition.* London: Routledge and Kegan Paul, 1967.

Rossetti, Christina. *The Complete Poems of Christina Rossetti.* Ed. R. W. Crump. 2 vols. Baton Rouge: Louisiana State UP, 1979.

———. "The World." *The World Split Open: Four Centuries of Women Poets in England and America, 1552–1950.* Ed. Louise Bernikow. New York: Random House, 1974. 126.

Rossetti, Dante Gabriel. *Poems Ballads and Sonnets.* Ed. Paul Franklin Baum. Garden City, N.Y.: Doubleday and Doran, 1937.

———. *Rossetti's Poems.* Ed. Oswald Doughty. London: Dent, 1957.

Rowland, Beryl. *Animals with Human Faces: A Guide to Animal Symbolism.* Knoxville: U of Tennessee P, 1973.

Rukeyser, Muriel. *The Collected Poems of Muriel Rukeyser.* New York: McGraw-Hill, 1978.

Sackville, Lady Margaret. *Lyrics.* London: Herbert & Daniel, 1912.

Sanday, Peggy Reeves. *Female Power and Male Dominance: On the Origins of Sexual Inequality.* Cambridge: Cambridge UP, 1981.

Sanger, Margaret. *Woman and the New Race.* New York: Brentano's, 1920.

Sarton, May. *Collected Poems (1930–1973).* New York: Norton, 1974.

———. *Letters from Maine.* New York: Norton, 1986.

Schwartz, Delmore. "The Heavy Bear Who Goes with Me." In *Bear Crossings.* Ed. Ann Newman and Julie Suk. Newport Beach, Calif.: New South, 1978. 64–65.

Scott, Duncan Campbell. "At Gull Lake: August, 1810." In *The New Oxford Book of Canadian Verse in English.* Ed. Margaret Atwood. Toronto: Oxford UP, 1982. 53–56.

———. *Selected Poems.* Ed. Glenn Clever. Ottawa: Tecumseh Press, 1974.

Scott, F. R. "Old Song." In *The Oxford Anthology of Canadian Literature.* Toronto: Oxford UP, 1973. 483.

Scully, Vincent. "The Great Goddess and the Palace Architecture of Crete." In *Feminism and Art History: Questioning the Litany.* Ed. Norma Broude and Mary D. Garrard. New York: Harper and Row, 1978.

Shelley, Percy Bysshe. *The Poetical Works of Percy Bysshe Shelley.* Ed. Harry Buxton Forman. 4 vols. London: Reeves and Turner, 1877.

Shenstone, William. "A Description of the Leasowes." *Works.* London, 1764. As quoted in James G. Turner, "The Sexual Politics of Landscape, Images of Venus in Eighteenth-Century English Poetry and Landscape Gardening." In vol. 11, *Eighteenth-Century Culture.* Ed. Harry C. Payne. Madison: U of Wisconsin P, 1982. 343–66.

Sherwin, Judith Johnson. "First Dance: God Who Walks Like a Bear from Three Power Dances." In *Bear Crossings.* Ed. Anne Newman and Julie Suk. Newport Beach, Calif.: New South, 1978. 115.

Sichel, Edith Helen, ed. *Gathered Leaves from the Prose of Mary Elizabeth Coleridge.* New York: n.p., 1910.

Siebers, Tobin. *The Mirror of Medusa.* Berkeley: U of California P, 1983.

Silko, Leslie Marmon. *Storyteller.* New York: Seaver Books, 1981.

Sill, Edward Rowland. *Poems.* New York: Houghton Mifflin, 1887.

Simmons, St. John. *Wilderness Images.* Frederickton, New Brunswick: Fiddlehead Poetry Books, 1983.

Sitwell, Edith. *The Collected Poems of Edith Sitwell.* New York: Vanguard Press, 1954.

Slater, Phillip E. *The Glory of Hera: Greek Mythology and the Greek Family.* Boston: Beacon Press, 1968.

Works Cited

Smith, A. J. M. *The Classic Shade: Selected Poems*. Toronto: McClelland and Stewart, 1978.

———. "The Lonely Land." In *An Anthology of Canadian Literature in English*. Ed. Donna Bennett and Russell Brown. 2 vols. Toronto: Oxford UP. 1: 361.

Smith, Andrea. "For All Those Who Were Indian in a Former Life." *Woman of Power* 19 (Winter 1991): 74–75.

Smith, Bessie. "Dirty No Gooder Blues." In *The World Split Open: Four Centuries of Women Poets in England and America, 1552–1950*. Ed. Louise Bernikow. New York: Random House, 1974. 276–77.

Smith, Patricia Clark. "Ain't Seen You Since: Dissent among Female Relatives in Contemporary Native American Women's Poetry." Paper delivered at the Midwest Modern Language Association meeting, 1979.

———, with Paula Gunn Allen. "Earthy Relations, Carnal Knowledge: Southwestern Indian Women Writers and Landscape." In *The Desert Is No Lady: Southwestern Landscapes in Women's Writing and Art*. New Haven: Yale UP, 1987. 174–96.

Snyder, Gary. *The Back Country*. New York: New Directions, 1968.

———. *Mountains and Rivers without End*. London: Fulcrum Press, 1967.

———. *Myths and Texts*. New York: New Directions, 1978.

———. *The Practice of the Wild*. San Francisco: North Point Press, 1990.

———. "Praise for Sick Women." In *The New American Poetry*. Ed. Donald M. Allen. New York: Grove Press, 1960. 307–308.

Spenser, Edmund. *The Faerie Queene*. Ed. A. C. Hamilton. New York: Longman, 1977.

Stanford, Ann. *In Mediterranean Air*. New York: Viking Press, 1977.

———, ed. *The Women Poets in English*. New York: McGraw-Hill, 1972.

Steele, Jeffrey. *The Representation of the Self in the American Renaissance*. Chapel Hill: U of North Carolina P, 1987.

Stone, Lawrence. "Sex in the West." *New Republic* 8 (July 1985): 25–37.

Stone, Merlin. *When God Was a Woman*. New York: Harvest Press, 1978.

Swanton, J. R. *Tlingit Myths and Texts*. Bulletin 39. Washington, D.C.: Bureau of American Ethnology, 1909.

Swinburne, Algernon Charles. *Selected Poems of Swinburne*. Ed. Edward Shanks. London: Macmillan, 1950.

Tallman, Warren. "Wolf in the Snow." In *Context of Canadian Criticism*. Ed. Eli Mandel. Chicago: U of Chicago P, 1971. 232–53.

Teasdale, Sara. *The Collected Poems of Sara Teasdale*. New York: Macmillan, 1946.

Terrell, John Upton and Donna M. *Indian Women of the Western Morning: Their Life in Early America*. Garden City, N.Y.: Anchor Books, 1976.

Thiébaux, Marcelle. *The Stag of Love: The Chase in Medieval Literature.* Ithaca: Cornell UP, 1974.

Thomas, Dylan. "Notes on the Art of Poetry." In *A Garland for Dylan Thomas.* Ed. George Firmage and Oscar Williams. New York: Clarke and Way, 1963. 147–52.

———. *The Poems of Dylan Thomas.* Ed. Daniel Jones. New York: New Directions, 1971.

Thomas, Gwen. "The Androgynous American: The Strong Black Woman." Paper presented at the Popular Culture Association convention, 1977.

Thomas, Keith. *Man and the Natural World: A History of the Modern Sensibility.* New York: Pantheon, 1983.

Thompson, John. "The Bread Hot from the Oven." *The New Oxford Book of Canadian Verse in English.* Ed. Margaret Atwood. Toronto: Oxford UP, 1982. 345.

Thompson, Stith. *Tales of the North American Indians.* Bloomington: Indiana UP, 1966.

Toomer, Jean. *Cane.* New York: Harper and Row, 1969.

Travitsky, Betty. *The Paradise of Women.* Westport, Conn.: Greenwood Press, 1987.

Turner, Frederick. *The Cost of Living.* New York: Godine Press, n.d.

Turner, James G. "The Sexual Politics of Landscape: Images of Venus in Eighteenth-Century English Poetry and Landscape Gardening." In vol. 11, *Studies in Eighteenth-Century Culture.* Ed. Harry C. Payne. Madison: U of Wisconsin P, 1982. 343–66.

Turner, Walter James. "The Seven Days of the Sun." In *The Oxford Book of Modern Verse 1892–1935.* New York: Oxford UP, 1936. 298–304.

Virgo, Séan. *Deathwatch on Skidegate Narrows and Other Poems.* Victoria, B.C.: Sona Nis Press, 1979.

Von Franz, Marie-Louise. *Problems of the Feminine in Fairytales.* Zurich: Spring Publications, 1976.

Waddington, Miriam. *Driving Home: Poems New and Selected.* Toronto: Oxford UP, 1972.

Wagner-Martin, Linda. *Sylvia Plath: A Biography.* New York: Simon and Schuster, 1987.

Wakoski, Diane. *The Collected Greed, Parts 1–13.* Santa Barbara: Black Sparrow Press, 1984.

———. *Dancing on the Grave of a Son of a Bitch.* Santa Barbara: Black Swallow Press, 1980.

———. *The Magician's Feastletters.* Santa Barbara: Black Sparrow Press, 1982.

———. *Medea, the Sorceress.* Santa Rosa: Black Sparrow Press, 1991.

Works Cited

———. *The Motorcycle Betrayal Poems*. New York: Simon and Schuster, 1971.

———. *The Rings of Saturn*. Santa Barbara: Black Sparrow Press, 1986.

———. *Waiting for the King of Spain*. Santa Barbara: Black Sparrow Press, 1976.

Walker, Barbara G. *The Crone: Woman of Age, Wisdom, and Power*. San Francisco: Harper and Row, 1985.

———. *The Woman's Encyclopedia of Myths and Secrets*. San Francisco: Harper and Row, 1983.

Walker, Cheryl. *The Nightingale's Burden: Women Poets and American Culture Before 1900*. Bloomington: Indiana UP, 1982.

Walker, Margaret. "Molly Means." In *Modern and Contemporary Afro-American Poetry*. Ed. Bernard W. Bell. Boston: Allyn and Bacon, 1972. 74–76.

Wall, Kathleen. *The Callisto Myth from Ovid to Atwood: Initiation and Rape in Literature*. Kingston: McGill-Queen's UP, 1988.

Walters, Anna Lee. "Hartico." In *The Third Woman: Minority Women Writers in the United States*. Ed. Dexter Fisher. Boston: Houghton Mifflin, 1980. 110–12.

Warner, Marina. *Alone of All Her Sex: The Myth and the Cult of the Virgin Mary*. New York: Knopf, 1976.

Weaving, Willoughby. *Star Fields and Other Poems*. Oxford: Blackwell, 1916.

Webb, Phyllis. "A Tall Tale." In *15 Canadian Poets Plus 5*. Ed. Gary Geddes and Phyllis Bruce. Toronto: Oxford UP, 1978. 155–56.

Wehr, Demaris. *Jung and Feminism: Liberating Archetypes*. Boston: Beacon Press, 1987.

White, Hayden. "The Forms of Wildness: Archaeology of an Idea." In *The Wild Man Within: An Image in Western Thought from the Renaissance to Romanticism*. Ed. Edward Dudley and Maximillian E. Novak. Pittsburgh: Pittsburgh UP, 1972. 3–38.

Whiteman, Roberta Hill. "Dream of Rebirth." In *That's What She Said: Contemporary Poetry and Fiction by Native American Women*. Ed. Rayna Green. Bloomington: Indiana UP, 1984. 282.

———. "Star Quilt." In *That's What She Said*. 281–82.

Whitman, Sarah Helen. *Poems*. Boston: Houghton Osgood, 1879.

Wilbur, Richard. "She." In *Today's Poets: American and British Poetry since the 1930s*. Ed. Chad Walsh. New York: Scribner, 1964. 277–78.

Wilcox, Ella Wheeler. *Poems of Passion*. Chicago: Bedford, Clarke, 1883.

Wilkinson, Anne. "Winter Sketch." In *An Anthology of Canadian Literature in English*. Ed. Donna Bennett and Russell Brown. 2 vols. Toronto: Oxford UP. 1:527.

Williamson, Marilyn, ed. *The Female Poets of Great Britain*. Detroit: Wayne State UP, 1981.

Winters, Yvor. "Quod Tegit Omnia." In *Bear Crossings*. Ed. Anne Newman and Julie Suk. Newport Beach, Calif.: New South, 1978. 11.

Witherell, Louise R. "Camille Claudel Rediscovered." *Woman's Art Journal* 6 (Spring–Summer 1985): 1–7.

Wolkstein, Diane, and Samuel Noah Kramer. *Inanna, Queen of Heaven and Earth*. New York: Harper and Row, 1983.

Wright, James. "March." In *Bear Crossings*. Ed. Anne Newman and Julie Suk. Newport Beach, Calif.: New South, 1978. 23.

Wyatt, Sir Thomas. "CLXXII: Venus, in sport, to please therewith her dear." *The Complete Poems of Sir Thomas Wyatt*. Ed. R. A. Rebholz. New York: Penguin, 1978. 230–31.

Wylie, Elinor. *Black Armour*. New York: George Doran, 1923.

———. *Collected Poems of Elinor Wylie*. New York: Knopf, 1932.

Ywahoo, Dhyani. *Voices of Our Ancestors: Cherokee Teachings from the Wisdom Fire*. Ed. Barbara Du Bois. Boston: Shambhala, 1987.

Zaturenska, Marya. *The Listening Landscape*. New York: Macmillan, 1941.

Index

African American poetry, 30, 49–50, 67–72, 188–97, 204, 230–38; African American female poets, 51, 67–70, 74, 215–16, 230–38; African American male poets, 70–71, 188–97; gender comparisons, 70–71, 195–96, 230–31
African American women, 68, 191, 194–95, 204, 215–16
Aiken, Conrad, 165, 168–69, 188
Alexander, Lewis, 191–92
Allen, Grant, 162–63, 166
Allen, Paula Gunn. *See also* Native American critics
Aphrodite (Venus), x, xv, 22, 64, 65, 200, 283, 285, 295, 296, 297, 359, 364, 373; degradation of, 101, 107–108, 111, 115, 160, 223, 242, 332; liminality of, 112–13; as cosmic force, 113–14, 125–26, 134, 135, 140n1, 189, 246, 326; as war goddess, 113, 125, 133, 137, 198, 226, 228, 229, 307–308; Venus's origins, 115–16; scale of attitudes toward, 123–24, 145, 167, 184; deep background of, Chapter Four *passim*, 123, 134, 208. *See also* Part Two *passim*
Archetypal empowerment, 5, 35, 44, 51, 63, 65, 67, 70, 71, 73, 100, 109, 119, 126, 131–32, 200, 218, 221, 227, 235, 278, 286, 287, 300–301, 304, 332, 333, 347, 348, 368
Archetypal quests, 179, 363; men, for rebirth, 6–7, 173, 238, 253, 284, 305; women, for rebirth, 7, 204, 219, 220, 226, 227, 228–29, 229–30, 238, 242, 247–48, 277, 304; for maternal blessing, 20, 34, 42, 61–62, 64, 66, 67, 69–70, 226, 227, 229–30, 233–34, 276–77, 277–79, 364, 367; for goddesses, 30, 44, 174, 176–77, 178, 179, 181, 182, 217, 234, 238, 279, 293, 298, 301–302, 346, 364–66, 368; Canadian, for rebirth, 76–77, 78–79, 88, 92; men's and women's quests compared, 228–29; Native American

healing quests, 329–30, 334–38, 346, 347
Archetypal theory, xii; Carl Gustav Jung on, xii, xvii, 5–7, 12, 42–43, 75, 165–66, 315, 316, 364; Erich Neumann on, 6, 43, 45, 75, 165–66, 169, 187, 295–96, 315–16; Marija Gimbutas on interacting layers of images, 21–23, 28, 109–110; Paul Friedrich on interbraided imagery, 23, 42, 112, 113, 129; Marie-Louise von Franz on, 100; James Hillman on, 316
Archetypal theory, feminist, 371; Merlin Stone, 25–26, 29, 289; Karen Elias-Button, 33, 63, 40–41, 59, 63; Buffie Johnson, 36, 350; Hazel E. Barnes, 37, 38, 40, 54–55, 73; archetypal dialectics, 42, 101, 117, 119, 123, 134, 161, 186, 223, 226, 233, 238; Estella Lauter, 69, 284, 287; Christine Downing, 100; Eleanor Amico, 103, 107; Jean Shinoda Bolen, 161; archetypes interacting in a field, 161, 162, 200, 235–36, 255, 274, 288, 324, 343, 353, 356–57, 358–59, 365, 369, 373–74; Betty Meador, 304, 307–308; Gloria Orenstein, 347
Archetypes: methods for teaching of, ix–xi, xxi–xxii, 101; definitions of, xi, xvii, 5, 100, 161, 347, 359; deep background of, xi, 8, 176, 204, 222, 223, 230, 339, 349, 369; signatures, xvii, 8, 42, 161, 173, 176, 178, 188, 190, 221, 234; methods for finding, xvii–xix; shadow, 7, 17, 204, 228, 229, 243, 257, 313, 316, 320; green world lover, 7, 152, 201, 218, 306, 349; crones/hags, 8, 56, 269, 274–75, 276, 296, 303, 309, 333, 354, 365; wild woman archetype, 9, 145, 284–87, 292, 315; snakes, 13, 23, 24–35, 59–60, 70, 85; Lamia, 15, 29, 30, 33, 122, 134; in needlework, 19, 20, 40, 239–40, 336–37; stones, 23, 56, Chapter Three *passim*, 180, 211, 215, 221–

Index

Index

Medusa, 67–70. *See also* Part One *passim*

Merrill, James, 48

Merwin, William, 57, 198–99, 238, 253

Millay, Edna St. Vincent, 223–24, 227, 302–303

Montagu, Lady Mary Wortley, 154

Mora, Pat, 330

Morris, Sir Lewis, 15–16

Mothers, 3, 11–12, 38, 41, 44, 45, 47, 50, 55, 64, 68, 75, 84, 100, 118, 178, 188, 201, 212, 222, 229–30, 258, 276–77, 290–91, 354; in psychological development, ix, 52–53, 63, 74; "Mother Goddess" hypothesis, xv, 20–21, 25, 43, 105, 109, 118, 122, 164, 166, 168, 174, 175, 187, 308, 364; our mothers' lives in patriarchy, 3–4, 42, 61–62, 64, 66; "terrible mother," 6, 7, 41, 43, 70, 82, 85–86, 122, 178, 179, 187, 188, 214, 217, 256, 295, 328; "Black (or dark) mother," 30, 69–70, 72, 230, 232, 233–34, 237, 278, 283, 304, 308, 313, 314; male conflation of maternal/sexual, 46–47, 48, 58, 73–74, 167, 168, 170, 180, 184–85, 186–87; women poets blocked by, 51–54, 58, 73–74; the "Mother Right" hypothesis, 163, 164, 166; Native American, 328–30; the Bear Mother, 344, 352, 364–68. *See also* Archetypal quest for maternal blessing; Goddesses, Demeter

Mouré, John, 271

Musgrave, Susan, 85–86, 87, 91, 257, 279

Mythology: history of myth scholarship, 20–21, 146, 163–65; Jane Ellen Harrison on, 20, 26, 31, 36, 38, 44, 62; Joseph Campbell on, 20–21, 31, 284–85; Minoan, 20, 23, 26–27, 28, 29, 31, 289; J. J. Bachofen on, 21, 163; Greek, 21–22, 23, 24, 28, 31, 39, 111–12, 223, 310, 353–54; Celtic, 39–40, 111, 133–34, 174, 179, 180–83, 265, 275, 289, 292, 293, 294, 307–310, 318, 350–52, 364; in Roman Britain, 39–40, 307; Europagan, 39–40, 145, 146, 265, 274, 275, 308–310, 315, 318–19, 339, 345–46, 347–55, 362, 365, 375; Robert Graves on, 58–59, 136–37, 174–79; Canadian, 76–78, Chapters Three and Eight *passim*; Sumerian, 101–105, 307–308; Ugaritic, 103; Mesopotamian, 104–108; Indo-European, 109–111, 289;

Hindu, 111; Arthurian legends, 111, 133, 350; Roman, 115–18, 302; J. G. Frazer on, 136–67, 164; Tannhäuser legends, 145, 285; the Cambridge School, 164–65; Dylan Thomas on, 179–83; Gary Snyder on, 183–84, 356–57; Robert Duncan on, 183–86; Robert Bly on, 184, 186–88; Muriel Rukeyser on, 226–27; Margaret Fuller on, 300–301

Native American critics: Andrea Smith, 317, 318, 338; Geary Hobson, 317; Wendy Rose, 317–18, 338; Paula Gunn Allen, 319–20, 321, 323, 326, 327–28, 331, 334, 336, 363

Native American women, 326, 327–29, 332, 333, 343–44

Native Americans, xviii; Native Peoples of Canada, xvii, 81, 90, 91, 95, 265–74; Indian policy, 267–68, 308; Iroquois, 90, 268; culture usurped by Europeans (white shamanism), 91, 185, 227, 257, 266–68, 273, 305–306, 313–19, 336–39, 356–57; in non-Native American poetry, 260, 261, 263, 265–74, 298–99, 300, 301; Salteaux, 266; Onondaga, 268, 346; Ojibwa (Chippewa), 268, 319, 326, 327, 328, 331, 341, 344, 345–46, 347; Salish, 269–70; Blackfoot, 271, 345; Haida, 271, 274, 356; Kwakiutl, 271; Cherokee, 319, 325, 332–33; Hopi, 319, 326; Zuñi, 319; Keres, 320, 326, 329, 333; Navajo, 320, 322, 333, 363; Botowatomie (Potowatomie), 321, 341; Tlingit, 321, 334, 344; Yokuts, 321, 344–45; Laguna, 322; Nootka, 322, 329, 338; "totemism," 323, 324–25, 341–42; Sioux, 323; Omaha, 323–24; Anishnabeg, 329–30; Chicana, 330; Creek, 332; Inuit, 333, 342; Apache, 333; Mohawk, 334; Papago, 334; Crow, 334; Native American bear archetypes, 340–47; Diné, 341; Ute, 341; Ottowa, 341; Winnebago, 341–42; Yukon, 343, 344; Comanche, 344; Chitimacha, 346; Tewa, 346; Kishkatenaw, 357. *See also* Chapter Ten *passim*; Theology

Nemerov, Howard, 48

Neumann, Erich, 108, 120–22, 295. *See also* Archetypal theory

Newlove, John, 271–73

Nowlan, Alden, 264

406

Index

ANNIS PRATT taught English and Women's Studies at the University of Wisconsin in Madison for twenty years and is the author of *Archetypal Patterns in Women's Fiction*. She has used archetypal theory to develop a transformational pedagogy for the classroom and continues to seek ways to enhance personal growth and ecological community through archetypal empowerment.